BESTSELLING
BOOK SERIES

Cruise Vacations For Dummies® 2005

T4-AVA-485

Cheat Sheet

The Caribbean Islands

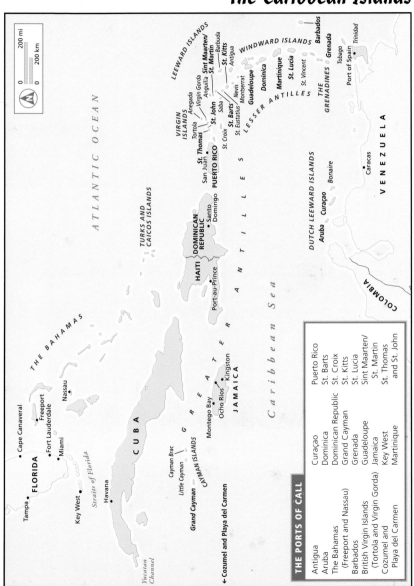

THE PORTS OF CALL

Antigua	Curaçao
Aruba	Dominica
The Bahamas	Dominican Republic
(Freeport and Nassau)	Grand Cayman
Barbados	Grenada
British Virgin Islands	Guadeloupe
(Tortola and Virgin Gorda)	Jamaica
Cozumel and	Key West
Playa del Carmen	Martinique

Puerto Rico
St. Barts
St. Croix
St. Kitts
St. Lucia
Sint Maarten/
St. Martin
St. Thomas
and St. John

Southeast Alaska

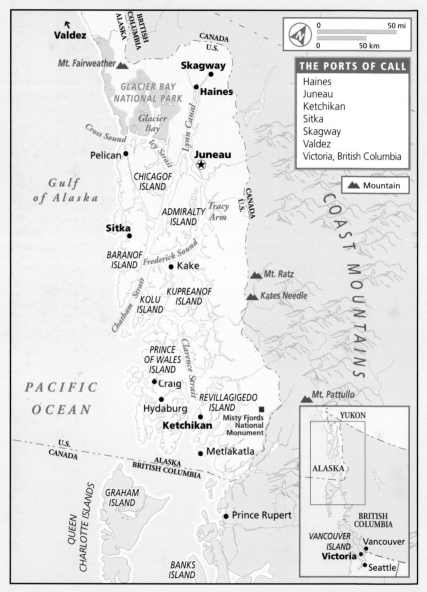

Valdez

BRITISH COLUMBIA
ALASKA

Mt. Fairweather

Skagway

CANADA
U.S.

GLACIER BAY
NATIONAL PARK

Haines

Glacier
Bay

Cross Sound

Icy Strait

Lynn Canal

Pelican

Juneau

CHICAGOF
ISLAND

Gulf
of Alaska

ADMIRALTY
ISLAND

Tracy
Arm

CANADA
U.S.

Sitka

Frederick Sound

BARANOF
ISLAND

Kake

Chatham Strait

KUPREANOF
ISLAND

KOLU
ISLAND

Mt. Ratz

Kates Needle

COAST MOUNTAINS

PRINCE
OF WALES
ISLAND

Clarence Strait

Craig

Hydaburg

REVILLAGIGEDO
ISLAND

Mt. Pattullo

Ketchikan

Misty Fjords
National
Monument

PACIFIC
OCEAN

U.S.
CANADA

Metlakatla

ALASKA
BRITISH COLUMBIA

QUEEN CHARLOTTE ISLANDS

GRAHAM
ISLAND

Prince Rupert

YUKON

ALASKA

BANKS
ISLAND

BRITISH
COLUMBIA

VANCOUVER
ISLAND

Vancouver

Victoria

Seattle

| 0 | | 50 mi |
| 0 | | 50 km |

THE PORTS OF CALL

Haines
Juneau
Ketchikan
Sitka
Skagway
Valdez
Victoria, British Columbia

▲ Mountain

FOR DUMMIES®

The fun and easy way™ to travel!

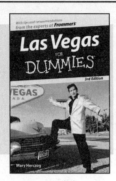

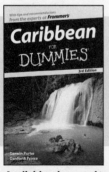
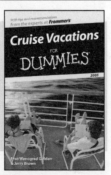

Cruise Vacations FOR DUMMIES® 2005

by Fran Wenograd Golden
and Jerry Brown

WILEY

Wiley Publishing, Inc.

Cruise Vacations For Dummies® 2005

Published by
Wiley Publishing, Inc.
111 River St.
Hoboken, NJ 07030-5774
www.wiley.com

For general information on our other products and services, please contact our Customer Care Department within the U.S. at 800-762-2974, outside the U.S. at 317-572-3993, or fax 317-572-4002.

For technical support, please visit www.wiley.com/techsupport.

Wiley also publishes its books in a variety of electronic formats. Some content that appears in print may not be available in electronic books.

Library of Congress Control Number: Library of Congress Control Number is available from the Publisher.

ISBN: 0-7645-6941-4

Manufactured in the United States of America

10 9 8 7 6 5 4 3 2 1

1B/RV/RR/QU/IN

WILEY

About the Authors

Fran Wenograd Golden is travel editor of the *Boston Herald*. She is also the author of *TVacations: A Fun Guide to the Sites, the Stars, and the Inside Stories Behind Your Favorite TV Shows* (Pocket Books, 1996), and coauthor, with Jerry Brown, of *Frommer's Alaska Cruises & Ports of Call* and *Frommer's European Cruises & Ports of Call*. Raised mostly in West Hartford, Connecticut, she lives north of Boston, and is the proud parent of Erin and Eli.

Jerry Brown was born in Scotland and worked as a reporter for Scottish newspapers before joining the news department of the *London Daily Mail*. Later, for 31 years, he was the West Coast Bureau Chief for a leading U.S. travel trade newspaper. Now he co-writes books with Fran (see above) and writes travel stories on a freelance basis. He and his wife, Margaret, have two grown sons, two daughters-in-law, a granddaughter, Victoria Rose, and a grandson, Mason Patrick.

Authors' Acknowledgments

No book of this scope could be possible without more than a little help from our friends. We'd like to send a special thank you to contributors Art Sbarsky (cruise reviews), Mark Chapman (gambling and activities/entertainment chapters), Felicity Long (family and Caribbean chapters), the cruise lines' public relations departments, and our patient editor Amy Lyons. And a big thanks to our families, for putting up with us.

Publisher's Acknowledgments

We're proud of this book; please send us your comments through our Dummies online registration form located at `www.dummies.com/register/`.

Some of the people who helped bring this book to market include the following:

Editorial

Editors: Traci Cumbay, Project Editor; Amy Lyons, Development Editor

Copy Editor: Josh Dials

Cartographer: Elizabeth Puhl

Editorial Manager: Jennifer Ehrlich

Editorial Assistant: Melissa Bennett

Senior Photo Editor: Richard Fox

Cover Photos:
Front Cover: © Roger Paperno/ Index Stock Imagery; Back Cover: © Harvey Lloyd/ Corbis

Cartoons: Rich Tennant, `www.the5thwave.com`

Composition

Project Coordinator: Ryan Steffen

Layout and Graphics:
Lauren Goddard, Joyce Haughey, Stephanie D. Jumper, Barry Offringa, Melanee Prendergast, Heather Ryan, Jacque Roth, Julie Trippetti

Proofreaders: Joe Niesen TECHBOOKS Production Services

Indexer: TECHBOOKS Production Services

Publishing and Editorial for Consumer Dummies

Diane Graves Steele, Vice President and Publisher, Consumer Dummies

Joyce Pepple, Acquisitions Director, Consumer Dummies

Kristin A. Cocks, Product Development Director, Consumer Dummies

Michael Spring, Vice President and Publisher, Travel

Brice Gosnell, Associate Publisher, Travel

Kelly Regan, Editorial Director, Travel

Publishing for Technology Dummies

Andy Cummings, Vice President and Publisher, Dummies Technology/ General User

Composition Services

Gerry Fahey, Vice President of Production Services

Debbie Stailey, Director of Composition Services

Contents at a Glance

Maps at a Glance

Table of Contents

Introduction

*Y*ou're probably a lot like us: You want to take a cruise but may be a little worried about committing and putting down a deposit because you don't know what to expect.

We once felt the same way. After we got our first assignments to write about cruises many years (and cumulatively more than a hundred cruises) ago, we cringed at the thought. Neither of us could imagine spending a week on a cruise ship. Yuck! Fran was worried about getting seasick; Jerry thought he'd be bored and feel trapped; and we weren't even sure we wanted to interact with other people on the cruise (after all, we'd seen *The Love Boat*).

As it turned out, not only were our fears groundless, but they were also just plain wrong. After one week on the ship during her first cruise, Fran cursed herself for not booking a longer trip; Jerry wanted to move onboard permanently.

Why? Because although you may envision yourself alone in a dark, dank cabin, head-over-toilet with seasickness, in reality we found that taking a cruise can be the most relaxing, stress-free, and even luxurious vacation experience.

And yes, it was fun, too!

Part of the cruise experience has to do with the sea and scenery, but more important, from the moment the friendly crew ushers you aboard, all seems right with the world. You feel pampered and taken care of. All you have to do is wave your hand or make a quick phone call and a steward brings you whatever you need. You don't have to do anything you don't want to do.

Dummies Post-it® Flags

As you're reading this book, you'll find information that you'll want to reference as you plan or enjoy your trip — whether it be a new hotel, a must-see attraction or a must-try walking tour. Mark these pages with the handy Post-it® Flags included in this book to help make your trip planning easier!

Each day on a cruise ship is filled with many "difficult choices" — but you get used to it. Should you

- ✔ Go to the gym and work out?
- ✔ Sit on the deck and chat with the other passengers (who often turn out to be likeable people from all walks of life)?
- ✔ Find a quiet place to read?
- ✔ Have a massage?
- ✔ Take a nap or watch a movie in your cabin?
- ✔ Go for a swim?
- ✔ Participate in one of the goofy deck games?
- ✔ Take one of the organized shore excursions on days when the ship stops in port or just head off on your own?

With so much to do, you can't possibly do it all, and if you choose to just stare off into sea and do absolutely nothing, that's okay, too. No one demands anything other than your satisfaction.

On top of it all, cruising is a great value vacation: For one price, you get your cabin, all your meals and entertainment for the week, and a whole slew of onboard activities. Plus, you get to visit any number of different places and you have to unpack only once. It all adds up to one heck of an attractive vacation experience.

About This Book

We want to make sure that you have a delightful, varied, and stress-free cruise vacation, which is why we joined forces to write this book.

We tried to anticipate every question you may have about the cruise experience and provide the answers. For first-time cruisers, we describe what to expect from the cruise experience, pre-cruise to post-cruise, with the nitty-gritty on everything from looking at your first cruise brochure to clearing Customs at the end of the trip. The goal is to make the experience easy and familiar, even if you haven't cruised before.

If you're not a first-timer, you probably picked out this book because you don't want to waste a lot of time on trip planning. You want a quick and easy, yet comprehensive, source of information, which is exactly what we aim to give you here.

Of course, you don't have to read the whole book. And you don't have to start at the beginning either. This is a reference book. Check out the table of contents or the index and read the parts that answer your specific questions.

Besides being practical, this book is meant to give you the idea that the whole subject of cruising should be just plain fun, so don't expect any dry lectures — boring isn't our style.

Conventions Used in This Book

This guide is designed for easy reference. We include reviews of all the best cruise lines; overviews of the most popular cruise ports in the Caribbean, Alaska, and the Mediterranean; and a quick-and-easy introduction to everything you're likely to experience in planning and taking a cruise. The attractions, along with telephone numbers, are often in **bold** type to draw your attention to them, and the ship names appear in *italic*. If an attraction, hotel, restaurant, or what-have-you has a toll-free number, we list that number first, in bold type, right after a tiny little telephone, which looks like this: ☎.

For sanity and brevity, whenever we talk about temperatures, the degrees are in Fahrenheit; and when we talk about prices, we mean U.S. dollars unless otherwise noted.

People rarely pay full price for a cruise. For easy comparison purposes, however, we list the full brochure rate. Think of this rate as the "sticker price." You can expect to pay substantially less (in some cases up to 60 percent — and sometimes even more — off the brochure rate). We list the prices in the ship review chapters in Part IV for a one-week, seven-day cruise (that means seven nights on board the ship). In cases where a particular ship doesn't do one-week cruises, we note the exception and show the appropriate rates. Be sure to check out the "Super deals" section in each cruise line review to get a handle on good discounts.

We list the range of brochure prices based on the following three basic types of accommodations:

- ✔ Inside cabin (one without windows)
- ✔ Outside cabin (one with windows)
- ✔ Suite

Foolish Assumptions

As we wrote this book, we made some assumptions about you and your needs as a traveler. We assumed the following:

- ✔ You may be an inexperienced traveler looking for guidance about taking a cruise and how to plan for it.

- ✔ You may be an experienced traveler who hasn't had much time to cruise and wants expert advice for when you finally do get a chance to go to sea.

✔ You may be an experienced cruiser who wants a handy guide to the many cruise lines and their respective itineraries and ports of call.

✔ You've cruised before in the Caribbean but want to venture this time into Alaska or the Mediterranean.

✔ You don't want a book that provides all the information available about cruising. Instead, you're looking for a book that focuses on covering the ships that can give you the best experience for your particular taste.

If you fit any of these criteria, *Cruise Vacations For Dummies 2005* gives you the information you want!

How This Book Is Organized

This book is organized in a roughly chronological fashion (although you don't have to read it that way), taking you from the basics of choosing a cruise through the particulars. We detail the reasons you're going to sea: visiting great ports of call and having a ball on board as you sail from one port to the other.

Part I: Getting Started

We start with the best of the best, our recommendations of top ships, top destinations, and top things to do onboard. We explain why a cruise is a great vacation choice and knock down some common misconceptions about cruising — that it may be too expensive or that you may get bored, for example. And we offer some suggestions of how to find the cruise and cruise experience that best suits you

Part II: Planning Your Cruise

Part II helps you start figuring out what your trip may cost. We take you through the process of finding and booking a cruise, including how to find a good travel agent or make your reservations over the Internet. We also tell you what you need to know before you get on the ship — from buying travel insurance, to getting there, to packing tips, to passport requirements and how much cash to bring.

Part III: All Aboard: The Cruise Experience

Part III covers everything you can expect to experience shipboard during your cruise vacation, including entertainment, food, spa offerings, shopping, and gambling. We devote a chapter to families cruising with children. We also offer tips on tipping and answer your questions about Customs regulations.

Part IV: Ship Shapes: Cruise Lines and Cruise Ships

Part IV discusses the major cruise lines and their vessels and offers honest reviews to help you target the ship most likely to give you the vacation experience you desire.

Part V: Landing at the Ports of Call

To find out where the ships sail from and to, check out Part V, which offers specifics on points of embarkation and ports of call. We offer advice on how to make the most of your time if you plan to stay a few days in the port city before or after your cruise. And we offer insights into what to see and do in the major ports of call in the Caribbean, Alaska, and the Mediterranean, highlighting the top attractions and best shore excursions.

Part VI: The Part of Tens

The Part of Tens includes a synopsis of the most classic onboard experiences and special ways you can enhance shipboard romance.

Appendix: Quick Concierge

The Appendix lists toll-free phone numbers for cruise lines and airlines and a directory of top travel agencies.

Icons Used in This Book

Keep an eye peeled for these icons, which appear in the margins:

Find money-saving tips and/or great deals next to this icon.

Check out the Cruise Fact icon for odd little facts of life at sea. But be forewarned that this represents our repository for quirkier items and just-plain-fun tidbits.

Watch for the Heads Up icon to identify annoying or potentially dangerous situations such as tourist traps, unsafe neighborhoods, rip-offs, and other things to be aware of.

Look to the Kid Friendly icon for attractions, hotels, restaurants, and activities that are particularly hospitable to children or people who travel with kids.

Find useful advice on things to do and ways to schedule your time when you see the Tip icon.

This icon marks our choices for the best ships, destinations, and activities.

Where to Go from Here

Now you're ready to go! Get that Hawaiian shirt out of the closet, put some reggae on the stereo, fix yourself a frosty drink, and settle down to pick out the cruise of your dreams. Don't worry; if your dream doesn't include loud shirts and party music, voyages exist for us mellow folk, too!

Part I
Getting Started

The 5th Wave   By Rich Tennant

In this part . . .

Think of this part of the book as your quick introductory course, where you discover that a cruise ship is more than just a boat in the water. You find out about the very best cruising has to offer, why you should cruise, where you can cruise, and how you can afford a cruise; and you can match your vacation goals to the type of ship that best meets your needs.

Chapter 1

Discovering the Best of Cruising

In This Chapter

▶ Revealing the top cruise lines

▶ Finding the best ship to fit your interests

▶ Uncovering the top ports of call around the world

*O*kay, as cruise writers, we get this question a lot: "What's your favorite cruise?" It's a hard question to answer because we like so many different things about so many different ships. When we want pampering, we may think of one ship. When we're in a party mood, we may make another choice. When we think back on family trips, our minds wander in one direction. When we think of romance . . . well, you get the point. And then we have to add itineraries — some are more memorable than others — and factors like shore excursions, amenities, and cuisine to the discussion. And service — don't forget service.

The ongoing debate makes our heads hurt. But on your behalf, we did some deep thinking and came up with a list of favorites — our picks of the best cruising has to offer.

 You can find the "Best of the Best" icon signaling the contents of this chapter throughout the book.

The Best Ships for Luxury

Chapter 15 gives you the complete lowdown on each of these ships, but here's a summary:

✔ **Crystal Cruises:** Crystal's dream ships offer the best of two worlds: pampering service and scrumptious cuisine on ships large enough to offer plenty of outdoor deck space, generous fitness facilities, four restaurants, and over half a dozen bars and entertainment venues. Crystal's California ethic tends to keep the atmosphere more mingly and chatty than aboard the more sober ships, such as Seabourn.

✔ **Cunard Line:** *QM2* has her very own niche in the luxe market — and in the cruise market as a whole, for that matter. Although she's too enormous to offer the kind of intimate luxury you get with Silversea, Seabourn, and SeaDream, she can give you a pretty close idea of what life aboard the great old ocean liners was like — a pretty luxe perk all in itself.

✔ **Seabourn Cruise Line:** Small and intimate, Seabourn's sleek, modern ships are floating pleasure palaces bathing all who enter in doting service and the finest cuisine at sea. You luxuriate in unprecedented amounts of onboard space and an almost 1 to 1 passenger to staff ratio, with service worthy of the grand hotels of Europe.

✔ **Silversea Cruises:** Although a little less high-brow than Seabourn, Silversea operates bigger ships (296 to 382 passengers against Seabourn's 204).

The Best of the Mainstream Lines

Turn to Chapter 14 to find out more about these outstanding mainstream cruise lines:

✔ **Celebrity Cruises:** All the lines are coming out with fabulous new ships, but we particularly like the ships in the Celebrity fleet (especially the Millennium-class ships — *Millennium, Infinity, Summit, and Constellation*). They make up the classiest affordable ships out there. Attractive features include cutting-edge art collections, modern decor, stunning dining rooms, over-the-top alternative restaurants, and lavish spas.

✔ **Princess Cruises (Diamond class & Coral class):** Princess's huge but cozy *Diamond Princess* and *Sapphire Princess* are its most beautiful ships to date. They combine gorgeous exterior lines with wood-heavy, old-world lounges, an innovative dining plan, and a great covered promenade that allows you to stand right in the ship's bow. The smaller *Coral Princess* and *Island Princess* are big winners too, with similar decor and a size that lets them traverse the Panama Canal.

✔ **Royal Caribbean International (Radiance class & Voyager class):** The most elegant vessels Royal Caribbean has produced to date, *Radiance, Brilliance, Serenade,* and *Jewel of the Seas* combine a sleek, seagoing exterior; a nautically themed interior; and acres of windows. The Voyager ships — *Voyager, Explorer, Adventure, Navigator,* and *Mariner* — are the archetypal activities ships and maybe the first vessels to satisfy the old "city at sea" cliché.

The Best Ships for Families

Chapter 10 clues you in to family-oriented cruising activities, and Chapter 14 gives you more information about mainstream family-oriented cruise lines. The following are our favorites:

- **Carnival Cruise Lines:** Carnival has made the move from party line to family line, with kids a particularly big focus, facility-wise, on the line's Destiny-, Spirit-, and Conquest-class vessels.

- **Disney Cruise Lines:** Kids are becoming a large part of the big cruise ship experience, and, of course, Disney knows how to keep kids (and parents) as happy as mice: with the most well developed children's programs at sea.

- **Princess Cruises:** Nothing beats the giant *Golden Princess* in this category. The vessel has a spacious children's playroom, a fenced-in outside deck area designated as kids' space (with a kiddie pool and a fleet of red tricycles), and a teen center complete with computers, video games, a sound system, and even a teens-only hot tub and sunbathing area. Supervised activities are offered for kids ages 2 to 17, and the ship also has amenities designed to please adults and kids alike, including a pizzeria, basketball and volleyball courts, and a virtual-reality game room (including a motion-simulator ride).

- **Royal Caribbean International:** Royal Caribbean's Voyager-class ships, with their rock-climbing walls, ice-skating rinks, in-line skating tracks, miniature golf, and **Johnny Rockets** restaurants, are the absolute best choice for active families — particularly those with teens.

The Best Romantic Cruises

Some cruise lines cater to the amorous. Our top picks include the following:

- **Cunard Line:** Like real royalty, *Queen Mary 2* was born with certain duties attendant to its station, and one of its biggest duties is to embody the romance of transatlantic travel and bring it into the new century. Take a stroll around that promenade deck, dine in that fabulous dining room, and thrill to be out in the middle of the Atlantic on nearly a billion dollars worth of ocean-faring thoroughbred. See Chapter 15.

- **SeaDream Yacht Club:** SeaDream's small vessels are ultra luxurious in a comfortable way. You have plenty of opportunities on these ships for holding hands, whether you stroll the deck under the stars, enjoy fine cuisine at a table for two, or lounge in the *Balinese DreamBeds* (puffy outdoor mattresses). See Chapter 15.

✔ **Windstar Cruises:** Pure romance is a day with your loved one in a private cove or other secluded spot with *Wind Surf* or *Wind Spirit* anchored offshore, bobbing calmly on the waves, sails furled. Windstar offers a truly unique cruise experience, giving passengers the delicious illusion of adventure (by stopping at small coves and such) and the ever-pleasant reality of first-class cuisine, service, and itineraries. See Chapter 16.

The Best Party Cruises

Looking for a party at sea? Try one of these cruise lines:

✔ **Carnival Cruise Lines:** A lot of men and women in their 20s, 30s, and 40s seek out Carnival's *fun ships* for their wild-and-crazy decor and around-the-clock excitement. What else would you expect from ships with names like *Fantasy, Inspiration,* and *Sensation?* The Pool Deck is always bustling (especially on the 3- and 4-nighters), with music playing so loudly that you have to go back to your cabin to think, and the discos and nightspots hop until the early morning hours. The ships are big, offering many places to meet and mingle. See Chapter 14.

✔ **Royal Caribbean International:** This line draws a good cross section of men and women from all walks of life. As with Carnival, a decent number of passengers are singles and in their 20s, 30s, and 40s, especially on the short 3- and 4-night weekend cruises. For an exciting Saturday-night-out-on-the-town barhopping kind of experience, the Voyager-class ships feature a truly unique multideck, boulevard-like promenade running down the center of every ship. Each ship's ground floor is lined with shops, bars, restaurants, and entertainment outlets, with a multistory atria at either end. See Chapter 14.

✔ **Windjammer Barefoot Cruises:** If you have an informal attitude, Windjammer cruises are a great getaway. You can dress-down and be very, very casual. The wind, waves, stars, and moonlight spark up your social skills — and the free rum punch, $2 beers, and visits to legendary Caribbean beach bars don't hurt either! You can find a handful of rowdy, singles-only cruises annually — erotic tart-eating contest, anyone? See Chapter 16.

The Best Ships for Shoppers

If shopping is your thing, we recommend these cruise lines:

✔ **CelebrityCruises:** Celebrity has high style shopping malls on its *Millennium, Infinity, Summit,* and *Constellation,* with name brands like Escada Sport, Tommy Hilfiger, Swarovski crystal, and Fossil watches and a plethora of souvenirs and logo items among the items for sale. See Chapter 14.

✔ **Cunard Line:** *Queen Mary 2* is all about brands, with H. Stern, Dunhill, Hermes (for cruisers who want $900 sneakers), Harrod's logo items, and other big names. You can find less expensive souvenirs as well. *QE2* wins shopping points not only for providing nifty around-the-world souvenirs (you can buy things from all the neat places the ship visits, even if you don't actually go there on your cruise), but also for its bookshop and the nautical antiques it sells. See Chapter 15.

✔ **Royal Caribbean International:** Royal Caribbean has some of the best shops at sea, stocking items from local ports as well as jewelry, liquor, perfumes, collectibles, and nearly every logo-ed souvenir you can imagine. *The Voyager of the Seas* and its sister ships also have Tommy Hilfiger boutiques. See Chapter 14.

The Best Ships for Cuisine

Food and cruising go hand and hand. Find the best dining on these cruise lines:

✔ **Celebrity Cruises:** It doesn't get any better than the alternative restaurants on the Millennium-class ships, which are all supervised by chef and restaurateur Michel Roux of the **Waterside Inn,** one of England's most highly rated restaurants. Reservations are required in these intimate, elegantly designed spots. *Millennium*'s **Olympic** restaurant boasts the actual gilded French walnut-wood paneling used aboard White Star Line's *Olympic,* sister ship to *Titanic,* and sister ships *Infinity, Summit,* and *Constellation* have restaurants themed around artifacts from the SS *United States, Normandie,* and *Ile de France.* A highly trained staff dotes on diners with tableside cooking, musicians play elegant period pieces, and the entire decadent experience takes only about three hours. It costs $25 a person, but the experience is well worth the price. See Chapter 14.

✔ **Crystal Cruises:** Although all the food you get on Crystal ships is first-class, their reservations-only Asian specialty restaurants are the best Asian cuisine at sea. Master Chef Nobuyuki "Nobu" Matsuhisa is behind the outstanding Asian food on *Serenity,* and the restaurant on *Harmony* serves up utterly delicious, fresh Japanese food. The accouterments help set the tone, too — chopsticks, sake served in tiny sake cups and decanters, and sushi served on thick blocky square glass platters. An Asian-themed buffet lunch, offered at least once per cruise, gives passengers an awesome spread, from jumbo shrimp and chicken and beef satays to stir-fry dishes. See Chapter 15.

✔ **Seabourn Cruise Lines:** Nothing quite compares to dining on the outdoor deck of *Legend* and in *Pride*'s **Veranda Café**, which offers casual dinners most nights. With the ships' wakes shushing just below, you have a rare opportunity to dine with the sea breezes and starry night sky surrounding you. Asian, Mediterranean, and steakhouse-style menus are featured. See Chapter 15.

✔ **Silversea Cruises:** Depart at sunset from port and the windowed, candlelit **Terrace Cafe** alternative restaurant on each of this line's four ships becomes a window to the passing scenery and a home for some of the best food at sea. Reservations are required for the fixed theme menu: Asian night starts with sushi and sashimi, and a French feast begins with foie gras, followed by a scallop and rata- touille salad, beef tenderloin, and a warm chocolate tart with rasp- berries. (Excellent wines and all spirits are included in the cruise rates.) See Chapter 15.

The Best Ports of Call

You don't spend all your cruise time on the water. The following ports are particularly intriguing:

✔ **In Alaska:** **Juneau** and **Skagway** are our favorites. Juneau has to be the prettiest state capital anywhere in America; it's fronted by the Gastineau Channel, backed Mount Juneau and Mount Roberts, close to the Mendenhall Glacier, and otherwise surrounded by wilderness. Skagway offers Alaska Gold Rush history in a perfect setting, with buildings so well preserved that you think Disney cre- ated the place. See Chapter 19.

✔ **In the Caribbean:** We like **Cozumel** for its wonderful Mexican flavor, party atmosphere, great buys on crafts, nearby ruins, and excellent snorkeling. **Key West** is a pure delight with its street performers, food, bars, funky history, colorful characters, water opportunities . . . well, we like just about everything. **St. Barts** is exclusive, pretty, lush, and loaded with celebrites. Need we say more? See Chapter 18.

✔ **In the Mediterranean:** **Venice** is our favorite, a city where every view is museum-quality. A stop in **Kuşadasi** (Turkey) brings you not only close to Ephesus, an amazing ancient archeological site, but also to vendors selling wonderful rugs at affordable prices. You can't top **Athens** or **Rome** for history. For quaintness, you can't beat **Portofino** (Italy), and **Santorini** (Greece) has the most dra- matic port scenery. Other faves include **Barcelona** and **Istanbul** — both impressively exotic. See Chapter 20.

Chapter 2

Introducing the Cruise Experience

. . . .

In This Chapter

▶ Discovering the advantages of cruising

▶ Understanding how cruising developed

▶ Exploring the seven seas

▶ Getting a feel for the activities

▶ Figuring that you *can* afford it

▶ Tossing your excuses overboard

. . . .

A cruise is a dream vacation — both fun and easy. You get to go to interesting places; you're pampered by attentive crew who are there to help you relax; you get to experience the sea and view gorgeous coastal scenery; and you have to unpack your bags only once. Best of all, your accommodations, food, and entertainment all get lumped into one easy bill that you pay in advance — and it can be a comparatively small bill at that. What could be better?

Getting On Board with Cruising

People choose a cruise vacation for a variety of reasons: It's easy to plan; their friends tell them great things about cruising; it allows them to go to several different countries rather than just one; they want to try something new; or they find out about a great deal. Whatever leads you to your decision to explore cruising, you're on the right track.

The cruise industry in 1970 catered to only a half million passengers. The number of cruise passengers was, for the first time, expected to surpass the 10 million mark during 2004. About 80 percent of passengers who try cruising are likely to want to repeat the experience. Why? Well, consider these top reasons that first-time cruisers gave the Cruise Lines International Association (CLIA; the marketing group for the cruise industry) for preferring a cruise to other vacations:

- ✔ Being pampered
- ✔ Relaxing and getting away from it all
- ✔ Having the opportunity to visit several destinations in one trip
- ✔ Experiencing a variety of activities
- ✔ Getting good value for the money
- ✔ Enjoying high-quality entertainment
- ✔ Making the trip a romantic getaway
- ✔ Resting in comfortable accommodations
- ✔ Taking delight in the trip as a learning experience
- ✔ Trying out a vacation area with the thought of returning to it

Entering the modern cruising era

Until only a few decades ago, cruising was considered mostly a form of transportation. Getting on a ship, no matter how luxurious, was designed to get you from point A to point B, and sometimes also to points C and D.

In 1958, a sea change occurred. Pan Am flew the first nonstop jet flight from New York to Paris and rendered cruise transportation somewhat obsolete. People now had a quicker transportation option.

But as the jet age emerged, so did a new concept in the cruise industry. Cruises lines marketed their ships not as transportation vehicles, but as moving vacations — a hotel that floats.

In 1966, Ted Arison, who would later form Carnival Cruise Lines, and Knut Kloster, who would later form Norwegian Cruise Lines, introduced the *Sunward*, a converted car/passenger ferry that debuted as a Caribbean cruise ship. The *Sunward* began offering 3- and 4-day cruises from Florida to the Caribbean and back again, and the success of the venture quickly drew competition.

In the years that followed, Carnival Corporation (the industry's biggest success story by far) did much to enhance the idea of the cruise ship as a vacation destination, and the Caribbean became and remains the cruising industry's top destination.

Embracing the Love Boat age

In the 1970s, the cruise industry shed what had been a mostly white-gloved-old-lady reputation and became a truly mass-market phenomenon.

Cruising through history

To understand how cruising developed into a successful industry, you have to take a brief look at the past. Today's cruise industry actually has its roots dated to the early 1840s.

Among the earliest cruise passengers was author Charles Dickens, who booked passage in 1842, along with 86 fellow travelers, on a mail ship called *Britannia* (operated by Canadian Samuel Cunard, founder of the Cunard Line). Writing in *American Notes* about his journey from Liverpool to Halifax, Nova Scotia and Boston, Dickens describes the cramped quarters, coffinlike cabins, and passengers, including himself, getting seasick (although he claims that he just felt woozy).

Conditions had somewhat improved by the time Mark Twain took a transatlantic voyage on the steamship *Quaker City* in 1867. Twain described his cabin as having "room to turn around in, but not to swing a cat in, at least with entire security to the cat." Well, at least he didn't get sick. In *The Innocents Abroad,* Twain wrote, "If there is one thing in the world that will make a man peculiarly and insufferably self-conceited, it is to have his stomach behave himself, the first day at sea, when nearly all his comrades are seasick."

Okay, so Dickens and Twain probably weren't quoted much in early cruise promotions. But despite the bad press, passenger cruise ships became increasingly popular.

The industry got a big boost in 1977 with the introduction of the ABC television series *The Love Boat.* Using the real Princess ships *Island Princess* and *Pacific Princess* as floating sets, the show was virtually a weekly one-hour primetime commercial for the cruise industry.

The show's weekly vignettes about love and romance nearly always had a happy ending, which didn't hurt the image of cruising one bit.

Cruising today

Cruising is so popular today because it really does offer something for everyone, whether you're an outdoor adventurer or someone who prefers glitzy Las Vegas-type attractions. Small, casual, adventure-type vessels can explore remote islands, and massive megaships compete with land-based resorts by offering lavish gyms and spas, exciting casinos and clubs, extravagant shows, and even golf (on mini courses or using simulators). Royal Caribbean's *Voyager of the Seas* and its sister ships *Explorer, Adventure,* and *Navigator* have ice-skating rinks; Cunard's *Queen Mary 2* has a planetarium; and the *Caribbean Princess* features *Dive-In* movies, shown under the stars on a big screen at the mid-ship pool area. What's next? Take your best guess.

Keeping It Fresh

Cruise lines have launched most of the ships that currently cater to North American cruisers within the past 10 years, and bigger and better ships appear all the time. In fact, 12 new ships were scheduled for intro-duction in 2004; the first introduced in April 2004 was Cunard's *Queen Mary 2*, the world's largest ocean liner. The new ships offer enticing extras, such as cabins with private verandas (a wonderful feature worth the extra bucks), expanded spas, and fancy or casual alternative dining choices (you often pay an extra fee to dine at the fancy venues). And the ships put an emphasis on providing a place for relaxation — some people come on a cruise just to take it easy.

Cruise lines are spicing things up by adding new destinations, new activ-ities on and off the ship, new motifs, and more realistic cruise lengths (not everyone can take off for a week at a time). They bring ships closer to travelers' doors by offering sailings from places including Baltimore, Boston, Charleston, Galveston, Houston, Long Beach, New Orleans, New York, Norfolk, Philadelphia, San Diego, San Francisco, Seattle, Whittier (Alaska), and even Bayonne, New Jersey. Even in Florida, the lines are expanding to new ports such as Jacksonville. For people who need it, cruise lines offer airfare options and transfers as well as optional pre- and post-cruise hotel stays, making it easy for vacationers to plan a trip in one shot. Cruise information is also available on the Web, making it easier to compare services and prices.

But the best news for consumers is that the competition to fill all the new ships keeps the prices low. In fact, given the spate of discounts, the price of cruising has actually gone down in recent years. Travel jitters because of world conditions, compounded by an unstable economy, only add to this trend, bringing some of the biggest discounting ever over the past three years.

Seeing the World

You can cruise in North America, Central America, Europe, Greenland, Asia, Africa, South America, the South Pacific, Australia, New Zealand, and even Antarctica. Cruising in the Middle East used to be common, but in the aftermath of 9/11, most of those itineraries were cancelled after the ships moved to safer ports. World cruises take vacationers who have the time (we're talking months) to several regions all over the globe. In this book, we highlight the most popular cruising regions: the Caribbean for fun in the sun and gorgeous island vistas; Alaska for a sense of the vast wilderness, wildlife, Native culture, and scenery like you've never seen before; and the Mediterranean for history brought to life and a chance to immerse yourself in various cultures. All these regions are good destinations whether you're a first-timer or a repeat cruiser.

If you want something different, remember that when it comes to cruising, the sky's the limit — or more aptly, the sea's the limit. One of the great benefits of cruising is that you can experience exotic locales such as Vietnam, Antarctica, or the countries along Africa's coast and return to the familiar comfort of your ship at night. You have the best of both worlds.

Appealing to All Types of Travelers

Although demographics vary from ship to ship and from cruise line to cruise line, cruising companies provide something for everyone when it comes to cruise vacations — young and old, singles and couples, honeymooners and families. And, with all the bargains out there, you don't have to be rich to cruise: If you can afford a vacation, you can afford a cruise. Cruising can, in fact, be a bargain when compared to many land-based vacations.

Who cruises? People like you. According to CLIA, the average cruise passenger is 50 years old, but 30 percent of cruisers are under 40. The average age of new cruisers is 43. Some 78 percent of cruise passengers are married, with an average household income of about $79,000 per year (but 15 percent of cruisers have household incomes of $40,000 or less).

An all-inclusive Caribbean cruise vacation including port charges costs on average about $1,000 per week, based on double occupancy (two people sharing a room). But with discounts, you may find options from about $100 a day to less than $70 a day. Shorter cruises typically start at about $299 for a three-night sailing.

Remember, your fare includes your accommodations, six meals or more a day (if you can eat that much), a plethora of onboard activities (including sports), resort-style amenities such as swimming pools and gyms, nighttime entertainment, and stops at interesting ports of call. And in most cases, if you choose, you can book a package that includes airfare and transfers from the airport to the ship (with the option of an add-on hotel stay at your port of embarkation or disembarkation). All in all, it adds up to a great vacation value.

Table 2-1 illustrates how the price of an average cruise vacation compares with that of an average land-based vacation. We tried to come up with realistic estimates, but obviously these depend on how budget-minded you are — you can cut land-based costs by staying at a cheap motel and eating fast food at every meal, for example. Airfare is extra, but a benefit of cruises is, of course, you can drive to the port.

Table 2-1	Cost Comparison by Land and by Sea	
Expense	*Bahamas Resort (7 Nights)*	*Caribbean Cruise (7 Nights)*
Cruise fare	N/A	$1,000
Room	$700	Included
Ground transfers	Included	Included
Meals and snacks	$350	Included
Alcoholic beverages	$120	$100
Activities	Additional	Included
Entertainment	$55 or more	Included
Tips	$90	$70
TOTAL	$1,315 (plus activities)	$1,170

Checking Your Hassles at the Door

The whole cruise experience is designed to help you relax. Sure, you may have to wait in line to get aboard, but after you get through that process your experience should be relatively stress-free — just unpack your bags and let your floating hotel take you to interesting ports. Head up to the pool deck and wave your hand for a cold beer or a piña colada. No need to make dinner plans: The kitchen crew is busy preparing the evening's delights. Entertainment options abound, and you don't have to pour over a map or hire a taxi to get to the fun.

The crew feeds, pampers, and takes care of you. You don't even have to worry about money because you paid upfront; and for the extras, such as drinks, the ship operates with a cash-free system (of course, the cruise line charges your credit card for that beer or piña colada at the end of the cruise).

When you get to port, you can take an excursion offered by the ship, or you can go off exploring on your own. It's your choice. This vacation is yours.

A resort by day . . .

Just because you're on a ship doesn't mean you have to give up the kind of daytime activities available at land-based resorts. Most cruise ships, especially the newer and bigger vessels, boast lavish spas with beauty parlors (where for a fee you can splurge on a soothing massage or a manicure) and gyms, often with ocean views. Extensive children's programs are designed to keep your kids well occupied so that you have a chance to play, too. The ships also organize activities that range from silly pool games to craft classes (on some of the newer Princess ships you can even do pottery), art auctions, bridge tournaments, and lectures.

Sports enthusiasts may find (depending on the ship) basketball, racquetball, tennis, trapshooting, golf, rock-climbing, billiards, and/or in-line skating, as well as the traditional shuffleboard and ping-pong. Some ships offer scuba classes. And at the ports, if you go to a warm-weather destination, you have ample time to enjoy the beaches and additional water sports offerings, including snorkeling.

Want more? How about video arcades and movie theaters showing first-run releases? You can shop on the ship for souvenirs and even diamonds or pearls (all duty-free). And thanks to satellite technology, you may even be able to watch a live sporting event. You can also stay in touch by sending and receiving e-mail at the ship's Internet cafe.

Or you can focus on eating. Start with an early risers' continental breakfast at 6 a.m., followed by a full breakfast (buffet or sit-down), a lunch at a buffet or in the dining room, and pizza and/or afternoon tea. But save room for dinner, and don't forget the midnight buffet!

. . . a total entertainment experience by night

Nighttime is one of the liveliest times on a cruise ship. You have the multi-course dinner to look forward to, for one thing. And then, depending on the ship, you can dance, try your luck in a casino, sip drinks at a piano bar, light up a stogie at a cigar bar, see a Vegas- or Broadway-style show, or just walk on the deck and stare at the stars until sunrise.

Best of all, nearly all activities are included in your cruise fare. You don't pay admission charges to any of the entertainment offerings; you pay only for your drinks (which are usually quite reasonably priced) and, of course, for any bets you place at the casino. If you're in a port at night, you can check out the local nightlife, including shows, casinos, and clubs.

Overcoming Your Cruising Anxieties

Just as everyone has an opinion on politics, everyone has reasons for not cruising before. Often, those excuses are just cover-ups for long-held misconceptions. We answer the nagging questions of the cruise-curious in the following sections.

Can I afford it?

The upfront price may shock you, but remember that it includes your cabin, food, amusements, shows, and the option of reduced-rate airfare and transfers. Often, a cruise costs less than a land-based vacation (refer to Table 2-1). Remember, you're likely to get a discount off those prices in the cruise brochures.

Can I bring my kids?

Cruise companies know that many of their target customers have kids. Consequently, the lines today are very kid-friendly. They offer free, supervised activities for youngsters from toddlers to teens, especially during school vacation periods. Most lines also offer baby-sitting for an additional charge.

What if I get seasick?

Most cruise ships nowadays are so large and well stabilized that you can barely tell you're on water. Plus, most cruises stick to calm seas, especially in the Caribbean and Alaska's Inside Passage.

You probably won't have any problems, unless you're extremely sensitive or the ship passes through rough water. If you do feel queasy, try taking an over-the-counter medication such as Dramamine or Bonine. Most ships stock medicines for less sea-hardy passengers, and you can sometimes get them for free from the purser's office. You can also go to your doctor before you leave home for the Transderm patch, available by prescription. Alternative remedies include ginger capsules, available at health food stores, and acupressure wristbands, which most pharmacies carry.

Is there a doctor on board?

The big ships have fully equipped medical facilities and staff, with one doctor (sometimes two) and several nurses, to handle medical emergencies, including minor surgery. If something really bad happens, such as a stroke or heart attack, the cruise line calls for a helicopter or boat to evacuate the passenger to the nearest port. Smaller ships stick closer to the mainland, and although they may not have doctors on board, they can usually get to a land-based doctor quickly.

Will I be bored?

You practically need a map and several days to explore some of the largest ships around today, and you can find something to do in just about every nook and cranny. You can listen to guest speakers, chug down a beer at the sports bar, or even participate in a sport yourself. Take a swim, watch a flick, go to the gym, get pampered at the spa, or go shopping.

And besides, you aren't *on* the ship for a week. Remember, ships go places. Which leads me to . . .

Where will my ship go?

Cruise ships visit some 1,800 ports worldwide — just about any place you can go for a coastal vacation. Some cruise lines even take you to places you can't visit otherwise, such as their own private beach resorts!

Obviously, the activities you can do at a port of call vary depending on which port you visit. Climb a mountain, go scuba diving, sunbathe on a beach, haggle with street vendors, visit ancient landmarks, see the scenery on a helicopter tour — you can find something interesting whether you explore on your own or go as part of a ship-organized group.

What if I don't like crowds?

Cruising, especially on larger ships, provides plenty of opportunities for social interaction, but if you feel like lounging on a deck chair or taking a nap in your cabin, no one is going to make you socialize or participate.

But, with that said, cruising is by nature a group-travel experience. Although most cruise lines are good at dispersing crowds, you still may have to wait your turn at the buffet or to get off the ship at a port. Meals are very much a social high point of the experience. You can't easily find a table for one (or a table for two, for that matter), and if you really don't like to be around other people, you're better off rethinking a cruise vacation.

 If you prefer to steer clear of large groups of people, try a cruise on a small ship. The atmosphere is generally more laid-back and fewer passengers are aboard.

Won't I get fat?

Although the rumor is that the average person gains about five pounds on a one-week cruise, opportunities are available for you to actually lose weight. Many vessels offer special low-fat options on their menus, and buffets include healthy alternatives such as fresh fruits and salads. Continuing your low-carb diet on a cruise ship is easy. Also, you can keep up with your exercise regimen by working out in the ship's gym, speed walking or jogging around the various decks, and booking physical activities at the ports such as mountain biking, kayaking, or hiking.

How can I stay in touch?

Most ships offer CNN on in-room televisions and a daily news sheet that features news headlines from major newspapers and/or the wire services. And almost all ships offer direct-dial satellite telephone service from your cabin (although making calls from the ship is pricey — from $6.95 to $16.95 per minute). Someone can call you on the ship, too, for a large fee. To save money, wait until the ship docks and hit the pay phones at the ports.

Be wary of individuals hovering around the pay phones; they may want your phone credit card number.

Most ships have Internet access as another communication option. Some ships, including those in the Norwegian Cruise Line fleet, even have *Wi-Fi* (Wireless Fidelity, or wireless Internet that you can use from your cabin or anywhere on the ship with access). At the onboard Internet cafes, expect to pay 50 cents to $1.50 per minute. If you plan to be online a lot, buy a package (sold in 60-, 90-, or 120-minute increments; an unlimited use package may also be available). You can also find cheaper Internet cafes at many ports.

Is cruising safe?

Safety and technology have come a long way since the *Titanic* went down, and today's ships must follow numerous rules and regulations that assure passengers' (and crew members') safety while on board.

Unfortunately, no place exists for you to check on a specific cruise ship's safety records. The Coast Guard conducts rigorous quarterly inspections of all ships operating from U.S. ports, looking to make sure that they comply with its emergency-response requirements. To check out what those requirements are, visit the consumer section of the Coast Guard's Web site at `www.uscg.mil/hq/g-m/cruiseship.htm`. You can look at another section of the Coast Guard Web site, (`cgmix.uscg.mil/psix/psix2`), to find incident reports and recommendations made to the cruise lines, but the information is technical in nature and, as one Coast Guard official told me, can be easily misinterpreted by novices (for example, a 2-inch hole may sound bad, but isn't). You can also log on to the National Transportation Safety Board's Web site (`www.ntsb.gov`) to read past accident reports.

In the area of health inspections, the Centers for Disease Control and Prevention (CDC) regularly inspects cruise ships arriving at U.S. ports for drinking water quality and conditions that could lead to food contamination as part of its Vessel Sanitation Program. The CDC then issues a *Green Sheet,* grading the vessels (86 is a passing mark). You can view the scores at `www.cdc.gov/travel`.

Within the first 24 hours of sailing, everyone on your ship is required to participate in a safety drill that includes trying on a nifty orange life jacket and locating your assigned lifeboat. Pay attention to the information, just on the odd (and rare) chance that you need to use it.

What about this Norwalk virus?

Repeated reports have surfaced over the past few years of passengers experiencing gastrointestinal ailments, including nausea and diarrhea, linked to the Norwalk virus. The increase of incidents is, in part, a result of better reporting procedures. Cruise lines are required to report outbreaks to the Centers for Disease Control (CDC). The CDC works with cruise lines to make sure that the affected ships are properly sanitized. But the CDC also said ships aren't to blame for the outbreaks. Norwalk is passed hand-to-hand, so you can get it from touching, say, a banister someone else touched. Our advice? Take a cruise, but wash your hands frequently.

What about fire safety?

When it comes to fire safety, cruise ships operate under international rules known as *Safety of Life at Sea (SOLAS)*. The rules require ships to have smoke detectors and low-level emergency lighting for escape routes and, as of October 2005, sprinkler systems.

How tight is onboard security?

In the wake of the 9/11 attacks, cruise-ship security was increased. In January 2003, new international rules were established that require all ships and ports to have both security officers and security plans. In addition, regulations mandated by the 2002 Maritime Transportation Security Act became effective on November 23, 2003. For passengers, this means you may see National Guardsmen overseeing the boarding process. When you board any vessel, your hand luggage is X-rayed, and you walk through an airport-type security screening system. You may also be subject to an additional interview and hand search. When the ship leaves port, you may observe Coast Guard vessels standing watch.

Cruise lines are now required to report the names of passengers before each sailing, presumably so officials can check the passengers against lists of known terrorists. The lines strictly enforce a policy that guests and crew must provide identification when boarding and re-boarding a vessel (passengers are issued special boarding cards; some ships have a machine that takes and stores your photo for identification purposes). Another recent change is a ban on allowing passengers to visit the bridge.

Generally, visitors are not allowed on a ship. Just as you would in a hotel, exercise caution when inviting unknown visitors into your cabin on a cruise ship.

Chapter 3

Choosing Your Ideal Cruise

. . . .

In This Chapter

▶ Determining your cruise taste

▶ Deciding on your destination

▶ Picking a cruise that suits your special circumstances

. . . .

So, the cruise bug just won't leave you alone. During those few idle moments you enjoy each day, you find your thoughts roaming to fantasies of hopping aboard a cruise ship and sailing away from your daily routine.

Before you lose sight of dry land, you need to consider what you like to do, what places hold appeal for you, what climates feel most comfortable, and what type of accommodations you prefer. This chapter lays out your options and gives you a running start toward the right gangplank.

The cruise lines' snazzy brochures aren't your best tools for making choices about a ship or destination. *Every* brochure looks lovely — what you see is a staged portrayal of people and places.

 Cabin photos, for instance, tend to show the fancier suites and cabins — low-end staterooms are rarely featured. Ports may be as beautiful in real life as in the pictures — as long as you don't wander off the beaten path. As for the people in the brochures, well, you can be sure that not everyone on your cruise will look like these movie-star types. You may, however, be able to pick up a few hints from the photos as to the typical age of the line's clientele.

Choosing Your Cruise

Cruises come in all sizes, shapes, and designs, so we created the following categories to help you find the cruise that, ahem, floats your boat. Sail over to Chapters 17 through 19 for specifics on the cruise lines and ships that cater to these categories. Make sure to note the overlap — for example, a ship easily may be both a resort cruise and a family cruise.

✔ **Family cruises:** Some cruise lines specialize in family vacations, and they take great pains to plan for all age groups. If you want your vacation to be a family affair, look for a line that caters to adults *and* children. Expect a crowd during holidays and other school break periods. (Find more on the best cruises for families in Chapter 13.)

✔ **Luxury cruises:** You say money is no object? If you can afford a top-of-the-line ship, you're in store for impeccable service, luxurious accommodations, first-class cuisine, and a sophisticated ambience.

✔ **Party cruises:** On these voyages, the passengers tend to party hearty — definitely at night (the disco hops until dawn) and sometimes during the day, too. People groove to the Caribbean steel-band tunes on the Pool Deck (even if the ship isn't in the Caribbean) and bar areas are crowded.

✔ **Resort cruises:** Activities and amusements are the key to resort cruises. These cruises are very popular with folks who want a vacation experience that includes the pool, the spa, aerobics classes, a state-of-the-art gym, sports offerings, kids' programs, and constant activities, such as scuba diving, snorkeling, water sports, golf, educational lectures, and a lot of goofy onboard contests.

✔ **Romantic cruises:** The romantic ambience on a cruise ship is unmistakable. With the rolling sea as a backdrop, *amour* seems ever-present. Some lines promote romance with onboard wedding, honeymoon, or vow-renewal ceremony packages. If your idea of romance is privacy (or relative privacy), you may want to look at a ship where quiet time for two is easy to come by.

✔ **Adventure and educational cruises:** If exploring and getting in-depth knowledge about a destination is first on your list of priorties, an adventure/educational cruise is best for you. You can attend lectures that pertain to the region you travel through or participate in guided nature walks or history tours. Some cruises make kayaking, hiking, and nature observation the focus of the trip.

Most ships offer at least a taste of all these cruise categories. But by knowing your priorities, you can easily find the cruise that best fits your needs.

Finding the right ship

The difference between the experience of being on a modern megaship (with anywhere from 1,750 to more than 3,000 passengers) and being on a small ship with 400 passengers or less (sometimes as few as a dozen) is huge. Ditto for the difference between being on a glitzy new megaship and a midsize traditional-style ocean liner.

Cruising with a theme

Your personal interests don't stay behind when you pack up for vacation. So cruise lines offer theme cruises that take peoples' passions into account. Special thematic cruises range from food and wine (on Crystal and Silversea, among others), to theater (Cunard), to Big Band music (Holland America), and even to quitting smoking (on Carnival). Check with your travel agent or contact the lines directly for a current schedule of themed cruises.

Gauging your time away

Seven nights is a nice round number for a reasonably paced cruise. Ships usually depart on a Saturday or Sunday afternoon and return early the following Saturday or Sunday. However, booking a 3- or 4-night getaway is a good alternative to a full-week cruise — especially if you're traveling the waterways for the first time or simply don't have the cash for a longer cruise. A shorter cruise can give you a chance to enjoy some land-based options during a week's worth of vacation by combining your cruise with, say, a visit to Disney World or time on the beach in Miami. Not wanting to miss any marketing opportunities, the cruise lines offer an array of pre- and post-cruise packages that make it easy to plan a combo vacation.

The shorter the cruise, the more party-oriented the passengers tend to be — something to keep in mind if you're looking for a quiet time.

Picking a Destination

Almost as important as deciding what kind of cruise experience you want is deciding where you want to go. The most popular cruising region in the world is the Caribbean, followed by Europe and Alaska. Most first-time cruisers choose the Caribbean, with an itinerary that may include a port of call in Mexico. See Part V for specifics on each destination.

If a particular destination doesn't immediately speak to you, consider the following guidelines: Caribbean cruises attract the younger, active sun-worshiper; Alaskan cruises appeal to the older, active (or not) nature lover; and European cruises generally interest those, young and old, who appreciate history and culture.

Warming up to a Caribbean cruise

If you want a tan — and some palm trees, rain forests, interesting cultures, and great shopping — consider cruising in the Caribbean. The biggest draw is the climate, which is so temperate that cruises run year-round.

Caribbean cruises, which generally run from three to seven nights, are popular with the younger set, families, and travelers who enjoy plenty of activity on their vacations. On board, people tend to spend time on the open decks, hanging around the pools, and participating in amusements organized by the ship's cruise director.

Most Caribbean cruises include stops at several islands where passengers can enjoy special events and activities such as beachside barbecues, snorkeling, hiking, and shopping.

Typical itineraries

Eastern Caribbean itineraries tend to sail from one of the Florida home ports — most from Miami, Fort Lauderdale, or Cape Canaveral — and visit several islands such as San Juan, St. Thomas, St. Croix, and St. Maarten or to a private island (possibly owned by the cruise line) or the Bahamas.

Most Western Caribbean itineraries sail from a Florida port (Miami, Fort Lauderdale, Cape Canaveral, or Tampa) to the Cayman Islands or Jamaica (or both); Cozumel and sometimes Calica or Costa Maya, Mexico; Key West, Florida; or to a private island. Cruise lines also offer itineraries from San Juan, Puerto Rico that cover a southern Caribbean route and include stops at several islands such as Grenada, Antigua, St. Thomas, Dominica, Trinidad, Barbados, Tortola, and St. Barthélemy (commonly called St. Barts). See Chapter 21 for details on these locations.

Caribbean cruises are also offered regularly from New Orleans and Galveston/Houston, Texas and occasionally from ports including Mobile, Alabama; Norfolk, Virginia; and Charleston, South Carolina. And thanks to a new generation of fast ships, some Caribbean cruises now depart from New York and Bayonne, New Jersey.

Smaller, more adventure-oriented lines offer Caribbean itineraries that depart from the Caribbean islands themselves (you fly to the island to catch the ship).

On a big ship in the Caribbean, expect to visit three to five popular islands during a 7-night cruise. That leaves one to three days spent at sea — your chance to participate in all the fun shipboard activities or just relax.

If you want to check out more islands and some special spots off the beaten tourist path, such as a quiet cove with great snorkeling and scuba opportunities or an isolated beach, book a passage on a smaller ship. We detail the hot spots at each popular cruise port in Chapter 21, but if you want even more detail, check out *Caribbean For Dummies* (Wiley).

Caribbean sailing seasons

High season for the Caribbean runs from the third week in January to the Easter/spring-break period. The sailings most likely to sell out, however, are those during school holiday periods (when you see a lot of families on board), such as Christmas and New Year's and during the summer season. Chapter 4 shares the inside scoop on finding off-season bargains.

If you're anxious about hurricane season, which spans from approximately June 1 to November 1 in the Caribbean, you can take solace in the readiness of modern satellite warning systems to alert ships to any danger. Although ships usually have plenty of time to steer clear, you may be in for a slightly bumpier ride or, in an extreme situation, a course deviation that may prevent you from stopping at an island you really want to see or disrupt your shore excursion plans.

In some rare instances, brewing or active storms may prevent a ship from returning to its homeport, and you may have to take a longer trip back from another port.

Cozying up to an Alaskan adventure

Travelers opt for Alaska to see wondrous sights and scenery more than for fun in the sun. Even in August, the rain or the chill is likely to keep you away from the pool. But you can expect to be on deck for the ship's passage through Alaska's display of resident wildlife and postcard-perfect mountains, glaciers, fjords, and forests.

Alaskan cruises attract an older audience, often (but not always) 55 and up. However, these cruises are becoming increasingly popular with families. Although the typical passengers may be less into partying than their cruise-the-Caribbean counterparts, a trip through the 49th state promises plenty of excitement and vigorous adventure, and you may want to try activities such as kayaking, mountain biking, river rafting, flightseeing (by helicopter or floatplane), salmon fishing, or dog sledding.

In addition to the natural attractions, rich cultural and historical sightseeing opportunities abound on shore.

Typical itineraries

Most Alaskan cruises depart from Seward, Alaska, or Vancouver, British Columbia, with a new homeport in Whittier, Alaska. Ships also sail from Seattle and San Francisco, and some smaller vessels leave from Juneau and other ports. Routes follow two distinct areas, known generically as the Inside Passage and the Gulf (short for Gulf of Alaska).

Inside Passage itineraries typically sail round-trip from Vancouver and visit the narrow strip that runs from the Canadian border in the south to the start of the Gulf in the north. The trip passes through glacier areas (possibly including the famous Glacier Bay), various islands, and the port towns of Juneau, Haines, Ketchikan, Skagway, and Sitka (which is not technically in the Inside Passage, but close enough).

The Gulf routes normally travel one-way between Vancouver and Anchorage/Seward or Whittier, and they include visits to glacier areas in south-central Alaska and to Inside Passage ports. A typical Gulf itinerary stops at Ketchikan, Juneau, Sitka and/or Skagway, the port of Valdez, either Glacier Bay or Hubbard Glacier, and College Fjord. A smaller ship in Alaska normally stops by smaller ports of call such as Haines and Petersburg. It may also visit popular ports such as Juneau and great natural areas such as Glacier Bay and Tracy Arm, however. If you get lucky, you see some small bays, fjords, and wilderness areas that are off-limits to big ships.

We detail the best things to see and do at Alaska's ports in Chapter 22, but for even more information, you can also check out *Frommer's Alaska* or *Frommer's Alaska Cruises & Ports of Call* (both published by Wiley).

Alaskan sailing seasons

Cold weather the rest of the year limits Alaska's tourist season to the summer (generally early or mid-May through late September), although smaller ships may venture out as early as April. The warmest months are June, July, and August, when temperatures generally range from 50 to 80 degrees during the day with a slight dip at night. During the shoulder-season months — May and September — travelers can take advantage of lower rates.

Moving on to the Mediterranean

The Mediterranean — whose ports include Barcelona and Lisbon in the west and Athens and Turkey in the east, plus everything in between — is a destination for people who appreciate history and culture. Your journey introduces you to buildings and monuments that date back thousands of years, small towns where you can sit at a tavern and take in the local scene, and high culture — from art museums to gourmet restaurants and excellent shopping. The ports are close together, and your itinerary typically includes several countries.

Sailing in Europe provides a much more diverse experience than you can find in the Caribbean or Alaska, and the ship's passenger mix reflects the international flavor. Your fellow travelers are likely to be an assortment of older passengers, younger couples, families, and honeymooners.

Activities center on museum hopping, touring ancient ruins, and absorbing the cultural landscape steeped in history; depending on the ship, activities may also include water sports.

Cruises range from 3-day sailings around the Greek Isles to 10- or 12-day voyages that visit ports in both the eastern and western Mediterranean. Also available are plenty of 7-day options that focus on a single region.

Typical itineraries

Mediterranean itineraries vary greatly, but most ships leave from Barcelona, Athens, Istanbul, Rome (actually Civitavecchia, which is a port near Rome), or Venice. Some small ships sail from the Greek Islands or from smaller ports in Turkey or France.

Three regions make up the cruising territory of most lines: the Western Mediterranean, the Greek Isles/Eastern Mediterranean, and the Riviera. Some ships offer itineraries that take in all the areas; others concentrate on a particular locale.

The area typically described as the western Mediterranean stretches from Barcelona or Lisbon to Civitavecchia and includes port calls in Spain, France, and Italy.

The Greek Isles/eastern Mediterranean area includes the Aegean Sea and sometimes the Adriatic, with ports including Piraeus (near Athens), the Greek Islands (Rhodes, Santoríni, Mykonos, and so on), and Kuşadasi and/or Istanbul (both in Turkey). Some cruises also visit Venice and Dubrovnik, Croatia.

Riviera itineraries include such French ports as Nice, Cannes, and Saint-Tropez; Monte Carlo; and small Italian Riviera ports such as Portofino. Riviera cruises may also include Rome (Civitavecchia). A large ship may stop at a different port every day; on some days, you may even visit two ports — one in the morning and another in the afternoon — or stay in a port overnight (giving you more than a day to explore). Many Mediterranean itineraries last longer than one week, and having more than one day a week at sea is rare.

 On a smaller ship, you hit some of the same ports as the big ships do, but you may also stop at smaller towns such as Portofino and Portoferraio in Italy.

We give details on all the major ports in Chapter 23, but if you want even more info, check out the relevant *For Dummies* book (France, Spain, or Italy) or a *Frommer's* guide — you can find a full book for every country we discuss in Chapter 23. (Both series are published by Wiley.)

Mediterranean sailing seasons

The Mediterranean cruise season generally runs from April through November, although some operators cruise there year-round. Temperatures in-season can reach 80 degrees Fahrenheit or higher, but nice breezes along the coast help refresh you. Portugal tends to be cooler (more like mid-70s) but with more rain. Greece and Turkey are the hottest, and if you don't enjoy warmer weather, you should visit these countries from April to June or mid-September through the end of October.

Meeting Special Situations

If you're a single traveler, a honeymooner, a traveler with disabilities, or a gay or lesbian traveler, you may have particular considerations when you decide on a destination and book a cruise. These sections offer a little practical advice.

Solo cruisers

Hoping to meet Mr. or Ms. Right on your cruise vacation? Cruise ships are inherently romantic places. One in four cruise passengers today is single; so, statistically speaking, the odds of meeting other singles work in your favor.

The cruises that offer more of a party atmosphere, such as Carnival and Royal Caribbean's 3- and 4-day Bahamas or Mexico sailings, generally attract more singles. If you want to leave nothing to chance, Windjammer Barefoot Cruises offers singles cruises, and most other ships host singles get-togethers during the first day of the cruise to let you know who's in the same boat (so to speak).

You may also consider booking a cruise through a travel company that specializes in bringing singles together. These companies include **Cruiseman** (☎ **800-805-0053;** www.cruiseman.com) and **Discount Travel Club** (☎ **800-393-5000;** www.singlescruise.com).

Obviously, not every person who travels alone intends to pair up with a fellow passenger. If you're interested in casual conversation, however, ships provide a perfect atmosphere — after all, you're part of a captive audience. To improve your chances, ask to sit with other singles at dinner, hang out at the disco (especially late at night), and participate in group activities and shore excursions. If you're into athletic types, check out the gym; or you may be able to find a fellow bookworm in the library or attending a lecture.

To find a ship that fits your single needs, consider these questions:

  ✔ Does the cruise line offer cabins designed for single passengers? If not, do they charge outrageous sums when a solo passenger books a cabin designed for two?

  ✔ Alternatively, does the line offer a cabin-share program so you can split the cost with another single?

✔ Does the line attract passengers in your age group?

✔ What sort of social programs for singles does the line host?

We know of at least two cases where women went on cruises and ended up meeting and marrying the ship's captain.

Honeymoon cruisers

Imagine strolling on the promenade deck with your new spouse, sipping champagne as the ocean breeze whispers to you softly. Cruising to a romantic destination tops many couples' lists of post-wedding desires. Typically, one-week cruises depart on either Saturday or Sunday, so look carefully at sailing times as you plan your wedding weekend. Also, consider these questions before you book:

✔ Are honeymoon packages available?

✔ Does the line offer special perks for honeymooners, such as free champagne?

✔ What kind of accommodations can you expect: double-, queen-, or king-sized beds, bathtubs in staterooms, or a Jacuzzi?

✔ Are private verandas — preferably with room for a couple of lounge chairs — available? And are they really private or can your neighbors peek in?

✔ Can you book a table for two in the dining room?

✔ Are there likely to be other couples your age on board?

✔ If the line offers room service, can you order a romantic dinner from a full menu or are you limited to sandwiches?

See The Part of Tens in the back of this book for suggestions on finding romance at sea.

Gay and lesbian cruisers

Gay and lesbian travelers are, of course, not limited to charter cruises when making vacation plans. If you're researching mainstream cruises, you may want to consider these questions:

✔ Would you prefer cruising in a predominately gay environment, or do you enjoy spending time with a more diverse crowd?

✔ Will you feel comfortable on the ship being openly affectionate with your partner? Dancing together?

✔ How gay-friendly are the ports the ship visits? (Same-sex partners who show affection in the Bahamas and on Grand Cayman can elicit hostility.)

Getting married on board

Cruise ship captains generally conduct marriage ceremonies only in movies and on television, but on several of Princess's newer ships you can get married at sea. Ships such as the *Golden Princess* and *Star Princess* have their own wedding chapels and captains who can lead the proceedings. And your friends back home can even watch the ceremony via the Internet thanks to the line's special Wedding Cam on some of the vessels. You can get married on Alaskan cruises in the chapel of Carnival's *Spirit*.

More common, however, is for ships to bring a clergyman or a civil official on board at an embarkation port. Your friends can come on board during the ceremony and either see you off on your honeymoon at the pier or join you on the cruise — a prerequisite of shipboard weddings is that at least the bride and groom take the cruise.

You can also get married shipboard at a port of call, such as a Caribbean island. Some lines also help you arrange a wedding off-ship at a port of call. Princess, Royal Caribbean, and Carnival are among the lines that offer wedding packages with all the trimmings.

Keep in mind that you need to make the ceremony and party arrangements and get a license in advance.

Already married? Check out vow-renewal ceremony packages offered by several lines.

Windjammer Barefoot Cruises (☎ 800-327-2601) offers a few gay-only sailings in the Caribbean and/or South America each year. The line has a special Web site that features these cruises at www.gaywindjammer.com. For these sailings, the line brings special entertainment on board, including drag performers.

Other cruise lines don't organize such cruises themselves — they work with travel agencies that specialize in gay travel to organize special full-ship charter sailings for gay men and/or lesbian women. Usually, these organizations bring their own entertainment and coordinate onboard activities. A few companies to consider include the following: **RSVP Cruises,** 2800 University Ave. S.E., Minneapolis, MN 55414 (☎ **800-328-7787;** www.rsvp.net); **Olivia Cruises and Resorts,** 4400 Market St., Oakland, CA 94608 (☎ **800-631-6277;** www.oliviacruises.com); and **Pied Piper Travel,** 330 W. 42nd St., Suite 1804, New York, NY 10036 (☎ **800-TRIP-312;** in New York, ☎ 212-239-2412; www.piedpiper.com).

For additional operators, contact the **International Gay & Lesbian Travel Association,** 52 W. Oakland Park Blvd., #237, Wilton Manors, FL 33311 (☎ **800-448-8550;** www.iglta.org). The organization has more than 1,000 travel industry members.

You may want to check out *Frommer's Gay & Lesbian Europe* (Wiley), the well-known *Out & About* travel newsletter ($39 print, $20 electronic for one year; to subscribe, call ☎ **800-929-2268** or visit www.outandabout.com), or *Our World* travel magazine ($25 a year by mail or $12 online to subscribe; call ☎ **386-441-5604** or visit www.ourworldpublishing.com) for articles, tips, and listings on gay and lesbian travel.

Wheelchair cruisers

Cruise lines have made an effort in recent years to make their ships more accessible to disabled travelers. The newest ships now commonly feature two-dozen or more wheelchair-accessible cabins they offer at a variety of price points to give wheelchair passengers a good choice of accommodations.

Holland America Line, for example, installed on all its ships an industry-first system to comfortably transfer wheelchair passengers to tenders (launches). The system uses lifts and the guest doesn't have to leave his or her wheelchair during the process. And Princess's *Golden Princess* has a handicapped-accessible pool (with a lift).

On older ships, however, the cruising experience remains a struggle. You may encounter narrow doors and other frustrations like entranceways with lips (to prevent flooding). You may even find that some public rooms are simply not accessible. Small ships rarely have elevators, much less accessible cabins, so they may not be able to accommodate you at all.

A handful of experienced travel agencies specialize in booking cruises for disabled travelers. **Accessible Journeys** (35 W. Sellers Ave., Ridley Park, PA 19078; ☎ **800-846-4537**; www.disabilitytravel.com) publishes a newsletter and can provide licensed health-care professionals to accompany travelers who require aid.

We recommend that when you gain interest in a particular ship, contact the line's special services desk and make sure you understand all the nuances of traveling on that ship. Be aware that some lines require an able-bodied person to accompany a traveler with a disability. Passengers with chronic illnesses may have to present a doctor's note stating clearance for travel.

When you talk with a prospective line, consider these issues:

- ✔ What wheelchair-accessible cabins are available? How are they equipped?

- ✔ Are all public rooms wheelchair accessible? Do I have to maneuver over lips in doorways?

- ✔ Are there a good number of elevator banks (so I don't have to wait long), and are the buttons low enough to reach?

✔ At the ports of call, does the ship pull into dock or use tenders (small boats) to go ashore? Can the tenders handle wheelchairs?

✔ Does the line have any special procedures for boarding and disembarking travelers with disabilities from its ships?

After you board, seek the advice of the tour staff before you choose shore excursions; some may not be wheelchair accessible.

 Make sure the cruise line knows that you use a wheelchair when it makes dining-room table assignments. Some dining rooms are huge, and maneuvering between the tables may not be the easiest thing to do.

Part II
Planning
Your Cruise

The 5th Wave   By Rich Tennant

"Don't worry, they may be called St. Croix, St. Thomas, and St. John, but you're not required to act like one while you're there."

In this part . . .

*H*ere's where we give you the lowdown on cost and the booking process: navigating the Web, finding the travel agent who can give you the best bang for your buck, choosing a cabin, and selecting dining-room seating. We offer tips on what to pack, how much cash you need, and what documents you must bring. We also talk about getting to the ship and the things you need to know for the end of your cruise, such as Customs requirements and how much to tip the crew.

Chapter 4

Managing Your Money

. . . .

In This Chapter

▶ Figuring out the cost of your cruise
▶ Sniffing out savings
▶ Estimating prices for extending your stay
▶ Planning for cruise extras
▶ Monitoring your spending

. . . .

*A*lthough cruise vacations may once have been for the A-listers, the economy-conscious can now afford to cruise too. But you need to develop a realistic budget for your cruise. You should consider a variety of factors, including the cruise price itself, costs of getting to the ship (whether by plane or car), what you expect to spend on board, how much to set aside for shopping, deciding if you want to book the ship's organized shore excursions (and if not, what it costs to tour the ports on your own), whether you need a hotel room before or after the cruise, and if you want to extend your vacation with a land tour.

Understanding Cruise Pricing

Don't let the rates in cruise brochures scare you off — you *can* afford a cruise.

Think about buying a cruise the same way you think about buying a car: Don't pay the sticker price. Here's why: Cruise line brochures typically feature the highest rate for the cruise — the rate the cruise line executives would charge if they had no competition and could get away with charging whatever they wanted, with a guarantee of filling all their available berths. The reality is, however, that cruise lines do have competition — a lot of it — and have to do whatever it takes to fill as many cabins as possible on every sailing, whether they get their asking price or just a fraction of it.

So, except on some of the smaller, niche-market lines, you shouldn't have to pay the brochure price unless you want to travel at a peak time such as Christmas, New Year's, or sometimes during school vacation periods. And even then, early-bird discounts may apply. We list brochure rates for individual cruise lines and ships in Chapters 17 through 19.

Saving Bucks on Your Booking

Naturally, the biggest cost of your cruise vacation is the cruise itself, so this section gives you the best strategies for saving.

Book early, book smart

You don't have to book your cruise a year in advance, but we advise booking at least a few months in advance because cruise lines offer early-bird discounts that range from 15 to 60 percent off for those who book ahead. Company policies vary, and cruise lines don't necessarily state in their brochures how far out you need to book to get the early-bird rate, or even what the actual early-bird rate is, but the discount is worth investigating.

Not only do you save money by booking well in advance, but you also have your best shot at getting your first choice of cabin. Both the nicest and cheapest cabins tend to sell out first.

So how early is early? Lines usually announce their itineraries 10 to 14 months before a sailing. People typically book longer cruises farther out, such as a cruise in Europe 6 to 9 months in advance. Expect people to book shorter cruises 3 to 6 months in advance. Major changes took place in the aftermath of 9/11 because many travelers were hesitant to book cruises more than 60 days before a sailing. Cruise lines adjusted their early booking prices accordingly. Whether this pattern continues or not remains to be seen, but if you want to cruise during a popular period on any itinerary, our advice is to book as early as possible.

Even if a better deal comes along after you book at the early-bird rate, the cruise line may make good and give you the lower rate *if* you happen to notice the rate change. Of course, you or your travel agent must ask for the lower rate; the cruise lines generally don't notify you.

Take a risk by booking late

If a ship approaches the sailing date with empty berths, the cruise line usually offers last-minute discounts that trim 50 to 60 percent (sometimes more) off the cruise fare. These deals are in proportion to the cruise line's anxiety about filling the ship and may appear in the marketplace anywhere from four to eight weeks before the cruise is due to depart. As cruise lines add more new ships, spontaneous travelers find that such last-minute discounts abound (cruises as low as $399 or $499 per week are not uncommon during certain travel periods, such as late fall).

On the other hand, you may not have a variety of cabins to choose from, and although the cruise fare may be great, you may have a hard time getting a good deal on last-minute airfare. We don't recommend that you go the last-minute route unless you have flexible travel plans or you're desperate at the last minute to get away.

Choose off-season cruising

Another surefire way to cut the cost of your cruise is to book slightly off-season — in what's known as the *shoulder season* (the front and back ends of a high season) or in a low season. Table 4-1 lists the shoulder seasons for key cruise locales.

Table 4-1 Off-Seasons for Some Popular Destinations

Dream Cruise Spot	Best Times for Savings
Alaska	April, May, and September
Bermuda	May and September
Caribbean	September to right before Christmas, the first and second weeks of January, and April to June
Europe	April, May, September, and October

Cruise lines often offer the best bargains for fall cruises because the September to mid-December months (with the exception of Thanksgiving week) are traditionally the cruise lines' slowest.

Go on an introductory or repositioning cruise

When a cruise line moves one of its ships from one market to another each season, say from New England to Florida or from Florida to Alaska, it typically offers repositioning cruises at a value price. Experienced cruisers love these cruises, not only for the deals they represent, but also because they tend to include more days at sea than typical itineraries.

Likewise, the lines tend to offer cut rates when they introduce a new ship or move into a new market. So it pays to keep track of what's happening in the industry when you look for a deal. Check cruise line brochures and Web sites such as www.cruisemates.com and www.cruisecritic.com.

Pack more people into your cabin

Into togetherness? Enjoy rubbing elbows with friends and loved ones? You can get discounts by booking extra people for your cabin.

Here's how the cruise lines pull it off: They book the first two passengers at the regular fare and give the third and fourth passengers a pretty big discount. And if your extra passengers happen to be your kids, the line may offer rates just for them. Note that kids under age 2 often can go on the cruise free of charge.

Go with a group

One of the best ways to get a cruise deal is to book as a group, so you may want to gather family for a reunion or convince your friends or colleagues that they need a vacation, too.

A group is generally a minimum of 16 people in 8 cabins. The savings include not only a discounted rate but also at least the cruise portion (but not the air) of the 16th ticket is free (on some upscale ships, you can negotiate one free ticket for groups of eight or more). You and the gang can split the savings from the free ticket or maybe hold a drawing to see who sails for free. If your group is large enough, you may get some freebies from the cruise line, too, such as a cocktail party or added onboard amenities.

Share with another single

Cruise lines want to get the most out of every available cabin, so they base rates on double-occupancy and often require singles who want to room alone to pay what they call a *supplement.* This is no bargain. Supplements can range from 130 percent of the per-person double-occupancy rate to an outrageous 200 percent.

As an alternative, if you're willing to share quarters, most lines guarantee to match you up with a same-gender roommate. (Royal Caribbean, however, doesn't.) If they fail to find you a roommate, you get to enjoy having the whole cabin to yourself at the cheaper shared rate. For extra savings, sign up for a shared quad (a room for four), available on some ships.

Use your seniority

Some lines take 5 percent off the top for passengers 55 and older, and you get that rate even if you share your cabin with a younger passenger. You don't have to be a member of a senior citizens group (such as the AARP), but it doesn't hurt. Sometimes memberships get you extra savings.

Pay in advance

Cruise lines love to get your cash in their hands as early as possible. So some of the pricier lines offer discounts — sometimes up to 15 percent — to folks who pay their whole cruise fare ahead of time.

Take advantage of value-added deals

Some cruise promotions may include extra treats such as pre-cruise hotel packages and/or cabin upgrades. Some lines may even give you a shipboard credit for onboard purchases (you start your cruise with a balance you can spend). In some cases, you may even see an offer of free airfare (normally with European sailings).

Use repeat-passenger discounts

If you enjoy your first cruise, try it again: Cruise lines appreciate repeat business, so if you sail on a line you've traveled with before (even if you were just a kid with your parents), let the line or your agent know that you've come back for another round. The line may provide special discounts or at least extra onboard amenities. If they leave truffles by your bedside on your second cruise, imagine what kind of perks you could get for your tenth cruise anniversary!

Book your next cruise on board

Book your next cruise while you're still aboard your first! When they still have your undivided attention, cruise lines often offer incentive deals to bring you back another time. Be sure to ask if you can combine the discount the line offers on board with other deals it may offer later. Your travel agent can still handle your reconfirmation and tickets as long as you tell the line his or her name when you sign up for your next cruise.

Stay aboard for a bonus cruise

Bonus cruise bargains are for people who get hooked on cruises like most of us get hooked on potato chips: You can't stop after just one. By booking back-to-back cruises (where the same ship covers two different routes, one right after the other), you can get up to 50 percent off the second cruise. You may even be able to combine short cruises (such as Carnival's 3-day cruise to the Bahamas with its 4-day cruise to Cozumel and Key West). You lengthen your vacation and increase the number of ports you see along the way, all while saving money — in fact, if you go for two weeks, you may get a third week free. Ka-ching ka-ching!

Find the deals

All the deals we mention in this section are terrific, you say, but how can you discover which lines offer special rates? Certainly it pays to keep an eye on the Travel section of your Sunday newspaper, but remember that some of these discounts are easier to spot than to assess. Given the number of variables that can affect how much you save, you probably still want to consult a cruise-savvy travel agent (in person, on the Web, or by phone) before you make your booking. And it pays to comparison shop, too.

Tracking Additional Costs

Your cruise fare includes your accommodations, meals, and entertainment, but keep in mind what's *not* included when you plan your budget. Extra costs can really swell your vacation tab.

Figuring in tips

Although you choose how much you want to tip the crew (unless you sail on one of those rare "no tipping" ships), the cruise line offers plenty of guidance — such as tipping cheat sheets and special tipping envelopes. Some lines now add tips automatically to your shipboard account. The best approach to avoid tipping shock is simply to plan ahead. Figure about $70 per week (or $10 per day) to cover tips for your waiter, bus person, and room steward. You pay for all these basics at the end of the cruise; tip for extras, such as massages, whenever you receive the service.

Don't worry about tipping the bartender unless he or she is a *really* good listener — on most ships, your bar tab includes a 15 percent gratuity.

Budgeting for shore excursions

Shore excursions are sightseeing tours that help you make the most of your time at the ports your ship visits; however, they can add a hefty sum to your vacation costs, ranging from about $29 for a short bus or walking tour to $300 or more per person for flightseeing by plane or helicopter. You may not stay in port long enough to take more than one option, but the costs can add up pretty fast.

Some tours are worth the money. This is particularly true, we've found, with active tours, such as those involving kayaking or mountain biking, or for tours that take you far beyond the port city (you may be better off taking the prearranged transportation rather than a cab).

Be aware that sometimes a shore trip means seeing the sights from a packed tour bus with some ho-hum spiel and a stop for souvenirs.

A little planning early on can save you big bucks and help you avoid regrets about missing out on something cool later. Before you set sail, read up on your cruise's ports of call and figure out what you may want to see at those places (the chapters in Part V of this book can help). Adding up admission costs and then comparing the price of doing it your way with the cost of doing it their way can help you determine whether to go the excursion route or not.

You generally book shore excursions on board, not in advance (although some lines, including Princess, Royal Caribbean, Celebrity, and Holland America, offer an advanced-booking option). You have time to ask questions of the ship's tour staff before you make your decision — the tour staff offers lectures on the excursions, but be aware that these lectures often come off more like sales pitches. Tours are a money-making area for the cruise line, and the role of the onboard tour folks is to get you to buy.

Paying taxes and port charges

Be sure to ask whether taxes, port charges, or other such fees are included in your total fare. If not, you may find yourself paying up to $200 in additional charges on a typical one-week cruise in the Caribbean.

You can find information on whether such charges are included or not in most cruise brochures. If you don't find the info there, ask your travel agent or call the cruise line.

Estimating onboard costs

Cruise lines make a substantial amount of their revenue on board. Sometimes when you get on a ship, particularly a big mass-market ship, it seems as if everyone tries to sell you something, from the bar staff with the enticing umbrella drinks to the roving photographer to the salespeople promoting everything from clothing to art auctions.

You pay for the cute professional photo of you and the kids by the pool, for the sweatshirt with the ship's logo, for the cocktail someone so kindly offers you the minute you step aboard, for that relaxing massage, and for the video arcade games. Just like at home, be mindful of your budget for these treats and goodies.

Be aware that the ship's fancy alternative restaurant may charge a service fee of as much as $25 a head, and you may have to pay extra for treats such as an espresso, cappuccino, or gourmet ice cream. Turn to Chapter 8 to find out more about the finer points of at-sea dining.

Table 4-2 can help you determine how much to set aside to cover onboard costs. Keep in mind that these prices are averages and may vary by ship.

Table 4-2	Typical Costs of Cruise Extras
Service	*Charge*
Alternative dining (service charge)	$5 to $25
Babysitting for two kids (group)	$6 to $8 per hour
Babysitting for two kids (private)	$10 per hour
Beer	$3.25 to $3.95
Cruise line souvenirs	$3 to $50
Dry cleaning (per item)	$2.50 to $7.50
E-mail (per minute)	50 cents to $1.50
Haircut (men)*	$32
Haircut (women)*	$57 to $77
Massage (50 minutes)*	$89 to $109
Mixed drinks	$3.95 to $6.75 (and up)

(continued)

Table 4-2 *(continued)*

Service	Charge
Phone calls (per minute)	$6.95 to $16.95
Photos (5 x 7)	$6.95 to $8.95
Soft drinks	$1.50 to $2.50
Shore excursions	$29 to $300
Wine with dinner	$15 to $300 per bottle

* Standard prices of Steiner, which has contracts to provide spa and beauty services on most ships.

After you calculate your cruise fare (figuring in discounts but also including port charges and any other additional taxes and fees) and cost of transportation, plan on setting aside about $50 to $60 per person per day, not including tips, to cover other expenses. Plan for more or less based on your specific wants and needs: If you want to take that $300 helicopter tour, buy a bauble in the ship's jewelry store, or enjoy fine champagne and cognac, you need to budget a little more.

If you plan to gamble, have bucks on hand for the ship's casino. And don't forget to set aside money to spend at the ports.

Paying Up When the Party's Over

The cruise-bill fairy visits your cabin late on the last full day of the cruise with your final bill, slipping it under your door or leaving it on your bed. If you find any error or if you want to pay by cash, traveler's check, or personal check, you need to go stand in line at the purser's or guest relations desk with your cruisemates. If it all adds up right and you simply want it billed to your credit card, you don't have to lift your weary head from the pillow.

Keep tabs on your spending

You should keep track of your shipboard expenditures so that you aren't surprised when you get the final tab at the end of your voyage. You can do this by keeping your receipts — you get one every time you sign with your onboard credit card. On some lines, you can also take advantage of the interactive television features in your cabin, which allow you to review your account regularly at the push of a button or two. And you always have the option of stopping by the purser's desk to check the ship's listing of your expenditures (you may have to wait in line to do this, particularly late in the cruise).

Chapter 5

Getting to Your Port of Embarkation and Boarding Ship

- -

In This Chapter

▶ Arriving from the airport

▶ Preparing to board ship

▶ Finding your cabin

▶ Getting acclimated

▶ Showing up for the all-important safety drill

▶ Anticipating the cruise days ahead

▶ Making arrangements for shore excursions

- -

*T*he moment has finally arrived for you to embark on your trip. The ship's crew is set to welcome you aboard, and in no time at all you'll be sipping down a luscious tropical drink. Just a few minor details left — and then all aboard!

Flying to Your Port of Embarkation

So you're about to begin your trip. Pack your suitcases and don't forget to put your name and address on the tags. If you can check your bags through to the ship, fill out the cruise line tags with the appropriate information — including the sail date, ship name, and your cabin number.

Keep your tickets, cruise documents, passport and identification, keys, valuable items, and medicine in your carry-on bag rather than in your checked luggage (see Chapter 7 for packing tips). You may also want to pack an extra set of clothes in case you get to the ship before your bags do and want to change into something more comfortable — or in the unlikely case that your bags get misrouted.

Calling the airline before you leave home to ensure that your flight is on schedule is a good idea. Also, especially with increased security concerns, allow yourself ample time at the airport to check your bags and get through security screening.

Arranging transfers through the cruise line

After you get off the plane, a cruise line representative (carrying a clip-board that displays the cruise line's name) greets you either at the gate or at the baggage claim. If you booked transfers to the ship through the cruise line, the representative lets you know what to do next.

If you arrive in another country, you need to clear Customs and Immigration, which includes showing your passport and any forms crewmembers gave you to fill out on the plane. Follow the appropriate signs. When you get through the checkpoints, a cruise line representative awaits.

If you bought a pre-cruise package, read your trip documents to familiarize yourself with what to do at the airport (remember, you arrive earlier than other passengers on your trip).

If you checked your luggage through to the ship, you can head right for the cruise line's transportation (often a bus or van), which takes you to the ship. You probably have to turn over your transportation voucher to the bus driver, so have it handy (it should be in your cruise documents).

If you didn't check your luggage through to the ship, you have to reclaim your bags and turn them over to the bus driver yourself (again, make sure that they have the proper tags). You may not see your bags again until they arrive in your cabin (porters remove them from the bus, and crew members deliver them to your cabin).

Handling transfers on your own

If you didn't book the cruise line transfers, gather your luggage from the baggage area and head to the pier via taxi or whatever mode of transportation you previously arrange.

Find out in advance what the trip from the airport to the port should cost to avoid getting ripped off. Don't forget to put the luggage tags (displaying your ship name, sailing date, and cabin number) from the cruise line on your bags. When you get to the pier, a porter stands nearby to take your bags and ensure that they arrive on the right ship. The porter expects a tip (around $1 a bag), and some porters are less shy than others in soliciting you for it.

Some cities have multiple piers, and you can help your cab driver by having the pier number and directions to the ship handy. The line should include this information with your cruise documents. If not, you can get it in advance by contacting the line.

Dealing with a delayed flight

If your flight is delayed, don't panic. Let the airline personnel know that you're a cruise passenger who has a ship to catch that day. A different flight may be available. Have the cruise line's emergency number handy in your cruise documents so that the airline can call the cruise line right away and tell it about the delay. Other passengers from your ship may be on the flight as well, so the line may hold the ship's departure until your arrival. If not, the line may put you up at a hotel for the night and then fly you, drive you, or take you by boat to the next port.

 Be aware that the cruise line is under no obligation to pick up these extra expenses even if you book your air through the cruise line (the fine print in your cruise contract probably relieves them of any responsibility). Some types of travel insurance provide coverage if you're delayed en route. See Chapter 7 for more information about travel insurance.

Checking In at the Pier

What happens when you reach the cruise terminal depends on the ship, but the check-in process can be a real pain. Expect to wait in line (so you're thrilled if you don't see one). And expect the atmosphere at the pier to be chaotic. Remember, the check-in area is filled with people who *need* a vacation, so nerves can get frazzled. Think ahead to that comfy deck chair and the sunshine on your face.

Getting an early start

Checking in early is your best bet for a smooth process. You probably can't board the ship until about two or three hours before you sail (sailing time is normally around 5 or 6 p.m., but check with your line for specifics) because the ship has a million things to do before you and the other cruise passengers board, including unloading passengers from the earlier cruise, shuffling paperwork (including customs documents), and preparing the ship for your journey.

The crowds tend to be worse earlier in the embarkation process; however, if you want lunch and spa appointments, you may have to grin and bear it. Getting on the ship early in the embarkation process affords you some advantages, such as getting your seating preferences for meals and signing up for the time of your choice for popular spa treatments. And, if you time it just right — depending on the ship and departure time — you can also get lunch, which is usually served until 3 or 4 p.m. on the first day.

If you get to the pier really early, you may want to drop off your bags and grab a cab to see the local sights. Make sure you're back at least an hour before departure.

To make the boarding process as carefree as possible, keep the following in mind:

- ✔ Before you get in line, make sure that you fill out all the documents the cruise line sent you (the ones marked "Be sure to fill these out in advance").

- ✔ Before you board is the time to make any phone calls that you need to make. Calls from the ship are expensive (ranging from $6.95 to $16.95 per minute), even when the ship is docked. Pay phones at the pier are cheaper.

- ✔ Fix your hair, put on your lipstick, and tidy yourself up a bit (you, fella, tuck in your shirt!), because the ship's photographers are waiting to snap you before you step aboard (you can purchase the picture later for about $6 to $8 a pop).

Getting set to sail

During the check-in process, a crewmember examines your papers and you set up your onboard credit account by turning over a major credit card or making a deposit with cash or traveler's checks (usually $250). You may also receive your cabin key at this time (or it may be waiting in your cabin), along with a boarding card you need to show when you get on and off the ship. Sometimes your onboard credit card doubles as your cabin key and boarding card. On some ships, the crew checks only your papers at this point; the process of setting up your onboard account takes place later in the purser's office.

If you booked a suite or you have a disability, someone may direct you to a priority check-in area (which typically has shorter lines). Otherwise, boarding lines generally form alphabetically by last name.

Check-in is often when you get your dining-room table assignment, although this varies by ship. Some ships give you your assignment before you board (it may even be noted on the documents you received at home). If you don't like your assignment, take care of it during check-in. Make sure your seating time (early or late), table size, and choice of smoking or nonsmoking section (where applicable) is as you want (see Chapter 8 for more dining info). The cruise line does its best to honor your requests. Make sure that the cruise line knows of any special dietary needs you have.

All passengers must clear security before boarding the ship, which includes an X-ray of your handheld luggage. Note that increased security measures and the addition of National Guardsmen at major ports have added time to this process. Be patient.

Stepping Aboard and Checking Out Your Digs

After you walk up the gangway, a photographer asks you to pose for a picture. Don't worry. You aren't obligated to buy the photo, but if you want to you can find it on display later at the ship's photo gallery. You may also be asked to pose for a tiny camera that records your face for the ship's security system (copies of this photo are *not* available).

After you're actually aboard the ship, a crewmember directs (maybe even escorts) you to your cabin, where it makes sense to spend a little time checking things out. Your steward may stop by to see that everything is okay. Make sure that you know how to operate the air conditioning and heating (assuming the system is individually controlled, which is not the case on all ships), the television, the safe (if you find one), the shower, the telephone, and any other nifty gadgets in the cabin. Your steward can help you with all this. Feel free to let the steward know of any special needs you may have — extra pillows, for example — or if something seems amiss in your cabin.

Don't be put off by the big WHOOSH!!! of the toilet. The sound is normal — ship toilets typically use a vacuum system. Don't put anything into the bowl other than the toilet paper provided — foreign objects can clog up the works.

A daily program in your cabin tells you what's on tap for the rest of the day (including meal times) and outlines safety procedures (see the upcoming "Attending the Safety Drill" section).

Your bags may not arrive at your cabin until after the ship leaves the pier, but don't be concerned. 5,000 or more bags travel on the bigger ships, and it takes some time to get them properly distributed. Dinner on the first night, consequently, is always casual — you may not have your bags in time to dig out a change of clothes. If you start to worry as the night goes on, give the purser's office a call.

If your luggage does get lost, the crew immediately contacts the applicable airline and ground operators to find out what's going on (let them make the calls because it costs you a pretty penny if you try to do it yourself). Missing luggage often turns up at the airport or pier and arrives at the ship the next day after being driven or flown to the first port of call. If you don't get missing luggage the first night, you can get an overnight kit, with such items as a toothbrush, toothpaste, and a razor, from the purser's office.

If your luggage doesn't show up on the second day, you get to go shopping in the ship's stores for proper attire if you purchased baggage insurance. If you don't have insurance, the cruise line and/or airline, at their discretion, may offer you a cash compensation of about $50 a day, which at least gets you clean underwear and a t-shirt. If the second night is formal, the line may be able to provide a tux for a man and may have a small collection of dress-up clothes available for a woman to borrow. You shouldn't get too worried about this situation, however: Luggage is rarely lost for more than a day.

A few other bits of info you should know:

- ✔ Your room is outfitted with a Do Not Disturb sign (important for nappers), order forms for room-service breakfast (if offered), and forms and bags you need to use if you want to send out your laundry or dry cleaning.

- ✔ The ship may provide bottled water (the tap water is probably perfectly drinkable, but may have a strong chlorine taste or may be on the warm side), but just because the bottles are there doesn't make them free. Check before you open them. Items in the minibar are not free (unless you sail on a really swanky vessel). A card nearby should indicate the prices.

- ✔ Find out how to make calls to other passengers and ship personnel, as well as how to dial home from the ship (directions should be located near the phone). Remember that calls to places off the ship are incredibly expensive! You can ring up hefty bills in a very short amount of time.

Exploring the Ship

We suggest that you spend some of your time on the first day exploring the ship. But before you do, remember to lock your cash and valuables in the safe. If your room doesn't have a safe, you can use one at the purser's desk. Carry your shipboard credit card (in case you want to buy a drink) and your cabin key with you, as well as a deck plan that you can probably find in your cabin (if you don't see one, try to get one at the purser's office).

If you're timid about exploring on your own, some ships, especially the really big ones, offer escorted tours of the public rooms. If you want to skip the organized tour, head up to the Pool Deck, which is the usual place for the welcome-aboard buffet, and start your own tour with a snack.

Make an appointment right away if you know you want any spa or beauty treatments during your cruise. Prime times — such as appointments with the hair stylist right before dinner on formal nights — go fast. Sometimes the spa staff also offers an introductory tour.

You may also want to check out the library for the latest bestsellers (and newly-released videos) before the rest of the passengers get the same idea (it opens sometime during the first evening).

Note that the casino and shops are closed until the ship is actually at sea, in accordance with government regulations. Sometimes the swimming pool is also covered until after embarkation.

You may want to be on the deck, drink in hand, when the ship leaves the pier. Some ships offer complimentary champagne to get you started.

Attending the Safety Drill

Ships are required by law to hold a safety drill within 24 hours of departure, and most lines get it out of the way either right before or right after sailing out of port. Ships require your attendance. You get the message from the daily program and in announcements over the loudspeakers; your cabin steward lets you know, too.

In your cabin, you should find a bright-orange life jacket for each passenger, including special life jackets for any kids in your cabin (if not, let the cabin steward know immediately). Features on the jackets include a whistle and a light that shines when it hits the water.

When you hear the loud emergency signal, grab your jacket and follow the signs to your designated *muster* (meeting) *station* (the number is written both on the back of your cabin door and on the lifejacket). You go to this place in case of a real emergency, too.

Although some drills are very brief, others can go on for a half-hour or more. (We've even been on cruises in Europe where the captain inspected all passengers to make sure we wore our life jackets correctly.)

Signing Up for Shore Excursions

Another important errand to do your first day on the ship is to sign up for any shore excursions you want to take (unless, of course, you're on a ship that allows you to do this in advance). You may have until the second day to make your choices, but the earlier you sign up, the better: The excursions are offered on a first-come basis, and popular offerings tend to sell out fast. A shore excursion manager gives a short briefing/sales pitch. You may be able to glean some useful information from the lecture even if you plan on exploring on your own, such as the local transportation situation and what safety issues you should consider.

The person running the session may make a big push for certain shops on shore (usually jewelry stores) that you just *have* to hit. In some cases, the cruise line gets advertising fees for recommending the shops and a commission on sales, too. Be aware of this when you consider the suggestions, but also keep in mind that the shops your cruise line recommends are less likely to swindle you because they depend on the line for business. For info on what you can bring back home after the cruise, check out Chapter 12.

Gearing Up for the Days Ahead

You made it aboard ship, cast off from the pier, and now your vacation stretches out before you, as full of *Whoopee!* (or as free of it) as you want it to be.

In general, life on a big ship can seem to follow a kind of bipolar logic: On the one hand, you're taking a trip to visit some great ports of call, and on the other you have great things to do right on the ship, from lounging around in the sun and getting a massage in the spa to playing virtual golf. Smaller ships focus more on the ports than on the shipboard activities, which are fewer because small ships just don't have the space (or the philosophical inclination) to provide you with a lot of distractions.

The following two sections detail what you can expect when the ship is at sea and in port.

One if by land: Days ashore

Map out your days in port to make sure you get to see all that the destination offers. Decide ahead of time whether you want to lunch locally or on the ship, and find out where the shopping and other hot spots are. (Check out the chapters in Part V for specifics on the ports of call.) To make sure that you don't miss the boat, literally, take careful note of your ship's departure time.

Some ports allow cruise ships to dock at the pier so that you can walk right off the ship via a gangplank. Other ports require ships to anchor offshore so that you have to take a small boat (called a *tender*) to reach the pier. To catch a lift on a tender, you usually go to a lounge area and take a number. Although you get a lower number and get ashore earlier if you get to the lounge earlier, the lines tend to be longer first thing in the morning, so sometimes you're better off lingering over a second cup of coffee than rushing to the lounge to wait in line. If you signed up in advance for a shore excursion, you generally get to disembark ahead of everyone else.

Don't feel like you have to get off at every port of call, but you may want to at least stretch your legs and get some exercise. On big ships especially, some people stay on the ship, which takes on a haunting yet appealing aura when the crowds disappear. The pool may be closed, but you can still sit on the sun deck, take spa treatments, use the gym (which is less crowded on port days), play cards, eat lunch, and enjoy some quiet time. On port days, the ship generally offers fewer organized activities, but you can still find offerings such as movies, live music poolside, a few seminars, and lighthearted sports competitions.

Two if by sea: Days at sea

If you sail on a big ship (small ships rarely spend entire days at sea), brace yourself for a staggering array of sea-day activities — especially in the Caribbean, where typical offerings include exercise classes, movies, rum swizzle parties, beauty seminars (such as "How to Fight Cellulite"), pool games, and contests that range from golf putting to knobby knees (the knobbiest wins).

An onboard who's who

Anyone who's seen *The Love Boat* knows that a ship has a captain, a purser, a cruise director, a doctor, and a bartender, but their jobs are not to make love matches. Here's what they really do:

Captain: The big boss (may also be referred to as The Master); he's in charge.

Staff Captain: The second in command; normally in charge of navigation and safety.

Hotel Manager: In charge of passenger services, including restaurants, bars, and accommodations (if you need someone to complain to in these areas, the buck stops here).

Chief Engineer: In charge of all the onboard machinery, including the engines.

Purser: In charge of information and financial matters (this person delivers your bill at the end of the cruise).

Chief Steward: In charge of making sure all cabins and public rooms are cleaned and maintained.

Cabin Stewards: The people who clean the cabins.

Dining Stewards: A fancy name for waiters.

Cruise Director: In charge of all activities and entertainment; also gets to act as the ship's emcee.

Shore Excursion Director: In charge of land tours; often doubles as the port lecturer.

Entertainment Director: Heads the show team.

Head Chef or Chef de Cuisine: In charge of the kitchen (galley) and the menus.

Maitre d': In charge of the dining room operation.

Doctor: In charge of medical care.

Sea days on Alaskan cruises are packed with beautiful scenery and sights to enjoy; wildlife and glacier experts are on board to explain more about the area's natural wonders. In fact, the ship may reduce the number of other activities at times when the ship is scheduled to sail by one of Mother Nature's more extravagant offerings, such as a famous Alaskan glacier or fjord.

In Europe, the activities are somewhat lower key than on North American sailings, but you still find a good selection, including lectures by archeologists and historians and the occasional Mr. Universe-style contest.

Chapter 6

Booking Your Cruise

. . . .

In This Chapter

▶ Using an agent (in person or online)
▶ Researching online
▶ Finding the best cabin
▶ Evaluating your dining room seating options
▶ Getting the skinny on air add-ons
▶ Booking pre- and post-cruise travel
▶ Paying a deposit

. . . .

A plethora of new ships and fierce competition have ushered in the age of the discounted fare. So how do you find the bargains? Traditionally, people book their cruises through travel agents. You may wonder in this Internet age if the travel agent has gone the way of typewriters and cassette tapes. Well, not exactly. Travel agents are alive and kicking, although airline commission cuts have changed the equation (you may have to pay a fee for your airline ticket), and the Internet has staked its claim alongside travel agents and knocked some out of business. Many traditional agencies now operate their own cruise Web sites to try to keep pace.

So what's the best way to book a cruise these days? Good question. The answer may be by using both the Internet *and* a travel agent. If you're computer savvy and have a good idea of what cruise you want (and you probably will after reading this book), Web sites are a great way to trawl the seas at your own pace and check out last-minute deals, which can be dramatic. On the other hand, you don't get personalized service as you search for and book a cruise online. If something goes wrong or you need help getting a refund or arranging special meals, you're on your own. So if this is your first cruise, you should seek the advice of an experienced agent.

Hiring a Travel Agent

The process of booking a cruise is probably more complex and confusing than you realize. Think about it: What you basically arrange when you book your cruise is a contract for transportation, lodging, dining, entertainment, housekeeping, and assorted other services that the ship provides you over the course of your vacation. These services involve a lot of people. Because of this complexity, the majority of cruise passengers use agents to book their cruises. And these agents, if they possess any talent, can help you get the right ship and the right kind of cabin for your needs. They can also help you put together an easy package that gets you from home to your ship and back again quickly and cleanly.

For the most part, cruise lines let agents handle the booking process. They, unlike the airlines, don't have large reservation staffs. Not only do lines such as Carnival, Holland America, Royal Caribbean, Celebrity, and Norwegian accept Web bookings, but they also offer links from their sites to agency sites; therefore, the specials that lines offer on their sites tend to be the same deals available through land-based travel agencies. When you see a great cruise bargain over the Internet, an online agent, rather than a cruise line, is normally responsible.

Your agent may even have a deal that a line hasn't yet posted on the Web site or even put in print. Agents (especially those who specialize in cruises) frequently communicate with cruise lines that alert them to the latest and greatest deals and special offers. The cruise lines tend to contact their preferred (or top-selling) agents first about such deals before they clue in the general public. Some of these deals are only offered through agents.

 Cruise lines run promotions where you can book a category of cabin (rather than a specific cabin), and the line guarantees you a cabin in that category or better. A smart agent knows about these offers and may be able to direct you to a category where few cabins are available, increasing your chances of an upgrade. The cruise lines may also upgrade passengers as a favor to their top-producing agents or agencies. You can ask your agent to write a letter on your behalf.

Each agency is different, and they offer various booking incentives and ways to save you money. Here are some deals to ask about:

- **Back-office systems:** After you book your cruise, some agencies use a *back-office system* to check the very latest deals to make sure you got the best rate available. Your agent may be able to adjust the rate if you didn't get the best one.

- **Group rates:** Some agencies buy big blocks of space on a ship in advance to offer to their clients at a reduced group rate — available only with that agency.

- **Newsletters:** Agencies are aware of special rates and promotions before the general public and can quickly send out a newsletter, e-mail, or postcard that alerts you, the client, to specials (although they may charge you a small fee for this service).

- **Price-matching:** Some agencies are willing to negotiate with you, especially if you find a better price somewhere else. Go ahead and ask; you could be pleasantly surprised.

> ✔ **Rebates and incentives:** To get you to buy a package, some agents may share part of their commission from the cruise line. The incentive may be money or a nice gift, such as a free bottle of champagne or a free shore excursion.

In addition to these services, a good agent can also help you make decisions about your dining-room seating preference, pre- and post-cruise land offerings, air add-ons, and travel insurance.

If you decide to book a cruise yourself, keep in mind that if your trip doesn't go as planned, you can't blame anyone but yourself.

Choosing an agent

By using a *cruise-only agency* (an agency that specializes in selling cruises) or a *cruise specialist* (an agent who specializes in selling cruises), you ensure that you're dealing with someone who knows cruises. If you call a *full-service agency* (an agency that handles all types of travel), ask for the cruise desk.

If you don't already have an agent, ask around for a referral. Interview the agent, and ask what ships or lines he or she has personally cruised on. If you don't feel comfortable with that agent, move on to another one.

Not all agents sell all cruise lines. In order to be experts on what they sell and to maximize the commissions that the lines pay them (they pay more based on volume), some agents may limit their product to one luxury line, one mid-priced line, one mass-market line, and so on. Your agent should still offer enough variety, however, to steer you in the right direction in your cruise choice.

 If your heart is set on a particular line after you read through our cruise line reviews in Part IV of this book, you can call that line (or check its Web site) to ask a representative to recommend an agent in your area who can help you book your cruise.

 Keep in mind that *discounters,* which you can find with great come-on rates in Sunday papers and on the Internet, aren't necessarily into service as much as price (they typically specialize in last-minute offers), and their staffs are more likely to be ordertakers than advice-givers. Go to them only after you know what you want.

Going with a specialist

Contact the **Cruise Lines International Association (CLIA)** at ☎ 212-921-0066 (www.cruising.org) or the **National Association of Cruise Oriented Agencies (NACOA)** at ☎ 305-663-5626 (www.nacoaonline.com) to find experienced agencies with good reputations. Members of both groups are cruise specialists, and the groups monitor the ethics of their members.

Membership in the **American Society of Travel Agents (ASTA)** similarly ensures that the agency is monitored for ethical practices, although this doesn't in itself designate cruise experience. Contact ASTA at ☎ **800-275-2782** (www.astanet.com).

Cruise specialists with the **Certified Travel Counselor (CTC)** designation have completed a professional-skills course the **Institute of Certified Travel Agents (ICTA)** offers. The designation guarantees in-depth knowledge of the industry. You can find the institute's Web site at www.icta.com.

Acting as Your Own Travel Agent

If you decide to make your own cruise arrangements, the Internet is the place to go for information on itineraries and prices. Even if you take the travel-agent route, information on the Internet can help you become an informed consumer, enabling you to take a peek at some of the amenities on various ships.

Making use of the Internet

You can find plenty of great information about cruises on the Web. Most major lines have their own sites and fill them with facts, photos, itineraries, and brochure rates (the appendix in the back of this book has a complete list). Some sites feature virtual tours of specific ships and interactive programs to help you match your interests and pre-ferred travel dates to a particular cruise. Most sites provide links to the line's preferred travel agents, and on some you can actually book your cruise.

Some good sites on the Web specialize in providing cruise information rather than selling cruises. Among the best are the online magazines www.cruisemates.com and www.cruisecritic.com. Both offer reviews, tips, postings of cruise bargains, and more.

If you do find a better rate online than your agent offers, you can always ask your agent to match the price.

Dealing with online agencies, discounters, and auction houses

Buying a cruise via the Web is a lot more complicated than buying an airline ticket, especially if you haven't booked a cruise before. You have a wide range of choices, such as what kind of cabin is best for you (we discuss cabin choices in the "S, M, L, XL: Finding a Cabin that Fits" section later in this chapter) and which cruise gives you the best fit with the other passengers (for example, children don't have much fun on a singles- or seniors-oriented cruise).

A good agent can help you avoid making mistakes. In many ways, so can reading this book carefully. But no matter how nicely you phrase your questions, this book can't give you an answer like a real live person can. Similarly, finding answers on the Web isn't always so easy, although the situation is improving. Sites such as www.uniglobe.com, for example, allow you to chat live with an agent. And www.icruise.com has developed an excellent research database.

Cruise Web sites offer great deals. But do your homework — a deal isn't a deal unless you really know what you're buying!

 Whether you work in person with an agent or evaluate an offer at an online site, be sure you understand what's included in the fare that the agent or site quotes you. Are you getting a price that includes the cruise fare, port charges, airfare, taxes and fees, and insurance? Or are you getting a cruise-only fare? One agent may break out the charges in a price quote and another may bundle them all together. Know the situation as you make price comparisons. When you check a Web offer, make sure you look for an extra charge for shipping and handling (some land-based agencies now also charge handling fees). Read the fine print!

Web sites that sell cruises include

- ✔ Online travel agencies that sell all types of travel (www.travelocity.com, www.expedia.com)

- ✔ Agencies that specialize in cruises (www.icruise.com, www.cruise.com, www.cruise411.com)

- ✔ Travel discounters (www.bestfares.com, www.1travel.com, www.lowestfare.com)

- ✔ Auction houses (www.allcruiseauction.com, www.priceline.com)

See the appendix for more details, including a listing of top land-based cruise agencies.

Buyer beware!

Keep in mind that if you hear of a deal that sounds too good to be true, as the saying goes, it probably is. If you get a solicitation by phone, fax, mail, or e-mail that doesn't sound right or if your agent gives you the heebie jeebies, contact your state consumer protection agency or local office of the Better Business Bureau (www.bbb.org). You can also call the cruise line directly and ask them about the agency. And be wary of working with any company, be it on the phone or the Internet, that refuses to give you its street address. You can find more advice on how to avoid scams at the **American Society of Travel Agents** Web site, www.astanet.com.

S, M, L, XL: Finding a Cabin that Fits

After you figure out where you want to go and what kind of ship you want to cruise on, you have to figure out what kind of cabin you want to stay in. Several types are available, from extremely small, windowless spaces to spacious suites with large, private verandas and hot tubs.

To figure out what cabin fits your needs, you need to take into account price and vacation style. Do you want to be on the go all the time, using your room only to shower and sleep, or do you plan to spend ample time in your quarters, relaxing and reading books or watching movies?

If you want to just chill out and don't plan on leaving your cabin much, choose the biggest cabin you can afford. On the other hand, folks who plan to participate in every activity and see every show spend very little time in their cabins. If you're this type of person, save some money and get a smaller cabin.

Figure 6-1 shows a sample deck plan and indicates some of the factors you should take into consideration when you choose a cabin.

Understanding cabin basics

You can be fairly certain that every cabin has a private bathroom with a shower. You have to get a more expensive room if you want a bathtub — a luxurious perk on ships.

The twin beds in standard cabins convert into double or queen-size beds. Some cabins have bunk beds, which are obviously not convertible to anything; they are, however, a boon to three- or four-person families. Some rooms can accommodate a fifth, portable bed. If you need two cabins, ask about booking connected cabins. Fancier suites may have king-size beds.

Most cabins (but not all) have televisions. Some also have extras, such as safes, mini-refrigerators, VCRs, bathrobes, and hair dryers. Amenities like soap, shampoo, and hand lotion are either hotel variety (small bars and containers) or in dispensers on the wall.

Keep in mind that the most-expensive and least-expensive cabins on any given ship tend to sell out first, so if you want either of these options, book early.

Evaluating cabin sizes

Most ships offer several types of cabins — sometimes up to a dozen or more different varieties — as outlined by deck plans in the cruise line's brochure. Figure 6-2 shows sample cabin floor plans. The lines normally describe cabins by price (highest to lowest), category (using words such as *suite, deluxe, superior, standard,* and *economy*), and furniture configuration ("sitting area with two lower beds," for example). Cabin diagrams are often available.

Lines also list cabins as *inside* (no windows) or *outside* (with windows). Because most people like natural light, outside cabins are pricier.

 You may enjoy having natural light shine into the cabin and a view of the ocean, but keep in mind that equipment (such as a lifeboat) may obstruct your view or you may look out onto a public area (not good if you want privacy). Although your cruise line's deck plans may indicate lifeboats near your window, the vessels are sometimes slightly above or below the sightlines, allowing you to enjoy the view. Your travel agent's experience can guide you in the right direction in this area. Although we like a cabin with a window because it creates a feeling of openness (visually, at least, as the windows don't usually open), if you don't plan to spend a lot of time in your cabin, you may want to get an inside cabin and save some money.

Usually, the higher on the ship the cabin is located, the nicer — and pricier — it is, which is why luxury suites are often located on upper decks. Cabins on lower levels may be the same size as their upstairs neighbors, but they may have downgraded decors to go with their downgraded price tags. The flip side of the higher-up cabins is that you may notice more of the ship's movement the higher up you go, which isn't good for passengers prone to seasickness. You don't notice the movement as much on the middle and lower decks.

Choosing a cabin size

Cruise line brochures list the size of a cabin in terms of square feet. You may want to measure a room or two at home to give yourself an idea of the size and keep the following guidelines in mind:

- ✔ Smaller rooms are less than 120 square feet and feel like a closet.

- ✔ Standard rooms are 120 to 185 square feet, depending on the cruise line. Standard can also mean cramped toward the 120 foot measurement — you claustrophobes out there may want to get a room that measures at least 180 square feet.

- ✔ Suites are generally 250 square feet and larger.

A newer (and more expensive) feature on some cruise ships is a veranda, or balcony, connected to your cabin. Verandas vary in size and amount of privacy, so make sure that the space is big enough for whatever plan you have for it, whether it be sunbathing or enjoying the night breeze.

Considering the noise factor

The sounds you can hear from your cabin depend on your location in the ship. A lower deck cabin may be close to the engine room, and a cabin near the dance floor may have you doing the rumba in your dreams. If noise is a factor for you, try to avoid cabins near elevators, laundry areas, and the galley.

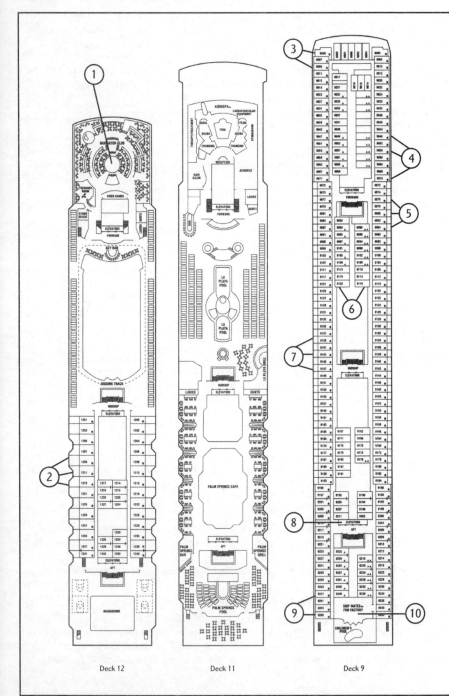

Figure 6-1: A sample deck plan.

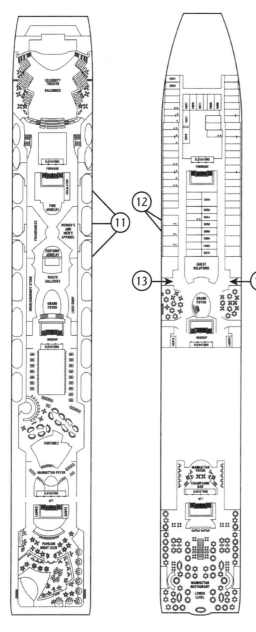

Deck 7

Deck 5

Cabin Choice Considerations

1 Make note of public areas that may be loud — the ship's disco, for example. Although the nightclub on this ship is far from any cabins, it doesn't hurt to request that your cabin not be close to or below such a sleep-inhibitor.

2 Upper-deck cabins are not a good bet if you're susceptible to seasickness because the upper decks feel more of the sea's motion.

3 The motion-sickness warning also holds for cabins in the ship's bow.

4 Outside cabins without verandas are represented as undivided rectangles.

5 Outside cabins with verandas show up as divided rectangles.

6 You can save big by booking an inside cabin without windows.

7 The cabins least affected by the motion of the sea are amidships, especially cabins amidships on the lower levels.

8 The cabins next to elevator shafts may be noisy. Of course, they're also very convenient.

9 Cabins in the stern can be affected by the motion of the sea, and also are prone to vibrations from the ship's engines.

10 Cabins near children's areas may be fairly noisy during the day.

11 Lifeboats sometimes obstruct the view from cabin windows. The lifeboats on this illustrated ship are near public rooms, so private cabins aren't affected.

12 Ideally, disabled vacationers have cabins near the ship's entrance **(13)** and an elevator.

(The Mercury's *deck plan is provided by Celebrity Cruises.)*

Typical outside cabins
- Twin beds (can often be pushed together)
- Upper berths for extra passengers fold into walls
- Bathrooms usually have showers only (no tub)
- Usually (but not always) have televisions and radios
- May have portholes or picture windows

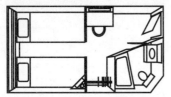
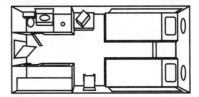

Typical suite configurations
- Queen-size or double beds
- Sitting areas (sometimes with sofa beds for extra passengers)
- Large bathrooms, usually with tub
- Refrigerators (sometimes stocked, sometimes not)
- Stereos and televisions with VCRs are common
- Large closets
- Large windows or outside verandas

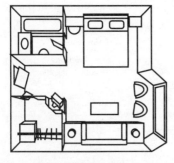
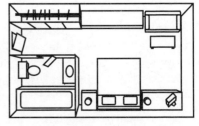

Figure 6-2: Sample cabin layouts.

Dining Decisions

Do you want to have time after dinner to take in a show, or do you prefer to linger over an after-dinner drink? Do you want to spend (relatively) private time with your loved one(s) during meals, or are you looking forward to socializing with your fellow passengers over surf'n' turf? This section helps you make these decisions.

Timing is everything

The logistics of trying to fit all the passengers in a dining room at the same time are generally impossible, so you often have to sign up for a designated time to eat, especially for dinner (see Chapter 8 for more dining info). Some ships, including those in the Norwegian Cruise Line and Princess fleets, make exceptions to this rule by offering restaurant-style, open-seating options in their dining rooms. Assigned seating is not normally required on smaller or ritzier ships. But on most ships, table space is still reserved.

If you like to eat early, go to the *main* or *early seating* around 6 p.m. Advantages and disadvantages exist for early and late times, so it basically comes down to whatever you prefer. Families, seniors, and people who don't like larger crowds generally go to the early seating. You may feel like you need to eat quickly because the staff rushes around to get things ready for the late diners. However, because your food doesn't have to sit for hours under warmers, it may be fresher. You may find that activities right after dinner are less crowded, and you may get better seats to shows while the other half of the passengers eat. And after a good night's dancing, you feel famished just in time for the midnight buffet.

Late seating falls around 8:30 p.m., giving you time for a nice long shower or one last game of shuffleboard before dinner. Your meal isn't rushed at all — unless you want to catch the 10 p.m. show. Unlike the early diners, you may not be hungry again at midnight, which can be a good thing if you want to watch your waistline.

The dining room assigned-time rules are supposed to be in effect during breakfast and lunch, too; however, most ships are fairly lenient during these times. Crowds in the dining room are typically only an issue at dinner. If you show up before or after your assigned time at breakfast or lunch and your assigned table is occupied, the staff seats you elsewhere. Alternatively, you can also eat at one of the more casual eateries on the ship.

In a bid to be more flexible with its main dining room seating policy, Carnival Cruise Lines offers four assigned dining times: 5:45 p.m., 6:30 p.m., 8:00 p.m., and 8:45 p.m. You still have to pick your preferred time in advance of your sailing, however.

Tabling seat assignments

Dinner on a cruise ship is a very sociable time and an ideal situation to meet some of your fellow passengers. You can choose to sit at a table of 1, 2, 4, 8, 10, or even 12 people, although the smallest tables are the hardest to come by. You can wait and see what you get, or you can indicate your seating preference when you book your trip (travel agents can make these arrangements). The cruise line assigns a table to you based on your request. The assignment may show upon your ticket, or you may not get it until you board the ship. If you don't get the assignment you want, try to change it. A tip for the maitre d' can inspire him to find an opening for your party.

In some cases, you can make known your preference for either a smoking or nonsmoking section of the dining room in advance of your cruise. Many cruise lines — including Carnival, Celebrity, Princess, and Royal Caribbean — ban smoking completely in their dining rooms, making this point moot.

If you have any special dietary requirements, alert the cruise line when you make your reservation.

Adding Air Travel

You usually have a choice of booking your air through the cruise line or on your own. The cruise lines negotiate group fares with the airlines based on the volume of business they do, and although these fares are decent, they may not be the lowest available.

Booking air travel with the cruise line

An advantage of taking the cruise line's *air add-on* is that the line can keep track of you. If your flight is delayed, for example, the cruise line knows that and may even hold the ship (especially if other passengers are on your flight). If you travel on your own and miss the ship, you have to find your own transportation to the next port. Cruise lines typically list their airfare offerings in the back of their brochures.

By booking through the cruise line, you can rest assured that it books your flight for the correct day and time. Believe it or not, cruise lines report that a good number of do-it-yourselfers manage to get the departure date or departure time wrong and end up literally missing the boat.

Most lines include *transfers from the pier* in their air add-on rates, which means that a cruise line representative meets you at the airport, assists you with your luggage, and shows you to a bus that takes you to the ship.

If you book air on your own, you still may be able to get the transfer service. Otherwise, you have to hassle with getting a cab on your own.

A downside to booking air through the cruise line, in addition to the fact that you may not get the very lowest airfare, is that you usually can't pick which carrier you fly on (and you may not get a nonstop flight). You also may have to fly at odd hours, and you normally can't get frequent-flyer credits for the flights.

Most cruise lines have an *air deviation program* that allows you to personalize your air request (for a specific airline or routing) for an additional fee (about $50). Additional fares may also be required (in some cases making the add-on deal a lot less of a deal).

 If you prefer traveling on land, see if the line has a deal with Amtrak. In some cases, you can qualify for bus service to the ship if you don't live too far away.

Booking air travel on your own

If you decide to book air travel on your own, ask your agent for a price quote or check out the airfare deals offered by online agencies (such as www.travelocity.com and www.expedia.com) or the airlines' own Web sites (where you may find Internet-only specials). You may also want to check out the offers of discounters such as www.cheaptickets.com. Or you can even try making a bid for a ticket at www.priceline.com.

Keep in mind that generally you can get the best airfare deals by booking at least 30 days in advance. And, especially when you have a ship to meet with a set sailing time, you want to lock in a flight as soon as possible. If you want to grab a last-minute cruise offer (see Chapter 4), the Internet is a good place to look for eleventh-hour airfares.

 If you want to use your frequent-flyer credits for the flight, book your flight far in advance (for European destinations, you may need to book your frequent-flyer flight a year in advance).

Extending Your Vacation

Many of the cities that cruise lines use as home ports are fantastic destinations in their own right, so you may want to lengthen your vacation with a hotel stay, especially if you plan to travel far — to Europe, for example. Just as with airfare, you can buy a hotel package from the cruise line or make arrangements on your own.

When you compare cruise line packages, check the fine print to see what each covers. For example, does the line provide transportation from the airport to the hotel? From the hotel to the cruise ship? What hotel does the line use? Where is it located? Are escorted tours included? Admission to local attractions? Meals? Is a rental-car deal available if you want to explore on your own?

Depending on where you cruise, your line may offer you an opportunity to extend your trip for up to a week by adding an escorted *cruisetour.* These land tours, which allow you an opportunity to see inland sights in addition to coastal attractions, are particularly popular on Alaskan and European sailings. In Alaska, Princess and Holland America are major tour operators, even incorporating their own hotels, buses, and trains. Royal Caribbean has set up its own Alaskan tour company, too.

The prices for cruisetours are generally favorable (based on group rates), and the planning is made easy, with hotel accommodations, sightseeing, admission to attractions, some meals, ground transportation, and transfers typically included. You're picked up at the ship and taken to a hotel, and then you embark on your tour (mostly by bus or train). And at the end of the tour, your transportation drops you off at the airport for your flight home.

You may want to compare prices with other non-cruise tour operators, just to be sure you get a good deal. Or if you're the independent sort, you may want to calculate the cost of putting together your own land-tour program.

If you don't want a complete tour, opting instead for a stay in a port city for an extra day or two, you may also want to see if the cruise line offers hotel stays with reasonable rates (based on the amount of business they do with the hotel). The cruise line may even throw in transfers from the ship (saving you cab fare).

Putting Down a Deposit

After you review your cruise vacation package and give it a thumbs-up, your agent or the line asks you to put down a deposit — sometimes a fixed amount, sometimes a percentage of the total cost of the cruise. The cruise line sends you a receipt in the mail for the amount and asks you to pay the balance by a set date. Check with your agent or the line to make sure you understand the rules.

When you book your trip, have your travel agent notify the line if you're celebrating a special occasion, such as a birthday or anniversary, while on board the ship. The cruise line may provide special treats.

Chapter 7

Taking Care of the Remaining Details

. . . .

In This Chapter

▶ Having your identification and passport in order

▶ Verifying all the info in your cruise documents

▶ Dealing with money — on board and on shore

▶ Deciding if you should get travel insurance

▶ Packing for your trip

▶ Double-checking your flight

▶ Checking all the things that most people forget

. . . .

*B*efore you head to the airport, you have some chores to do. You need to make sure that you have the proper papers to get on board, verify all your cruise documents, figure out how you plan to pay for stuff on board and at the ports, make sure that you have insurance, and — well, you get the idea. You're at the right place to get the scoop. Just read on.

Identifying Yourself with the Right Documentation

You don't think you can just walk on the ship, do you? First you need to prove who you are. And not just any documentation does the trick.

The following are need-to-know identification facts for you:

✔ You need to bring photo identification and proof of citizenship. If you don't have a passport, an official copy of your birth certificate works as a proof of citizenship — but only one that has a raised seal.

You can't board your ship without proper identification (and a driver's license alone doesn't cut it). This rule applies to everyone, including infants and children.

✔ If you have to fly to get to the ship, keep your identification in your carry-on bag, wallet, or purse — not in checked luggage. You don't want to lose it.

✔ If you send your child on a cruise with, say, Grandma — or with just one parent — you may have to (depending on your itinerary) present written permission from the absent parent(s) for the child to take the cruise (check with your cruise line for more on this).

✔ If you're not a U.S. citizen, but you live in the United States, make sure that you bring your alien-registration card and passport. You also need your passport (and sometimes you must have a visa, too) if you're a non-U.S. citizen visiting from your home country.

Keep in mind that U.S. Immigration, not the cruise line, sets the rules on documents. With that said, you can most likely call the line's toll-free number to find out which documents you need for the cruise. Typically, the line details this information in the packet that comes with your tickets. Read this information carefully.

Getting Your Passport

For most cruise destinations we cover in this book — the Caribbean, Mexico, Alaska, Canada, and Hawaii — you don't need a passport. That's right: You *don't.* But if you have one, go ahead and bring it along. Your passport helps you get through customs and immigration faster because the authorities consider it a preferred form of identification.

You do need a passport if you travel to Europe or another overseas destination and, in some cases, if your ship embarks from one of the Caribbean islands rather than Florida.

Getting a passport is easy (you can apply at some 4,500 public places), but completing the process takes some time. First-timers can get a passport in person at one of these locations:

✔ A designated post office

✔ One of 13 passport offices throughout the United States (travel.state.gov/agencies_list.html)

✔ Various federal, state, or probate courts

You need to bring proof of citizenship, which means a certified birth certificate. Also, bring along your driver's license, state or military identification, or any other identifying documents. You also need two *identical* passport-sized photos (2 x 2 inches) taken within the last 6 months. Many photo and copy shops have special cameras that take identical pictures. You *cannot* use the strip photos from one of those photo vending machines.

For people 16 years old and over, a passport is valid for 10 years and costs $85. For kids 15 and under, a passport is valid for 5 years and costs $70 total. If you're over 15 and have a valid passport issued less than 12 years ago, you can renew it through the mail by filling out an application available at the places we describe in the preceding bulleted list and at the State Department Web site (travel.state.gov). If you renew by mail, the cost is just $55.

Apply for your passport at least two months before your trip — preferably even earlier than that. Processing takes four weeks on average, but it can run longer during busy periods (especially in the spring and other school vacationing months). You can help speed things along by writing a departure date that falls within the next three weeks on the application. To expedite the processing of your passport, visit an agency directly and pay an additional $60 fee (or go through the court or post office and have it overnighted). For more information, and to find your regional passport office, consult the State Department Web site (travel.state.gov) or call the National Passport Information Center at ☎ **877-487-2778** for automated service or the National Passport Agency at ☎ **202-647-0518** for general information.

If you lose your passport while abroad, go directly to the nearest U.S. embassy or consulate. Bring all the forms of identification you have so the officials can start generating you a new passport.

Reviewing Your Cruise Documents

Your cruise documents usually arrive in your mailbox about a month before your cruise. Sometimes, however, they don't get to you until a week before your cruise. Plenty of important items are included, such as

- ✔ Your airline tickets (if you bought them from the cruise line)
- ✔ A boarding document that contains your cabin assignment and sometimes your dining table assignment
- ✔ Boarding forms to fill out
- ✔ Luggage tags
- ✔ Your prearranged bus-transfer vouchers from the airport to the port (if you arranged for this option)

You may also get descriptions of the various shore excursions available for purchase after you board the ship (and in some cases in advance), as well as materials that cover the details you need to know before you sail.

Carefully read through and verify the info on every one of your cruise documents. Confirm that your cabin category and dining preferences are right. Check that your airline tickets show the correct flights and arrival times. And definitely make sure that enough time is available for you to reach the port at least an hour before the ship is scheduled to depart.

When the big day arrives, keep your cruise documents with you in your purse, briefcase, or carry-on. You can't easily get on board without them.

Paying Up

With cruises, your onboard money isn't a big pain. You pay the biggest hunk of the money in advance of your trip, so get ready for some smooth sailing.

Spending on board

You have some choices as to how to pay for your onboard expenses. When you check in at the cruise terminal, you can supply a major credit card and have all your expenses billed to your card at the end of the cruise. Or you can pay your account with cash, traveler's checks, or sometimes even a personal check. (The cruise line's brochure spells out specific rules for paying by personal check.) Note that if you decide to pay cash, you may have to put down a deposit — on a one-week cruise, you normally pay about $250.

Regardless of how you plan to pay your account, the line usually gives you a special ship charge card for use during the cruise. You use this card to pay for your drinks at the bar, shore excursions, gift-shop goodies, or special services (such as a massage or a hair cut). In many cases, the card also doubles as your boarding card (which you show every time you get on or off the ship), and sometimes, if the ship has electronic locks, the card serves as your room key. (Note that on very small ships, you don't get special ship charge cards. The number of people on board is so small that you just give your name and cabin number once, and the staff remembers you from then on.)

After you get your special ship charge card, you basically don't need much cash at all on board — well, not until the end of the cruise when you pay tips to the staff, although several lines now let you charge tips, too. You may want to keep some coins on hand to use in the laundry room and a few dollars to pass on to the bartender if he or she does an above-and-beyond job. In general, you need cash for the casino, but check to see if your ship allows you to put gambling dollars on your shipboard account.

 If you find that you need more cash, some ships have their own ATMs — often located, not surprisingly, in the casino. The ATMs give out U.S. dollars. Some ships operating in Europe also have nifty cash conversion machines that make it easy to change cash back and forth between various currencies. Otherwise, you can usually convert bucks at the purser's desk. In all cases, you pay a fee for the service.

 Play it smart: *Don't* keep large amounts of cash around your cabin. Lock your cash in your in-room safe or in a safe at the purser's office.

Settling up on shore

Almost all the stores at the ports take credit cards, and most restaurants do too, but you need some cash on hand to pay for taxis, to buy small items (including those you purchase at markets, which don't usually accept charge cards), to buy soft drinks and munchies, and to tip tour guides. Having some small bills on hand is helpful. (You can go to the purser's desk to get change.)

Pretty much all the Caribbean, Mexican, and Canadian ports we describe in Part V accept U.S. money. If you want to use the local currency, you can often find exchange counters, banks, and ATMs that give out local currency (but not U.S. dollars) somewhere close to the docks. In Europe, you need to convert your cash to local currency, which in several countries is now the euro. When you fly to a European embarkation point, you may want to arrive with at least enough local cash to buy a newspaper and a cup of coffee or to get you to your hotel or the ship (if you don't prearrange for a transfer).

 To check conversion rates before your trip, use the currency calculator at www.bloomberg.com. After you board, ask a crewmember at the purser's desk for an updated exchange rate for the ports you plan to visit.

Purchasing at the ports

In places where you have to exchange money, such as in Europe, the easiest way is to use an ATM. You can plug your bank card into a machine in, say, Nice, France and get euros without having to walk into a bank or exchange service — and you usually get a better rate and a lower fee.

Twelve countries in Europe now use the euro as official currency: Austria, Belgium, Finland, France, Germany, Greece, Holland, Ireland, Italy, Luxembourg, Portugal, and Spain. Old currencies, such as lire and francs, are no longer legal tender. This monetary unity is quite a boon for travelers: You don't have to switch currencies anymore when you travel between these countries.

Using ATMs means that you don't have to carry large amounts of traveler's checks or cash from the United States (you can pick up money on the road). We usually carry some traveler's checks or cash, however, in case of an emergency (such as if all the banks' computer systems suddenly go down).

 Before you leave home, be sure any cash you intend to access is in the checking part of your account if your ATM card allows you to access from both savings and checking — some foreign machines allow you to withdraw only from your checking account and don't offer you the option of transferring money between accounts.

You can find ATMs at most ports — even the tiny ones. Don't take out more money than you need that day or you may end up with a bunch of bills that you have to convert back at the end of your trip (you can't usually convert coins, so spend, spend, spend them). And be sure that you have at least a rough idea of what the exchange rate is before you try to make your withdrawal so that you take out the proper amount.

Personal checks are pretty much useless for cruise travel purposes, except as accepted on your ship (check with the cruise line for its policy on personal checks).

Buying Insurance

Three primary kinds of travel insurance are available: trip cancellation, medical, and lost luggage. Trip cancellation insurance — the insurance we most recommend — is a good idea if you pay a large portion of your vacation expenses up front (which is often the case in booking a cruise). It typically costs six to eight percent of the total value of your cruise vacation and should cover bankruptcy or default of a cruise line. Medical insurance and lost luggage insurance don't make sense for most travelers. Your existing health insurance should cover you if you get sick while on vacation (although if you belong to an HMO, check to see if you're fully covered away from home). Homeowner's insurance should cover stolen luggage if you have off-premises theft protection. Check your existing policies before you buy any additional coverage.

The airlines are responsible for up to $2,500 on domestic flights (and $9.07 per pound, up to $640, on international flights) if they lose your luggage; keep anything more valuable than that in your carry-on bag.

Some credit cards (American Express and certain gold and platinum Visa and MasterCards, for example) offer automatic flight insurance against death or dismemberment in case of an airplane crash. If you feel you need more insurance, try one of the companies we give you in the following paragraph. But don't pay for more insurance than you need; for example, if you only need trip cancellation insurance, don't buy coverage for lost or stolen property.

Some reputable issuers of travel insurance are

Access America (☎ 866-807-3982; www.accessamerica.com); **Travelex Insurance Services** (☎ 888-457-4602; www.travelexinsurance.com); **Travel Guard International** (☎ 800-826-4919; www.travelguard.com); and **Travel Insured International, Inc.** (☎ 800-243-3174; www.travelinsured.com).

Decking Yourself Out: What to Pack

Some people worry about packing for their cruise. Don't. Seriously, you probably have everything you need right in your closet. Cruise vacations are fairly casual, attire-wise. Case in point: One time Fran was eating at the outside grill on a ship and a passenger — lunch tray in hand — walked by wearing nothing but what looked to be plain ol' boxer shorts. That may be an extreme example, but it goes to show that pretty much anything goes — at least out on the deck and by the pool.

 Repeat after us: *I will not overpack.* That's the most important tip we can give you. Although cruise lines don't usually limit how much luggage you can bring on board, the airlines sure do. Generally, they let you bring two checked bags and one carry-on bag per person, and your checked bags can't weigh more than 70 pounds or you have to pay an extra fee. Also, remember that you have limited storage space in your cabin.

The following sections give you the inside scoop on what to bring.

Packing your carry-on

Your carry-on bag should, well, carry your passport (or other necessary identification), cruise documents, credit or ATM cards, cash and/or traveler's checks, house and car keys, claim checks for airport parking, and airplane tickets.

 Don't forget your prescription medicines. Bring an ample supply (get refills if necessary before you leave.)

Try to pack valuables such as jewelry, binoculars, cameras, video equipment, and eyeglasses in your carry-on as well. And you may also want to put in a change of clothes in case your checked suitcase ends up at the wrong destination.

Throw in some reading material, seasickness medication (in case you have a bumpy flight), and chewing gum. Also, because most airlines have cut down on food service, take some granola bars or other snack so you don't starve!

Relaxing by day

Daytime on cruises is a very laid back environment. If you're going on a tropical cruise, shorts and a T-shirt or a swimsuit and a cover-up do the trick — regardless of the itinerary. If you're going on an Alaskan or other cold-weather cruise, pack sweatshirts and jeans or sweatsuits or jogging outfits (probably too cold for shorts). You should also keep a waterproof jacket handy, as well as a warm sweater, because even summer temperatures can be cool in Alaska.

 Before you leave for your cruise, check the weather for your destination. Tune in to The Weather Channel or call ☎ **900-WEATHER**, which connects you to a service operated by The Weather Channel that gives weather reports and forecasts for nearly 1,000 cities. (Note that the call costs 95 cents per minute.) Or you can check (for free) The Weather Channel's Web site at www.weather.com.

We know from experience that packing tight-fitting clothes is a bad idea — they may not fit by the end of the cruise. So if your "winter weight" means you can't get into those summer shorts, you may want to get an extra pair.

Dressing for dinner

You may need to get spiffed up at dinnertime. Your cruise brochure describes the ship's dress code, and the cruise line lets you know before the trip exactly how many dressy occasions it has planned for your particular cruise. In their daily bulletins, ships advise you of the proper dinner attire for the night — formal, informal, or casual (keep in mind that these dress codes apply to the main dining room and not to alternative dining venues). On most 5- to 7-day cruises, you have two formal dinners and two informal dinners; the rest are casual. On most 2- to 4-day cruises, you have one formal dinner. (Some lines, however, are beginning to eliminate formal nights entirely.)

Here's what the labels mean in cruise lingo:

- ✔ **Formal:** Traditionally, men should wear a tux or dark suit with a tie, and women should wear a cocktail dress, long gown, or dressy pantsuit. In reality, however, especially on shorter cruises and budget cruises, people don't seem to pay much attention to the dress code and just show up in comfortable shirts and slacks. So the rule here is get as dressy as you want.

  Don't own a tux? You may be able to rent one through the cruise line's preferred supplier (who delivers right to the ship). If you're interested, check your cruise documents to see if they have info on this service or check with the cruise line. But, on most cruises, you no longer have to go to the trouble unless you sail on a very posh line or you just like wearing your tux. Aboard most ships, a dark suit with a tie works fine. (If you do bring your tux, remember, remember, remember to bring your cufflinks and cummerbund — all *very* expensive items in the onboard shops.)

- ✔ **Informal:** Men should wear a jacket and dressy slacks or a casual suit. A tie is optional, depending on the ship. Women should wear a dress, a skirt and blouse, or dressy slacks. Jeans are a no-no.

- ✔ **Casual:** Men should wear a polo shirt or a dress shirt with slacks. Some also wear a jacket. Women can wear a more casual dress — a sundress, a skirt and blouse, or pants. Jeans are also okay.

  Even on a casual night, you shouldn't wear shorts except on really, really casual lines like Windjammer Barefoot Cruises.

If you don't like to get dressed up, ever, you can avoid the hubbub of the main dining room on formal nights on many ships by choosing the alternative casual dining area (or you can always eat in your skivvies in your cabin). Conversely, many ships now offer fancy, reservations-only restaurants where you can dress up even on casual nights.

Planning for theme nights

Some ships have a theme night during the cruise — country-western night, Caribbean night, whatever. Or they may throw a masquerade party or a talent show. Ask the cruise line before your trip if it has any theme nights planned, and then you can pack what suits your fancy. You're under no obligation to participate, however.

Must-haves for warm-climate cruises

To give you an idea of what you probably need for a weeklong cruise in the Caribbean, the Mediterranean, or any other warm-climate destination, we put together Table 7-1, which lists essential warm-climate items.

Table 7-1	Warm-Climate Cruise Essentials	
Item	*Men*	*Women*
Two swimsuits (one if you don't plan to actually swim)	X	X
A cover-up		X
Two pairs of shorts	X	X
Four tops (polo or t-shirts work fine)	X	X
Two sundresses or casual skirts/blouses or pants outfits		X
Two pair of lightweight slacks (one can be jeans)	X	
Two formal outfits		X
A tux or dark business suit	X	
Two or three nice but less formal dresses or outfits		X
Two or three pairs of dress slacks and three dress shirts	X	
Two belts (one dressy and one casual)	X	
Neckties	X	
A light suit (optional)	X	
Dress shoes	X	X
Accessories	X	X
A light sweater or jacket (for air-conditioning and evening strolls)	X	X
A sports coat	X	
Pajamas (some cruise lines provide robes)	X	X

(continued)

Table 7-1 *(continued)*

Item	Men	Women
One pair of sandals	X	X
One pair of walking shoes or rubber-soled sandals	X	X
Nylons		X
Underwear	X	X
A light raincoat and/or an umbrella	X	X
Gym clothes and sneakers if you plan to exercise	X	X
A sun hat or other hat	X	X
Sunscreen	X	X
Toiletries (most ships provide shampoo)	X	X
Bug spray (you may encounter mosquitoes)	X	X
Sunglasses	X	X
A camera and film	X	X
A good novel and/or magazines	X	X

Must-haves for cold-climate cruises

For an idea of what you probably need for a weeklong cruise in Alaska or some other cold-climate destination (such as the Norwegian fjords), see Table 7-2.

Table 7-2   Cold-Climate Cruise Essentials

Item	Men	Women
A lightweight, waterproof coat or jacket	X	X
A sweater or warm vest	X	X
A warm hat and gloves	X	X
Two or three pairs of pants or jeans	X	X
Several polo shirts, blouses, and/or light sweaters	X	X
A blazer		X
A sports coat	X	
A warm-up suit	X	X

Item	Men	Women
Gym clothes and sneakers if you plan to exercise	X	X
Pajamas (some cruise lines provide robes)	X	X
A swimsuit or two	X	X
Walking shoes (two pairs in case one pair gets wet)	X	X
Three dresses or skirts and pants outfits (for informal or casual nights)		X
Two pairs of dress slacks and three dress shirts	X	
Two belts (one dressy and one casual)	X	
Neckties	X	
Two formal outfits		X
A tux or dark business suit	X	
Accessories	X	X
Underwear	X	X
Dress shoes	X	X
Nylons		X
A warm coat (optional if you prefer layering)	X	X
Toiletries (most ships provide shampoo)	X	X
Bug spray (yes, you may need it)	X	X
Sunscreen	X	X
Sunglasses	X	X
A camera and film	X	X
A good novel and/or magazines	X	X
Binoculars	X	X

Nice-to-have odds and ends

If you plan to bring electronic devices (from curling irons to laptop computers), check with the cruise line first. Not all ships use 110 current (although most in North American fleets do). Even if the ship is 110, you may find only two-pronged jacks rather than three-pronged, so you may need an adapter. And if you stay at a foreign hotel before or after your cruise, you need a converter kit and different plugs.

You may not need to bring a hair dryer. Some ships provide them (although the ship's model is rarely very powerful). Check with the cruise line before your trip.

Here are some other things for you to consider:

- ✔ Packing a few hangers is a good idea, in case your cabin doesn't have enough. And you may want to pack a few large safety pins to keep the curtains closed. (The morning light is bright indeed.)

- ✔ A beach bag, backpack, or the like is great for days at the beach. Most cruise lines provide beach towels for you to take to shore

- ✔ A couple of freezer-size zip-closure bags come in handy for protecting your camera and/or binoculars if you participate in water activities (like kayaking). And you can also use them to pack damp bathing suits for the trip home.

- ✔ If you want to bring your own gear for sports such as golf or scuba diving, check with your airline for the best way to transport such items.

- ✔ Most ships have a telephone wake-up service, but you may prefer to bring your alarm clock.

- ✔ Bring plenty of film for your camera and blank cassettes for your camcorder. That stuff often costs more at tourist-y areas.

- ✔ Learn from our mistakes: Don't take brand-new shoes that you haven't worn in. (Or pack a bunch of adhesive bandages if you do.)

Confirming Your Flight

Airplanes' arrival and departure times are always subject to change, so take some time to confirm your flight a day before your departure. (Do it three days before departure if you're taking an international flight.) To avoid getting stuck waiting at the airport, call the airline again the day you leave to make sure that your flight is operating on time. Also be sure to arrange any in-flight meal requests in advance.

Get to the airport early. For domestic flights, plan to get there two full hours before your plane is scheduled to depart. For international flights, plan to get there three hours before departure.

Remembering Other Important Stuff

Before walking out the door, be sure to

- ✔ Call the post office and arrange for it to hold your mail. Similarly, arrange to stop delivery of the newspaper, or ask a friend to collect your post and papers for you.

✔ Make copies of your passport or identification, your airline tickets, and any credit cards you plan to use just in case they get separated from you for any reason. Pack the copies in your luggage separately from the actual documents (which should be in your carry-on) or leave them with a friend.

✔ Write down the ship's phone number (it should be included with your cruise documents) and leave the number and a copy of your itinerary with a friend or relative.

✔ Put luggage tags on your bags. Luggage tags with the cruise line's name, identifying you as a passenger of the line, come with your cruise documents. Fill in your departure date, port, cabin number, and so on (check your cruise documents for the specifics), and put a tag on each bag.

✔ Be sure to put your name and address *inside* your bags just in case your luggage tags fall off.

✔ Avoid carrying scissors, straight razors, or any other sharp objects in your hand luggage. Due to increased air travel security, you're no longer able to bring these items into the passenger cabin. You can pack them in your checked baggage, however.

✔ Keep a separate record of your traveler's checks' numbers. If you lose your traveler's checks, you have to report the numbers.

✔ Carefully read all the pre-trip material the cruise line provides you.

Part III

All Aboard: The Cruise Experience

The 5th Wave

By Rich Tennant

"Oh look! Isn't that Raoul, the ship steward you refused to tip after he fished your watch out of the pool?"

In this part . . .

Now you can find out what cruises are all about, from the lively onboard activities and mouth-watering food presentations to the lavish spa treatments.

In this part of the book, we give you the scoop on meals, entertainment, shipboard activities, the gambling scene, and (if you need a rest) the quiet spots. We also include information for shoppers and families.

Get ready for the time of your life.

Chapter 8

Wining and Dining

. . . .

In This Chapter

▶ Getting the scoop on cruise ship menus

▶ Taking charge of your table arrangements

▶ Dining formally and informally

▶ Discovering the best gourmet cruises

▶ Doing breakfast and lunch

▶ Minding your dining room manners

. . . .

*W*hen it comes right down to it, people love to eat — especially on vacation! Cruise lines know this, and like suitors trying to impress their dates, they woo you with food. In particular, dinner in the ships' main dining rooms can be an over-the-top blast of luxury and theatrical extravagance, particularly on the new megaships. For breakfast, lunch, and midnight snacks, cruise ships serve buffets that, although more casual than dining room dinners, rival ancient Roman feasts. And as if all this isn't enough, most cruise lines now have alternative dining options such as casual eateries (sushi bars, Irish pubs, pizzerias, and hamburger grills) and specialty restaurants (steakhouse, Italian, Asian, and so forth). Many lines have also added in-cabin pizza delivery and more to their room-service menus.

 Whether the sea air makes everyone hungrier or a sense of self-indulgence arises from being away from home and work, even the most disciplined eaters are tempted to blow their calorie allowance on board. The usual statistic we hear is that people gain five pounds on a weeklong cruise, but you don't necessarily have to: Check out the tips Chapter 2 gives you for burning off the extra calories.

Grazing Throughout the Day

Excess: The key word for cruise ship eating. In fact, cruise ships may offer organized activities just to help distract you from the endless edible offerings. Check out this typical meals listing from one cruise line to see what's meant by that old joke, "You come on as a passenger and you leave as cargo":

✔ **Top o' the morning:** (6:30 a.m.) Coffee and simple pastries.

✔ **Buffet breakfast:** (8 to 10:30 a.m.) Daily specials, sweet rolls, fruit, eggs, bacon, cereal, yogurt, croissants, coffee, juice, and tea.

✔ **Breakfast in the dining room:** (Main seating begins around 7 a.m.; late seating around 8 or 9 a.m.) Full breakfast, including omelets, eggs, French toast, pancakes, breakfast meats, potatoes, fish, cereal, oatmeal, fruit, yogurt, and juices.

✔ **Mid-morning snack:** (10 a.m.) Sweet rolls, muffins, coffee, and tea.

✔ **Buffet lunch:** (11:30 a.m. to 2:30 p.m.) Full hot and cold lunch offerings, including salad bar and pasta station.

✔ **Lunch in the dining room:** (Main seating at noon; late seating at 1:30 p.m.) Full luncheon with a rotating menu of hot dishes, salads, sandwiches, pastas, grilled items, and desserts.

✔ **Afternoon tea:** (3:30 to 5:00 p.m.) Tea and cake.

✔ **Snack time:** (All afternoon) Ice cream and fat-free frozen yogurt.

✔ **Dinner in the dining room:** (Early seating at 6 p.m.; late seating at 8:15 p.m.) Gourmet cuisine, including popular international and American dishes served in seven courses with desserts.

✔ **Midnight buffet:** (Guess!) Extravagant offerings of hot and cold entrees, desserts, salads, cold meats, breads, cheeses, and fruit.

As if you could still require more eating opportunities, your ship may also have a pizza parlor, an ice cream parlor, or maybe even a sushi bar. Some ships, particularly the newer and larger ones, may also boast coffee bars, which tend to offer sweets, and champagne bars, where you can have caviar with all the trimmings. (Be aware of an extra charge for the caviar, as well as possible charges for espresso, cappuccino, and gourmet ice cream.)

Sitting Pretty at Seatings

To ease the logistics of feeding more than 3,000 passengers three square meals a day, many ships use timed seatings at each meal. Until recently, the norm was two seatings, with guests booking the early or late seating. You chose a time, the ship assigned you to a table that seated four, six, eight, or more people, and you sat with the same group for every meal you took in the main dining room.

Recently, however, major megaship cruise lines have tried hard to make dining arrangements more flexible. Carnival, for instance, now offers four seating times on all its ships that have two dining rooms (but only two seatings on ships with one dining room). And Norwegian Cruise Line and Princess Cruises, taking a page from the smaller and ritzier lines, offer restaurant-style open seating — you decide where, and with whom, you want to dine. (On Princess ships you decide in advance of your cruise whether to dine the traditional way or with open seating.)

Sitting at a table with eight seats gives you enough variety among your companions that you don't get bored. This also allows you to steer clear of a particular individual you really don't like. Don't feel that the chair you sit in the first night needs to be your place every night — the ship assigns you to a table, not a specific seat. Shake things up by choosing a different seat each night. Your variation sometimes confuses the waiters who may try to remember guests' special requests by remembering which seat they were in, but it allows you to meet everyone at your table (and avoid anyone you don't particularly like). Be friendly enough so that the waiter remembers you by face or name and doesn't rely on the seating.

Don't panic if you end up sitting next to some obnoxious type who chews with his mouth open and keeps shouting "What's with all these forks?" Try to change your table by speaking with the maitre d' (greasing his palm may help).

If you get tired of the whole formal dining room routine, many ships have alternative casual dining options that you can check out. And the newest fad is fancy reservations-only restaurants for an extra fee (up to $25). Choose this option to enjoy a more intimate, and often more expertly prepared, meal.

Dining as a Matter of Courses

Dinner aboard a cruise ship provides more than a five- to seven-course meal: It serves as one of the main social events of the day. With the multiple courses served at a relaxed pace and your table dressed in china, silver, fresh flowers, and starched linens, you can't get further from a fast-food experience.

Expect to be at your table for at least an hour and a half. Here's what you're likely to find:

- Overall, count on Continental (international) cuisine in the dining room.

- Meals often feature specialties particular to the region you cruise through, such as salmon in Alaska and lobster in New England.

- The courses consist of an appetizer, soup, salad, main course (with starch and vegetables), and dessert, and on some ships a pasta, fruit, and cheese course as well.

- Most lines provide at least one healthy selection in each category, listing the fat, salt content, and number of calories on the menu. In the spring of 2004, Carnival became the first cruise line to join the low-carb craze, offering special menu items for followers of low-carb diets.

- Many ships feature daily vegetarian selections.

 ✔ Children's menus are more commonly appearing on the cruise-ship dining scene.

 ✔ On some nights the ship builds the menus around a theme, such as Caribbean or Italian night.

Feel free to make a culinary request if you have an urge for something in particular, but remember that the chef can prepare dishes only with what's available in the larder (no running out to the grocery store here). Make your requests the day before so the chef can prepare.

Savoring the best lines for gourmet cuisine

These cruise lines get special props for the culinary talent they have on display, which rivals most restaurants on land:

✔ **Crystal:** The best Asian food afloat, as well as creative California cuisine. A guest chef series brings celebrity chefs aboard. A new addition is a Kosher-dining program that offers a selection of specially prepared dishes.

✔ **Seabourn:** Celebrity chef Charlie Palmer consults on cuisine that reflects California and Pacific Rim influences but also includes favorites like broiled lobster and beef Wellington. Celebrity chefs (Palmer and friends) may be on board offering specialties.

✔ **SeaDream:** This line does just about everything right, with the chefs using fresh ingredients in creative ways. And no special request gets denied.

✔ **Seven Seas Cruises:** Combining traditional and new cuisine, Seven Seas menus reflect the regions where the ship cruises. The *Seven Seas Mariner* and *Seven Seas Voyager* also have specialty restaurants overseen by chefs from the prestigious French cooking school *Le Cordon Bleu*. On some sailings, these chefs offer cooking classes.

✔ **Silversea:** French-influenced recipes and great steaks cooked to order, as well as themed buffets, guest chefs, and a specialty restaurant by Spain's renowned chef Joachim Koeper.

Although not quite as extravagant, these lines are also worth a mention . . .

✔ **Cunard:** On the *Queen Mary 2* Cunard assigns you to a restaurant based on your cabin category, and if you're in the Queen's or Princess Grill, expect the best. Celebrity chef Todd English also has his first shipboard restaurant on this vessel.

✔ **Oceania:** Excellent alternative dining at a steakhouse and Italian restaurant, each with beautiful decor and huge portions.

✔ **Celebrity:** Consulting chef Michel Roux creates a meal that lasts a luxurious three hours and thrills the palate for the reservations-only alternative restaurants on the *Millennium, Infinity, Summit,* and *Constellation*.

✔ **Windstar:** Top Los Angeles restaurateur Joachim Splichal consults on fresh and creative menus that go way beyond what you may expect from a sailing ship.

If you're a big soda drinker, see if the line has a deal where you pay for your soda in advance instead of doling out the usual $1.50 a pop (excuse the pun). Carnival has a program where you can get a soda pass to use for unlimited sodas: For a one-week cruise the cost is $22.95 for kids under 21 and $34.44 for adults. Royal Caribbean has a similar soda program ($20 for kids 18 and under and $33 for adults for a weeklong cruise) and also provides a card good for 12 mock-tails (normally $4 apiece) or other drinks sans alcohol ($24.95 for kids and $29.95 for adults).

 Unsure about how to select wine? Consult the wine steward (if your ship has one) or see if the ship offers a wine tasting. A small fee may be involved (probably $5 or $10), but you get to sample several varieties, and if you find something you like, you can order on the spot (a waiter delivers your wine later to your table in the dining room). You may even get to buy the wine at a discount if you attend a wine seminar.

Choosing other dining options

If formal dining isn't your style but you love fine cuisine, you may, on some nights (depending on the ship you choose), have the option of dining in a smaller gourmet restaurant. The lines usually decorate these venues in upscale decor and focus on one type of cuisine — Italian, Asian, French, and steakhouses are the most popular. You typically have to pay a service fee (up to $25 per head) and reserve your table in advance (do so early on in the cruise or you may not get a spot).

Many ships also offer a free casual alternative dinner option — an open-seating, no-reservations-required, casual dress affair, most often on the Lido Deck (Pool Deck). You can get either a buffet or a short menu with simple food such as steaks, grilled fish, pasta, and salads. This option may be available overnight for night owls.

Of course, the ultra-casual alternative is room service. The menu may be limited, but you don't have to put on your formal duds — or any duds at all!

Making special dietary requests

 If you have any special dietary needs, make arrangements with the ship when you book your cruise. After you board, check with the maitre d' your first day out to make sure that the kitchen got your request. Some lines offer kosher menus and most have vegetarian, low-fat, low-salt, or sugar-free options.

Enjoying Breakfast and Lunch

Breakfast and lunch in the dining room are also multi-course events. Menus generally change daily. As with dinner, the service isn't rushed, making the meal more about having an experience and less about filling your belly. If you're in a hurry or just don't want to deal with the formalities, you can take advantage of a casual buffet — check near the Pool Deck. (Also, sticking with fresh fruit for breakfast is a great way to save up calories for a splurge later in the day.)

For lunch, you may have a deck-side grill option with hot dogs, burgers, and chicken. And the newest ships offer even more: On Royal Caribbean's giant *Voyager of the Seas* and its sister ships, for example, a **Johnny Rockets** diner caters to cruisers who crave a good burger and shake.

Mastering dining room etiquette

Even the most socially polished cruisers may need some pointers on shipboard dining. Here are the highlights:

Do's

Display good manners in the dining room by following these tips:

- ✔ **Arrive in the dining room on time.** Dining hours are listed in the daily program.

- ✔ **Display your understanding of what the members of the dining staff do.** Order from the waiter, not the bus boy.

- ✔ **Offer wine to the others at your table.** If your tablemates are as polite as you are, one of them will order the next night's bottle.

- ✔ **If you don't finish your bottle of wine, ask your waiter to have it corked.** You can have it held for the next night.

- ✔ **Consider the waiter's suggestion about menu items or specials.** The waiter can tell you the most popular menu items.

Don'ts

To keep from embarrassing yourself or your dining companions, don't do the following:

- ✔ **Don't start eating until the waiter serves everyone at your table.** Good etiquette no matter where you dine.

- ✔ **Don't show up dressed inappropriately for the evening.** Check your daily bulletin for the dress code for the evening and prepare accordingly.

- ✔ **Don't use the incorrect silverware.** Use your silverware moving from the outside in. The first fork on the left is the one that you use for the first course.

- ✔ **Don't feel as if you have to eat a meal you don't like.** Feel free to send food back and ask for something else if you don't like your selection.

- ✔ **Don't try to smoke in a no-smoking section.** Or, even worse, in a no-smoking dining room.

Chapter 9

Heading into Activities

· ·

In This Chapter

▶ Digging into your daily bulletin

▶ Lounging, playing, and learning by day

▶ Hamming it up for big productions on board

▶ Finding the cruise lines with the best nighttime entertainment

▶ Keeping up with life on land

· ·

*B*ecause cruise ship vacations offer more activities than practically any other kind of vacation, you don't get bored on board. And if you just need to get away from it all, you have the opportunity to do absolutely nothing — your choice.

Reading the Cruise News

All the cruise ships print and distribute a daily bulletin filled with information to help you plan your day and get the most out of your cruise experience. The bulletin is delivered to your cabin in the evening and includes the following:

✔ The next day's activities schedule and entertainment offerings

✔ Hours of operation for the bars and shops (with sales and specials noted)

✔ The evening dress code for the main dining room (see Chapter 8 for more dining info)

✔ Listings of television channels and movie presentations

✔ A schedule for exercise classes

✔ Tips for playing some of the casino games

✔ Details about upcoming ports of call (such as shopping hot spots and top attractions)

✔ Facts about the region you're sailing through

The bulletin may also offer summaries of the day's top news stories from the real world, taken from wire services or top newspapers. Typically, the bulletin is loaded with advertisements for the ship's shops or for shops in ports.

Depending on the line you sail with, your bulletin may offer up to 50 activities for a single day! Sure, it seems like an insane amount of things to do, but remember that cruise ships aim to satisfy a lot of different people who have wildly varying tastes. So you can choose to bid in the art auction, play in the slots tournament, take in an enrichment lecture, or grab a book and head to a comfortable lounge chair for some peace and quiet.

Enjoying Daytime Activities

On days at sea especially, you're faced with something most folks don't often get in their daily lives: a full day to do anything you want, at any time you want. Rise with the sun or sleep until noon. Bound from one activity to the next or spend the day quietly with a book and/or movie.

You may want to just flop down and relax for the first day or two and then loosen up and join in the festivities as the week goes on, but how much or how little you do is always up to you.

Lounging at the pool

The pool deck is the center of daytime activity on most ships, especially in the Caribbean. If you want to spend a day lounging poolside on a bigger ship, get there early so that you can stake out a lounge chair in a good spot. Lounging is more active than you may think: From your chair you can take in poolside games and contests, listen to a live band, sip a piña colada, and work on your tan.

Although a few cruise lines, such as Disney, Princess, Royal Caribbean, and Carnival (Spirit-class ships), have gotten hip to the notion that some people prefer their pool experience to be calm and quiet — they provide a separate pool (more than one on some ships) sealed off from the bands, games, and kids — this is the exception, not the norm. If you want to relax and read in a quiet area, the pool is often not the place for you. We don't call it the center of activity for nothing.

Surprisingly, you may not get to swim much at all while on board; most ship pools are just too tiny. The pool is more of a place for taking a quick dip to cool off or standing on the side with your drink, checking out how the other passengers look in their swimsuits (don't worry — you'll never see these people again!) rather than a place to do laps. If you want quiet sunning, try the sun deck — usually the uppermost deck — or hidden spaces, usually in the stern, where you can soak up the rays without as much foot traffic.

Finding other diversions

If you prefer a really quiet day or you spent too much time in the sun the first day, you can visit the library, available on nearly all ships. In addition to books, some libraries make CDs available and a few even have specially equipped chairs with headphones where you can listen to the CDs. On ships that offer rooms or suites with VCRs, a selection of videos may be available. (The Yachts of Seabourn has a particularly nice selection; see Chapter 15.) Most ship libraries have set hours — some have very limited hours and others are open all day when not in port — so check your bulletin for details.

Another appealing area is the ship's card room, where you can expect bridge to be the most popular game. Some ships have a bridge instructor on board and offer tournaments. The card rooms often provide decks of cards. You can also borrow board games such as Monopoly and Scrabble from either the card room or the library.

Bigger ships may have their own movie theaters. Disney Cruise Line, whose ships offer marvelous movie theaters with stadium seating, big screens, comfy chairs, and first-run films (from Disney-owned studios, of course), is the unquestioned leader here (see the section "Taking in a show" later in this chapter for more Disney info, or check out Chapter 14). Some Holland America ships have dedicated movie theaters, too, with free popcorn. On ships without theaters, you can still catch a movie shown in a bar or lounge (not always the most comfortable arrangement). Although the flicks aren't current releases, they're at least recent.

You can always check out the offerings on your in-room television. The daily bulletin or separate television guide provides listings, and the selection has come a long way in the past few years. Many ships offer Arts & Entertainment, Discovery Channel, ESPN, HBO, History & Biography, TNT, and free in-house movie channels. Royal Caribbean has 29 free channels including French, Spanish, Italian, Portuguese, and German-language offerings. Some of the newer ships (including those in the Royal Caribbean and Celebrity fleets) also offer pay-per-view options; you may even be able to order up adult movies.

Another viewing option is, well, you. A few ships videotape activities to make sure that no one misses anything and replay them on the TV system. You may be able to watch yourself doing the limbo at a poolside party from your own room — which may make for good or bad viewing, depending on the kind of night you had.

Learning as You Lounge

Ships offer a variety of lectures, demonstrations, and seminars. If you haven't already caught the online fever, you may be able to sign up on board (sometimes for a fee) to discover how to boot up, get online, send and receive e-mails from the ship, and use processing programs such as Word and Excel. On the lighter side, and for free, you can figure out how the kitchen staff makes vegetables look like flowers or napkins look like birds; take in a demonstration on makeup or hair styling; or, for a minimal fee, participate in a wine-tasting seminar or spend an hour mixing drinks.

If you seek learning opportunities, experts such as historians, marine biologists, and U.S. forest rangers may offer lectures in their areas of expertise. Some ships feature seminars in the arts from professionals: photographers on photography, artists on drawing and painting, and authors on books. Cooking classes are all the rage, sometimes taught by visiting celebrity chefs.

Crystal has an excellent new offering: You can learn to play piano on your vacation. You get instruction in a piano lab filled with Yamaha electronic keyboards. You may not come home sounding like Chick Corea or Van Cliburn, but you just may get a start on a lifelong hobby.

Crystal's learning program also includes acting and cabaret workshops, event planning, feng shui, alternative medicine, estate planning, and more. (Flip to Chapter 15 to find out more about Crystal.)

Not to be outdone, Cunard has gone for big name activities on its new *Queen Mary 2*. Passengers can hear lectures from Oxford University professors or chefs chosen by *Gourmet* magazine and participate in workshops with members of the *Royal Academy of Dramatic Arts* (who also perform onboard). The world's biggest ship is also the only one with its own planetarium. Discover more about the megaship in Chapter 15.

On Princess ships, you can earn your scuba certification from the Professional Association of Diving Instructors (PADI). The newer Princess ships also offer pottery classes. The line offers much more, and we offer the info in Chapter 14.

Small ships offer fewer activities, but the offerings may be of higher quality than those geared toward the masses on larger ships; you're more apt to find a distinguished celebrity giving a lecture on a smaller, luxury Seabourn or Silversea ship than on a Carnival megaliner.

Both large and small ships offer the popular galley tour, a behind-the-scenes look at the ship's food-preparation area. Some ships (including those in the Costa and Holland America fleets) even offer their midnight buffet in the galley once during each cruise, giving you a chance to raid the biggest fridge you're ever likely to encounter.

Several of the big-ship lines — most notably Celebrity, Princess, Royal Caribbean, and Holland America — spend millions of dollars on their onboard art collections, which include pieces by well-known artists.

Inquire at the purser's office about a group tour of the collection or for a printed description and map so that you can take a tour on your own.

Finding Entertainment after Dark

As ships get bigger and competition grows, after-dark entertainment options increase. Most cruise passengers want to step out after dinner: take in a show, listen to some music, maybe hit the dance floor, or head for the casino. Megaships like the Grand Class Princess vessels, Carnival's Conquest and Destiny classes, and Royal Caribbean's Voyager-class ships have a multitude of options; small ships such as those in The Yachts of Seabourn and Silversea fleets are more limited. And quality varies greatly from line to line and from ship to ship.

Taking in a show

Big-ship cruising means high-tech shows that feature dazzling laser-lighting effects, pyrotechnics, video backdrops, actors "flying" in and out, and large casts of singers and dancers performing everything from Stephen Sondheim and Andrew Lloyd Webber ensembles to fast-paced, contemporary tunes. Show casts range from solo singers on small ships to around 16 or 18 performers on many Carnival and Celebrity ships. Cruise lines spend literally millions of dollars on each extravagant production, and the effort normally translates into fulfilling results. The large shows are often as good as anything you see in New York.

Smaller ships favor cabaret shows over glitzy stage productions. These shows may have dancers or just a vocalist with a combo; either way, the emphasis is on old-fashioned music without the frills. A few older ships still offer small-scale theatrical revues. Some of the larger ships are more cutting-edge than others, but you can count on an enjoyable evening at the theater, especially on Royal Caribbean, Carnival, Crystal, and, of course, Disney.

Disney, in fact, raises the bar for at-sea entertainment. Offering three family-friendly productions on 3- and 4-day cruises and a fourth (a magic show) on its 7-day sailings, the Mouse spares no expense in creating Broadway-caliber shows at sea (albeit in one-hour versions). The shows feature the same carefully crafted sets, costumes, and special effects that you find at the Disney parks and, within limits, in Disney movies.

What you see on stage may be spectacular, but most ships invest less in the music than the sets and costumes. Whereas several lines used to have up to 16-piece bands, today the norm is between 6 and 10, with most on the lower end of the range. Some lines don't have live bands playing at the shows at all — they use recorded music. And although featured vocalists sing live, the dancers in most cases are actually lip-synching to a recording.

Many lines try to find their niche with their productions. The following list tells you what some of the lines offer (see Part IV for more details):

- **Carnival:** Large-scale musical revues that rank among the best in the business. Over the past year, the line has added new production shows, including some magic shows, on *Glory, Conquest, Pride, Imagination, Miracle, Valor, Paradise,* and *Ecstasy.* Still to come in 2005: two new shows on the *Liberty,* a new show for *Ecstasy,* and new shows on *Fascination. Miracle* features a Beatles show (a good production, although some passengers may find it awkward hearing "Hey Jude" to a Latin beat).

- **Celebrity:** Some of the finest megaliner theaters at sea. Celebrity has added 13 new shows since 2003. The *Fantasea* show offers Cirque du Soleil-like aerial acts. The *Century* ship features performances of Broadway tunes that range from classics to contemporary shows such as *Hairspray, The Producers,* and *Wicked. Constellation* has a multimedia show that plays beautifully to your senses. Also on Celebrity: big names like Tommy Tune, Manhattan Rhythm Kings, and Stephen Sorrentino.

- **Costa:** Stage revues that don't appear as professionally delivered as the production shows on some American ships; however, the Italian line wins points for at least having its dancers attempt something akin to modern ballet (and with a certain degree of success). And because Costa ships attract a multi-language clientele, you also find mimes, acrobats, magicians, and multi-instrumental musicians performing pretty much non-verbally.

- **Crystal Cruises:** Broke new ground by introducing *Repertory Theatre at Sea.* Here, Crystal guests are likely to see excerpts from works by authors ranging from Neil Simon to Edgar Allen Poe and William Shakespeare, along with scenes from contemporary Broadway plays.

- **Radisson Seven Seas:** Offers up something different for its *Seven Seas Voyager* vacationers. *On a Classical Note* treats the audience to an operatic show with English subtitles on a screen. Music and dance numbers include selections from *La Traviata, La Boheme, The Marriage of Figaro,* and some Gilbert & Sullivan. *Beyond Imagination* includes music from Puccini, Mendelssohn, and more, and *Here, There and Everywhere* is a tribute to the Beatles.

- **Royal Caribbean:** Known for the biggest and best revue shows and its occasional "name" entertainers, Royal Caribbean adds the spice of ice to its *Voyager, Explorer, Adventure, Navigator,* and *Mariner* ship lines. All these giant ships have ice skating rinks and offer ice shows with special effects similar to those in the main theaters. The most recent addition: *Tango Buenos Aires,* aboard *Jewel of the Seas.*

Most ships offer productions twice a night to correspond with traditional first and second seating dinner times; usually you see the show after dinner, but, on some nights, you may have the option of seeing the show before dinner. And on lines that increasingly push "freestyle" or "personal choice" dining options, which allow for dinner whenever you want it (notably Princess and Norwegian), shows may be scheduled only once a night and repeat later in the week.

Mixing with variety acts

Vaudeville is alive and well on cruise ships, which you may or may not think is a good thing. On-ship variety acts include acrobats, jugglers, magicians, and ventriloquists. Ritzier lines like Crystal and Celebrity often feature classical pianists or violinists (real music fans may scoff at the fact that they tend to only play short, familiar works) and vocalists who have appeared on Broadway or London's West End. Good old-fashioned standup singers seem to be out of favor with cruise lines, although given the popularity of television shows like *American Idol* and *Star Search*, this may change. Carnival has added some full-length, heavily produced magic shows to its onboard lineup on its biggest vessels; Princess likewise emphasizes the art of deception on some ships.

Occasionally, ships carry some well-known singers and other performers, such as Maureen McGovern, Joel Grey, and Lorna Luft. You may also see some excellent performers who may not be household names or a singer who was famous back in the day crooning oldies but goodies. On a Seabourn cruise, we found Phillip Huber — he created and manipulated the puppets for the hit cult film *Being John Malkovich* — and his Huber Marionettes.

Lounging around

Although you still encounter the occasional lounge singer who seems to have lost interest in the craft, listlessly rendering a cliched set of standards in a cheap tux, the quality of small-room entertainment has improved in the past decade, due no doubt to increased interest in the lounge genre on shore. Princess, Royal Caribbean, and Carnival seem to have taken the lead here by spending a bit more money to lure engaging entertainers to their ships.

Lounge entertainment varies not only from ship to ship, but also from room to room on the same ship, providing enough variety to please passengers with varying tastes (after all, one person's music is another person's Muzak). Combos or solo acts pop up all over most large ships at night, with at least one band playing dance tunes. If a quiet piano bar isn't your thing (or it has given way to electronic background tracks), you can hit the disco. Many smaller ships, however, often have just one room with danceable music and/or a piano bar.

Carnival has come up with the best innovation in years. The Spirit-class ships offer an old-fashioned supper-club cabaret (in the reservations-only, alternative restaurant). The music, often featuring two singer/musicians aided by synthesized accompaniment, is usually high quality, and the food and service are superb. Make your reservations early for this attraction.

Celebrity recently converted its **Michael's Club** rooms from cigar bars to piano and jazz lounges. Royal Caribbean ships have the **Schooner Bar,** which tends to feature a talented pianist-vocalist. The line's *Navigator of the Seas* added a Latin jazz bar and a "cool jazz" lounge as well. On Princess, check out the musical offerings on the Promenade or Atrium lounges. Crystal has the excellent **Avenue Saloon.**

As ships have gotten bigger, music venues have multiplied. On the biggest Royal Caribbean and Carnival ships, you may find eight or nine choices at night — from background guitar to karaoke, from sing-a-long piano bars to classical chamber groups.

 Prowl the decks in the wee hours to catch a musical treat you don't find listed in your bulletin: On the big ships, musicians sometimes gather late at night in one of the larger lounges to jam, producing some high-quality improv jazz.

Strutting your stuff on stage

If you fantasize about being the next Sinatra, Streisand, J-Lo, or Seinfeld, your ship has come in: Virtually all large ships have passenger talent shows. You need to audition, but upon passing that test you get to perform in the main theater or in a smaller lounge. Remember to pack your sheet music (although a skilled accompanist may be able to wing it) and whatever costume and props you need. If you want to do a stand-up comedy act, remember the cardinal rule of comedy: Know your audience. Don't tell X-rated jokes to a G-rated crowd.

Don't want to audition but still want to perform? Try karaoke, which provides many an introvert an opportunity for spontaneous performance. Most larger ships offer karaoke several times during the trip. For the uninitiated, *karaoke* involves people taking turns singing to recorded back-up tracks, which usually — but not always — sound more or less like the original recording, as lyrics scroll across a television screen. You choose the song from a book and the master of ceremonies calls each participant in turn to the microphone. Everyone gets into the spirit at these sessions, and no one — regardless of talent level — should be embarrassed or fear getting the hook.

Singing and dancing waiters

Especially if you cruise on a big ship, you get to sit back and watch your waitstaff engage in a sing-along (whether they want to or not). The traditional grand presentation of the Baked Alaska dessert entails the waitstaff parading around the room in song.

In many cases, the staff participates in at least one theme night on 7-day cruises, dressing up according to the theme — country and western, the '50s, Italian, or Greek, for instance (Norwegian Cruise Line has added Latin Night). You may be invited to dress up as well. Both the menu and the after-dinner entertainment may also reflect the theme. On Carnival ships, the staff serenades you nightly with choreographed routines.

Living Everyday Life on Board

Who said cruising was all fun and games? Well, mostly it is, but you may be wondering about a few more practical issues — such as how to send postcards home, how to keep up with the news, how to attend religious services, or how to get medical attention. This section gives you the scoop.

Dropping a line

To send mail from the ship, drop by the purser's office to find a mailbox and local postage. Remember, your U.S. stamps don't work in foreign countries.

Getting the news

Although most people go on a cruise to relax, you may still want to hear the nightly news — stressful as it may be! Most new ships offer CNN on their in-room televisions (in Europe — and sometimes in the Caribbean — you get CNN International or the BBC). Almost all ships post the latest scoop off the wire services outside the purser's office. Some lines also offer daily excerpts from the world's top newspapers, such as *The New York Times,* either delivering a printout to your cabin daily or leaving copies in the library. If you don't mind paying a fee, on most big ships you can go online (see the following section) and check your favorite newspaper via the Internet.

E-mailing from paradise

If your idea of fun is surfing the Web, you're in luck. Internet cafes and/or computer centers are all over the high seas. At these venues, you can e-mail to your heart's content, as long as you don't mind paying 50 cents to $1.50 per minute (the fee varies per line). Be aware, however, that time flies when you surf online, and the charges can pile up fast. Most lines offer a cheaper rate if you commit in advance to a certain time period (say, 60 minutes). You may also be able to purchase unlimited access for the duration of the cruise for a set price. (If you plan to check e-mail daily, this option may be the way to go.) Some computers may even be equipped with cameras, allowing you to send a hokey e-postcard of yourself from the ship (usually for a fee of $3.95 to $4.95 per postcard). If you choose a ship without access, you can probably find an Internet cafe at the ports of call.

Keeping the faith

Depending on the ship and the inclusion of clergy on board, most lines offer a nondenominational service on Sundays; some lines (including Costa and Cunard) offer Catholic mass every day. Typically, a passenger conducts Jewish Sabbath services on Friday nights. The ship provides prayer books. On both Jewish and Christian holidays, large ships may bring clergy aboard to lead services. Some ships have chapels, and Cunard's *QE2* even has its own synagogue.

For Friday-night Jewish Sabbath services, the ship organizes the service; notes it in the daily schedule; and leaves out prayer books, yarmulkes, challah, and wine. The passengers conduct the service themselves — usually one passenger agrees to be the leader.

Seeking a doctor

Nearly every ship carrying more than 100 passengers has a medical facility staffed by a doctor and a nurse who are ready to handle health emergencies that may arise at sea. The biggest ships now carry two doctors and between two and four nurses to handle the large number of passengers, and some facilities have become quite elaborate. Your shipboard doctor may even be able to link to a top hospital on land via computers and video displays so he or she can get another opinion. A dentist and chiropractor may be on board on longer cruises. Ships with less than 100 passengers and less-extravagant health services tend to sail closer to land, so in the event of an emergency the ship heads for shore.

Just like at home, a ship's medical center has set office hours, but you can get to a doctor 24 hours a day should an emergency arise. Most shipboard ailments are fairly minor, such as seasickness, a sprained ankle, or the flu (ships stock antibiotics on board for the latter), but the doctors can also perform minor surgery if necessary.

Should you develop a serious medical problem, you're taken off the ship at the nearest port for treatment or possibly flown by helicopter to a hospital. And be aware: Your regular health insurance means nothing on the ship. Medical facilities charge you a significant amount of money for emergency treatments (although you can get seasick pills free from the purser's office), and an airlift at sea can be very expensive. You can try to collect from your health provider later, but it may not cover the charges. You should invest in travel insurance to cover away-from-home emergencies. (For details about travel insurance, see Chapter 7.)

If you have existing health problems, let the shipboard doctor know in advance of your sailing so that he or she can make any necessary preparations.

Chapter 10

Catering to the Kids: Activities for Children and Teens

. . . .

In This Chapter

▶ Getting the full scoop on childrens' and teens' programs

▶ Knowing which questions to ask before you book your family cruise

▶ Arranging for baby-sitting on board

▶ Informing your kids about cruise-ship rules

▶ Identifying the best cruises for families

. . . .

*F*act A: Baby Boomers make up an ever-increasing percentage of cruise passengers. Fact B: Baby Boomers have kids. Fact C: Baby Boomers with kids take family vacations. Fact D: Cruise lines recognize this and try to cater to parents who want it all — to keep their kids happy and entertained and to rest and relax themselves. (And who needs a rest more than parents?)

In this chapter, we point out cruises and cruise lines that help you make the most of family vacation time. See the section "The Best Family Cruises" later in this chapter to get information on which particular ships are tops.

Keeping the Children in Mind

To meet the needs of families, cruise lines now provide great facilities for all ages. Children and teens can enjoy planned, supervised programs throughout the day and evening, giving parents the freedom to enjoy their own fun. The lines are investing in the cruisers of tomorrow, spending today so that they can provide a memorable experience for kids (who grow up wanting to return to the good old cruise ship for vacations).

Today's cruises have quite a few kids on board. Carnival alone said it expected to carry nearly 450,000 kids (ages 2 to 17) on its ships in 2004. And Royal Caribbean now carries more than 300,000 kids a year.

The newer ships of the mass-market lines and premium lines, including Carnival, Royal Caribbean, Celebrity, Holland America, Norwegian, Princess, and (obviously) Disney, go all out with facilities for kids of all ages. Youngsters can entertain themselves in playrooms, splash pools, teen centers, kiddy theaters, ice cream parlors, and video arcades.

Some luxury outfits, such as Cunard and Crystal, set aside special facilities for the youngest cruisers and offer activities on a seasonal basis. Children's activities are included in the cruise fare and often go beyond the standard arts-and-crafts and video-movie offerings parents may expect. You pay only for extras like baby-sitting and shore excursions.

Not all ships are kid friendly, however. Some lines feature outdated facilities on older ships or actively discourage passengers from bringing children along. Others lines disallow kids outright. For example, American Canadian Caribbean Line doesn't permit children under 14. The tone on some ships, such as those in the Silversea and Seabourn fleets, is very adult (the line and other passengers expect kids that come onboard to be well behaved).

You find more kids on ships in the Caribbean, but Alaska is growing in popularity as a *three-generation destination* (children, parents, and grandparents) where youngsters can enjoy finding out about glaciers, native culture, and wildlife. Europe, too, is becoming more popular with family cruisers. A nifty thing about taking the kids on a cruise in Europe is that some of the kids in the children's program probably speak English only as a second language, if at all, so your kids can have a nice cross-cultural experience. (Alert your children to the possibility of this in advance so that they don't think the other kids are unfriendly.)

Summing Up Shipboard Activities for Kids

Cruise lines set up their programs by age, similar to a summer camp, so that children can get involved in age-appropriate activities with their peers. The programs start with children ages two or three (you yourself are the program for a child younger than two) and often require that toddlers are potty-trained. Ask your travel agent if specially trained youth counselors lead the programs and find out about the ratio of youth staff to kids, particularly if you have very young children.

Attractions vary with each cruise line; here are some ways kids can find entertainment:

- Participate in gooey science experiments
- Play with staffers dressed up as big-name cartoon favorites

✔ Learn to snorkel

✔ Pick up new computer skills and possibly access the Internet

✔ Try out a new language

✔ Take dance lessons

✔ Perform in a talent show

 Holland America (in Alaska) and Carnival (in the Caribbean) offer special shore excursions to introduce youngsters to the ports of call in an age-specific way. Some lines with private islands, including Disney and Royal Caribbean, offer kid-focused activities during stops (ask your travel agent about the extra cost of these activities). At night, ships offer pizza parties, movies, and other entertainment timed to give parents a chance to dine alone or take in a show.

Uncovering Kids' Cruise Criteria

You don't want to spend your precious vacation time and money on a disastrous cruise that resembles a Griswold family vacation from the movies. So don't be shy about grilling your travel agent for all the pertinent details. We fill you in on some of the areas to ask about in this section.

Program availability

Some ships offer children's programs only seasonally — during the summer and holiday periods when most families travel. Other programs run year round. Find out if the ship offers the advertised program during the time you plan to sail.

 Some ships operate programs for a specific age category only if 15 or more kids of that age are on board. Find out if your cruise has such restrictions, or you risk a frustrating time after you board.

Program hours

Some programs shut down during meal times, and they may not be offered during port calls. So if you want to take a shore excursion, you may have to bring the kids along, which can get expensive because most lines don't offer children's discounts on organized outings.

Teen-tivities

Even if your teen has stated plans to mope in the cabin, dressed in black, to protest the weeklong separation from the boyfriend/girlfriend back home, you should still make sure the ship offers a special program for his or her age group. A teen-friendly ship may offer dances, parties, and other opportunities for teens to stay up late with peers and get away from adult crowds — a bonus for all concerned. And your teen probably wants you to pick a ship with an Internet cafe, so he or she can keep up with what's going on at home. If nothing else, a teen program can act as an icebreaker for your teen to meet other kids his or her age, in turn improving everyone's mood.

Cost and comfort

Consider what kind of a deal you can get traveling as a family, figuring in airfare and cruise fare, as well as how much togetherness your family can survive. Ship cabins can get cramped very quickly (although with all the activities at your disposal, everyone may go back to the cabin only to sleep). If you think you run the risk of having to vote someone out of the cabin, see if your travel agent can swing you a deal on two cabins (interconnected or not). At the very least, consider a cabin with a terrace, which offers extra living space and helps counteract that claustrophobic feeling.

Program supervision

Most children's programs are designed so that kids — depending on their ages — can come and go. Planned activities are certainly less restrictive than day-care facilities at home. Counselors may assume that older kids have your permission to find other entertainment whenever they want. If you have concerns about your child spending time unsupervised, make your position clear to the program counselors and to your children. If you do grant your older kids wandering privileges, emphasize that the casino is off limits (officially, at least). Find out, too, if the ship requests that unsupervised children not visit the spa, gym, disco, or other adult-oriented areas. You may want to consider investing in hand-held walkie-talkies so that you and the kids can keep tabs on each other; cell phones don't normally work out at sea.

Even on ships with extensive children's programs, you're still responsible for your children's safety at the pool. For safety reasons, most programs don't take kids to the swimming pool, although younger kids may spend some time in a splash pool.

All cruise ships provide appropriate medical personnel and facilities, but be sure to bring any special medications or other items specific to your children's health needs. On any vacation, you should bring along a first-aid kit, complete with a thermometer, and you should check with your child's pediatrician about bringing along prescription medications. Think of the ship's medical facility as an infirmary rather than a hospital; check your insurance to see if it covers you in the unlikely event that someone needs to be transported ashore (as in the case of appendicitis). Also, take the time to instruct your children about proper hand washing, which experts say is still the best prevention against gastrointestinal problems and other diseases.

Baby-sitting on board

Want to get through your formal dinner without cutting up anyone's food? Most ships offer private baby-sitting in your cabin. Rates are generally about $10 an hour for two children, with a potential four-hour minimum. You may also be able to get group baby-sitting, which runs about $8 an hour for two kids. Check with your travel agent ahead of time — only some lines guarantee sitter availability. And group baby-sitting can fill up quickly, so ask if reservations are required.

Teaching Your Kids Important Rules

Safety is a big issue for the cruising parent. But a ship is a confined environment, so kids can get themselves into only so much trouble. Nevertheless, you still need to drill your kids on basic safety procedures before setting sail. The number one rule: Don't lean on the railings of open decks or verandas. Although most railings are high enough to not be of major concern for non-climbing little kids, make a strict rule about it to be on the safe side — particularly if you have active kids.

Another important rule is to make sure that your children don't go to the pool without telling you, because lifeguards aren't always present. Pools with waterslides often have staff members regulating the flow of traffic, but they don't get paid to watch for little ones swimming unsupervised.

 Make sure your children take the onboard safety drill seriously and that they understand the safety information you and the ship provide. (Check out Chapter 5 for more safety drill info.) Also, check that your cabin has appropriately sized life jackets.

As on any vacation, have your children memorize the home base information — the ship's name and their cabin and deck numbers — in case you get separated during the voyage.

Finding the Best Family Cruises

The top lines for family travelers offer not only great supervised programs for kids, but also special play areas and facilities. These sections run down the best fits for family cruisers. (Check out Part IV for more info on these lines.)

Carnival Cruise Lines

Carnival, home of the "Fun Ships," carries more families than any other cruise line and it shows. Carnival has the largest staff of trained counselors of any line, and its Camp Carnival program runs year-round. Recognizing the popularity of its kids' offerings, Carnival added other family-friendly extras, including a kids-only turn-down service with cookies at bedtime on the first and last night of the cruise, an updated children's menu, and a Fountain Fun Card, good for unlimited soft drinks for children under 21. All Carnival ships have 24-hour pizzerias. Kid-friendly amenities on some of the ships also include stroller rentals by the day.

A new children's dining program, available fleet-wide, includes supervised dining for kids so that parents can have a night off. Children's dinners are available nightly from 6 p.m. to 7 p.m., except for the first night
on 3- and 4-day cruises and the first and last night on longer sailings. In
addition to the usual burgers and hot dogs, the menu includes chicken
quesadillas, grilled salmon steak, and a 35-item salad bar.

To make kids feel warm and fuzzy, the line has a new mascot — "Fun
Ship" Freddy — who shows up to greet passengers and pose for photos.
To keep youngsters busy, science and geography programs feature hands-
on projects and experiments, as well as cake-decorating and pizza-making
sessions.

The Spirit-class ships, including the new *Carnival Miracle* (as well as the
Spirit, Legend, and *Pride*), feature a 2,400-square-foot play space divided
into three areas interconnected by tunnels. The ships have a computer
lab, an arts and crafts area — complete with spin art and candy-making
machines — and a playroom with toys for a range of age groups. High-
tech fun includes a video wall for movies and multi-lingual computer
games (also available on Destiny-class ships) and a separate, sizeable
video game room.

The outside deck section has a play area with mini-basketball hoops
and playground equipment, as well as four swimming pools (including
a wading pool) and a two-deck corkscrew waterslide.

The *Carnival Conquest,* the largest of the Fun Ships, boasts a whopping
4,200-square-foot indoor play space with four distinct areas. Features
include such arts-and-crafts offerings as spin art and candy making;
an all-ages playroom is equipped with toys, games, and puzzles; and
a video room with a computer/PlayStation 2 center. Also on board is
a teen recreation center with a DJ and a video wall that plays music
videos. The *Conquest's* sister ships *Carnival Glory* and the upcoming
Carnival Valor and *Carnival Liberty* feature a 3,300-square-foot play
area with a family recreation section, teen club, and video game room.

On all Fantasy-class vessels (*Ecstasy, Fantasy, Fascination, Imagination,
Inspiration,* and *Sensation*), kids get two playrooms. Even more elaborate
are the two-level, indoor/outdoor, 1,300-square-foot playrooms on the
Destiny-class vessels (*Destiny, Triumph,* and *Victory*). As if those options
aren't enough, these ships and the newest Fantasy-class ships (*Elation*
and *Paradise*) also feature high-tech video game centers. On all the ships,
families traveling during the school year can take advantage of homework
help sessions.

Camp Carnival divides kids into four groups, with appropriate activities
based on age: The toddlers group covers ages 2 to 5, juniors are ages 6
to 8, intermediates are ages 9 to 12, and the teens group includes ages
13 to 15. Group baby-sitting, available even for children under three,
takes place in the children's playrooms from 10 p.m. to 3 a.m. under the

supervision of the Carnival youth staff for $6 an hour; $4 for siblings. No private baby-sitting is available.

Rollaway beds and cribs are available. Carnival Conquest- and Destiny-class ships feature some specially designated family staterooms with picture windows. The *Spirit, Pride,* and *Legend* offer 52 connecting cabins.

Celebrity Cruises

Although Celebrity has welcomed children for years with a kids club and supervised activities, the line has put an emphasis on adult luxuries such as fine dining and upscale spa treatments. This year, however, the line is getting serious about the small fry. The new Celebrity Scientific Journeys programs, part of the Family Cruising Program, are available fleet-wide for children ages 3 to 12.

Hands-on activities include Buccaneer's Bounty, learning about pirates; Earthworks, discovering pollination, biomes, and the solar system; Environmentation Station, exploring natural phenomena and natural disasters; and Get Buggy, delving into the world of insects and spiders. A Sounds of the Sea program lets kids listen in to communications between dolphins, whales, and other creatures, and Wacky Weather explores everything from tsunamis to thunder.

Each program is a half-hour to an hour long and runs at 9 a.m. to Noon, 2 p.m. to 5 p.m., and 7:30 p.m. to 10:00 p.m. whether the ship is in port or at sea.

Celebrity's programs are available in summer and on major holidays or whenever 12 children who want to participate are on board. Children are divided into four age categories. Ship Mates, for kids ages 3 to 6, offers Legos, T-shirt painting, make-your-own sundaes, and computer games. This age group has its own Ship Mates Fun Factory on the *Century, Constellation, Galaxy, Mercury, Millennium, Infinity,* and *Summit.* Celebrity Cadets, for children 7 to 9, features pool Olympics, fitness programs, and team trivia contests. Ensigns, for children 10 to 12, and Admiral Ts, for those 13 to 15 and 16 to 17, have activities such as karaoke, movies, scavenger hunts, and pool parties.

The Ship Mates Fun Factory playroom features giant animal sculptures for the younger set to climb on. The *Mercury, Millennium, Infinity,* and *Summit* also have ball pits for kids to jump around in, and the *Millennium, Infinity, Summit,* and *Constellation* have a fenced-in outside deck area with a wading pool.

Group baby-sitting for kids ages 3 to 12 is available on Celebrity ships from noon to 2 p.m. on port days and 10 p.m. to 1 a.m. every night; private baby-sitting is available on a limited basis for up to two children per family, but you should book ahead — the service isn't guaranteed.

In summer, the youth program offers early shore excursion hours, opening 30 minutes before departure of the first shore excursion (and no later than 9 a.m.), so parents can get off on time.

The drinking age on Celebrity sailings is 18 for beer and wine whenever a ship is in international waters, but parents have to sign a waiver stating their awareness of this rule. If parents don't sign, the age is 21.

Many cabins on Celebrity ships can accommodate three or four passengers, and cribs are available. Kids' menus also are available at dinner.

Costa Cruises

The Italian Costa Cruises offers the Costa Kids Club, which breaks up kids into four groups on its Caribbean sailings: ages 3 to 5, 6 to 8, 9 to 12, and teens. The ship provides at least four counselors on board; and a greater number when more than 12 kids sail or during Christmas and Easter vacations. On European sailings, you find three groups: the Baby Club, ages 3 to 6; the Junior Club, ages 7 to 12; and the Teen Club, ages 13 to 17. (Teen Club's operation is dependent on the number of teens on board.)

Video game tournaments, galley tours, karaoke, face painting, and ice-cream sundae socials are featured for the younger set, and teens can take advantage of sports and fitness offerings, guitar lessons, and dance parties.

The new *CostaFortuna* and *CostaMagica* have a designated children's area called the Squok Club with its own enclosed swimming pool. Designed to accommodate Costa Activity Clubs, the onboard youth center also features a video arcade.

The *CostaVictoria* has a teen center that includes a disco and a video arcade. The *CostaAtlantica* has a video arcade and teen hours in the adult disco, along with a kiddie pool and waterslide. Teen activities are also offered in the basketball/tennis/volleyball courts of the *CostaAtlantica, CostaEuropa,* and *CostaVictoria.* The new *CostaMediterranea,* sister ship to the *CostaAtlantica,* and the *CostaFortuna*, which entered service at the end of 2003, are both outfitted with basketball courts.

European ships don't come equipped with the same extensive facilities the American lines offer, but how many ships offer Italian language lessons? European Costa Cruises do.

Group baby-sitting is available for children ages 3 (out of diapers) and older, at no charge, from 6:30 p.m. until 11:00 p.m. on most cruises. You can stay out until 1 a.m. by advance arrangement with the Information Desk.

Some cabins on the ships can accommodate four people, and some suites can accommodate six (including six suites on the *CostaRomantica* that have Murphy beds). The ships have a special children's menu, and pizza and Italian ice cream are also available. Keep in mind that the kids' club is closed at lunch and dinner, but the ships offer two Parents' Night Out dinners when kids attend their own buffet or pizza party. For Caribbean sailings, children ages 3 and under cruise free; kids 4 to 14 sail for a 10 percent discount off adult prices.

Disney Cruise Line

You expect great kids' programs on a Disney cruise. In fact, both the *Disney Magic* and *Disney Wonder* not only offer extensive programs designed to appeal to specific ages and interests, but they also dedicate an incredible 15,000 square feet (nearly an entire deck) to children's facilities, with a full-service nursery, playrooms, various high-tech offerings, a designated teen club, a children's pool area, and a special family lounge. Disney films often premiere on the ships the same day they debut in theaters, and the ships also show the company's animated classics.

This year, the line wants to focus on extended families and groups of friends traveling together and has tweaked some of its public space accordingly. The former **Common Grounds** teen club, for example, is now the **Cove Café** lounge for adults. Teens now have their own dedicated space called **The Stack,** formerly the **ESPN Skybox,** where they can dance, watch multiple televisions, snack, and access the Internet.

Also new is *The Golden Mickeys*, a Disney musical with a mix of animation, special effects, and live theatrical performances.

Just like at Disney World, costumed Disney characters appear at scheduled times during the voyage so that passengers can line up for hugs and photos or avoid them altogether, depending on their inclination.

The Disney line employs more children's counselors — 50 in all — than any other company (presumably because the line expects to host more kids than other ships). The children's program offers 20 new age-appropriate activities for kids ages 3 to 4, 5 to 7, 8 and 9, 10 to 12, and 13 to 17.

Activities include Mouseketeer Training for children 3 and 4 on the *Magic*; Escape from Hook for ages 5 to 7 on the *Wonder;* and Gases in Action for ages 5 to 7 on both ships. Aladdin programs, including treasure hunts for "jewels" in the Cave of Wonders, and magic carpet "rides" also are available on both ships. Kids 10 to 12 get a Splish and Splash pool party.

Disney's **Flounder's Reef Nursery** on both ships holds as many as 30 children with a child/counselor ratio of four to one. The cruise line recently updated the nursery with a new reception area, new toys, a toddler area twice the size of the old one, and a one-way porthole for mom and dad to peek in on the kids. 7-night cruises offer extended hours so parents can dine alone, try a spa treatment, or sneak off for a shore excursion. Best of all, unlike on other cruise lines, Disney's nurseries welcomes infants as young as 12 weeks old to 3-year-old toddlers. The center is open from early morning through late evening, but be sure to book at the time of embarkation because space fills up fast. One particularly neat feature is that Disney ships give parents beepers, so the ship can alert them if their kids have any problems in the children's center.

Castaway Cay, Disney's private island, offers kids' activities such as a trip to **Scuttles Cove,** an oversized sandbox with a whale dig site, archaeology tools, and beach toys; Disney character visits; and private beaches for teens and adults. Naturally, you can book your cruise in combination with a visit to **Disney World.**

Kids can have dinner with the counselors on some nights; private babysitting isn't available.

The line's cabins all sleep at least three (many can sleep four or five), and most spaces come with separate shower/bath and toilet compartments.

Holland America Line

Holland America is gearing up for a huge expansion of its children's offerings, including a Kids Center and Youth Program scheduled for completion by the end of 2005.

In the meantime, the line offers Club HAL, a year-round kid's program that provides supervised activities on board plus special kids' shore excursions at some ports. The program is available on all ships and all sailings, but activities are based on the number of children sailing and their ages. All the ships have some sort of kids' space. On the older ships, these places are pretty drab because they double as meeting facilities when no kids are on board, but the newer ships have special facilities such as playrooms, video-game areas, and wading pools.

Every ship has at least one full-time Club HAL youth director on board, and the ratio of counselors to children is 1 to 30. Teen staff members may also be on board on larger youth sailings.

Activities for kids ages 5 through 8 can include story telling, fabric painting, indoor games, ice-cream sundaes, or pizza parties. Children 9 through 12 can learn to putt golf balls, participate in sports tournaments, or watch movies and videos. Youth Olympics are held for all ages.

The *Maasdam,* a year-round ship in the Caribbean, features an expanded Club HAL kids area called the KidZone and a teen center called the Waverunner. The line plans for 150 to 200 children on each sailing during the summer and on short jaunts. The new big-for-HAL (at 85,000 tons), Vista-class ships *Zuiderdam, Oosterdam,* and *Westerdam* feature a KidZone, complete with inside and outside play areas, a computer and video game area, and the Waverunner teen area with its own video game center, large-screen movie corner, and dance floor.

When enough kids are on board, Club HAL divides them into 3 age groups: kids 5 to 8, tweens 9 to 12, and teens 13 to 17. The kids enjoy pastimes such as Ping-Pong, disco parties, face painting, casino night, karaoke, and pool parties. Youth activities begin at 3 p.m. when the ship is in port.

Kids are encouraged to eat with their parents; kids' menus are available. The ships offer private baby-sitting on a first-come, first-serve basis.

Cabins can hold up to four passengers if you use upper berths or fold-away sofa beds. If you want to bring an infant, reserve a crib ahead of time with Ship Services — cribs are in limited supply.

 Just-for-kids shore excursions are available on all Alaskan sailings, escorted by a Holland America youth coordinator or naturalist. Groups are divided into tweens ages 9 to 12 and teens ages 13 to 18. If you sail in the Caribbean, the line has its own private island, called **Half Moon Cay**, which offers age-appropriate kid activities that give parents time to snorkel, sail, or have a massage.

Norwegian Cruise Line

Norwegian unveiled a Junior Star Seeker passenger talent competition in 2004 as part of its Kids Crew program. Contestants are given three minutes to perform before a panel of judges, and the ship awards the winners a free NCL cruise.

Other Kids Crew activities include the innovative Circus at Sea, a program that turns kids into circus performers. Norwegian has also expanded its year-round Kids Crew children's program to accommodate children as young as 2, supervised by trained youth counselors. Kids are now divided into four age groups: The Junior Sailors program (ages 2 to 5) offers storytelling, face painting, and magic shows; the First Mates program (ages 6 to 8) includes wacky cooking classes and sandcastle building; the Navigators program (ages 9 to 12) features video games, camp outs, and scavenger hunts; and the Teens program (ages 13 to 17) has disco, basketball, and pool parties.

Because of delays in the completion of the *Pride of America*, the *Pride of Aloha* was poised to take over the 7-day, inter-island Hawaiian cruises at press time. The Kids Korner, located on the International Deck, offers a dedicated playroom, and Splashes, the children's pool, offers a waterfall and hot tub. Teens can hang out at The Club, which is a teen center by day and a teen-only disco at night.

The *Norwegian Dawn* has nearly 5,550 square feet of space for its children's facilities. The T-Rex Childcare Center for little children boasts a jungle gym and playroom, a Flicks movie theater, a Clicks computer center, a Doodles art-and-crafts area, and a Snoozes cozy nook for naps. The T-Rex pool features water slides, a kids-only hot tub, and a wading pool for toddlers. Older kids can enjoy the Teen Club on the *Norwegian Dawn*, with its teen-only disco, video wall, cinema, and Video Zone.

The *Norwegian Star*, a sister ship to the *Norwegian Dawn*, offers nearly identical children's facilities, but the facility itself is called Planet Kids. The *Norwegian Wind, Norwegian Dream, Norwegian Majesty, Norwegian Sky*, and the new *Norwegian Sun* each have a Kids Korner playroom, and the *Sky* and *Sun* also have kiddie pools and teen activity centers.

Norwegian also caters to kids by offering eight separate kids menus, as well as a special children's area in the **Garden Café** with a shorter serving counter and kiddy-sized tables and chairs. Norwegian caters to kids and teens by publishing separate daily *Cruise News* bulletins just for them so they can keep track of all the activities. A Kid's Crew backpack contains a baseball cap, souvenir T-shirt, and other goodies.

Group baby-sitting, which takes place in designated public rooms, is available on port days from 9 a.m. to 5 p.m. (The ships give pagers to the parents of children who aren't potty trained, and then calls them if their child needs a diaper change.)

On all ships, you can now book cabins that can accommodate up to four passengers. The *Norwegian Dream, Norwegian Sky, Norwegian Sun*, and *Norwegian Star* offer connecting cabins. The *Norwegian Sun, Norwegian Star*, and *Norwegian Dawn* also offer mini-suites suitable for families.

Princess Cruises

The three Princess Kids programs are the Princess Pelicans, for ages 3 to 7; the Princess Pirateers, for ages 8 to 12; and Off Limits, for kids 13 to 17. A Teen Spa program offers kid-friendly spa packages such as henna tattoos, body and hair glitter, face painting, and body art.

An "edu-tainment" program designed in conjunction with the Los Angeles–based California Science Center provides kids with hands-on activities on Mexican Riviera sailings. Activities include stargazing, studying ocean and coral reef habitat, building and racing sailboats, launching rockets, and dissecting gooey squid.

Budding naturalists can take advantage of activity books and other learning materials provided by the National Wildlife Federation. The new programs were designed to complement the line's Junior Ranger program in Alaska and the Save our Seas environmental program, which operates fleet-wide. Children who participate in Princess Kids events receive a Pete's Pal plush animal souvenir.

The Princess Teen Club, for ages 13 to 17, offers a teen-only disco on the newer ships, karaoke and lip-sync shows, pizza parties, computers, video games, shipboard Olympics, and a murder-mystery game. Young cruisers aboard all Caribbean sailings can participate in the Miami Seaquarium program, which offers fun activities about sea life.

Princess includes a full schedule of activities for kids on port days, including lunch.

The new *Caribbean Princess*, *Diamond Princess*, and *Sapphire Princess*, as well as the *Coral Princess* and *Island Princess*, offer three separate play areas for kids along with the full Princess Kids program. The Pelican's Pool is a dedicated children's pool; Off Limits, a Teen Center for young adults ages 13 to 17, offers activities such as video games and teen disco; The Fun Zone is a center for Princess Pirateers (ages 8 to 12); and the Pelican's Playhouse is a children's center for ages 2 to 7. Youth Center staff host a daily schedule of age-appropriate activities.

All Princess ships built since 1994 (*Sun Princess* and those thereafter) offer fully equipped Youth and Teen Centers, featuring a toddler's play area and theater, a doll's house, a splash pool, a castle, and computers. The *Grand Princess*, *Golden Princess*, and *Star Princess* also have sizable fenced-in outside decks dedicated for kids only, with a whale's tail slide splash pool and even a fleet of Big Wheels; both the *Grand Princess* and *Golden Princess* offer a separate Jacuzzi and deck area for teens. The big ships also feature huge virtual-reality centers. The children's centers on the *Diamond* and *Sapphire Princesses* (scheduled to join the fleet before the end of 2004) will be slightly expanded versions of those available on the Grand-class ships (*Star*, *Grand*, and *Golden*).

The line's older ships don't have such extensive facilities. And the children's program is available on the *Royal* and *Pacific* only when 15 or more children ages 2 to 17 are on board.

A new program allows junior cruisers to dine with friends and counselors twice on each cruise. On other evenings, kids are encouraged to dine with their parents and get priority seating, if desired, in the 24-hour alternative restaurants available on most ships.

Group baby-sitting is available in port between 9 a.m. and 5 p.m. and at night between 10 p.m. and 1 a.m. in the children's centers, and kids receive cookies in their stateroom every day.

 Caribbean sailings visit the line's private Bahamas beach, **Princess Cays,** where kids can participate in activities under the supervision of youth staff. Shore excursions at other ports feature children's rates, and a new rating system that helps parents pick out excursions best suited for kids.

Many cabins can accommodate three or four passengers, and on the larger ships (*Grand Princess*, *Golden Princess*, and *Star Princess*) the Grand Suites can sleep eight. The *Coral Princess* and the *Island Princess* have 90 percent of their staterooms outside, most with private balconies. Children's programming from the television network *Nickelodeon* is shown on the in-cabin television. Princess has lowered the age limits aboard its ships to six months on all itineraries except for select exotic destinations (such as South America, Africa, Asia, Australia, and the South Pacific), where the age limit is 12 months.

Royal Caribbean International

Royal Caribbean's Adventure Ocean program, already considered one of the best programs in the business, introduced the Sail Into Story Time program this year for kids ages 3 through 8. Stories such as *Where the Wild Things Are* and *The Stinky Cheese Man* are followed by activities built around the themes of the books.

The free Adventure Family program offers planned activities that parents and kids ages 3 to 11 can participate in together, such as talent shows, shipbuilding regattas, and scavenger hunts.

The line also has a partnership with Crayola Crayons to create art projects that tie in with the culture of the destinations that kids visit. Children traveling to the Caribbean, for example, can make Mexican Huichol masks, and kids on their way to Europe make Greek Theater masks. Other creations include an Eskimo oil lamp for Alaska and Great Barrier Reef aquatic dioramas for the South Pacific.

A strong component of the Adventure Ocean program's success continues to be the quality of the youth staff. All staffers are college graduates with four-year degrees in education, recreation, and/or preschool or a related field, and most staffers are certified in CPR and first aid.

The program offers five age groups and drop-off times 30 minutes before departure on all morning shore excursions. The five age groups are Aquanauts, 3 to 5 years (must be potty-trained); Explorers, 6 to 8 years; Voyagers, 9 to 11 years; Navigators, 12 to 14 years; and Guests, 15 to 17 years.

Supervised daily activities, available fleetwide and year-round on all the line's ships, run 9 a.m. to noon, 2 to 5 p.m., and 7 to 10 p.m. while the ship is at sea; drop off until 5 p.m. and 7 p.m. to 10 p.m. while in port. Teen hours and activities vary.

One highlight of the Adventure Ocean program is Adventure Science, which offers such hands-on science experiments as Staggering Through the Stars, Alien Encounter Laboratory, Forensic Fun Laboratory, Wacky Water Workshop, and Mystery of the Motion of the Ocean.

Combined activities for all kids include the Adventure Science, Adventure Art, Movie Madness, and Late Night Party Zone, and Island Activities feature hermit crab hunts, beach volleyball, and Waterball. Youth facilities include the Club Ocean (a playroom and meeting room for kids) and colorful ball pits for kids to jump in.

 For participating in events, kids earn Adventure Ocean Coupons, which they can trade in for gifts.

The *Navigator of the Seas* and *Mariner of the Seas* offer 22,000 square feet of children's space — some 6,000 square feet more than the other ships in the Voyager-class. Facilities include computer stations, a video arcade, nightclubs, and a teen-only sun deck. In addition, at least 13 full-time Adventure Ocean youth staffers stay on board. All Voyager-class ships have an ice-skating rink, rock-climbing wall (now on all Royal Caribbean ships), in-line skating track, and a **Johnny Rockets** restaurant.

The new *Serenade of the Seas* and *Jewel of the Seas* both feature a Fuel nightclub as well as a dedicated space for each of the younger age groups. Both also feature a video arcade and a kids' pool with a waterslide.

In a unique arrangement, the *Explorer of the Seas* hosts a few small labs staffed by scientists from the National Oceanographic and Atmospheric Administration, the University of Miami, and elsewhere, which kids can visit. It also has a display area (like a mini-science museum) that explains facts about the sea. The *Radiance, Brilliance*, and *Serenade* boast a big pool area for little kids and teens (with a big water slide).

Group baby-sitting for potty-trained children ages 3 and up is available nightly from 10 p.m. to 1 a.m. (When in port, hours are noon until the ship sails.) Private baby-sitting by a crewmember for infants ages six months and up is available, but you must book 24 hours in advance.

The ship is continuing its Youth Evacuation Plan, designed to help children and parents find each other at their muster stations during emergencies if they separate.

Royal Caribbean's newest ships — *Brilliance, Voyager, Explorer, Adventure, Serenade, Jewel, Mariner, Navigator,* and *Radiance* — have special family cabins that can accommodate six. Cabins on the older vessels tend to be pretty small, although some can hold a third or fourth passenger in upper berths. Kids' menus are available, and children can eat either with their families or at special group meals just for kids on designated evenings. An Adventure Ocean Potion Card entitles children to 12 non-alcoholic drinks per sailing. The *Navigator* also offers a **Ben & Jerry's** ice cream parlor.

 Royal Caribbean has lowered the drinking age fleetwide to 18 years old for wine and beer when the ship sails in international waters, but parents have to sign a waiver stating their awareness of this rule. If parents don't sign, the age is 21.

Chapter 11

Taking Care of Those Final Details

* *

In This Chapter

▶ Tipping made easy

▶ Settling your shipboard account

▶ Packing up and getting off the ship

* *

*Y*ou knew it had to happen: It's almost time to leave the ship. You can always stay aboard, of course (if you're rich or are willing to mortgage your grandmother), but you have an everyday life to return to. Cheer up and think about it this way: After you disembark, you walk off a veteran cruiser. You know your stuff. Now you can start planning for your *next* cruise.

In this chapter, we take you through the nuts and bolts of actually getting off the boat.

 On your final day at sea (the day before you actually get off the ship), the cruise director holds a briefing to talk about everything you need to take care of before you disembark. During this meeting, you find out about exciting things such as settling your onboard account, tipping, packing your bags, dealing with Customs and Immigration, and following the ship's precise disembarkation plan. Although spending your last day in the sun may sound infinitely better than this, you or someone you're traveling with should turn up for the talk. Even though the directions for coming ashore are printed in your daily bulletin and you may catch the talk on ship television, the session is your only real shot to ask questions. Attending the session saves you hassles later, and if you're lucky, you may even get a prize for showing up!

Taking Care of Tips

Tipping is an area that some people find confusing. First, recognize that most lines expect you to tip the crew — in particular, your cabin steward, waiter, and busboy. With few exceptions, cruise lines pay these people the way most American restaurants pay their waitstaffs: badly, with the expectation that the crewmembers can earn most of their salary through gratuities. Keep in mind that many of these crewmembers support families back home on their earnings.

To eliminate some of the confusion, several lines now automatically add tips to your shipboard account. Carnival, for instance, has a standard tip of $9.75 per passenger per day. Norwegian Cruise Line and Princess Cruises automatically add tips of $10 per passenger per day. In these cases you can adjust the amount up or down as you see fit based on the service you receive. You can decide to remove the tip from your account and give out cash if you prefer.

Your line doesn't shy away from encouraging you to tip, and it may even give you envelopes printed with the titles of crewmembers so that you know whom to tip. Some ships (many small ships, in particular) ask passengers simply to put their tips into one envelope in a lump sum, which is split up among the crew after you depart. Generally, however, you reward people individually.

If you have spa or beauty treatments, you can tip the workers at the time of the service (sometimes the ship automatically adds it to your shipboard charge account). You may also want to give cash to room service waiters (especially if you have a teenage son who calls them often). But otherwise you normally give tips on the last night of your cruise.

Most lines suggest that you tip in cash, but some also have the means to allow you to tip via your shipboard account (if the ship has an automatic tipping policy, tips are on your shipboard account). Bar bills throughout your cruise automatically include a 15 percent tip, but if you're fond of a particular bartender or if the dining room wine steward serves you particularly well, you can slip him or her a few bucks, too.

If a staff member gives you particularly great service, send a letter to that person's superior when you get a chance. It may very well earn him or her an "employee of the month" honor and maybe even a bonus.

Most of the luxury lines either include tips in the cruise fare or have a no-tipping-required policy, meaning that you have no tip obligation, although the staff members on these ships gratefully accept any tips proffered.

Alternative and sailing ships have varying policies, so we offer a list in Chapter 16 with tipping suggestions specific to these vessels.

Paying the Purser

Your onboard account actually stays open until a few hours before disembarkation. However, before your account officially closes, you receive a preliminary bill in your cabin. If you want to pay with a credit card, just make sure that all the charges on the bill are correct. If you spot a mistake, go to the purser's office to report it and prepare to deal with a long line. If you decide to settle up with cash or traveler's checks, the ship usually asks you to settle your account at the purser's office the day or night before you disembark the ship. A crewmember delivers the final invoice to your cabin before you depart.

We suggest that you hold onto the many receipts that you accumulate throughout the cruise. Not only do you avoid going into shock when the bill arrives, but this system also makes the chore of checking to make sure the bill is correct much easier.

Checking Out

On the final full day of your cruise, don't forget to

- ✔ Place any last-minute liquor and/or cigarette orders at the duty-free shop. A crewmember delivers the items to your cabin later in the evening.

- ✔ Make arrangements with the purser's office for an early disembarkation if you have to catch an early flight the next morning. You normally receive a priority time for getting off the ship.

- ✔ Shop the last-minute sales at the ship's stores. Shops close the night before the ship lands and don't open on disembarkation day (rules prohibit their opening in port).

- ✔ Pick up any pictures you ordered from the ship's photographer.

- ✔ Claim any prizes you earned if you participated in a fitness rewards program.

- ✔ Check out the repeat-passenger offerings. Cruise lines know that one of the best times to get you to book another cruise is while you're aboard ship and having a good time. Many times you can receive a generous discount for your next cruise.

- ✔ Return any games, videos, or books you borrowed from the ship's library.

- ✔ Fill out the passenger questionnaire/comment card, if your ship hands one out. The ship may even have a prize drawing for the respondents.

Packing Procedures

Because the crew handles a large amount of luggage, big ships normally require you to have your bags packed and available for pickup the night before you disembark. Generally, you leave your luggage outside your cabin for crewmembers to pick it up sometime after midnight, and you claim it in the cruise terminal after you walk off the ship.

The packing process is kind of a pain because you have to figure out everything you need on disembarkation day (don't forget clean underwear!) and pack the rest. You need to leave room in your carry-on (or in this case, carry-off) for your nightclothes, toiletries, and so on.

For bags you want to send off the ship in advance, attach one of the luggage tags a crewmember gives you on the final night to each bag. Note how these tags differ from the tags you affixed to your bags before you boarded the ship: The tags are color-coded, indicating your deck number and disembarkation order, and the crewmembers group the bags together on the pier based on this info. If you need more tags, ask your cabin steward.

 Don't pack medications, expensive possessions, breakable items (including alcohol or perfume), travel information and papers, or any items that you may need the next day. Instead, carry these items off the ship yourself, just to be on the safe side.

You should put any items you purchased during your trip into one suitcase so that you can have them handy in the unlikely event that Customs stops you (see Chapter 12).

If you happen to stay up late partying your last night on board and find that the crew collected all the luggage before you put yours out, contact the purser's office so that someone can retrieve your bags for you. If you don't want to leave any of your luggage for pick-up, you have to carry it all yourself the next morning.

Getting off the Ship

Public address systems start bellowing early in the morning to let you know that your cruise has come to an end. But don't expect a stampede. In fact, you have to wait (usually about 90 minutes) until Customs and the port authorities clear the ship before you can get off. Ships rarely unload passengers before 9 a.m., and even then the process doesn't go frantically fast: Disembarkation is generally done by number order — the ship allows passengers with earlier flights and people booked in suites to leave first.

Plan for roughly two hours of unloading and get comfortable. Grab your book and head out on deck, watch a movie, or have a relaxing breakfast — anything is better than standing around with your bags and feeling your blood pressure rise.

Most times, the ship requires you to leave your cabin by 8 a.m. to give the ship crew enough time to prepare everything for the next set of passengers arriving just a few short hours after you leave. You can usually get away with leaving your overnight bag in one of the cabin's corners so you don't have to carry it around all morning.

 You aren't allowed to get off earlier than the time designated by your tag, but you can get off later. So if you don't have a flight to catch, feel free to take your time.

If the process of disembarkation becomes too long for you and you start worrying about missing your flight, don't hesitate to contact a crewmember.

Mostly, you need patience. The disembarkation process takes longer than anyone would like it to, so please be tolerant.

 Don't be concerned if you feel a little woozy for the first day or so after you get off the ship — it can take some time to get used to the world *not* rocking under your feet.

Chapter 12

Coming Home: Customs, Regulations, and Taxes

· ·

In This Chapter

▶ Going through Immigration

▶ Clearing Customs (or, Why You Can't Bring Home a Goat)

▶ Getting refunds on VAT and GST

▶ Handling departure taxes

· ·

*W*ant to bring back a salami? Think again. Tempted by those Cuban cigars? Don't try it. Why? Because the law says you can't — and you may just get caught.

This chapter explains some of the customs of Customs and provides an initiation to Immigration in a more digestible form compared to that salami — and it doesn't stink up your suitcase nearly as much.

Understanding Immigration

Immigration authorities used to do a blanket clearance of a whole ship when the time came to disembark at a U.S. port. That way, only non-U.S. citizens or green card holders needed to meet with authorities. But in recent times, with security concerns over terrorists entering the United States, every passenger may be required to appear before authorities at some point during the cruise. If so, the public address announcements give you details about the clearance meeting. You usually meet in some sort of lounge, all family members must attend, and you need to bring the necessary papers (the ship's crew can give you details).

In any case, when you leave the ship, even if you don't expect to go through the entire Immigration process, have your passport or identification handy just in case.

Getting through Customs

When you leave the ship after visiting a foreign country, you must fill out a Customs Declaration form (one per family). Rules for what you can and can't bring back are enforced in the United States by the U.S. Customs Service, and although inspectors don't actually check each and every bag that comes back into the United States, you don't want to get caught breaking the rules — say, for trying to sneak in Cuban cigars or more alcohol and cigarettes than law allows. Customs applies stiff fines for doing so.

If you sail on an Alaskan cruise that plans to disembark in the United States, you receive your Customs form the last night of your sailing and clear Customs at the pier when you arrive. (Going through Customs is necessary, because most Alaskan cruises either start in or call at Canadian ports such as Victoria and Vancouver.) If you get off the ship in Canada, you clear Customs at the airport when you get back to the United States (or at a border point if you drive).

On Caribbean cruises that disembark in the United States (including the U.S. Virgin Islands and Puerto Rico), you clear Customs at the pier when you arrive. On cruises that end in other Caribbean islands, you go through Customs at the airport when you arrive back on U.S. soil (either one of the 50 states or Puerto Rico, if your flight connects there). On European sailings, you clear Customs at the airport when you get back home.

Comprehending duty free

When you see the term *duty free* at all those shops in the Caribbean or in Europe, it doesn't mean that the items are duty-free when you get back to the United States; it just means that your current destination sells them free of taxes. The items still count in your standard exemption when you get back to the United States (see the next section for exemption information). So, if you buy a $2,000 ring, you have to pay tax on it.

Also, everything you buy on the ship counts toward your tax-free total. Duty-free booze and cartons of cigarettes are sold in the shops on board, but you use them when you get home (not on the ship). To assure this, the cruise lines don't let you pick up your items until the end of the cruise — they tell you when.

Filling out forms

Read and review your Customs form thoroughly. Make sure that you fill in the spaces correctly (if you mess up, ask for another form). You need to fill out only one form per family.

The standard allowance for a U.S. citizen was recently raised to $800 in duty-free goods if you return from anywhere other than a Caribbean

Basin country or a U.S. possession (such as the U.S. Virgin Islands). That can include 1 carton of cigarettes or 100 cigars and 1 liter of alcohol if you're over 21. Green-card holders and non-U.S. residents who plan to stay no more than 72 hours in the United States have the same standard allowance.

Everybody counts! A couple gets $1,600 in duty-free allowances. Kids get the $800 allowance, too, so a family of four can bring back $3,200 worth of goods. But kids can't bring in booze.

 You need to list individual purchases on the form only if you exceed the limits.

If you travel to certain countries, allowances for what you can bring back are different. For example, when you sail to specific Caribbean islands (including Antigua, Aruba, the Bahamas, Barbados, the British Virgin Islands, Grenada, Guadeloupe, Jamaica, St. Lucia, and St. Kitts), the duty-free limit is $600 and two liters of alcohol. You can bring back $1,200 worth of goods duty-free from the U.S. Virgin Islands, and because Puerto Rico is part of the United States, goods you purchase there are entirely duty-free. Likewise, any goods produced (and purchased) in Mexico and Canada are also duty-free when you bring them back to the United States.

The situation is fairly complicated for cruise passengers who visit multiple countries, however. If you go to an island with a $600 exemption and then to the U.S. Virgin Islands, you're taxed on anything over $600 from the first island, but you can spend another $600 in the U.S.V.I.

Works of fine art and some other luxury items are tax-free! (Check with the U.S. Customs Service to see if it counts that recycled plastic hula skirt as art; don't even try calling it a luxury item.)

 The **U.S. Customs Service** provides all kinds of help sorting out the complexities of bringing stuff back. It has computer kiosks in the departure lounges at major airports (including Atlanta, Dallas, Los Angeles, Miami, and New York) to answer your questions via a touch screen. You can also visit the Customs Service Web site at www.customs.gov. Or pick up the very informative booklet *Know Your Customs Before You Go, Customs Hints for Returning U.S. Residents* from your local Customs Service office. If you prefer, you can order it through the Web site or write for the booklet and further information: U.S. Customs Service, P.O. Box 7407, Washington, D.C. 20044.

Getting busted

Oops. Lost track of how much all your souvenirs cost? If you go over the legal limit, you must report your purchases on the Customs form. After filling out the form, you usually see a Customs official (sometimes on board or sometimes at the port); any amount over the limit may be subject to a 10 percent tax. You can pay this in cash (U.S. dollars only), by personal check, or, at most airports, by MasterCard or Visa. If you want to play it safe and you don't know if you've exceeded your limit, ask a Customs official to help you fill out the form.

Failing to declare your purchases when you exceed the limit is a serious offense and you face fines and penalties if Customs catches you. And just because you bought an item as a gift doesn't mean that it doesn't count in your exemption — it does. "But I bought it for my mother . . ." gets you nowhere.

Customs inspectors have some pretty sophisticated ways of checking for limit violations. Their computer tracking systems can coordinate information from law enforcement databases to target suspect passengers. In addition, the ship's staff must report passengers who make a bundle at the casino or cruisers who spend a bundle at the onboard shops. And, of course, Customs officers have the right to do random (and not-so-random) baggage inspections.

Suppose an inspector picks little old innocent you for a spot-check of your luggage. Don't be surprised if he wants to see everything you bought; therefore, we recommend that you pack all your purchases in one suitcase and keep the receipts within easy access to prove what you paid for each item. Without receipts, the Customs officials base the value of your purchases on what you would pay in the United States. On board is not the time to haggle over their calculations: If you want to contest the determination, write to the Customs Service later.

Mailing stuff home

You're allowed to mail home items valued at less than $200 duty-free, and they don't count in your standard exemption (either the $600, $800, or $1,200 duty-free allowance, depending on where you travel). If you choose to go this route, you have to mark on the outside of the package that the items inside are for personal use, what the items are, and their approximate value. You can also send your friends and relatives gifts, marked as gifts, as long as the value totals less than $100.

Following rules for regulated items

Some items are specifically forbidden from a Customs perspective, and we're not talking just plutonium. In addition, watch out for some items typically sold as souvenirs that may pose safety risks. This section covers some key no-nos.

Antiques

Some countries, including Greece, consider antiques (items more than 100 years old) national treasures and don't want you to take them out of the country. If you try, Customs can seize the items and you can be fined. Americans have even been arrested and prosecuted for buying antiques without a permit from street vendors. If you buy something that looks like an antique but is really a reproduction, have the vendor document it as such. If you want a real antiquity, you may have to apply for a permit in advance, sometimes to the country's national museum, although a reputable vendor may be able to obtain a permit for you. Watch out for disreputable vendors and their fake permits, however (do research before your trip or ask a reputable dealer in the states for advice).

Ceramics

If you buy ceramics abroad, be aware that they may contain lead, which makes them unsuitable for use with food or beverages. You can avoid this problem by buying from a firm with an international reputation (like all those fancy European china and crystal shops whose goods are sold at discounted prices in the Caribbean). The U.S. Food and Drug Administration (FDA) recommends that you have any non-name-brand ceramic tableware tested or that you use it for decorative purposes only.

Cuban cigars

Got a hankering for a Cuban cigar? Sure, you see them for sale in Canada, Mexico, and countries in Europe. But if the government can make a case that you bought, sold, traded, or otherwise engaged in transactions involving illegally imported Cuban cigars, you may face civil penalties of up to $55,000 and criminal charges. So, buy a few and smoke them at the port or enjoy them on the ship. Just don't try to bring them home.

Fresh produce and meat

You can't bring back fresh fruit, vegetables, meat products, plants in soil, and many other agricultural products from abroad because they may have insects or diseases that can damage U.S. crops and livestock. You can bring back bakery items and certain hard cheeses, however. If you try to bring in a prohibited item, Customs confiscates and destroys it. Customs has dogs that can sniff out these items at airports.

And yes, that apple from the fruit basket on the ship counts.

Live animals and endangered species

Some items are flat-out not allowed into the United States. These include live animals (messy and difficult to pack into your suitcase anyway) and items made of endangered species, such as anything made of elephant ivory (unless you have documentation showing it to be more than 100 years old), sea turtles, coral reefs, crocodile leather, or fur from certain kinds of wild cats. If you try to sneak in any of these souvenirs, Customs inspectors can confiscate them at the airport and you may face penalties.

Other random prohibitions

The list of things you can't bring back into the United States gets into pretty crazy territory when you read all the rules. For instance, you're not allowed to bring back the following:

- ✔ Byzantine-period ritual or ecclesiastic objects from Cyprus

- ✔ Absinthe or liquors that contain an excess of *Artemisia absinthium*

- ✔ Pre-Columbian monumental and architectural sculpture and murals from countries in Central or South America

- ✔ More than one copy of any particular CD, video, book, cartoon-character toy or T-shirt, or other copyrighted item (because of distribution restrictions)

- ✔ More than $10,000 in currency (you can't bring this out of the United States either)

- ✔ Anything from embargoed countries such as Cuba (see the preceding section "Cuban cigars"), Serbia, and the Sudan

- ✔ Any narcotics, including drugs you can buy in America with a prescription (you incur severe penalties for buying drugs abroad, and dogs at the airport have been trained to sniff them out)

- ✔ More than one of each type of $12 "Rolex" watch, $18 "Armani" jeans, and other fakes — you can't bring them back for all your friends.

Taking Back Value-Added Tax and Goods and Services Tax

As if dealing with U.S. Customs restrictions isn't confusing enough (see the previous section for Customs info), other countries have tax oddities that you need to pay attention to, if only because you may actually get money back!

In Europe

European countries levy a tax called *VAT (value-added tax)* on all items (already included in the price you see). Despite the name, VAT doesn't add value at all, but it can cost you significant bucks; the tax ranges from 15 to 35 percent (it varies by country). The good news is that you may be able to get it refunded if you spend a designated amount (normally between $50 and $200) in a single store.

Regulations vary by country (check when you get there or with your ship's purser), but generally you can either collect your refund at the airport as you leave Europe or have it mailed to you. To do this, you need forms and receipts from the stores where you made your purchases, and you may need to show your items to the VAT official at the airport. Allow at least an extra 30 minutes to get through the process (if you spend a lot, the hassle is well worth it).

Be aware that an administrative fee is deducted from your refund.

In Canada

Canada has what's called a *GST (goods and services tax)* of 7 percent that applies to goods, food, and hotel rooms. You can also run into an *HST (harmonized sales tax)* of 15 percent (which includes the GST) in the Maritime Provinces (such as Nova Scotia and New Brunswick) and a special 7.5 percent tax in Quebec called *TVQ (Quebec Sales Tax),* which the province charges in addition to the GST.

You can get a rebate for most purchases (excluding things such as alcohol and cigarettes) that you buy to bring home, as long as each item is worth more than C$50 and the total is at least C$200 (before taxes). You also get a rebate on your hotel bill. Keep your receipts and pick up a *Tax Refund Application for Visitors* at any Customs office or at most visitors centers, duty-free shops, department stores, and some hotels. Also, keep your boarding passes, which you may have to mail in with the form. If you leave the country by plane, car, or motor coach, you have to show your goods at the border (or airport) and get your receipts validated, or you can't get a refund. Be aware, while you calculate how much you can get, that Customs deducts an administrative charge from the refund amount.

For complete rules, write to the (in the U.S.) **National Tax Refund Service,** 1320 Route 9, Champlain, NY 12919, or fax to ☎ **450-434-6002.** Also find more information at www.nationaltaxrefund.com.

Dealing with Departure Tax

Something to remember if your cruise ends in a foreign country from which you plan to fly home: Some countries levy a departure tax on everyone who leaves. It normally, but not always, costs you less than $20. When you depart from Vancouver, you incur an airport improvement fee at Vancouver Airport. The fee is C$10 (about $7 U.S.), payable in U.S. or Canadian dollars. So don't spend every penny you have before you get to the airport. The airline can tell you the exact amount in advance.

Part IV

Ship Shapes: Cruise Lines and Cruise Ships

The 5th Wave   By Rich Tennant

"Do I like arugula? I love arugula! One of my favorite vacations was a cruise to arugula."

In this part . . .

Using our quick reviews of all the major cruise lines, you can decide which ship is right for you. In this part, we focus on the major lines that sail in the Caribbean, Alaska, and Europe (specifically the most popular Mediterranean ports). Why these destinations? Because you're probably a first-time cruiser, in which case you're unlikely to want to spend the big bucks for your first cruise in, say, China and the Far East. You may want to do this later, however, after you (ahem) get your feet wet. And many of the lines we feature also offer cruises in other parts of the world.

Chapter 13

Setting Your Sights on a Ship: Comparing Cruises

● ●

In This Chapter

▶ Using our reviews to find the right ship for you

▶ Keying in on ship specifications and ship itineraries

▶ Interpreting the prices listed in the reviews

● ●

*B*ecause you can classify cruises based on different criteria, we use a kind of shorthand in Part IV to help you sort ships according to your tastes in a range of areas that make a difference in your vacation experience. This chapter explains all those categories and what the different ratings and labels we use in this part mean. Reading through it saves you time by giving you key words and phrases to look for in the reviews in order to find the cruise lines and ships that most interest you.

Recognizing the Ratings

Each cruise line review begins with a quick and easy summary of the experience the line offers. You may be surprised at how much you can mix and match different interests (a good thing if you plan to travel with someone who isn't your psychological twin).

Sizing Up Your Ship

The size and type of a ship you choose can make a huge difference in the kind of experience you ultimately have. Fortunately, you have a tremendous range to choose from. Options run the gamut from giant megaships to the tiniest of tiny expedition-style ships. The following list gives you a handle on the various shapes and styles of ships that fall under each designation.

Note: A ship's size is expressed not in actual tons but in *gross registered tons (GRTs),* a figure that measures enclosed, interior space used to produce revenue on a vessel (cabins, dining areas, lounges, video game rooms, and so on). Tonnage, in ship terms, is a measure of volume rather than weight. One gross registered ton actually represents 100 cubic feet of enclosed, revenue-generating space.

- ✔ **Megaships:** Running about 70,000 GRT and up, megaships look and feel like floating communities. And, in actuality, they are, because they carry from about 1,750 to more than 3,000 passengers.

    Big on glitz, megaships promote loads of activities, attract families and a large share of the under-50 crowd, offer large public rooms (including fancy casinos and fully equipped gyms), and provide a wide variety of meal and entertainment options. They tend to visit crowd-pleasing ports, but in many ways the big attraction of these cruises are the ships themselves rather than the ports.

    The vessels of the Carnival and Royal Caribbean fleets all fit in this category, as do most of the ships in the Celebrity, Costa, Norwegian, and Princess fleets. Holland America also has some megaships, including the *Westerdam*.

- ✔ **Old (and new) oceanliners:** Remember the Cary Grant/Deborah Kerr movie *An Affair to Remember?* Once upon a time, people actually used ships to get from place to place on a regular basis. A few of these ships are still around.

    Launched in 1969, Cunard's *QE2*, for instance, is still as elegant as all-get-out — with prices to match. People who appreciate the romance of old ships, with their heavy steel doors, old teak decks, and brass detailing, swoon with delight on this vessel.

    Although big enough to deserve the label of megaship (and a super mega at that), Cunard's new *Queen Mary 2* has been carefully designed as an updated oceanliner.

- ✔ **Traditional-style ships:** These ships are modern with a traditional-style twist, often in the midsize range (carrying around 1,000 to 1,300 passengers). They generally provide subdued, old-fashioned decor and an onboard atmosphere geared primarily to older passengers. Many of the ships in the Holland America fleet fit into this category.

- ✔ **Modern midsize ships:** These ships run about the same size as the traditional-style midsize vessels but with a more contemporary decor and ambience. Some are simply smaller equivalents of their megasized sisters, providing the same kind of party atmosphere but with fewer partiers — Royal Caribbean's *Empress of the Seas* fits that description. Other ships, such as Celebrity's *Horizon* and *Zenith,* provide a more stylish, less party-oriented experience. Crystal's luxurious *Crystal Harmony*, *Crystal Serenity* (almost big enough to be a megaship), and *Crystal Symphony* are downright glamorous.

✔ **Small ships:** Small ships can negotiate shallow waters, which enables them to reach ports that larger ships can't manage. Often running at a more relaxed pace, smaller ships tend to have fewer children on board. In addition, the combination of smaller public space and less entertainment creates an atmosphere in which you spend a lot of time talking to other passengers. Some small ships (such as the Seabourn, Silversea, SeaDream, and Radisson Seven Seas vessels) are among the most luxurious afloat, whereas others (such as American Canadian Caribbean's vessels and some Glacier Bay Cruiseline ships) are downright rustic. Clipper, Cruise West, and Lindblad Expeditions vessels fall somewhere in between.

✔ **Sailing ships:** If you dream of doing the Errol Flynn thing, or if you're a purist when it comes to taking to the seas, a sailing ship may be your ticket to unforgettable adventure. Sailing ship experiences run the gamut among the lines currently in operation: from the bare bones Windjammer Barefoot Cruises to the extravagant Windstar line, with Star Clippers falling somewhere in between. The unifying factor among passengers who book these ships, however, is an appreciation for getting up close and personal with the elements. More than with any other type of cruising, if this is the type of cruise for you, you know it. No one is wishy-washy about a sailing ship. You either love them or you don't.

(Note that none of the sailing ships we review in Chapter 16 operate on sail power alone; all have engines, which often account for most of the ship's propulsion and are a necessary evil if you want to keep any kind of regular schedule.)

In a few cases, a ship falls between a couple of different categories, or it seems so unusual in one way or another that it doesn't *exactly* fit into one of these categories. We place these ships in what we think is the nearest fit.

Attending to the Details

Every review includes the information on the 2004/2005 season for each ship that was available at press time (because cruise lines tend to do some last-minute jostling, itineraries are subject to change), followed by some of the special features each line offers.

The number of days we list for each cruise represents the number of full days or nights — we don't count the hour or two you're on board on the last day of your cruise, waiting to get off the ship. For example, cruises that begin and end on a Sunday count as 7-day cruises, even though some cruise line brochures may refer to them as 8-day itineraries. Some itineraries also tack on an extra day (included in the cruise fare) for staying in a hotel at the beginning or end of the cruise, but we don't include those days in our numbers (although we mention where this kind of deal applies).

We also include a table that lists the vital statistics of all the line's ships in each review (with their size, passenger capacity, number of cabins, number of crew, and so on).

Getting a Handle on Prices

People rarely pay full price for a cruise. However, for easy comparison purposes, we list the brochure rates or *sticker prices*, which are the rates each line would love to get for its cabins if all was perfect with the world (from a cruise line executive's position, that is). You can expect to pay anywhere from 15 to 60 percent less (in some cases even more) than the rates the line lists. We go with the brochure rates because the amount of discount off these rates varies by line, ship, sailing, how far in advance you book, and in some cases even by day or hour (in other words, getting a good handle on it is hard). The brochure rates we list are for 2004. For each line, we also give quick tips on the kinds of special deals you can get. (For more detailed information on getting a bargain, see Chapter4.)

We indicate rates for a standard 7-day cruise. In cases where the ship sails in several markets, such as in the Caribbean and in Europe, we go with the Caribbean fare. In cases where the ship does only shorter or longer cruises, we note the rates accordingly.

We list prices for the following three basic types of accommodations:

- ✔ Inside cabin (one without windows)
- ✔ Outside cabin (one with windows)
- ✔ Suite

Cruise ships generally have several different categories of cabins within each of these three basic divisions, all priced differently; the prices we list represent a range for inside and outside cabins and suites. If you want to book a roomier, snazzier cabin in any category, the price is on the higher end.

Rates are generally cruise only (without airfare or hotel rooms), per person, and based on double occupancy. In cases where extras are included in the cruise fare, we note it.

Fares may vary depending on the sailing date and itinerary. We show them to give you an idea of the average price level based on the brochure rates.

Chapter 14

Mainstream Ships

. . . .

In This Chapter

▶ Introducing the major mainstream cruise ships in the Caribbean, Alaska, and the Mediterranean

▶ Getting the lowdown on the mainstream cruising experience

▶ Previewing the best new ships

. . . .

*T*he ships we feature in this chapter range from classic old ocean liners to new megaships — some of them so big they have room for such bizarre onboard features as ice-skating rinks and rock-climbing walls.

If luxury ships are more your style, see Chapter 15. At the other end of the spectrum, if you want a more down-to-earth experience, check out Chapter 16, where we discuss smaller, expedition-type vessels.

What Mainstream Ships Have

Some ships these days are so gigantic that they can offer more diversions than your average small town, but even ships that aren't *so* enormous have all the facilities you can imagine a cruise ship having and more. Mainstream ships have swimming pools, health clubs and spas of various sizes, nightclubs, movie theaters, shops, casinos, bars, special kids' playrooms, and open decks where you can take in the sun. You also find sports decks, virtual golf, computer rooms, cigar clubs, and martini bars. The state of state-of-the-art of ship designing nowadays allows that, even on the biggest vessels, you can find so many nooks and crannies that you can always have a place to be away from it all if you wish. Plus, the ships have many big public areas so you don't feel claustrophobic.

Mainstream ships have large dining rooms and buffet areas that serve more food with more variety and at more times than you can imagine or enjoy. Most ships offer formal nights when you can dine in your tux or gown if you like. Your ship may offer additional eating venues too, such as pizzerias; hamburger grills; ice cream parlors; alternative restaurants; patisseries; and wine, champagne, and caviar bars.

You can find onboard activities such as games and contests, classes and lectures, and a variety of entertainment options, including large-scale production shows, quiet pianists, not-so-quiet dance bands, operatic recitals, magicians, comedians, and more.

Mainstream ships offer modern comforts such as televisions and telephones in the cabins and, in some cases, safes, bathrobes, and minibars. The cabins themselves range from cubbyholes to large suites (depending on the ship and the category of accommodations you book). You may choose to upgrade your cabin with a veranda (available on most lines) that affords private, or at least semi-private, sea views.

The ships in this chapter tend to carry a lot of passengers, so you may have to wait in line occasionally when at the buffet or while you get off the ship in port. On the other hand, you don't get stuck with the same old faces for a week, because of the dining room options and those less frequented spots on board created by the vast amount of space.

The ships generally offer a comfortable cruising experience, with your well-being overseen by virtual armies of service employees. Ship stabilizers ensure that you have a fairly smooth sailing experience, too.

Where Mainstream Ships Go

The itineraries of the biggest ships in this chapter tend to include the tried-and-true ports where your ship may be one of several visiting that day (and where duty-free shopping may be a main attraction). But some smaller ships also visit alternative ports, away from the typical tourist crowds. All the lines offer shore excursions — some of them quite extravagant — so that you can see inland areas; visit places that you would have difficulty getting to on your own; or have a fun, adventurous, or educational experience set up for you in the short time you have in a port.

The rates we list in this chapter are brochure rates. As a general rule, you can expect to pay less — significantly less if you book early or snag a last-minute bargain (see Chapter 13 for more info on this topic or Chapter 4 to find out how to manage your cruise money).

Carnival Cruise Lines

3655 NW 87th Ave., Miami, FL 33178-2428; ☎ *888-CARNIVAL;* www.carnival.com

- ✔ **Type of cruise:** Family, party, resort, romantic
- ✔ **Ship size/style:** Modern, glitzy megaships

Thirty-three-year-old Carnival is the biggest fish in the industry, sporting a fleet of brash modern ships it designed for one thing alone: fun, Fun, FUN! Morning, noon, and night, you can find diversions on Carnival ships, as well as parties and party-hearty fellow passengers.

On an average week, Carnival ships carry about 50,000 guests, and it has one of the youngest passenger demographics in the industry — mostly under age 50 (30 percent under 35, 40 percent ages 35 to 55, and 30 percent over 55), including couples, singles, and a good share of families (the line carries more than 400,000 kids a year).

The decor on Carnival's mass-market ships is eclectic and glitzy, with a liberal use of neon and bold, bright colors, especially on the older ships. And expect a playful environment: a piano bar outfitted like King Tut's tomb here, a room with gilded representations of ancient Greek deities there — you get the idea. The *Carnival Victory* has sea-themed public rooms: The Ionian Room is Ionian Sea-themed (replete with Doric columns and ancient Greek vases), and the wine bar is evocative of the Caspian Sea region, taking its air of elegance from Russia. The *Carnival Pride,* believe it or not, offers a Renaissance decor in the Caribbean — complete with a life-size recreation of Michelangelo's famous *David.* And the *Carnival Conquest* boasts an Impressionist and post-Impressionist art theme, complete with rooms based on the works of van Gogh, Matisse, Gauguin, and others.

On Carnival ships, you have so much to do that the ports of call tend to take a back seat — although you have plenty of shore-excursion offerings. Carnival's ships spend more time at sea than their peers, giving people a chance to totally enjoy the Carnival floating-resort experience and its professionally delivered fun. Of course, this tactic also allows more time for passengers to increase the line's onboard revenue.

Food is usually well prepared and bountiful, geared toward a middle-American audience, and includes enhancements (depending on the ship) such as sushi bars; patisseries; Asian and deli sections in the buffet area (the *Carnival Conquest* also has a gourmet seafood section); and, on the *Carnival Spirit, Carnival Pride, Carnival Legend, Carnival Conquest, Carnival Glory,* and the new *Carnival Valor, Carnival Miracle,* and *Carnival Liberty,* a reservations-only supper club/steakhouse that serves big steaks (for an extra charge of $25 per person) and features live musical entertainment. All the ships offer a casual dining option at night called **Seaview Bistros,** and they also have 24-hour pizzerias and nightly midnight buffets. Carnival has moved from two to four assigned dining times on most of its ships in an effort to make the dining experience suitable to everyone's tastes and needs. (You still have to pick a time when you book and stick with it, however.)

Entertainment is, well, splendiferous, with each ship boasting lavish stage shows with dancers and singers, a 10-piece orchestra, and performances by comedians, magicians, and numerous live bands. And all the ships have big (in some cases giant) casinos and active discos. Service is not as refined as on smaller and/or fancier ships, but refinement is not the point here. All Carnival ships are well run, although you still experience minor annoyances such as long lines at buffets and disembarkation and frequent loud public announcements. Carnival doesn't promise deluxe this or luxury that; what it promises is fun! And the opportunities for fun on Carnival are myriad.

Drinking and off-color jokes are part of the onboard scene, as are goofy contests — for example, one contest features a blindfolded woman who has to pick her husband out of a lineup by feeling the contestants' chest hair.

For kids, Carnival offers Camp Carnival, an expertly run children's program with a plethora of kid-pleasing activities that keep them occupied so that you can enjoy some downtime.

Carnival actively courts the wedding and honeymoon market. Both *Brides* and *Modern Bride* magazines named Carnival the top line for honeymooners, and according to line officials, more weddings are conducted on Carnival ships than at Walt Disney World. You can even get married at sea on the *Spirit* (in Canada only). On the other ships, nuptials are conducted in port or at island locations (arranged by the cruise line).

Itineraries

Although Carnival's bread and butter is Caribbean sailings from Florida ports (Miami, Port Canaveral, Tampa, and more recently Fort Lauderdale and Jacksonville), the line broadened its base with ships home-ported year-round in Galveston, Texas; Mobile, Alabama; and New Orleans. The *Carnival Destiny* is based year-round in San Juan. The *Ecstasy* and *Carnival Pride* are based year-round in Long Beach (where Carnival recently opened its own dedicated port facility) on Mexican Riviera itineraries, and the *Carnival Spirit* stays in nearby San Diego for part of the year for Mexico service. The line offers cruises to Bermuda and Canada/New England from New York and Bahamas/Caribbean voyages from New York and Baltimore. Carnival also offers cruises in Alaska and some to Hawaii.

In the Caribbean, Carnival spices up its offerings with 8-day exotic itineraries, some of which include Belize, Costa Rica, and Panama on the *Carnival Legend* and *Carnival Spirit*. *Carnival Destiny* sails 7-day southern Caribbean cruises year-round out of San Juan. *Carnival Pride* sails 7-day Mexican Riviera cruises (from Long Beach) year-round. *Carnival Spirit* sails 7-day Gulf of Alaska cruises in summer, 8-day Caribbean cruises in the winter, 12-day Hawaii cruises in the spring and fall, and 14- to 16-day Panama Canal positioning cruises in the spring and fall. *Carnival Triumph* sails 7-day alternating eastern and western Caribbean cruises year-round. *Carnival Victory* sails 7-day eastern and western Caribbean cruises in winter and spring and 4- to 7-day New England/Canada cruises (from New York) in summer and fall. *Elation* offers 7-day western Caribbean cruises (from Galveston) year-round. *Inspiration* sails 7-day western Caribbean cruises (from Tampa) year-round. *Carnival Legend* sails 8-day, alternating eastern and western Caribbean cruises (from Fort Lauderdale) in winter and fall and 8-day Caribbean cruises from New York in spring, summer, and fall. *Carnival Glory* sails alternating eastern and western Caribbean (from Port Canaveral) itineraries year-round. *Carnival Conquest* (see Figure 14-1) sails 7-day western Caribbean cruises (from New Orleans) year-round. *Carnival Miracle* cruises from Baltimore in 7-day Bahamas/Key West voyages in the spring and fall and 7-day Bahamas/Orlando service in the summer. The line's newest ship, *Carnival Valor*, which entered service late last year, is in 7-day alternating eastern and western Caribbean service out of Miami.

The line offers a good selection of shorter cruises for people who can't afford to be away for a whole week.

Celebration sails 4- and 5-day Caribbean cruises year-round from Galveston. *Fascination* and *Ecstasy* sail 3-day Bahamas and 4-day Caribbean cruises year-round from Miami. *Fantasy* sails 3- and 4-day Bahamas cruises year-round. *Holiday* sails 4- and 5-day Caribbean cruises from Mobile, and the *Jubilee* and *Celebration* sail in 4- and 5-day Bahamas/Key West rotations from Jacksonville, Florida. *Imagination* sails 4- and 5-day western Caribbean cruises year-round. *Sensation* sails 4- and 5-day cruises from Tampa. *Paradise* is in the 3- and 4-day Mexico market out of Long Beach year-round.

(Photo: Carnival Cruise Lines)

Figure 14-1: The *Carnival Conquest*

Outstanding features

Carnival offers a *Vacation Guarantee program:* Any guests dissatisfied with the cruise while on board can disembark at the first non-U.S. port of call and receive a refund for the unused portion of their fare, plus reimbursement for air transportation back to the ship's home port. Carnival enforces a tough smoking policy, banning smoking in all dining rooms, including alternative Lido Deck dining areas and all showrooms. All the ships have 24-hour pizzerias and alternative dining at night. Room stewards entertain by turning bathroom towels into fluffy animals; all the ships offer Internet access; and the Fun Finance Plan allows you to cruise now, pay later (you get a branded credit card with an annual percentage rate of 9.9 percent and up). Carnival has a program where your tips ($9.75 per person, per day) are automatically added to your shipboard account (you can, of course, adjust this tip as you see fit). Alaskan sailings feature onboard marine biologists and Alaskan wildlife specialists. The fleet-wide golf program includes lessons and escorted golf excursions at selected ports of call.

Super deals

Carnival offers generous early-bird discounts, AARP discounts, a cabin-share program for singles, third- and fourth-passenger fares with special rates for those 12 and under, wedding and honeymoon packages, and packages that combine a 3- or 4-day cruise to the Bahamas from Port Canaveral or Tampa with a 2- to 7-day Universal Studios land vacation (including accommodations in Orlando). Carnival also offers Reunion Cruises for past passengers (offered from $599 per week). Table 14-1 provides Carnival rates.

Table 14-1	Carnival Rates		
Ship	*Inside*	*Outside*	*Suites*
Carnival Conquest [a]	$1,649–$1,749	$1,899–$2,099	$2,599
Carnival Destiny [a]	$1,649–$1,749	$1,899–$2,099	$2,599
Carnival Glory [a]	$1,649–$1,749	$1,899–$2,099	$2,599
Carnival Legend [b]	$1,799–$1,899	$2,099–$2,249	$2,799
Carnival Miracle [c]	$1,649–$1,749	$1,949–$2,099	$2,599
Carnival Pride [a]	$1,649–$1,749	$1,899–$2,099	$2,799
Carnival Spirit [d]	$1,919–$2,019	$2,269–$2,469	$3,269
Carnival Triumph [a]	$1,649–$1,749	$1,899–$2,099	$2,599
Carnival Valor [a]	$1,649–$1,749	$1,899–$2,099	$2,599
Carnival Victory [a]	$1,649–$1,749	$1,899–$2,099	$2,599
Celebration [e]	$849–$899	$979	$1,379
Ecstasy [f]	$699–$729	$789	$1,049
Elation [a]	$1,349–$1,449	$1,599	$2,199
Fantasy [e]	$849–$899	$979	$1,279
Fascination [g]	$699–$729	$789	$1,049
Holiday [h]	$999–$1,049	$1,149	$1,749
Imagination [h]	$999–$1,049	$1,149	$1,549
Inspiration [i]	$849–$899	$979	$1,279

Ship	Inside	Outside	Suites
Jubilee [e]	$849–$899	$979	$1,379
Paradise [a]	$1,349–$1,449	$1,599	$2,199
Sensation [h]	$849–$899	$979	$1,279

[a] For 7-day Caribbean sailings
[b] For 8-day Caribbean sailings from New York
[c] For 7-day Key West/Bahamas sailings
[d] For 7-day Gulf of Alaska sailings
[e] For 4-day Bahamas sailings
[f] For 3-day Mexico sailings
[g] For 3-day Bahamas sailings
[h] For 5-day Caribbean sailings
[i] For 4-day Caribbean sailings

Fleet facts

The *Celebration, Holiday,* and *Jubilee* are the older, non-megaships in the Carnival fleet, but they have roomy cabins.

The *Carnival Destiny* was, in her first year (1996), the biggest ship in the world (Princess's *Grand Princess* surpassed her in 1998, and Royal Caribbean's *Voyager of the Seas* surpassed both of them in 1999), and she offers a lot of the "wows" you expect of a ship her size, including huge spa and gym areas. The *Carnival Triumph* and *Carnival Victory* are the *Carnival Destiny's* slightly bigger siblings. A stretched version of these ships debuted in the fall of 2002, the *Carnival Conquest. Carnival Glory* similarly extended a year later. These ships are about 60 feet longer, with tonnage of 110,000 tons, and boast massive family recreation centers. The Conquest-class *Carnival Valor* is expected to debut in December 2004 and the *Carnival Liberty* in August 2005.

Carnival's Fantasy-class ships — the *Ecstasy, Fantasy, Fascination, Imagination, Inspiration, Sensation, Elation,* and *Paradise* — differ in their decor but not their size, use of space, or acres of teak decking or extravagance. Their cabins, although neat and tidy, are really nothing to write home about. The best way to tell the ships apart is by their names, which reflect their interior design.

In 2001, the line introduced a relatively small (by megaship standards) class of ship: the 2,124-passenger, 84,000-ton *Carnival Spirit,* which is a sister ship to Costa Line's *CostaAtlantica* and boasts an outdoor promenade, a supper club, and many cabins with verandas. *Carnival Pride,* done up in Renaissance style, followed in January 2002; *Carnival Legend* debuted in the summer of 2002; and *Carnival Miracle* arrived in spring 2004. These vessels all offer the most successful design elements of Carnival's earlier classes of ships, including many bars and lounges. Table 14-2 shows the current fleet specifications.

Table 14-2		Carnival Fleet Specifications				
Ship	Year Built	Passengers	Crew	Total Cabins	Tonnage	Length in Feet
Carnival Conquest	2002	2,974	1,100	1,487	110,000	952
Carnival Destiny	1996	2,642	1,050	1,321	101,353	893
Carnival Glory	2003	2,974	1,100	1,487	110,000	952
Carnival Legend	2002	2,124	920	1,062	84,000	960
Carnival Miracle	2004	2,124	930	1,062	88,000	960
Carnival Pride	2001	2,124	920	1,062	84,000	960
Carnival Spirit	2001	2,124	920	1,062	84,000	960
Carnival Triumph	1999	2,758	1,100	1,379	102,000	893
Carnival Valor	2004	2,974	1,160	1,487	110,000	952
Carnival Victory	2000	2,758	1,100	1,379	102,000	893
Celebration	1987	1,486	670	743	47,262	733
Ecstasy	1991	2,040	920	1,020	70,367	855
Elation	1998	2,040	920	1,020	70,367	855
Fantasy	1990	2,040	920	1,020	70,367	855
Fascination	1994	2,040	920	1,020	70,367	855
Holiday	1985	1,452	669	726	46,052	727
Imagination	1995	2,040	920	1,020	70,367	855
Inspiration	1996	2,040	920	1,020	70,367	855
Jubilee	1986	1,486	670	743	47,262	733
Paradise	1998	2,040	920	1,020	70,367	855
Sensation	1993	2,040	920	1,020	70,367	855

Celebrity Cruises

1050 Caribbean Way, Miami, FL 33132; ☎ *800-437-3111 or 305-539-6000;* www.celebrity.com

- **Type of cruise:** Family, resort, romantic
- **Ship size/style:** Modern, stylish midsize and megaships

Celebrity has the best vessels in the mid-priced category — the *Century*, *Galaxy*, *Mercury* (see Figure 14-2), and the newer *Millennium*, *Infinity*, *Summit*, and *Constellation*. All are works of art, combining an impressive sense of style, careful attention to detail, and formal yet friendly service that make the cruising experience truly exceptional. Passengers, who range in age from 20-something honeymooners to retirees, are pampered in a low-key, non-invasive way.

The Celebrity fleet is among the newest in the industry, and all the ships cut sleek figures. Painted in bright white and deep blue, each ship features a huge X on its smokestack, which is the Greek symbol for *ch,* as in Chandris (the shipping family that launched the line in 1990 and sold it to Royal Caribbean in 1997).

(Photo: Matt Hannafin)

Figure 14-2: The *Mercury*

Renowned designers from Europe and the United States worked on the interiors of Celebrity vessels, and it shows. The result is just the right amount of drama without the glitz. And the designers also managed to make the most of traditional nautical touches, such as etched glass and a lot of woodwork. The ships offer plenty of cushy lounges; open decks; windows (particularly valuable for sightseeing in Alaska); and an impressive array of intimate public rooms that include cigar clubs, champagne and/or martini bars, and coffee bars. The artwork on display throughout the ships is as good as you can find on the high seas.

The *Century*, *Galaxy*, and *Mercury* each feature the AquaSpa, a water-centered spa the equal of anything else the industry offers. Decorated in a variety of motifs — Japanese (on the *Century* and *Galaxy*) and Moorish (on the *Mercury*) for instance — the more recent ships have large *thalassotherapy pools,* a kind of giant New Age hot tub where water jets hit different parts of your body as you relax. In addition, a plethora of exotic spa treatments are available. The *Millennium*, *Infinity*, *Summit,* and *Constellation* top even this with their massive, 25,000-square-foot AquaSpa facilities and free use of their thalassotherapy pools (you have to pay a small fee on the other ships). Along with the water jets, the pools on the new ships offer a reverse-current area for resistance swimming, plus aromatherapy showers and other New Age offerings. Although the spas on the *Horizon* and *Zenith* don't offer thalassotherapy, they do have a range of other treatments.

The cabins on Celebrity ships are all good-sized and well organized — you can't really find a bad cabin — and provide plenty of storage space. The penthouse suites on the *Century, Mercury,* and *Galaxy* are huge, and the top penthouse suites on the newer *Millennium, Infinity, Summit,* and *Constellation* are among the largest afloat — a whopping 3,000 square feet, including the veranda. On the newer ships, 74 percent of outside cabins have verandas.

Entertainment aboard all the ships is usually good and in some cases extraordinary — especially the featured acts. The ships' stage productions try to be more Broadway than Las Vegas, and the ships provide unexpected treats such as roving a cappella singers. Activities include cerebral pursuits such as personal investing seminars and handwriting analysis.

Michel Roux, Celebrity's famous culinary consultant and one of the top French chefs in Britain, guides all Celebrity cuisine. In keeping with French tradition, the cuisine generally is high fat, although healthy alternatives are always available. The food offerings are fresh, plentiful, and served with style, and nighttime casual dining options are available on all ships. The waitstaff serves snacks at midnight in such venues as the casinos and lounges.

The *Millennium* has a special reservations-only dining room with a great feature: hand-carved wood panels that were created for the *Olympic* (sister ship to the *Titanic*) and graced that vessel's **A La Carte** restaurant from 1911 to 1935. The dining experience in the restaurant Celebrity created around these panels is leisurely and luxurious, styled after liners cruising in the Golden Age of sea travel (although at three hours, some may find it excessive). The line offers comparably fine restaurants with intriguing decor on the *Infinity, Summit,* and *Constellation.* The cost to dine at these venues is $25 per person. Be sure to make reservations as soon as you get aboard!

Art is an important aspect of the Celebrity experience, so each time the line introduces a new ship it increases its art-acquisition budget. The extensive collection on *Summit,* for instance, includes *Woman With Fruit,* a large bronze of a rotund woman by noted Colombian artist Fernando Botero (the sculpture overlooks the ship's thalassotherapy pool area), as well as an ART sculpture by LOVE artist Robert Indiana. You also see a mirrored flower by Jeff Koons and a series of truly ugly but fascinating beaded busts by Liza Lou, as well as a fun series of Barbie photos by David Levinthal that you can find in the ship's shopping arcade.

Those into more commercial pursuits may want to while away time in the ships' shops. The newer ships boast what amounts to small malls that feature Escada Sport, Tommy Hilfiger, La Perla, Swarovski crystal, Fossil watches, Fendi purses, and more.

The newer ships also offer Internet cafes and Internet access in all cabins (for a fee) and feature music libraries with thousands of listening selections (headphones are available at the purser's desk).

Celebrity offers a decent children's program in the summer, when there may be hundreds of kids onboard, and during holiday periods (a limited program is also offered other times of year whenever more than 12 kids are onboard). But if vacationing with kids is not your thing, you may want to try Celebrity Escape sailings, Celebrity's adults-only (21 and over) cruises.

Itineraries

Most of the line's sailings are in and around North America, including the Caribbean, Alaska, Bermuda, and the Mexican Riviera, but Celebrity ships also cruise in Europe, South America, and Hawaii. Embarkation ports include Baltimore, Philadelphia, and Jacksonville, Florida (Celebrity is the first big line to cruise from this port). You cruise out of Dover, England for Baltic sailings.

Century sails 7-day alternating eastern and western Caribbean cruises year-round. *Constellation* sails 12-day Mediterranean sailings in the summer; followed by a couple of months of Panama Canal crossings; and 7-day southern Caribbean cruises in late fall, winter, and spring. *Galaxy* sails in Europe in summer, Canada/New England in the fall, and eastern Caribbean itineraries from Baltimore the rest of the year. *Horizon* splits its time between Bermuda and the Caribbean, sailing in a 7-day western Caribbean pattern in winter and spring with 7-day Bermuda cruises (from New York) in the summer and fall. *Infinity* sails in 7-day rotation in Alaska in the summer and a mixed bag of 7-, 10-, 12-, and 17-day Hawaiian, Mexico, and South American cruises the rest of the year. *Mercury* sails 7- to 11-day Mexican Riviera routes in winter and 7-day Alaskan cruises in summer. *Millennium* sails 7-day eastern Caribbean cruises in winter and spring and 12-day Mediterranean cruises in the spring, summer, and fall. *Summit* sails 10- and 11-day Caribbean cruises in winter and 7-day Alaskan cruises in summer. *Zenith* does 11- to 14-day Caribbean programs in winter and 7-day Bermuda cruises (from New York) in the spring, summer, and fall.

Outstanding features

Suite passengers receive complimentary butler service, champagne, and other special amenities, including the chance to book an in-cabin massage and free access to thalassotherapy pools (others pay $10 per day on the *Century, Galaxy,* and *Mercury;* free on the other ships). The penthouse suites on the *Millennium, Infinity, Summit,* and *Constellation* are the largest at sea (and those on the *Century, Galaxy,* and *Mercury* aren't so far behind). You can gamble from your cabin on interactive television. The *Millennium* and its sister ships boast a bank of glass-enclosed elevators that face the ocean for fantastic views. Recent upgrades include free champagne mimosas at embarkation, massages offered on deck (for a fee), chilled towels poolside, and additional time for disembarkation (you don't have to rush off the ship).

Super deals

Early-bird discounts of up to 50 percent and discounts for third and fourth passengers are available. The line also offers prearranged spa packages, as well as honeymoon and anniversary packages. For more Celebrity rates, see Table 14-3.

Table 14-3	Celebrity Rates		
Ship	*Inside*	*Outside*	*Suites*
Century [a]	$550–$610	$700–$990	$1,150–$3,500
Constellation [b]	$1,729–$1,759	$1,949–$2,509	$3,649–$9,749
Galaxy [c]	$1,300–$1,390	$1,550–$2,480	$3,300–$8,600
Horizon [d]	$700–$800	$850–$1,030	$1,030–$2,500
Infinity [e]	$1,010–$1,135	$1,175–$2,000	$2,650–$6,800
Mercury [f]	$800–$920	$950–$1,325	$1,450–$4,650
Millennium [a]	$780–$900	$980–$1,130	$2,030–$5,530
Summit [g]	$1,000–$1,180	$1,200–$1,800	$2,500–$7,600
Zenith [d]	$750–$820	$850–$1,080	$1,450–$2,850

[a] For 7-day Caribbean sailings
[b] For 12-day E. Mediterranean sailings
[c] For 10-day W. Mediterranean sailings
[d] For 7-day Bermuda sailings
[e] For 7-day Alaska sailings
[f] For 7-day Mexican Riviera sailings
[g] For 10-day Caribbean sailings

Fleet facts

The oldest Celebrity ships, *Horizon* and *Zenith,* are great by any standards, but when the company moved into the megaliner business, it topped itself with the even more impressive *Century* and then topped itself again with the *Galaxy* and again with the *Mercury.* The line's 91,000-ton, French-built Millennium-class ships continue the trend.

These vessels — the *Millennium, Infinity, Summit,* and *Constellation* — are just plain stunning: comfortable, beautifully designed, and full of lovely rooms and varied diversions, such as an Internet center, a music library, and extensive high-fashion shopping opportunities. The *Infinity, Summit,* and *Constellation* even have a conservatory complete with benches and orchids — a botanical garden at sea, a respite from the hustle and bustle of daily sea life. The *Millennium* has a smaller version. Table 14-4 shows the current fleet specifications.

Table 14-4		Celebrity Fleet Specifications				
Ship	**Year Built**	**Passengers**	**Crew**	**Total Cabins**	**Tonnage**	**Length in Feet**
Century	1995	1,750	853	875	70,606	807
Constellation	2002	1,950	999	975	91,000	964
Galaxy	1996	1,870	909	935	77,713	858
Horizon	1990	1,354	645	677	46,811	682
Infinity	2001	1,950	999	975	91,000	964
Mercury	1997	1,870	907	935	77,713	860
Millennium	2000	1,950	999	975	91,000	964
Summit	2001	1,950	999	975	91,000	964
Zenith	1992	1,374	645	687	47,225	682

Costa Cruises

200 South Park Rd., Suite 200, Hollywood, FL 33021-8541; ☎ *800-33-COSTA;* www.costacruises.com

- ✔ **Type of cruise:** Family, resort, romantic
- ✔ **Ship size/style:** Modern midsize and megaships

The origins of Costa (which dates back to 1860 and the olive-oil business) are in Italy, and it shows in nearly everything the line offers. Costa exudes an Italian aura, from the food to the ships' sleek Italian design and Italian-speaking crews (although they don't all hail from Italy) and entertainers to the onboard activities, which include festive Roman toga parties on Caribbean sailings and Carnival and Circus nights in Europe. Miami-based Carnival Corporation now owns the line (and many others, including Carnival, Holland America, Princess, Windstar, Seabourn, and Cunard), but it maintains Costa's unique Italian style.

As the number-one cruise line in Europe, Costa boasts a modern fleet and is in the process of spending some $1 billion on expansion. The most notable additions are the *CostaAtlantica* and sister ship *CostaMediterranea* and two super-mega 105,000-ton vessels, the *CostaFortuna* and the *Costa-Magica.* All these ships entered service after 2000, with the *CostaMagica* named as recently as last year. The line has also become, it seems, a repository for older Carnival Corporation vessels: In 2001, the 1981-built *Tropicale,* previously with Carnival Cruise Lines, joined Costa as the *CostaTropicale;* and in June 2002, Holland America's *Westerdam,* built in 1986, joined the Costa fleet as the *CostaEuropa.* Costa extensively refurbished both ships. You can easily identify Costa ships by their blue and yellow smokestacks emblazoned with a huge letter C. The line doesn't design its ships strictly for an American audience, and therein lies their charm, although some passengers may be put off by announcements being translated into multiple languages (as many as five) and the fact that many passengers smoke like chimneys (in response to this, in late 2001, Costa banned smoking in all main dining rooms and main showrooms on all its vessels).

A good number of Italian-Americans represent the line's clientele on Caribbean sailings. On European sailings, Americans make up only about 20 percent of the passenger mix, which is predominantly Italian (especially on itineraries from Italy) but also includes a French, German, and British following, among others. The cruises draw a good age mix, including honeymooners (some sailings in Europe get dozens of couples) and families.

In addition to casual elegance, the Italian experience on Costa vessels has a warm, continental flair. On a Costa ship, your room steward likely greets you with *"Buongiorno!"* and your waiter encourages you to *"Mangia, mangia!"* If you don't know what these words mean, never fear: The line offers Italian language lessons along with lectures on Italian culture.

The food is flavorful (pasta is a best bet), as plentiful as you would expect, and presented with theatrical verve. On theme nights, staffers may dress as gondoliers and present red roses to all the women. Aside from the main restaurants, alternative dining venues include pizza cafes and patisseries serving espresso, chocolates, and pastries. You can also dine at a fancy alternative restaurant on the *CostaVictoria, CostaAtlantica* (see Figure 14-3), *CostaTropicale, CostaFortuna, CostMagica,* and *CostaMediterranea* (the fee to eat at these venues is $20 per person).

Costa offers well-developed activities programs for both kids and teens and provides at least one full-time youth counselor aboard each ship, year-round. Special activities coordinators keep the atmosphere hopping for adults into the wee hours (the disco on European sailings fires up at midnight). All the ships offer Internet access.

(Photo: Costa Cruise Lines)

Figure 14-3: The *CostaAtlantica*

Itineraries

Costa ships spend spring, summer, and fall in Europe, and the *Costa-Atlantica* and *CostaMediterranea* also spend winters in the Caribbean. The *CostaTropicale* operates expanded South American sailings in winter, visiting such ports as Rio de Janeiro and Buenos Aires.

CostaAllegra sails 10- and 11-day Mediterranean and North Cape routes in spring, summer, and fall (from Genoa and Rotterdam, respectively). *CostaAtlantica* sails 7-day alternating eastern and western Caribbean cruises in winter and 7-day Greece itineraries in spring, summer, and fall (from Venice). *CostaClassica* sails 7-day Greek Isles itineraries (from Venice) in the spring, summer, and fall. *CostaEuropa* sails 7-, 9-, and 11-day Mediterranean voyages in the winter, spring, and fall and Northern European cruises (including the Baltics and Norway) in the summer. *CostaRomantica* sails Northern European itineraries in the summer and a 10-day western Mediterranean cruise in fall, but it doesn't market the rest of the year to Americans. *CostaVictoria* sails 7-day Mediterranean itineraries (from Venice) in spring, summer, and fall and spends the winter doing South American cruises. *CostaTropicale* sails 7-day western Mediterranean itineraries in the spring, summer, and fall (from Savona) and moves to South America in winter. *CostaMediterranea* sails 7-day Mediterranean routes in summer and 7-day alternating eastern and western Caribbean itineraries in fall and winter. *CostaFortuna* operates itineraries in Spain, Morocco, and the Canary Islands. *CostaMagica* is in western Mediterranean service year round.

Outstanding features

Opportunities range from Mass being conducted almost daily in the chapel to a weekly toga party (in the Caribbean). In between, you can attend a Golf Academy at Sea program on Caribbean cruises, in which guests take onboard clinics and private lessons with PGA golf pros and participate in putting competitions and tournaments at some of the Caribbean's best-known golf courses. Costa's children's program offers Italian language lessons. Eastern Caribbean itineraries spend a night at the private **Casa de Campo** resort in the Dominican Republic.

Super deals

Passengers who book European cruises at least 120 days in advance receive a discount of up to $4,000 per couple. Costa offers early-booking discounts of up to $1,400 per couple in the Caribbean (if you book at least 120 days in advance) and friend and family rates in the Caribbean — you save $200 per cabin if you book two or more cabins at the same time. Passengers 60 years and older get an additional $200 off. In the Caribbean, children can sail for the special fare of $199 (17 and under), plus government taxes, when they share a room with two adults. Check out Table 14-5 for more Costa rate variables.

Table 14-5	Costa Rates		
Ship	*Inside*	*Outside*	*Suites*
CostaAtlantica [a]	$999–$1,149	$1,249–$1,599	$1,949–$2,349
CostaAllegra [b]	$2,699–$3,139	$3,499–$3,939	$5,059–$5,699
CostaClassica [c]	$1,699–$2,069	$2,179–$2,379	$3,059
CostaEuropa [d]	$2,699–$3,139	$3,499–$4,799	$5,699
CostaFortuna [e]	$1,839–$2,169	$2,429–$2,779	$3,199–$3,799
CostaMagica [f]	$1,839–$1,969	$2,429–$2,779	$3,199–$3,799
CostaMediterranea [a]	$999–$1,149	$1,249–$1,599	$1,949–$2,349
CostaRomantica [g]	$2,369–$2,929	$3,069–$3,279	$4,479–$5,059
CostaTropicale [f]	$1,669–$1,959	$2,039–$2,329	$2,759
CostaVictoria [h]	$2,099–$2,609	$2,709–$3,209	$3,629–$4,009

[a] For 7-night Caribbean sailings
[b] For 11-day North Cape sailings
[c] For 7-day Greek Islands sailings
[d] For 11-day Baltic sailings
[e] For 7-day Spain/Morocco sailings
[f] For 7-day western Mediterranean sailings
[g] For 10-day western Mediterranean sailings
[h] For 7-day eastern Mediterranean sailings

Fleet facts

CostaAllegra was built in the 1960s and completely updated into a more formal passenger ship in the 1990s. *CostaClassica* is a contemporary and stylish vessel that recently underwent a multimillion-dollar refurbishment. *CostaVictoria* is the ship that brought Costa into the megaship era — she is technologically advanced, sleek, and stylish, with spacious and dramatic interiors. *CostaAtlantica* debuted as Costa's largest ship and as the only ship in the fleet to have a large number of cabins with private verandas (nearly 65 percent of the ship's outside cabins). The vessel also boasts some other nice new features, including **Café Florian**, a replica of the landmark 18th-century Venetian cafe of the same name. The ship is similar in layout, but not decor, to its sister ship in the Carnival fleet, the new *Carnival Spirit.* A new 86,000-ton, 2,114-passenger ship (a slightly larger sister), *CostaMediterranea,* joined the Costa fleet in summer 2003. *CostaTropicale* underwent a $25 million refurbishment before it joined the fleet in 2001 (it previously cruised as Carnival's *Tropicale*), becoming a roomy vessel with good-sized cabins and a tropical decor (as the name would suggest). The 1,494-passenger *CostaEuropa* (formerly operated by Holland America as the *Westerdam*) was built in Germany and offers an old ocean liner ambiance (although the ship isn't that old). Two super-mega ships, *CostaFortuna* and *CostaMagica,* arrived in late 2003 and 2004, respectively. The ships weigh in at 105,000 tons and are somewhat like Carnival ships with an Italian slant. Table 14-6 shows the current fleet specifications.

Table 14-6 Costa Fleet Specifications

Ship	Year Built	Passengers	Crew	Total Cabins	Tonnage	Length in Feet
CostaAllegra	1992	820	450	410	28,500	616
CostaAtlantica	2000	2,112	920	1,056	84,000	957
CostaClassica	1991	1,308	650	654	53,000	722
CostaEuropa	1986	1,494	650	747	54,000	798
CostaFortuna	2003	2,700	998	1,359	105,000	976
CostaMagica	2004	2,700	998	1,359	105,000	976
CostaMediterranea	2003	2,114	920	1,057	86,000	960
CostaRomantica	1993	1,356	610	678	53,000	722
CostaTropicale	1981	1,022	550	511	36,674	660
CostaVictoria	1996	1,928	800	964	54,000	817

Disney Cruise Line

P.O. Box 10210, Lake Buena Vista, FL 32830; ☎ *888-325-2500;* www.disney cruise.com

| ✔ **Type of cruise:** Family, resort

| ✔ **Ship size/style:** Modern, stylish megaships with the Disney touch

Disney entered the cruise industry in 1998 with a mission: to be the best cruise line in the world. That's a pretty hefty goal that the line hasn't quite achieved yet, but you can't deny that both the *Disney Magic* (see Figure 14-4) and *Disney Wonder* are great ships, lavish enough to hold their own alongside such competitors as Princess, Holland America, and Celebrity. The ships reflect a beautiful mix of old and new, taking some of the best elements of classic liners — to appeal to the nostalgia crowd — and merging them into a modern, Disney-esque sphere to appeal to both first-timers (especially fans of Disney's vacation resorts) and the mega-ship crowd looking for a little something different.

(Photo: Disney Cruise Line)

Figure 14-4: The *Disney Magic*

In creating the line, Disney (being Disney) tried to rewrite the book on cruising and has succeeded with several of its innovations. The ships' cabins are larger than the industry average and are designed with families in mind (many, for instance, come with a bathroom divided into two sepa-rate compartments: one for the toilet and another for the shower/ bath). Entertainment, as you may expect, is among the best in the indus-try and includes original Broadway-style shows, first-run films (shown in a real movie theater), and even an occasional movie premiere at sea (coin-ciding with the movie's land opening). A stage show, *The Golden Mickeys*, takes the audience through the history of Disney films and animation in an Academy Award-type format. The line's recently updated kids' pro-grams are some of the best at sea and include a nursery for babies and toddlers, special activities for teens, and a Hawaiian Luau Welcome Party (à la *Lilo & Stitch*) for kids of all ages. Adult programs aren't too shabby, either. And the unique rotation dining system, in which passengers eat in a different dining environment each night, keeps the kids (and some adults) from getting bored with the traditional cruise ship dining experience (and in two of the three restaurants you don't even have to dress up). Kids particularly like **Animator's Palette,** where the whole room changes colors throughout the meal. **Palo's,** open only to adults and on a reservation-only basis (you have to book a table when you first get on board or you don't get one), serves excellent Northern Italian cuisine.

If you're looking for a wild nightlife, you can't find it on Disney ships. The vessels have no casino or disco, but they do provide nifty adults-only entertainment areas with dueling piano clubs, dancing areas, and quiet piano/jazz bars. More hopping are family-oriented activities such as late-night karaoke (which attracts a surprisingly large number of kids). Depending on the sailing, you may also find some '50s and '70s music theme nights.

Although Disney Cruise Line has gone out of its way to appeal not only to families, but also to seniors and honeymoon couples, adults who travel without kids should be aware that many youngsters travel on Disney vessels — sometimes representing as many as one-third of the passengers — and kids make noise. Youngsters are banned from the adults-only pool area, although they may occasionally sneak in (the ships have separate pools for kids and families). And the spa and gym are also for those 18 and older, but teens can go to the beauty parlor at designated times.

Itineraries

This year, for the first time, you can see the Disney Cruises livery on the west coast. Disney has been a purely Caribbean operator since its inception, but the line is moving the *Disney Magic* to Los Angeles this summer for a series of 7-day Mexican Riviera voyages. For the rest of the year it plans to continue its alternating 7-day eastern Caribbean and 7-day western Caribbean itineraries. The *Disney Wonder* offers shorter 3- and 4-day Bahamas cruises that the line usually (though not necessarily) sells as a part of 7-day vacation packages, combining the sailings with a Walt Disney World land experience. If you take the package option on the *Wonder,* you have a single check-in for both cruise and land accommodations — one key opens your cabin door on the ship and your hotel room at Walt Disney World.

Both ships (when in Florida) operate out of Disney's private $24 million cruise terminal in Port Canaveral, Florida and both spend a day at the beach at **Castaway Cay,** Disney's private Bahamas island, which features its own pier for easy accessibility (you don't have to get in a tender, or launch, to get ashore). The island offers snorkeling and water sports (including parasailing and banana boats), kids and family activities, and separate beach areas for families, teens, and adults. A massage in a cabana on the adult beach here is a must-do. When in California, the *Magic* sails round trip out of San Pedro, the port for Los Angeles.

Outstanding features

You dine in a different restaurant each night of your cruise, and your waiter moves with you. Each ship has an ESPN sports bar. The *Magic's* western Caribbean itinerary includes a late afternoon/evening port call in Key West to satisfy your nightlife cravings. You can reserve shore excursions in advance of your trip. The ships are each equipped with nifty *Segway Personal Transportation Devices*, which are electrically powered, two-wheel scooters you can rent for $15 for 20 minutes (you can use them on the deck or at Castaway Cay).

Super deals

Discounts are available for early bookings. The line offers special fare discounts of up to 50 percent (not including air) for kids 3 to 12 who travel as a third, fourth, or fifth passenger and share a cabin with two adults on either ship. See Table 14-7 for Disney rates.

Table 14-7	Disney Rates		
Ship	**Inside**	**Outside**	**Suites**
Disney Magic [a]	$1,399–$1,449	$1,540–$1,610	$1,870–$2,530
Disney Wonder [b]	$550–$699	$750–$910	$969–$1,220

[a] For 7-day Mexican Riviera sailings
[b] For 3-day Bahamas sailings

Fleet facts

The two Disney ships are nearly identical. Both pay tribute to the classic ocean liners with their deep blue hulls, twin smokestacks, and updated classic decor — Art Deco on the *Magic* and lighter Art Nouveau on the *Wonder*. Cabins are bigger than standard, and the 82 suites are particularly plush. Table 14-8 shows the current fleet specifications. Disney continues talk of building additional ships, but no announcements had been made at press time.

Table 14-8	Disney Fleet Specifications					
Ship	**Year Built**	**Passengers**	**Crew**	**Total Cabins**	**Tonnage**	**Length in Feet**
Disney Magic	1998	1,760	964	875	83,000	950
Disney Wonder	1999	1,760	964	875	83,000	950

Holland America Line

300 Elliot Ave. West, Seattle, WA 98119; ☎ *800-426-0327;* www.holland america.com

| ✔ **Type of cruise:** Family, resort, romantic

| ✔ **Ship size/style:** Traditional-style midsize ships

Holland America Line (HAL) has been in business for 130 years, and the line's experience shows in its fleet of modern ships, which reflect both nautical history and the line's Dutch heritage (the company now resides under the ownership of acquisitive Carnival Corporation, parent of other lines including Carnival, Cunard, and, most recently, Princess). In the public rooms you find nautical memorabilia, with some pieces dating back to earlier HAL ships.

The Holland America ships, all sporting names that end with -dam (*Rotterdam, Statendam, Westerdam,* and so on), are clean and lean, impeccably maintained, and not overly glitzy. Cruising with the line is a low-key experience — restful rather than boisterous, with not much late-night carousing. The crowds tend to be middle-American and more mature (in some cases quite elderly), the kind who appreciate an old-fashioned cruising experience, friendly service, and a consistent and well-priced product. Many passengers head to bed early, and you can't find much action after midnight.

The line has tried, with limited — but growing — success, to attract families by creating a well-planned kids' program (known as Club Hal), special children's shore excursions, and family cruisetours in Alaska. Some ships have been retro-fitted with kids' facilities and separate clubs for teens. The newest ships (the *Rotterdam* and those thereafter) were custom-built with kids' and teens' facilities.

Food on HAL ships is international, with the dining rooms offering traditional favorites as well as light and healthy cuisine, pasta selections, and a children's menu. Foodies may scoff at some of the results from the kitchen, but the grub generally seems to please the crowd on these vessels. The ships also offer alternative casual nighttime dining venues. The *Rotterdam* and all the ships built after its arrival in the fleet — the *Volendam, Amsterdam, Zuiderdam, Oosterdam,* and *Westerdam* (which entered service just last summer) — have fancy alternative restaurants operated on a reservations-only basis (at a $20 per person additional charge). The Dutch influence shines in the special Chocolate Extravaganza Late Show midnight buffet. Room service is offered on a 24-hour basis.

Entertainment includes fairly lavish productions complete with lasers and fancy costumes. Activities are plentiful and may include seminars, dance lessons, food demonstrations, bingo, deck games, galley tours, and nighttime country-western and Fabulous '50s parties.

Most of HAL's Caribbean and many of its Panama Canal cruises include a call at the line's private Bahamas island, the 2,400-acre **Half Moon Cay,** which offers a white-sand beach, a Spanish fort-style welcome center, a coral reef for snorkeling, a food pavilion, a water sports center, and various shopping venues.

Itineraries

Showing a marked tilt toward closer-to-home cruise destinations in the post 9/11, Iraq War environment, Holland America's main markets in 2005 include Alaska, where it has an impressive seven ships for the summer season, and the Caribbean, where it plans to operate eight vessels (most of them on a seasonal basis) including the *Zuiderdam*, which stays there all year-round. However, the line has shown some confidence in the market for Europe by scheduling three ships there for parts of 2005. The operative words are "flexibility in scheduling." The Seattle-based line doesn't hesitate to reposition ships elsewhere should the demand for Europe prove slow to develop. The line is also represented in South America, Antarctica, the Panama Canal, Mexico, Hawaii, Asia, and the South Pacific.

The *Prinsendam* begins 2005 with a 16-day positioning cruise from Fort Lauderdale to Los Angeles, followed by a 100-day world cruise by way of Hawaii, the South Pacific, Australia and New Zealand, Asia, the Mideast, the Mediterranean, and ending in New York. The ship moves to the Mediterranean for the summer and fall seasons. The *Amsterdam* does South America/Antarctica cruises in the winter and spring and 7-day Alaskan cruises (from Seattle) in the summer. *Maasdam* does alternating 10- and 11-day Caribbean rotation in the winter and spring and 7-day New England/Canada cruises in the summer and fall (between Boston and Montreal). *Oosterdam* begins 2005 with a 7-day eastern Caribbean cruise out of Fort Lauderdale followed by a 15-day Panama Canal sailing to San Diego, where it enters a 7-day Mexican Riviera rotation. In the summer, the ship moves north to Alaska (from Seattle) and ends the year back in Mexico service. *Rotterdam* does 10-day Caribbean/Panama Canal cruises in the winter and moves to the Mediterranean for the spring through fall seasons, ending 2005 with a 17-day cruise from Lisbon to Rio de Janeiro and two South America/Antarctic voyages at the end of the year. *Ryndam* does 10-day Mexico cruises (out of San Diego) in winter, spring, and fall and 7-day Alaskan cruises in summer. *Statendam* has a winter, spring, and fall schedule of 15- and 16-day Hawaiian cruises out of San Diego and 7-day Alaskan sailings in the summer (out of Vancouver). *Veendam* does 7- to 12-day Caribbean cruises in the winter and spring and 7-day Alaskan trips in the summer. *Volendam* (see Figure 14-5) does 7-day alternating eastern and western Caribbean cruises (out of Port Canaveral) in the winter and spring and 7-day Alaskan sailings in the summer. *Zuiderdam* does 4- and 7-day eastern and western Caribbean cruises year-round. It also does 4- and 7-day eastern and western Caribbean cruises in winter, spring, and fall and 7-day Alaskan cruises in summer. *Westerdam*, in HAL service since last spring, spends winter and spring in the Caribbean (7-day cruises out of Fort Lauderdale) and the summer in 7-, 10-, 12-, and 14-day service in the Mediterranean, North Cape, the Baltic, and in European Capitals.

(Photo: Holland America Line)

Figure 14-5: The *Volendam*

Outstanding features

After years of operating a "no tipping required" policy, which some passengers found a little bit confusing, HAL has instituted new rules. The line now expects you to tip cabin stewards, waiters, and the like on all its ships. All HAL vessels have self-service Laundromats. Each passenger gets a free canvas tote bag with the HAL logo. The line offers Big band theme cruises. Gentlemen hosts are brought on sailings of 14 days or more (and on all big band theme cruises) to socialize with single female passengers who want company. The line's Passport to Fitness program offers prizes to passengers who participate in sports and fitness activities. The line was one of the pioneers of Alaskan cruising and has developed the state's most extensive cruisetour (land) operation, including tours to the little-visited **Kluane National Park** in Canada — a program that it plans to extend this year. Alaskan sailings feature a Native Alaskan artist in residence, and each day a Huna tribal member is on board along with a National Park Service lecturer to offer commentary. Caribbean cruises visit **Half Moon Cay**, the line's private island, where you can also get married if you like (wedding packages are offered). Golf programs are available in the Caribbean and Mexico. Wheelchair-accessible tenders are available on all the ships. The line also offers Internet cafes fleet-wide. You can book shore excursions in advance online.

Super deals

HAL offers early-booking discounts of up to 65 percent, last-minute deals, low rates for third and fourth passengers who share a cabin with two full-fare passengers, flat-rate children's fares, and special past-passenger deals. You can also take part in the guaranteed share program for non-smoking singles (of the same sex), guaranteed cabin category program (the cruise line picks the cabin), and occasional free airfare offers. For more rates from Holland America, check out Table 14-9.

Table 14-9	Holland America Rates		
Ship	*Inside*	*Outside*	*Suites*
Amsterdam [a]	$3,207–$3,706	$3,826–$4,302	$5,382–$11,751
Maasdam [b]	$1,959–$2,177	$2,329–$2,677	$3,504–$12,914
Oosterdam [c]	$1,789–$1,969	$2,199–$3,079	$5,919–$14,119
Prinsendam [d]	$4,393–$4,772	$4,940–$6,820	$9,018–$30,720
Rotterdam V [e]	$2,578–$2,915	$2,999–$3,406	$4,249–$16,663
Ryndam [f]	$2,306–$2,665	$2,869–$3,213	$4,025–$10,565
Statendam [g]	$4,434–$4,950	$5,299–$5,757	$8,281–$23,274
Veendam [c]	$1,369–$1,519	$1,624–$1,864	$2,224–$8,124
Volendam [b]	$1,959–$2,177	$2,329–$2,677	$3,504–$12,914
Westerdam [h]	$3,032–$3,431	$3,456–$4,356	$7,167–$18,504
Zaandam [b]	$1,369–$1,519	$1,624–$1,864	$2,224–$8,124
Zuiderdam [c]	$1,789–$1,969	$2,199–$3,079	$5,919–$14,119

[a] For 12-day South American sailings
[b] For 10-day Caribbean sailings
[c] For 7-day Caribbean sailings
[d] For 14-day Mediterranean/Aegean sailings
[e] For 9-day Western Mediterranean sailings
[f] For 10-day Mexico sailings
[g] For 16-day Hawaii sailings
[h] For 10-day Mediterranean/Aegean sailings

Fleet facts

The *Statendam, Maasdam, Ryndam,* and *Veendam* are modern midsize ships built with the same design that features soaring atriums and wonderful viewing lounges. The flagship *Rotterdam VI* is a bigger vessel that sets new standards for ship design, although the basic layout of its public rooms is similar to that on the *Statendam* and its series of sister ships. The *Volendam* and *Zaandam,* which debuted in 1999 and 2000, respectively, combine features of both the *Statendam*-class and *Rotterdam VI.* The *Volendam* boasts a floral theme, and the *Zaandam* has a music theme that includes a pipe organ in the atrium and a baby-boomer collection of guitars autographed by Iggy Pop, the *Rolling Stones*, and *Queen*, as well as a saxophone that President Clinton played in Holland.

The *Amsterdam* is a sister ship to the *Rotterdam VI* and is the first ship in the fleet to feature a high-tech, environmentally friendly propulsion system that provides a smoother ride than the usual rumbling diesels. The *Amsterdam* and *Rotterdam VI* both offer enhanced spa and children's facilities, more cabins with verandas, Internet cafes, and alternative dining restaurants. The *Prinsendam*, which joined the fleet in 2002, operated for the luxury line Seabourn (also a Carnival Corporation company) and is akin to a floating Ritz-Carlton. Standout features include big, fancy suites for passengers at the upper-end. About 90 percent of the ship's cabins have ocean views (with nearly 40 percent offering private verandas). Holland America introduced its biggest ship ever in September of 2002: the 85,000-ton, 1,848-passenger *Zuiderdam,* which was later joined by the virtually identical *Oosterdam.* HAL designated these ships as Vista-class liners, identifying them as the line's largest vessels with the highest capacity. A third, the *Westerdam* (and the third ship in the line's history to have that name), joined the fleet in 2004; 80 percent of its cabins boast private verandas. All these ships have exterior elevators on the port and starboard sides for panoramic ocean views. The vessels also have 24-hour cafes and the largest spas in the company's fleet.

Missing from the HAL fleet this year is the *Noordam*. The ship — the third ever to bear that name — was built in 1984 and, as one of Holland America's senior citizens, has been sold to British tour operator Thomson Holidays, who plans operate it in Europe as the *Thomson Celebration*. Not to worry, however. By January 2006, another Noordam, a Vista-class vessel now under construction in Italy, will enter service. Despite the unusually large size (by HAL standards) of the Vista-class ships, on-board offerings are still distinctively Holland America. Table 14-10 shows the current fleet specifications.

Table 14-10   Holland America Fleet Specifications

Ship	Year Built	Passengers	Crew	Total Cabins	Tonnage	Length in Feet
Amsterdam	2000	1,380	647	690	61,000	780
Maasdam	1993	1,266	557	633	55,000	720
Oosterdam	2003	1,848	800	924	85,000	951
Prinsendam	1988	794	428	394	38,000	669
Rotterdam VI	1997	1,316	593	658	60,000	780
Ryndam	1994	1,258	557	629	55,000	720
Statendam	1993	1,258	557	629	55,000	720
Veendam	1996	1,266	557	629	55,000	780

(continued)

Table 14-10 *(continued)*

Ship	Year Built	Passengers	Crew	Total Cabins	Tonnage	Length in Feet
Volendam	1999	1,440	647	720	60,100	780
Westerdam	2004	1,848	800	924	85,000	951
Zaandam	2000	1,440	647	720	61,000	780
Zuiderdam	2002	1,848	800	924	85,000	951

Norwegian Cruise Line

7665 Corporate Center Dr., Miami, FL 33126; ☎ *800-327-7030;* www.ncl.com

> ✔ **Type of cruise:** Family, party, resort
>
> ✔ **Ship size/style:** Mixed bag of older and modern midsize ships and megaships

Norwegian Cruise Line (NCL) is a cruise company that has changed dramatically over the past several years, starting as an almost budget-oriented line and transforming into one of the more innovative players in the industry today. After several years spent claiming (some say defending) that its fleet of older, midsize, 40,000-ton ships offered a more personal experience, the line moved into the megaship age in 1999 with the 80,000-ton flagship *Norwegian Sky*, recently renamed *Pride of Aloha* (see Figure 14-6). The line subsequently introduced sister ship *Norwegian Sun* and the even larger, 91,000-ton siblings *Norwegian Star* and *Norwegian Dawn*. During that period, the ownership of the line changed hands as well, with Star Cruises of Malaysia making the purchase, creating the fourth largest cruise company in the world. Innovation followed quickly with the introduction of Freestyle Cruising, which offers a more casual experience with open-seating, restaurant-style dining and a resort-casual dress code (and an occasional optional formal night thrown in for good measure). The idea was to shake off the stuffiness of traditional cruising and make the experience more like a land-based resort vacation. The experiment has worked, because stuffy it ain't: Look no further than *Norwegian Dawn*'s salsa bands and brightly painted hull for proof. The line is also innovative in its itineraries, promoting Homeland Cruising options that depart not only from traditional ports like Miami, Port Canaveral, and San Juan, but also from Baltimore, Boston, New Orleans, New York, Philadelphia, and Houston, allowing more people to drive to the ship rather than fly.

High-energy folks, take note: You always have something to do aboard NCL's activity-packed ships. Onboard entertainment includes excellent (and, surprise, inventive) Broadway-style musical productions themed on Miami Latin culture and "Bollywood" Indian films. Name performers are also occasionally aboard for short stints. Recreational and fitness programs are well thought out, as are kids' programs such as Circus at Sea — kids learn circus acts and later stage a performance for their parents. The onboard atmosphere is informal and upbeat, with passengers mostly under 50 (slightly older in Europe) and a good many families. All the ships have casinos except the *Norwegian Star,* which operates in Hawaiian waters where gambling is illegal (the extra space is used for gift shops).

(Photo: Norwegian Cruise Line)

Figure 14-6: The *Pride of Aloha*

The line's cuisine was never a high point but has improved and gets big, big points for variety, providing up to eight different sit-down restaurants on the newest ships (including Italian, Asian, sushi, French, steakhouse, and Tex-Mex options), in addition to snack and sandwich options, ice cream parlors, and an occasional chocoholic midnight buffet. The older vessels have two main restaurants and the **Le Bistro** alternative restaurant, serving nouvelle French cuisine, plus snacking options. Dining Freestyle means you can eat at any of the restaurants within a specified period, wandering in just like you walk into a shoreside restaurant (with reservations at the fancier ones) and sitting wherever you like. Bye-bye assigned seating and night-after-night dinner companions, unless you *choose* to dine with the same folks, of course. Dress codes are also eliminated. As aboard most lines, the smaller, finer restaurants carry a cover charge that ranges from $10 to $17.50. Service is about what you find on the other mainstream lines — generally good.

All the ships feature spas run by **Mandara**, a company representing part of the Steiner ship-spa empire. They offer both Eastern- and Western-influenced treatments, with the spa facilities on the newest ships really standing out in the style department. All the vessels also offer sports bars, with ESPN coverage of games and the all-news channel CNN, and extensive sports and fitness facilities, including full-size basketball courts.

In May 2003, NCL announced the formation of a new U.S.-flagged brand, NCL America, for inter-island Hawaiian cruising. Alas, the project has yet to materialize in the intended form. The first of this brand of ships, the 2,146-passenger *Pride of America*, which was to enter service last summer, toppled on its side in 36 feet of water while under construction in Germany and was so extensively damaged that it remains unsailable. To take its place, the *Norwegian Sky* was reflagged and renamed *Pride of Aloha* and began Hawaiian cruises last July 4 (how's that for a patriotic date?). From the regular NCL fleet, *Norwegian Star* also plans to cruise in Hawaii throughout the winter and spring of 2005 on itineraries that include four Hawaiian islands and a call at tiny **Fanning Island** in Micronesia. The ship stops at this little-known dot in the vast Pacific Ocean because non U.S.-flagged ships must include a foreign port in their Hawaiian itineraries. From there, the *Star* makes its way to Alaska for the summer (filling in for the renamed *Norwegian Sky*) out of Seattle and then to the Mexican Riviera in the fall. *Norwegian Wind* sails 10- and 11-day Hawaiian cruises that include Fanning Island all year long. (In case we haven't made it obvious, NCL hopes to own the Hawaiian market.)

One great name that you don't see around this year is the *Norway*. The ship, which suffered extensive damage and some fatalities in a tragic boiler room explosion in May 2003 (also in Germany), has been sold for non-cruise uses and can never again carry passengers from the United States.

Itineraries

The line put a new emphasis on homeland cruising starting in 2002, positioning its vessels to depart from 13 ports in the United States and Canada. *Norwegian Dawn* sails 7-, 10-, and 11-day cruises year-round from New York, heading south and calling — depending on the cruise you choose — at such ports as Miami, Port Canaveral, Nassau (Bahamas), Bridgetown (Barbados), Tortola (BVI), Roseau (Dominica), and NCL's private island, **Great Stirrup Cay**. *Norwegian Star* sails in Hawaii during the winter and spring and spends the summer in Alaska (out of Seattle) and the fall in the Mexican Riviera (from Los Angeles). *Norwegian Sun* and *Norwegian Spirit* (formerly the *SuperStar Leo*) both sail 7-day Alaskan cruises in summer. The former does 5- and 9-day Caribbean voyages at other times and the latter stays in 7-day Caribbean rotation out of both New Orleans and Miami. Throughout the year, *Pride of Aloha* (formerly *Norwegian Sky*) does 7-day Hawaiian cruises out of Honolulu. *Norwegian Wind* does 10- and 11-day Hawaiian cruises year-round. *Norwegian Majesty* sails 7-day Bermuda cruises (from Boston) in spring and summer and 7-day western Caribbean cruises (from Charleston, South Carolina) in winter and fall. *Norwegian Sea* sails 7-day "Texaribbean" cruises (from Houston) through the spring when it transfers from the NCL fleet to the fleet of the parent company, Star Cruises. *Norwegian Dream* sails 10- and 11-day Alaskan cruises in summer from Seattle and 7-day Caribbean cruises out of New Orleans and Houston at other times. *Norwegian Crown* sails 7-day Bermuda cruises from New York and Philadelphia in the spring, summer, and fall and 14-day South American cruises in the winter. Most of the ships also offer Panama Canal and other repositioning itineraries between their cruising regions. Many Caribbean itineraries visit the line's private Bahamian island, Great Stirrup Cay.

Outstanding features

Each ship has multiple dining venues (*Norwegian Star* and *Norwegian Dawn* each have an impressive ten restaurants). The line automatically adds gratuities to your shipboard account ($10 per person, per day). Honeymoon packages and Internet cafes are available on all ships. If you're not in a hurry, the ships offer Freestyle disembarkation, allowing you to have a leisurely breakfast and disembark up until about 10 a.m. rather than hustling you off early, as most lines do.

Super deals

NCL offers early-booking discounts of up to 60 percent (plus good deals on unfilled cabins as sailing dates get close). The line also offers value-season rates, reduced rates for third and fourth passengers who share a cabin with two full-fare passengers, limited-time cabin upgrades, and special two-for-one promotions on some cruises. See Table 14-11 for more NCL rates.

Table 14-11	Norwegian Cruise Line Rates		
Ship	**Inside**	**Outside**	**Suites**
Norwegian Crown [a]	$1,800–$1,950	$1,975–$2,025	$2,615–$5,185
Norwegian Dawn [b]	$1,389–$1,469	$1,589–$1,889	$2,199–$16,819
Norwegian Dream [c]	$1,602–$1,732	$1,882–$2,892	$3,512–$4,372
Norwegian Majesty [d]	$904–$1,154	$1,264–$1,399	$4,104
Norwegian Sea [e]	$616–$691	$716–$896	$1,606–$1,986
Norwegian Spirit [f]	$994–$1,174	$1,254–$1,814	$2,574–$3,764
Norwegian Star [f]	$1,004–$1,114	$1,264–$1,634	$1,844–$13,674
Norwegian Sun [f]	$944–$1,114	$1,204–$1,764	$2,524–$3,714
Norwegian Wind [g]	$1,153–$1,199	$1,225–$1,921	$2,229–$3,109
Pride of Aloha [h]	$1,265–$1,442	$2,180–$2,304	$3,957–$5,040

[a] For 12-day Canada/New England sailings
[b] For 11-day Caribbean sailings
[c] For 11-day Alaska sailings
[d] For 7-day Bermuda sailings
[e] For 7-day Texaribbean sailings
[f] For 7-day Alaska sailings
[g] For 10-day Hawaii sailings
[h] For 7-day Hawaii sailings

Fleet facts

The 91,740-ton, 2,224-passenger *Norwegian Dawn* is a knockout, with a very Miami-esque feel. It offers ten restaurants; balconies on 70 percent of its outside cabins (with nifty tea/coffeemakers inside); bathrooms with separate toilet compartments; and, perched up on the top of the ship, outrageously large Garden Villa suites that sprawl out across 5,350 square feet and feature private gardens with hot tubs, separate living rooms, full kitchens, multiple bedrooms with mind-blowing bathrooms, and private butler service. (Amazing what $16,000 to $18,000 a week buys.) *Dawn's* older sister, *Norwegian Star,* debuted in late 2001 with basically the same layout and amenities.

The 77,104-ton, 2,002-passenger *Norwegian Sky* debuted in 1999 and offers such niceties as a glass-domed mid-ship atrium, sports bar, Internet cafe, champagne bar, wine bar, cigar club, and a cabaret lounge with what it bills as the longest bar at sea. (We forgot a ruler when we were aboard, so we can't confirm that.) Now, after an extensive refurbishment, the newly renamed *Pride of Aloha* (a sister ship of the 2001-launched *Norwegian Sun)* is tackling a new assignment in the Hawaiian Islands.

The *Norwegian Sea* is not a glitzy ship, but it has its loyal followers. Ditto for the *Norwegian Majesty, Norwegian Dream,* and *Norwegian Wind*, older vessels that NCL enlarged and refreshed in 1998 and 1999. *Norwegian Crown* has a very bright, metallic, 1980s design. The classic *Norway* (formerly the *SS France*) had a loyal following that misses the ship, due to its demise after suffering an accident in Germany. Although not the most modern kids on the block, the ships in this paragraph all have what it takes to give you an enjoyable vacation at sea. But beware: Cabins on some of the older ships tend to be small. Table 14-12 shows the current fleet specifications.

Table 14-12		Norwegian Fleet Specifications				
Ship	*Year Built*	*Passengers*	*Crew*	*Total Cabins*	*Tonnage*	*Length in Feet*
Norwegian Crown	1988	1,062	470	531	34,250	614
Norwegian Dawn	2002	2,224	1,318	1,120	91,740	965
Norwegian Dream	1992	1,748	614	874	50,760	754
Norwegian Majesty	1992	1,462	570	731	40,876	680
Norwegian Sea	1988	1,518	630	759	42,000	700
Norwegian Spirit	1999	1,996	920	1,120	76,800	879
Norwegian Star	2001	2,240	1,100	1,120	91,000	965

Ship	Year Built	Passengers	Crew	Total Cabins	Tonnage	Length in Feet
Norwegian Sun	2001	2,002	968	1,001	77,104	853
Norwegian Wind	1993	1,748	700	874	50,764	754
Pride of Aloha	1999	2,002	750	1,001	77,104	853

Oceania Cruises

8120 NW 53rd St., Miami, FL 33166; ☎ *800-531-5658;* www.oceaniacruises.com

> ✔ **Type of Cruise:** Upper premium, country club casual, gourmet
>
> ✔ **Ship size/style:** Midsize, classy

Oceania is a relatively new entrant into the industry after taking two of the midsize ships from the now-defunct Renaissance Cruises and beautifully refurbishing them into *Oceania Regatta* (see Figure 14-7), launched in 2003, and *Oceania Insignia,* launched in 2004. Headed up by industry veteran Joe Watters and Renaissance's former President, Frank Del Rio, the line made an immediate impact in terms of quality product delivery, highlighted by superb dining after the introduction of two outstanding alternative restaurants. A third ship, *Oceania Nautica,* joins the fleet in May 2005.

Decor is lovely, with a sort of English manor look: very traditional looking in the public areas with plenty of seating areas on large comfy chairs and sofas. Even the architecture of the stairways is different, with New Orleans-looking grillwork painted in gold and black. The overall color-scheme varies, with a lot of earth tones in certain rooms and brighter, bolder colors, such as blues and golds, in others. You see little or no glitz, and the overall takeaway is very classy.

The ships' libraries are the loveliest at sea, with comfy seating, excellent lighting, and an extensive selection of books. The ships have no real showroom, but the **Regatta Lounge**, where the line presents evening entertainment, has plenty of tables and chairs for relaxed seating and many high-top tables and chairs in the back areas — thus viewing is no problem. The open seating **Grand Dining Room** has plenty of tables for twos, fours, and larger groups.

The two alternative restaurants, **Toscana** and **Polo Grill** (about 90 seats apiece; reservations are needed for both), are appropriate for the style of food and each has a bar of its own. You don't feel like you're on a cruise ship; they appear just as attractive as shore-based upscale restaurants. The casual restaurant, **Terrace Café,** is spacious (110 seats) and doesn't have any of the cafeteria look that can be so depressing. When they set up the outside area of Terrace Café for the evening alternative dining, Tapas on the Terrace, the staff adds glass jars with candlelight and puts nicely done slipcovers on the chairs to create a whole new look.

The public Internet services are very good and somewhat expensive. About 20 computers are in the Oceania@Sea room, which is open for limited hours (should be longer) and closed to the regular guests when the ships provide computer classes. Two more are available 24/7 in the library. The casino is nicely sized for this ship and has slots, blackjack, and roulette. Spa services (all the usual) and fitness equipment (plenty of variety and quantity; a good schedule of organized fitness programs) are featured in nice rooms, with the outside spa pool and seating area providing a nice touch.

Largely because of the line's ship size, Oceania doesn't fit in any preconceived niche. Service is professional yet friendly (and fairly consistent, even with 47 nationalities represented among the 400 or so crewmembers). And the ships, at only 30,200 GRT (see Chapter 13 for more GRT discussion), are intimate, not floating cities. The ships are perfect for couples of all ages (well, mid-40s and up) but not for kids or partying singles.

(Photo: Oceania Cruises)

Figure 14-7: The *Regatta*

Oceania doesn't add service gratuities to the cruise fare. It does, however, automatically add a tip of 18 percent to the bill in the bars on each ship.

Itineraries

Oceania offers its guests a wide variety of sailings, with all voyages cruising 10-days or longer. The port content and ratio of days at sea to ports are excellent. *Insignia* starts 2005 with a series of South American cruises all the way around the horn. *Regatta* starts the year with Trans-canal and Caribbean cruises that also hit excellent Central American and Mexican ports along the way. All three ships in the fleet, after the *Nautica* makes its debut in May 2005, plan to sail all over Europe from spring through early November, concentrating in the Baltic and Mediterranean. The St. Petersburg 2-night call is excellent, as it allows guests to do the all-day excursion to Moscow. The line offers pre- and post-cruise hotel nights at all its ports of embarkation/disembarkation.

Outstanding features

In the cabins, the mattresses are delightfully firm and the 350-thread count Egyptian linens, plush comforter/silk-cut duvet, and four fluffy down pillows are exceptionally luxurious. The alternative restaurants are as good a pair as you can find on any ship at sea.

Super deals

Check out the early booking fares, along with special 2-for-1 deals, sometimes with airline discounts thrown in. Check out the line's Web site for details. Table 14-13 presents a complete rate chart.

Table 14-13	Oceania Rates		
Ship	*Inside*	*Outside*	*Suites*
Insignia	$3,998–$5,198	$4,398–$7,198	$7,198–$15,998
Regatta	$3,998–$5,198	$4,398–$7,198	$7,198–$15,998

Fleet facts

The fleet's two sister ships are quite new, and the refurbishment project that Oceania put them through before they became Oceania vessels was quite well done (you can presumably say the same in advance for the third ship, *Nautica*).

Of the 342 staterooms, 280 are essentially the same size (150 to 165 square feet). Of these, 170 have balconies, bringing the total room size up to 216 square feet. All the 62 larger penthouses and suites have balconies and range from 322 square feet to just less than 1000. The regular room, although below the size you may expect in this category, is very comfortable. The woods are dark, but the many mirrors make the room seem larger than it is. You have plenty of drawer and closet space. Lighting is a bit dark. Broadcast options are limited (no VCR or DVD), with an on-demand pay movie system. The bathroom is small, but you have enough shelf and counter space. The amenities are adequate, but the ships supply no upscale touches such as cotton balls or q-tips. Table 14-14 shows the current fleet specifications.

Table 14-14	Oceania Fleet Specifications					
Ship	*Year Built*	*Passengers*	*Crew*	*Total Cabins*	*Tonnage*	*Length in Feet*
Insignia	1998	684	400	342	30,200	594
Regatta	1998	684	400	342	30,200	594

Princess Cruises

24305 Town Center Dr., Santa Clarita, CA 91355; ☎ *800-PRINCESS;* www.princess.com

- ✔ **Type of cruise:** Family, resort, romantic
- ✔ **Ship size/style:** Modern, stylish megaships with a couple of small-ish and midsize, traditional-style ships thrown in for good measure

Princess has moved away from its *Love Boat* marketing as it tries to attract the younger audience who may not remember the old television series about the romance of life at sea. In fact, the real-life cruise line that served as a floating set for the TV show is one of the biggest and boldest cruise lines in the world today. Now owned by Carnival Corp. of Miami, Princess is both dynamic and diverse — a company able to please a wide variety of passengers, with ships ranging in size from 20,000 tons and carrying fewer than 700 passengers to 116,000 tons and carrying 3,100. All Princess vessels produced after the *Grand Princess* (see Figure 14-8), which debuted in 1998 as the then-largest ship afloat (Royal Caribbean's humungous *Voyager of the Seas* later beat it out), are show-stoppers that offer huge numbers of cabins with verandas. Princess ships also feature multiple show lounges with different after-dinner entertainment and several dining venues, which may include steakhouses or restaurants that serve Southwestern, Asian, Italian, or New Orleans cuisines. The *Island Princess* debuted in 2003 and three other ships — the *Diamond, Caribbean,* and *Sapphire Princesses* — joined the fleet just last year. This year, for the first time in ages, no new ship is set to join the Princess fleet. A massive megaship (dubbed internally as *Caribbean II)* is now under construction and should be ready early in 2006.

But even if no new build begins service this year, you can nevertheless see a change in the fleet. Princess pulled a switcheroo with its sister company, P&O Cruises of London, by swapping the *Royal Princess* for P&O's *Adonia.* The move represents something of a return for the Adonia. The 1,950-passenger vessel was built for Princess (as the *Sea Princess)* in 1998 and now regains its former name. P&O plans to extensively refurbish and rename the 1,200-passenger *Royal Princess.* A word of tribute to the departing *Royal* is in order here. The elegant (an overworked word, but we can really say nothing more appropriate) vessel, which entered service in 1984, was the first cruise ship to have all outside rooms, and it pioneered the concept of large numbers of stateroom verandas. Until then, ships tended to have private verandas in only a handful of their very best accommodations. *Royal Princess* changed all that. After its arrival, every new build for Princess and virtually every other line has been equipped with huge numbers of balcony rooms — sometimes as many as three-quarters of all the rooms on board.

(Photo: Princess Cruises)

Figure 14-8: The *Grand Princess*

Princess groups ships into three classes: the Grand Class (the *Grand, Diamond, Sapphire, Caribbean, Golden,* and *Star Princesses*), the Sun Class (*Sun, Dawn, Sea, Coral,* and *Island Princesses*), and the Royal Class (the *Royal* — until its departure, probably in the spring — *Pacific, Regal,* and *Tahitian Princesses*).

Although its megaships have megaresort facilities, Princess's vessels still manage to offer the kind of intimate spaces you can find on smaller vessels, including plush, quiet bars. To create a cozier feel in the dining rooms on the bigger ships, for instance, the line created two separate facilities, identical in every way and serving the same food, thus avoiding the giant spaces you find on some other ships. Princess built as many as five other restaurants on its latest ships. (One of the factors that led to the release of *Royal Princess* was that, because it's a smaller, older ship, Princess couldn't install as many alternative dining facilities as guests have come to expect.)

In general, decor on Princess ships is stylish and moderately upscale, but the line presents it in a conservative way, without the usual glitz. Princess ships are showcases for impressive art collections that include works by David Hockney, Helen Frankenthaler, Frank Stella, Andy Warhol, and Robert Motherwell. And Princess tends to decorate with plenty of foliage.

Princess devotes increasing attention to its onboard entertainment, with elaborate stage shows and cabaret acts along with the usual casinos and discos.

The line's cuisine doesn't match the level offered by lines such as Celebrity, but it still rises above many mass-market lines. You can find healthy dining and vegetarian options on the menus. The pizza served at the ships' pizzerias is exceptionally good, and the pastas, some prepared tableside, are outstanding. Dollops of caviar appear at the captains' parties and at formal nights, and the wine cellar on each ship stocks at least 10,000 bottles. Like other lines, including Norwegian Cruise Line and Carnival, Princess offers a more flexible restaurant option called Personal Choice Dining. Under this program, you can choose to have dinner in the traditional cruise ship style (at a set time) or restaurant-style (anytime between 5:30 p.m. and midnight). You select which option you prefer before your trip (although you may be able to switch on board). The *Sun, Dawn,* and *Sea* offer reservations-recommended steakhouses on Caribbean sailings (for a $7 cover charge), and some of the bigger ships have alternative Italian (for a $20 cover charge) and Southwestern ($8 cover charge, which includes a free margarita) dining venues. The *Coral Princess* offers a New Orleans-style restaurant. On the new *Diamond, Sapphire,* and *Caribbean Princesses* you can dine at four (count 'em, four) additional free restaurants that serve steak, Italian, Asian, and southwestern U.S. food. And, adding to the variety offered, diners in any one of those restaurants can also choose off the menu from the main dining rooms.

Service on Princess ships is gracious and relaxed. Cabins are spacious, especially on the newer ships, and offer niceties that include terrycloth bathrobes, fruit baskets, and chocolates on your pillow at night.

Activities include paddle tennis, virtual-reality golf, bingo, dance classes, cooking classes, lectures, bridge tournaments, and audience-participation shows, and all the ships have good libraries. In the summer of 1993, the line introduced an "edutainment" program known as ScholarShip at Sea, which permits passengers to discover more about photography, computers, estate planning, the stock market, and — a first for the cruise industry — pottery. Guests are encouraged to create their own art pieces that they fire in a special pottery kiln installed on board for the activity. If the activity doesn't produce any timeless works of art, it at least entertains the passengers and leaves them knowing more than they did before.

Passengers are a varied group and include couples, honeymooners, and singles. Singles should note, however, that despite the line's *Love Boat* image, Princess cruises are hardly for swingers. Passengers tend to be 45-plus and are generally younger on Caribbean sailings than on, say, Alaskan sailings. The line's newer ships, the *Sun* and those thereafter, attract more kids and teens than others, particularly on Caribbean itineraries. They have special facilities for both kids and teens and recently upgraded the kids' program. The line has lessened its earlier restrictions on infants: Babies can now travel on all itineraries at six months of age, except for select exotic destinations such as Asia, South America, and Africa/India.

Princess's well-organized shore excursions are among the best in the industry and offer great variety. The line is a major player in the Alaskan market, offering cruisetours that combine land tours with a cruise. The line owns its own sightseeing trains and five Alaskan hotels, including the spectacular **Mt. McKinley Princess Wilderness Lodge** on the edge of Denali National Park and the **Copper River Princess Wilderness Lodge** alongside Wrangell/St. Elias National Park.

Itineraries

Not surprisingly, given the size of its fleet — which stands at 14 mostly huge ships this year — Princess plans to sail in every corner of the globe in 2005. One of the company's main markets has long been Alaska (where it wants to station most of its biggest ships and the greatest numbers of berths in the industry this summer), but the line has expanded in a big way into the Caribbean as well, in which it plans to deploy four ships, including — on a year-round basis — its biggest vessel yet, the *Caribbean Princess*, which entered service in April of last year. And the line will sail four ships in Europe for the summer of 2005. Princess also wants a presence in markets as diverse as New England/Canada, the Panama Canal, the South Pacific, French Polynesia, Australia, and Asia.

Caribbean Princess works in a schedule of alternating 7-day Eastern and Western Caribbean cruises throughout the year — a sailing pattern that it began upon its arrival in the fleet last year. *Grand Princess* is in the Western Caribbean through the spring and then spends the rest of the year in the Mediterranean. *Sea Princess* takes over the *Royal's* summer Mediterranean/North Cape schedule when the two ships switch owners in late spring. Until that time, you can find the *Royal* in its scheduled South America service for Princess. *Golden Princess* sails 7-day Southern Caribbean cruises in the winter and spring, moves to Europe in the summer for 10-day Western Europe/Britain voyages, and spends the fall in New England/Canada. *Dawn Princess* is one of the line's Caribbean representatives, sailing there in the winter, spring, and fall in 10-day Southern and Western cruise rotations and moving to Alaska in the summer months for 7-day Gulf cruises. *Sun Princess* sails 10-day Caribbean cruises in winter, spring, and fall and 7-day Alaskan cruises in summer. *Regal Princess* does 12- to 18-day South America and Antarctic cruises in the winter, spring, and fall and 10-day Alaskan (from San Francisco) cruises in the summer. *Star Princess* does 10-day Mediterranean and 12-day Greek Isles sailings in spring and summer and then sets sail for the Caribbean. *Sapphire Princess* sails in Asia and the South Pacific for most of the year and spends the summer in Alaska. *Diamond Princess* sails 7-day Mexican Riviera cruises in spring, 7-day Alaskan cruises in summer, and 11- to 29-day cruises in Asia and the South Pacific thereafter. *Coral Princess* does 10-day Panama Canal cruises in winter, spring, and fall and 7-day Alaskan cruises in summer. *Island Princess* does 15-day Hawaiian cruises (from Los Angeles) in the spring, fall, and winter and 7-day Alaskan cruises in summer. *Tahitian Princess* cruises in Tahiti throughout the year. *Pacific Princess* does exotic itineraries including the South Pacific, Asia, and Africa year-round.

On eastern and western Caribbean cruises, Princess ships stop at the line's own private island, **Princess Cay**, off the southwestern coast of Eleuthera in the Bahamas. Passengers can enjoy fun in the sun with beach picnics and water sports activities.

Outstanding features

Worried about paying for your trip? How about taking out a cruise loan? The Princess Cruise Financing Program offers its customers special loans, repayable in 24, 36, or 48 months. The line approves the loan on an instant basis after you review your credit information on the phone with the participating bank. It comes with rates that can vary from 14.99 percent to 26.99 percent, depending on your credit history. Call ☎ 800-PRINCESS for details.

You can get married at sea in the wedding chapels on *Grand Princess, Golden Princess, Star Princess, Coral Princess, Island Princess, Diamond Princess,* and *Sapphire Princess.* And your friends back home may be able to watch your nuptials over the Internet thanks to the special Wedding Cam available on some ships.

The line has a Lotus Spa program with Asian-themed decor and treatments. Princess offers a PADI (Professional Association of Diving Instructors) scuba-certification program in the Caribbean. The line allows passengers to book shore excursions in advance of their sailing. All the ships offer Internet access, and the newer ships in the fleet have special AOL-branded Internet cafes. You can pre-book your shore excursions at the line's Web site (www.princess.com). The flexible Personal Choice Dining plan is available on all ships produced after the *Sun Princess — Dawn, Grand, Golden, Star, Crown, Diamond, Caribbean,* and *Sapphire.* The line automatically assesses tips of $10 per person, per day.

Smoking is banned in the main dining and other food service areas, as well as in the show areas of all ships. The medical centers on the Grand-class ships have tele-medicine facilities that allow shipboard doctors to link to land-based hospitals for consultations.

Super deals

Princess offers discounts of up to 50 percent (and sometimes more) for booking early. The line also offers low fares for third and fourth passengers who share a cabin with two full-fare passengers. Table 14-15 offers more info on Princess rates.

Table 14-15	Princess Rates		
Ship	*Inside*	*Outside*	*Suites*
Caribbean Princess [a]	$1,209–$1,349	$1,579–$1,959	$1,889–$3,549
Coral Princess [b]	$1,479–$1,569	$1,579–$1,919	$1,939–$3,249
Dawn Princess [b]	$1,159–$1,429	$1,499–$1,939	$2,399–$3,030
Diamond Princess [b]	$1,289–$1,489	$1,619–$2,124	$2,249–$4,369

Ship	Inside	Outside	Suites
Golden Princess [c]	$1,445–$1,655	$1,670–$2,120	$2,145–$4,595
Grand Princess [d]	$3,885–$4,265	$4,365–$5,065	$5,440–$9,415
Island Princess [b]	$1,479–$1,569	$1,579–$1,919	$1,939–$3,249
Pacific Princess [e]	$2,895–$3,045	$3,070–$3,745	$4,070–$4,720
Regal Princess [f]	$3,745–$3,945	$4,020–$4,845	$4,995–$5,895
Royal Princess [g]	N/A	$2,390–$3,565	$4,490–$9,045
Sapphire Princess [h]	$2,645–$2,895	$2,920–$3,885	$4,335–$7,035
Sea Princess [i]	$1,399–$1,599	$1,699–$2,189	$2,389–$3,739
Star Princess [j]	$2,685–$3,715	$3,815–$4,515	$4,890–$8,865
Sun Princess [d]	$1,159–$1,429	$1,499–$1,939	$2,399–$3,030
Tahitian Princess [k]	$2,095–$2,245	$2,295–$2,745	$2,945–$3,595

[a] For 7-day Caribbean sailings
[b] For 7-day Alaska sailings
[c] For 7-day Canada/New England sailings
[d] For 12-day Mediterranean sailings
[e] For 12-day Tahiti/South Pacific sailings
[f] For 18-day South America sailings
[g] For 14-day European Capitals sailings
[h] For 12-day Australia/New Zealand sailings
[i] For 7-day western Mediterranean sailings
[j] For 10-day Scandinavia/Russia sailings
[k] For 10-day Tahiti/South Pacific sailings

Fleet facts

The Grand and Sun Class ships are cutting-edge vessels that provide the latest and greatest abodes, including a large number of cabins with verandas. The biggest ships in the Princess fleet entered service in 2004 — *Diamond Princess* (116,000 tons), with 2,600 passengers, *Sapphire Princess* (113,000 tons), carrying 2,670 passengers, and *Caribbean Princess* (116,000 tons), with a passenger capacity of 3,100.

Designed by Renzo Piano, the same architect who did the Centre Pompidou in Paris, the *Regal Princess* was recently given a multimillion-dollar facelift. The renovation added a 24-hour restaurant and a children's center located on the top deck of the modern, dramatic ship. Table 14-16 shows the current fleet specifications.

Table 14-16	Princess Fleet Specifications					
Ship	**Year Built**	**Passengers**	**Crew**	**Total Cabins**	**Tonnage**	**Length in Feet**
Caribbean Princess	2004	3,100	988	1,550	116,000	951
Coral Princess	2002	1,970	900	987	88,000	964
Diamond Princess	2003	2,670	1,100	1,335	113,000	951
Dawn Princess	1997	1,950	900	975	77,000	856
Golden Princess	2001	2,600	1,100	1,300	109,000	951
Grand Princess	1998	2,600	1,100	1,300	109,000	951
Island Princess	2003	1,970	900	987	88,000	965
Pacific Princess	2002	680	330	340	20,000	594
Regal Princess	1991	1,590	696	795	70,000	811
Royal Princess	1984	1,200	520	600	45,000	757
Sapphire Princess	2004	2,670	1,100	1,335	113,000	951
Sea Princess	1998	1,950	900	975	88,000	960
Star Princess	2002	2,600	1,100	1,300	109,000	951
Sun Princess	1995	1,950	900	975	77,000	856
Tahitian Princess	2002	680	330	340	20,000	594

Royal Caribbean International

1050 Caribbean Way, Miami, FL 33132; ☎ *800-327-6700;* www.royalcaribbean.com

- **Type of cruise:** Family, party, resort, romantic
- **Ship size/style:** Mostly megaships, with a couple of modern mid-size vessels and a couple of absolutely gigantic super-megaships

What kind of cruise line puts a skating rink on a ship? Royal Caribbean. In 1999 this mega-cruise line (number two in fleet size only to Carnival) introduced the *Voyager of the Seas,* shown in Figure 14-9, the largest ship afloat at the time (recently unseated by Cunard's *Queen Mary 2*) and the first to offer interior cabins with views (of its large Royal Promenade shopping, dining, and entertainment street that runs through the center of the ship). Along with sister Voyager-class ships *Explorer of the Seas*, *Adventure of the Seas, Navigator of the Seas*, and *Mariner of the Seas*, the *Voyager* offers more bells, whistles, and innovations than some cruise lines have in their entire fleet.

(Photo: Royal Caribbean International)

Figure 14-9: The *Voyager of the Seas*

Royal Caribbean sells a cruise experience that seems a lot like a land-based resort vacation and that comes off reasonably priced and mass-market oriented. The line supplies enough activities to please almost everyone, except maybe people who hate crowds. The ships are all well run and the product consistent, with an army of service employees who pay attention to the day-to-day details.

The contemporary decor on Royal Caribbean vessels doesn't bang you on the head with glitz like, say, top competitor Carnival. The atmosphere is more subdued, with plenty of glass, greenery, and art throughout (the newer ships have very impressive modern art collections). The ships have outstanding public areas, including elaborate health clubs, spas, large swimming pools (some with retractable roofs), and open sundeck areas. Each also features the line's trademark **Viking Crown Lounge**, an airport control tower-looking observation area located in a circular glass structure on the upper deck (in some cases encircling the smokestack). The line's older ships — *Empress of the Seas* and the so-called Sovereign-class ships: *Sovereign of the Seas, Majesty of the Seas,* and *Monarch of the Seas* — have the smallest cabins in the fleet, but even the newer ships don't lavish you with too much floor space in the cabins. An exception is the Radiance-class fleet — *Radiance of the Seas, Brilliance of the Seas, Jewel of the Seas,* and *Serenade of the Seas* — which have bigger standard cabins than the other ships. A third class of ship, the Vision class — *Vision of the Seas, Splendour of the Seas, Grandeur of the Seas, Rhapsody of the Seas, Enchantment of the Seas,* and *Legend of the Seas* — is smaller than many of the others, with ships in the 70,000 to 80,000 ton range that carry fewer than 2,000 passengers. Nevertheless, you can't mistake them for anything but Royal Caribbean vessels.

The crowd on Royal Caribbean ships, like the decor, tends to be somewhat more subdued than on Carnival (more of a karaoke than a wet T-shirt crowd), although some short cruises attract their share of partiers.

Passengers represent an age mix from 30 to 60. A good number of families, particularly in the Caribbean, gravitate to the line's well-established and fine-tuned kids' program (the line hosts more than 300,000 kids annually).

Royal Caribbean placed a ban on student groups, because of their tendency sometimes to party a little too hearty, creating discomfort for other passengers. Those under 21 are required to share a room with an adult over 25 (with exceptions made for young married couples and for kids whose parents are in the next room).

Food on Royal Caribbean is okay for a mainstream line, although not as good as the gourmet fare offered by sister company Celebrity. You can dine at Italian specialty restaurants on the Voyager- and Radiance-class ships (for a $20 surcharge), and the *Radiance* and its sister ships, as well as the *Navigator of the Seas* and *Mariner of the Seas,* also have steakhouses (also a $20 fee). The Voyager-class vessels have **Johnny Rockets** outlets where the food is free but not the sodas and milkshakes.

Typical activities on the Royal Caribbean ships include line-dancing lessons, art auctions, horse racing, bingo, shuffleboard, and deck games. In addition, the line has special offerings such as its Golf Ahoy! program, which includes play at the best local golf courses in any of 28 ports. The ships all also offer an extensive fitness program called ShipShape, which gives prizes for participation. Royal Caribbean spends big bucks on entertainment, producing its own shows, and you can see it in the line's savvy, high-tech show productions that feature singers, dancers, and live bands. Headliners are often showcased on the line's larger ships. The line also provides a vast array of duty-free shopping choices and a Price Guarantee (where you receive a refund if you find an item cheaper on land).

Itineraries

Although the Caribbean remains the company's main cruising area, Royal Caribbean plans to employ 19 ships in the Caribbean, Mexico, Alaska, Europe, Bermuda, and the Bahamas throughout 2005. But you can't go wrong if you think Caribbean for this line. Its ships cruise at various times of the year from Miami, Fort Lauderdale, Tampa, Galveston, Baltimore, Los Angeles, various European ports, Port Canaveral, New Orleans, Vancouver, and even Bayonne, N.J. Recently, along with many other cruise lines, Royal Caribbean introduced a number of shorter itineraries, most notably from Fort Lauderdale and Los Angeles. The company has become a major player in the Alaskan market, where Princess and Holland America rule the roost in both ships and land tours. In a competitive move, Royal Caribbean formed its own tour company, **Royal Celebrity Tours**, to serve the passengers of its ships and those of its affiliate company, Celebrity. The tour company began offering land tours in 2001, using the largest domed rail cars in the world (built especially for the line) to offer optimum viewing opportunities.

Adventure of the Seas sails 7-day southern Caribbean cruises from San Juan year-round. *Brilliance of the Seas* sails 12-day Mediterranean itineraries in summer and fall and alternating 10- and 11-day Panama Canal/Caribbean cruises the rest of the year. The *Enchantment of the Seas* sails 4- and 5-day western Caribbean itineraries year-round. *Explorer of the Seas* sails 7-day eastern and western Caribbean alternating itineraries year-round. *Grandeur of the Seas* sails 7-day western Caribbean cruises out of New Orleans in the winter and spring and 5-day Bermuda and 9-day Caribbean itineraries out of Baltimore the rest of the year. *Jewel of the Seas* sails 6- and 8-day Caribbean cruises in winter and spring, 12-day northern European itineraries in summer, and 7- and 10-day New England/Canada routes in fall. *Legend of the Seas* sails 14-day Panama Canal and 10- and 11-day Hawaiian itineraries in winter and 7-day Mexican Riviera cruises (from San Diego) in summer. *Majesty of the Seas* sails 3- and 4-day Bahamas itineraries year-round from Miami. *Mariner of the Seas* sails alternating 7-day eastern and western Caribbean itineraries year-round (from Port Canaveral). *Monarch of the Seas* sails 3- and 4-day Baja Mexico routes year-round out of Los Angeles. *Navigator of the Seas* sails alternating 7-day western and eastern Caribbean cruises year-round. *Nordic Empress* sails 3-, 7-, and 11-day Caribbean itineraries in winter and spring from Tampa and 7-day Bermuda cruises in spring, summer, and fall out of New York. *Radiance of the Seas* sails 7-day alternating eastern and western Caribbean itineraries in winter and 7-day Alaskan cruises in summer. *Rhapsody of the Seas* sails 7-day western Caribbean cruises year-round (from Galveston, Texas). *Serenade of the Seas* sails 7-day Alaskan cruises from Vancouver in summer and 7-day southern Caribbean itineraries out of San Juan the rest of the year. *Sovereign of the Seas* sails 3- and 4-day Bahamas cruises year round. *Splendour of the Seas* sails 7-day western Caribbean cruises from Tampa in winter and spring and 7-day Mediterranean cruises from Barcelona in the summer and fall. *Vision of the Seas* sails 7-day Mexican Riviera cruises (from Los Angeles) in fall and winter and 7-day Alaskan itineraries in summer. *Voyager of the Seas* sails alternating 7-day western and eastern Caribbean cruises from Miami in winter and alternating 9-day Caribbean and 5-day New England/Canada cruises from Bayonne in spring, summer, and fall.

Royal Caribbean owns a private island, **CocoCay**, in the Bahamas and an isolated beach in Haiti called **Labadee**. Both destinations give cruisers on many Caribbean itineraries a venue for fun in the sun, complete with water sports and all the trimmings.

Outstanding features
Royal Caribbean offers Royal Romance specials — eight wedding packages and one vow-renewal package. The *Voyager of the Seas* and its sister ships have their own wedding chapel, but you can get married there only when the ships are in port. The line bans smoking in the dining

rooms on all its vessels. Many of the newer ships have indoor swimming pools with retractable roofs. All the ships have Internet cafes (cabins on the newer ships also have Internet-ready outlets) and rock-climbing walls. For golfers, Royal Caribbean has relationships with nearly three dozen courses around the world. Some ships offer driving ranges, mini-golf, and golf simulators.

Super deals

The early-booking program allows for savings of up to 50 percent. Additional savings may be available on select cruises. Third- and fourth-passenger rates, senior citizens rates, and sporadic resident specials (for people living in a particular market) are available on select sailings. Table 14-17 provides other Royal Caribbean rates.

Table 14-17	Royal Caribbean Rates		
Ship	*Inside*	*Outside*	*Suites*
Adventure of the Seas [a]	$1,029–$1,139	$1,229–$1,529	$1,979–$4,539
Brilliance of the Seas [b]	$1,829–$1,889	$2,319–$2,859	$4,499–$11,999
Empress of the Seas [c]	$779–$809	$929–$999	$1,359–$1,649
Enchantment of the Seas [c]	$529–$569	$689–$809	$1,099–$2,649
Explorer of the Seas [a]	$1,070–$1,204	$1,274–$1,624	$2,124–$3,574
Grandeur of the Seas [a]	$629–$669	$729–$1,029	$1,179–$2,879
Jewel of the Seas [d]	$849–$899	$1,049–$1,259	$1,599–$2,799
Legend of the Seas [e]	$1,199–$1,289	$1,499–$1,629	$3,229–$3,999
Majesty of the Seas [f]	$269–$299	$309–$409	$709–$1,829
Mariner of the Seas [a]	$779–$829	$849–$1,279	$1,629–$2,779
Monarch of the Seas [g]	$229–$254	$259–$329	$529–$1,709
Navigator of the Seas [a]	$799–$869	$999–$1,249	$1,549–$4,149
Radiance of the Seas [i]	$799–$889	$1,049–$1,374	$1,649–$5,699
Rhapsody of the Seas [a]	$679–$749	$779–$1,079	$1,229–$2,929
Serenade of the Seas [a]	$824–$884	$1,024–$1,474	$1,724–$3,024
Sovereign of the Seas [j]	$309–$334	$339–$429	$629–$1,809
Splendour of the Seas [k]	$749–$789	$809–$1,349	$1,649–$2,949

Ship	Inside	Outside	Suites
Vision of the Seas [l]	$749–$799	$814–$1,399	$1,699–$4,199
Voyager of the Seas [a]	$559–$609	$698–$1,049	$1,299–$2,299

[a] For 7-day Caribbean sailings
[b] For 12-day Mediterranean sailings
[c] For 8-day Bermuda sailings
[d] For 5-day Caribbean sailings
[e] For 8-day Caribbean sailings
[f] For 14-day Trans-canal sailings
[g] For 4-day Bahamas sailings
[h] For 4-day Mexico sailings
[i] For 7-day Alaska sailings
[j] For 3-day Bahamas sailings
[k] For 7-day Mediterranean sailings
[l] For 7-day Mexico sailings

Fleet facts

The *Grandeur, Legend, Splendour, Enchantment, Rhapsody,* and *Vision* are all part of Royal Caribbean's Vision series. As sister ships they seem nearly identical, aside from weight and interior design variations, and offer amazing activity and entertainment options — including 18-hole miniature golf courses on the *Legend* and *Splendour* (the *Voyager,* and all new ships that have come after, have mini-golf courses as well).

The *Majesty* and *Monarch* are mirror-image twins from the early '90s and sport more of a brass, chrome, and neon decor than their newer Vision-class sisters — they appear a bit dated and dull by comparison. Their forerunner, the *Sovereign of the Seas,* is similar but weighs a bit less. The *Nordic Empress* is the smaller, non-megaship member of the Royal Caribbean fleet. On the other end of the spectrum, the *Voyager of the Seas* and sister ships *Explorer of the Seas, Adventure of the Seas, Navigator of the Seas,* and the new *Mariner of the Seas* are the biggest ships ever and are highly innovative.

With the *Radiance of the Seas, Brilliance of the Seas,* and new *Serenade of the Seas* and *Jewel of the Seas,* which debuted last year, the company took a step back in terms of size (each weighing in at 90,090 tons). To compensate, it introduced pretty ships with plenty of glass for viewing the scenery, including 12-deck glass elevators facing the ocean and floor-to-ceiling windows in many public rooms. The *Radiance* and its sister ships boast billiards rooms with self-adjusting tables that ride with the waves; the *Radiance* also has a coffee shop/bookstore. The vessels are designed to sail far-reaching global itineraries and feature balconies on 70 percent of the outside cabins. Table 14-18 shows the current fleet specifications.

Table 14-18	Royal Caribbean Fleet Specifications					
Ship	Year Built	Passengers	Crew	Total Cabins	Tonnage	Length in Feet
Adventure of the Seas	2001	3,114	1,185	1,557	142,000	1,020
Brilliance of the Seas	2002	2,100	859	1,050	90,090	962
Enchantment of the Seas	1997	1,950	760	975	74,140	916
Explorer of the Seas	2000	3,114	1,176	1,557	142,000	1,020
Grandeur of the Seas	1996	1,950	760	975	74,140	916
Jewel of the Seas	2004	2,100	859	1,050	90,090	962
Legend of the Seas	1995	1,800	720	900	69,130	867
Majesty of the Seas	1992	2,350	822	1,175	73,941	880
Mariner of the Seas	2003	3,114	1,185	1,557	142,000	1,020
Monarch of the Seas	1991	2,354	822	1,175	73,941	880
Navigator of the Seas	2003	3,114	1,185	1,557	142,000	1,020
Nordic Empress	1990	1,600	671	800	48,563	692
Radiance of the Seas	2001	2,100	857	1,050	90,090	962
Rhapsody of the Seas	1997	2,000	765	1,000	78,491	915
Serenade of the Seas	2003	2,100	859	1,050	90,090	962
Sovereign of the Seas	1988	2,278	840	1,125	73,192	880
Splendour of the Seas	1996	1,804	720	902	69,130	867
Vision of the Seas	1998	2,000	660	1,000	78,491	915
Voyager of the Seas	1999	3,114	1,176	1,557	142,000	1,020

Chapter 15

Luxury Ships

· ·

In This Chapter

▶ Seeking out the major luxury cruise ships in the Caribbean, Alaska, and the Mediterranean

▶ Preparing for the luxury cruising experience

▶ Discovering the best new luxury ships

· ·

*T*he cruise lines in this chapter are the very best in terms of luxury and extravagance — think Ritz-Carlton meets the high seas. Discerning passengers travel on these vessels to be pampered with the best wines, gourmet food served on elegant china and crystal, and spacious accommodations decked out with down pillows, fine linens, walk-in closets, and marble bathrooms. On most of these ships, caviar is offered from silver serving dishes, champagne flows like water, and if you want a break from the elegant dining room, you can have a full dinner served to you in your cabin — by a white-gloved waiter, no less.

What Luxury Ships Have

Like their mainstream peers, luxury ships offer excellent swimming pools, health clubs, and spa facilities. Cabins usually have such amenities as televisions (sometimes with VCRs), telephones, minibars, bathrobes (and often slippers, too), safes, and hair dryers. The cuisine on these ships rivals the best land-based restaurants, and dinner is served with much pomp and circumstance. Entertainment and organized activities are more limited than on mainstream ships, because most guests on luxury vessels enjoy having time to amuse themselves. You're more likely to spend nights on these ships chatting about stocks with newfound acquaintances in a quiet piano bar than to watch a Las Vegas–style extravaganza (most elaborate on the Crystal line). Because passengers on luxury lines tend to be experienced travelers, shore excursions may be more elaborate than those mainstream lines offer. Chapter 3 goes into detail about the categories we use to describe the different types of cruises and the kinds of passengers they appeal to.

Several luxury vessels are small and intimate. And even on the bigger ships (such as Cunard's *QE2* and *QM2*, the largest passenger ship afloat, and Crystal's *Harmony, Symphony,* and new *Serenity*) you're unlikely to feel lost in a crowd. You feel like a member of a private club of experienced travelers who know what they want and are willing to pay for it. Passengers are mostly adults, although you may see some kids on the *QE2* and the Crystal vessels, which have children's facilities.

If you plan to cruise on Silversea, Cunard, or Crystal, you need to bring a tux (ladies, pack your fancy dresses), as well as a suit or jacket and tie. People on these ships tend to dress for dinner. On Radisson Seven Seas Cruises you don't need anything more than country club casual wear on Alaskan and Tahitian sailings, but on other itineraries men need a suit for certain nights. On Seabourn ships, bring the tux for formal nights; all other nights are casually elegant, with no tie required. On SeaDream, country club chic is acceptable any time (no need for the tux or ball gown).

What Luxury Ships Offer for Free

The ultra-luxury ships treat passengers like royalty. The following list samples what certain lines offer guests on a complimentary basis (or at least what they figure into their cruise rates):

- ✔ **Alcohol:** Seabourn, SeaDream, Silversea, and Radisson Seven Seas (offers wine with lunch and dinner on *Paul Gauguin;* dinner only on all other ships)

- ✔ **Free stocked minibar:** Radisson Seven Seas, Seabourn, Silversea, Crystal (top suites only), and Cunard (top suites only)

- ✔ **A shoreside event:** Seabourn, SeaDream, and Silversea (on select cruises)

- ✔ **Tips:** Included on Seabourn, SeaDream, Radisson Seven Seas, and Silversea

- ✔ **Transatlantic airfare:** Cunard (one-way with transatlantic cruises)

- ✔ **Unlimited soda water/mineral water:** Crystal, Seabourn, SeaDream, Radisson Seven Seas, and Silversea

- ✔ **Watersports:** Seabourn, SeaDream, and Radisson Seven Seas

Where Luxury Ships Go

Luxury ships tend to be much more eclectic in their itineraries than the mainstream ships we discuss in Chapter 14. They often sail from a different home port every week or stay in one region only long enough to offer a few itineraries and then move on to another part of the world. As many luxury ships are substantially smaller than the big mainstream ships, they also tend to visit smaller, less accessible ports.

Keep in mind that prices are based on brochure rates. You pay considerably less if you book early.

Crystal Cruises

2049 Century Park East, Suite 1400, Los Angeles, CA 90067; ☎ *800-820-6663;* www. crystalcruises.com

> ✔ **Type of cruise:** Gourmet, luxury, resort, romantic
>
> ✔ **Ship size/style:** Modern, midsize luxury ship

 With two ocean liner-size luxury ships, the *Crystal Harmony* (see Figure 15-1) and *Crystal Symphony*, and a larger, but no less luxurious new ship, *Crystal Serenity*, this Japanese-owned, Los Angeles-based line redefines first-class cruising. The state-of-the-art ships were created for a discerning clientele, and every facet of their operation is first-class and pleasing in a slightly glitzy, Beverly Hills manner. Passengers, who tend to be middle-aged or older, pay a pretty steep price for the experience. In return the line treats them to elegant and attentive service, outstanding food, luxurious accommodations, and the facilities of a megaship without huge crowds of fellow passengers. The top-quality entertainment varies from classical recitals to Broadway-style revues, and the casinos, operated by Caesars Palace, are among the best afloat. Gamblers are also offered drinks for free. Fitness centers are spacious, and spas are designed on the principles of feng shui.

(Photo: Crystal Cruises)

Figure 15-1: The *Crystal Harmony*

Many of the ships' plush cabins and enormous penthouse suites have verandas, plus all the latest amenities, with white-gloved butler service and Jacuzzi tubs. Concierge service is available to all passengers, as well as access to a business center and the Internet. Public rooms feature a glamorous, modern design, and the line spares no expense on the trimmings, such as fresh flowers, china, and the very best linens.

The food is expertly prepared from the best ingredients. In addition to the elegant dining room, the ships have two specialty restaurants for alternative dining — one Italian and the other Asian. Famed restaurateur Wolfgang Puck even provides some of the recipes. And the *Crystal Serenity* has a sushi bar and Asian restaurant, **Silk Road**, that features the creations of celebrity chef Nobu Matsuhisa (of **Nobu** in Los Angeles, among other venues). On the penthouse deck you can even get Nobu room service. On select evenings, each ship also offers casual dining at an open-air grill. Each ship's wine cellar stocks some 25,000 bottles and 171 varieties. For a stiffer drink, each ship has a martini bar.

Onboard activities include golf and bridge clinics, wine tastings, and classes in calligraphy, computers, and ballroom dancing. You can catch a fabulous lecture series that has featured such notables as Barbara Walters and Regis Philbin. Famous chefs come on board for the line's series of wine- and food-themed sailings. Destination experts are brought on board to talk about specific ports of call. Another typically Crystal touch: A PGA-accredited golf pro accompanies most of the cruises to offer lessons and share playing experiences between ports.

Itineraries

In 2005, Crystal's ships plan to sail around the world to 57 countries and 174 ports of call, including stops in the Mediterranean, Northern Europe, Asia, the Panama Canal, the Caribbean, Hawaii, South America, Canada/ New England, the Mexican Riviera, and Alaska (from San Francisco) on itineraries that range from one week to *Crystal Serenity's* 106-day world cruise. Ports the ships plan to visit in 2005 range from Antwerp, Belgium to Zadar, Croatia (A to Z, get it?). *Crystal Harmony* sails 11-day Panama Canal cruises between Costa Rica and Ft Lauderdale at the start of the year and does a series of Asian cruises in the spring. The *Harmony* serves as Crystal's representative in Alaska in the summer in 12-day rotation out of San Francisco and then spends winter in the Mexican Riviera (in 2006) for 10-day sailings out of Los Angeles.

Crystal Symphony is in South American service in the winter and then completes a short Caribbean and Panama Canal schedule through the spring before taking up position in Europe for a program of 7- to 12-day Mediterranean and Northern European cruises. The ship returns to the United States in the fall for Canada/New England cruises. The company's newest vessel, *Crystal Serenity,* starts the year with a 10-day Mexican Riviera cruise followed by a 106-day world tour, which the line markets as a whole cruise or by segments of 13 or 14 days in length. After the world cruise, the ship heads for Europe for 7- to 12-day Mediterranean service until late November when it returns to Ft Lauderdale for Panama Canal sailings.

Outstanding features

The line's Computer University @ Sea program offers computer lessons (for free) and e-mail/Internet access (for a fee) in a designated computer room. You can also access the Internet from your cabin (every cabin has dial-up access, and special laptop computers are available for rent). Televisions are closed-captioned for the hearing impaired. Gentlemen hosts are available to dance and socialize with solo female passengers. Theme cruises include health and fitness voyages and wine and food sailings with top-name chefs such as André Soltner and Nobu Matsuhisa (whose cuisine is also featured in the sushi bar and Asian restaurant on the *Crystal Serenity*). The line recently introduced an enhanced enrichment/lecture program on all ships, including language classes with Berlitz, music lessons with Yamaha, and Tai Chi through the **Bay Area Tai Chi Cultural Center.** At the Italian restaurants on each ship, you can enjoy a five-course **Valentino** dinner thanks to a special agreement between the famed Los Angeles restaurant and the cruise line.

Super deals

Rates are discounted up to 50 percent for passengers who book well in advance. A third passenger (age 12 and up) who shares a cabin with two full-fare passengers pays the minimum available fare. The line also offers repeat-passenger discounts and savings of 3.5 percent for full payment at least six months in advance of a sailing. Table 15-1 shows the rates for Crystal Cruises.

Table 15-1	Crystal Rates		
Ship	*Inside*	*Outside*	*Suites*
Crystal Harmony [a]	$5,305	$5,695–$9,683	$12,150–$22,355
Crystal Serenity [b]	N/A	$8,205–$13,425	$16,905–$27,165
Crystal Symphony [c]	N/A	$6,050–$11,070	$13,980–$20,430

[a] For 12-day Alaskan sailings
[b] For 15-day Panama Canal sailings
[c] For 10-day Mediterranean sailings

Fleet facts

Handsome ships by any standard, the *Crystal Serenity, Crystal Harmony,* and *Crystal Symphony* have some of the highest space-per-passenger ratios of any cruise ships in the industry. Cabins are large and well appointed, with almost half of them offering private verandas. The

Crystal Serenity is a bigger vessel at 1,080 passengers and 68,000 tons and offers guests even more room than the other two. The ship boasts expanded spa and fitness areas and more dining venues, entertainment lounges, penthouses (the biggest four are each a whopping 1,345 square feet), and deluxe cabins with verandas than the other ships. Table 15-2 shows current fleet specifications.

Table 15-2	Crystal Fleet Specifications					
Ship	**Year Built**	**Passengers**	**Crew**	**Total Cabins**	**Tonnage**	**Length in Feet**
Crystal Harmony	1990	940	545	480	49,400	791
Crystal Serenity	2003	1,080	635	550	68,000	820
Crystal Symphony	1995	940	545	480	51,004	781

Cunard Line

6100 Blue Lagoon Dr., Suite 400, Miami, FL 33126; ☎ *800-7CUNARD;* www.cunard.com

> ✔ **Type of cruise:** Luxury, elegant, classic, romantic
>
> ✔ **Ship size/style:** Grand ocean liner experience, multi-class

The British-bred grande dame of the cruise industry, Cunard comes with an impressive pedigree of famous ships such as the *Mauritania, Queen Mary,* and *Queen Elizabeth*. And the tradition continues under American owner Carnival Corporation, which bought the line for $500 million in 1998. *Queen Mary 2* (see Figure 15-2), the new Cunard ocean liner, debuted in January 2004 with the largest amount of publicity any ship has ever received. Although part of the acclaim is for being the world's largest, longest, widest, and most expensive ship (about $800 million) ever built, the ship is also a truly elegant — in a low-key rather than opulent way — and classic ocean-going vessel with exceptional public rooms and a wide variety of dining options. She's likely to become the most famous ship in the world. The fleet also consists of the legendary *QE2;* however, other than her World Cruise, QE2 now serves primarily the British market.

(Photo: Cunard Line)

Figure 15-2: The *Queen Mary 2*

Queen Mary 2 took over the classic Trans-Atlantic (New York to Southampton and the reverse) routes from the *QE2* in April 2004. Like the *QE2*, the *QM2* maintains the multi-class system (line officials prefer to use the term *categories*) where cabin level determines where one dines. Passengers in top categories of accommodations dine with other passengers from equivalent accommodations (on *QM2*, about 15 percent of all rooms warrant the upgraded dining rooms). Cunard passengers can expect ever-so-polite service delivered by an attentive white-gloved staff in very tasteful settings.

Passengers on the *QE2* tend to be experienced travelers, older and cultured, with previous Cunard sailings under their belts. With the newer, larger *Queen Mary 2*, the line wants to target a younger, more active, family-oriented audience (hence the addition of extensive children's facilities) along with the loyal Cunard-ers. The line is also particularly gay-friendly and often hosts large groups of gay travelers.

Cunard displays some big-name branding with its new vessel. *QM2* boasts **Todd English**, a branch of celebrity Boston chef English's **Olives** restaurant. And consulting on other menus is renowned chef Daniel Boulud. All the ship's china is Wedgewood. The ship boasts an extensive and impressive list of guest lecturers, including actors from the Royal Academy of Dramatic Arts and professors from Oxford University. Full-scale production shows and big-name guest performers also keep guests entertained. The ship has an extensive computer center that offers free classes for beginners and Internet access (for a fee).

Itineraries

The *Queen Mary 2* does 6-day Trans-Atlantic cruises (between New York and Southampton) from April to December. The ship also offers 12-day New England/Canada itineraries in the fall and some 12- and 14-day

European cruises (including the Mediterranean) in the summer and fall. In winter, *QM2* operates Caribbean cruises from New York City and Fort Lauderdale.

The *QE2* starts the year with a 110-day world cruise. After that, the *QE2* spends spring, summer, and fall in Europe, with cruises geared towards British travelers.

Outstanding features

The *Queen Mary 2* is truly a show in itself. The public rooms are impressive for both their range and quality. The spa, operated by the famous **Canyon Ranch,** is both beautiful and extensive, including a large hydrotherapy pool. It boasts the largest ballroom afloat and a planetarium that features reclining seats for the best viewing. The library is the largest and most fully stocked on any ship. Spaces of special note are the elegant **Veuve Clicquot** champagne bar, the very lively **Golden Lion Pub,** the classically designed casino, and the line's signature, nautically-decorated Chart Room. Even the ship's hospital is the largest afloat, with very advanced facilities should you need them.

Super deals

Early booking awards you savings of up to 20 percent. You can also find special deals of up to 50 percent off on selected sailings. Fares frequently include complimentary airfare deals. Trans-Atlantic crossings for the new *Queen Mary 2* come with free one-way airfare. Past passengers and people who book back-to-back cruises get special savings. You can find a more complete rate chart in Table 15-3.

Table 15-3	Cunard Rates		
Ship	*Inside*	*Outside*	*Suite*
Queen Mary 2*	$1,619–$2,499	$2,499–$4,249	$4,999–$27,499

For 6-day transatlantic crossings, including one-way airfare.

Fleet facts

Carnival Corporation promised to expand the fleet when it bought Cunard; it delivered on that promise with *Queen Mary 2.* The 151,400 GRT, 2,620-passenger vessel is designed to look like a big version of a classic French liner. The vessel features stunningly beautifully suites (173 in six different categories — some are outrageously large; all have private balconies) and 1,137 regular rooms (782 have private balconies). The ship provides 30 rooms for the disabled in a variety of categories. Five swimming pools (including a kiddie pool), a full promenade, and vast amounts of deck space highlight the outdoor areas.

Table 15-4 shows current fleet specifications.

Table 15-4		Cunard Fleet Specifications				
Ship	Year Built	Passengers	Crew	Total Cabins	Tonnage	Length in Feet
Queen Mary 2	2003	2,620	1,253	1,310	150,000	1,132

Radisson Seven Seas Cruises

600 Corporate Dr., Suite 410, Fort Lauderdale, FL 33334; ☎ **800-477-7500** or **800-285-1835**; www.rssc.com

 ✔ **Type of cruise:** Gourmet, luxury, romantic

 ✔ **Ship size/style:** Smallish and midsize modern luxury ships

Radisson Hotels Worldwide decided to translate its hospitality experience to the cruise industry back in 1992. Today, the fleet includes the *Radisson Diamond* (see Figure 15-3), *Paul Gauguin, Radisson Seven Seas Navigator, Radisson Seven Seas Mariner,* and *Radisson Seven Seas Voyager.* All the ships offer itineraries geared toward affluent travelers and provide an atmosphere in which an executive can kick back and enjoy the best in food and service. The ships cruise all over the world, including North America, Bermuda, Europe, Asia, South America, Africa, Australia, New Zealand, and Tahiti (some sailings include the Marquesas Islands). The line also charters the *Explorer II* (previously the *Minerva*) for sailings in Antarctica — it sails as the top-level ship in that market.

(Photo: Radisson Seven Seas Cruises)

Figure 15-3: The *Radisson Diamond*

The Radisson Seven Seas experience is about service, amenities, and first-class cuisine, and the company fits in well in this mold with its luxury line counterparts. Seating in the dining rooms is open, too, so you can choose your dining companions. Wine with dinner is complimentary. Tips are included in the cruise fare.

The *Radisson Seven Seas Mariner* and the new *Radisson Seven Seas Voyager* feature a signature restaurant called **Signatures**, with cuisine overseen by chefs from the prestigious French cooking school *Le Cordon Bleu*. And if you want to learn the chefs' techniques to bring home, they conduct intensive six-hour workshops (made up of three 2-hour sessions) on the ship for $395 per person. On occasion, free cooking demos are given. Both ships also offer dinner with American menus in **Latitudes**, a venue where the presentation is part of the entertainment. The onboard atmosphere on the ships is luxurious yet casual, with port-intensive itineraries designed for active, well-educated travelers, most of whom (but not all) are over 40; Radisson Seven Seas doesn't gear service toward kids. The line assumes that most of its passengers want to entertain themselves, so organized activities are reasonably limited. However, offerings do include lectures by well-known authors, movie producers, oceanographers, and more. You can play card, board, and shuffleboard games; take dance lessons; and, at night, watch cabaret and production shows. Local entertainers sometimes come aboard to perform.

All the ships have a pool, jogging track, health club, and spa; the *Navigator, Mariner, Voyager,* and *Diamond* also have whirlpools. The renowned **Carita of Paris** operates all spas. *Diamond* has a floating marina that crewmembers lower from the hull at various ports of call, offering a platform for water sports, including sailing, windsurfing, and water-skiing. The ships are popular with corporate groups — they sometimes charter the ships in their entirety for company meetings and incentive trips.

Itineraries

Radisson Seven Seas offers some of the most diverse and innovative itineraries in the luxury category. In 2005, *Voyager* is set to sail her first World Cruise, a 108-day Los Angeles to Fort Lauderdale extravaganza, followed by European (including Mediterranean) and Caribbean sailings. *Mariner* starts the year in South America and then sails the Caribbean/Panama Canal/Mexico, Alaska, and Far East routes. *Navigator* plans to cruise Caribbean, Bermuda, Canada/New England, and Northern Europe/Baltic routes. *Diamond* plans to concentrate on the Caribbean and Europe (including the Mediterranean) in 2005. *Paul Gauguin* sails 7-day Tahitian cruises year-round (see Chapter 21).

Outstanding features

Radisson Seven Seas follows a no-tipping policy. A headline entertainer (usually a soloist or comedian) sails with each cruise; you can also enjoy dancers, a five-piece band, and a resident quartet. Shore excursions tend to be more creative than the norm. Gentlemen hosts and bridge instructors are available on select sailings. The line offers a youth activities program on Alaskan sailings and select Bermuda and Baltic sailings. With the all-outside, all-suite design of *Navigator, Mariner,* and *Voyager,* combined with all the items included in the cruise fare, you can find some real values.

Super deals

Radisson Seven Seas offers early-booking perks such as half-off companion fares, two-for-one fares, and discounted fares for a third passenger who shares a cabin. Some fares include free nights at a deluxe hotel or other innovative pre/post cruise offerings. Prices quoted for the line sometimes include free airfare (when they don't, ask for low-cost air add-ons). The line may offer a modest supplement for single travelers. See Table 15-5 for more Radisson Seven Seas rates.

Table 15-5	Radisson Seven Seas Rates		
Ship	*Inside*	*Outside*	*Suite*
Radisson Diamond	N/A	$3,295–$4,395	$6,395
Radisson Seven Seas Mariner [a]	N/A	N/A	$2,795–$12,695
Radisson Seven Seas Navigator	N/A	N/A	$3,395–$9,195
Radisson Seven Seas Voyager [b]	N/A	N/A	$2,595–$9,095

[a] For 7-day Alaska sailings
[b] For 5-day Caribbean sailings

Fleet facts

The *Radisson Diamond* is a most unusual ship: The $125 million vessel is a giant catamaran, with twin hulls atop that sit the passenger areas — a design that makes for a very wide ship. Only 420 feet long, she is nonetheless only 2 feet thinner (at 102 feet) than the *QE2,* which measures more than twice her length at 963 feet. Inside, thanks to her design, the *Diamond* is very roomy; you can't tell she has such a unique bottom. All her cabins are suites. The *Radisson Seven Seas Navigator* is faster and bigger, and all her cabins are suites with ocean views (most with verandas). The French-built *Radisson Seven Seas Mariner* is even bigger and more advanced, and all her cabins are suites with balconies. The *Mariner* added an Internet cafe, **Club.com,** with 18 stations for sending e-mail and surfing the Internet; the cafe also offers computer classes. You can e-mail from the *Navigator* and *Diamond,* but from less elaborate setups. A sister ship to *Mariner* (but not its twin), the all-suite, all-balcony *Radisson Seven Seas Voyager* debuted in March 2003 and took the best of both Navigator and Mariner, especially Navigator's bathroom design. Mariner and Voyager are two of the most spacious, most luxurious ships afloat. Table 15-6 shows current fleet specifications.

Table 15-6		Radisson Seven Seas Fleet Specifications				
Ship	*Year Built*	*Passengers*	*Crew*	*Total Cabins*	*Tonnage*	*Length in Feet*
Radisson Diamond	1992	354	192	175	20,295	420
Radisson Seven Seas Mariner	2001	700	445	354	50,000	675
Radisson Seven Seas Navigator	1999	490	313	250	30,000	560
Radisson Seven Seas Voyager	2003	700	445	350	49,000	670

Seabourn Cruise Line/The Yachts of Seabourn

6100 Blue Lagoon Dr., Suite 400, Miami, FL 33126; ☎ *800-929-9595;* www.seabourn.com

- ✔ **Type of cruise:** Gourmet, luxury, romantic
- ✔ **Ship size/style:** Small luxury ships

The ships of Seabourn, marketed as *The Yachts of Seabourn*, are much like small, private clubs. The onboard ambience is one of elegant refinement. Seabourn is truly a line for cruisers who want to see the world from a vessel, not much larger than a private yacht, carrying a limited number of guests in the ultimate of quality. With that said, Seabourn isn't for everyone. The *Seabourn Spirit*, *Seabourn Legend* (see Figure 15-4), and *Seabourn Pride* are for the moneyed, and the discreet decor and environment prove it. The lucky few onboard these ships obviously like the product: The line's repeat-passenger rate of 50 percent is among the highest in the industry. Service is impeccable and the cuisine, innovative and expertly prepared, matches the quality of the best land-based restaurants. The dining rooms operate on an open-seating basis (so you can make your own dinner party). Dinner menus in the main dining room feature the creative influence of New York-based celebrity chef Charlie Palmer. An indoor/outdoor **Verandah Café** offers a more casual alternative-dining venue. On formal nights, most men on Seabourn wear tuxes and the women dress up like royalty. On other nights, even Seabourn loosens up a bit with a no-ties-required policy.

From past surveys, Seabourn has determined that most of its passengers have household incomes that exceed $200,000 a year. Many are retired, although the average age is 52, and their net worth may top $4 million. Families sometimes travel on Seabourn ships, but no organized activities exist for kids (bring along your nanny).

(Photo: Seabourn Cruise Line)

Figure 15-4: The *Seabourn Legend*

The atmosphere on board all the ships is calm and relaxing; you don't see people rushing around. Passengers and staff alike are well mannered and respect each other's privacy. By design, the *Seabourn Legend, Pride,* and *Spirit* offer plenty of space for passengers — after all, most of the passengers live in really big houses and are used to stretching out. During days at sea, passengers occupy themselves reading, chatting, or maybe playing Scrabble. Sometimes, Seabourn invites guest celebrities on board — including golf legend Arnold Palmer, ex-*Supreme* Mary Wilson, singer/actress Michelle Phillips, comedian Tom Smothers (of the Smothers Brothers), *Jeopardy* host Alex Trebek, and Frank Deford, a senior contributing editor for Sports Illustrated, in 2004 alone. A new chef series features notable chefs who offer cooking demonstrations and signature dishes for the ships' restaurants and participate in shopping excursions to local markets. Chefs on board in 2004 included Dean Fearing of Dallas' **Mansion on Turtle Creek**, Jean Marie Lacroix of **Lacroix at the Rittenhouse** in Philadelphia, Todd Gray of **Equinox** in Washington, D.C., Gerry Hayden and Claudia Fleming from New York's **Amuse**, and Rob Feenie of Vancouver's **Lumiere**. Nighttime entertainment is low-key: A few singers perform in the main show lounge and a piano man entertains in a bar. Shore excursions are creative and suitably upscale. All three ships have Internet centers that offer Internet access.

Itineraries

Seabourn offers an enticing array of sailings for the 2005 season with most ranging from 7 to 18 days. Because ports are not usually repeated, the line combines many of the 7-day cruises into longer sailings without repetition. *Seabourn Pride* starts the year in South America and heads for the Mediterranean and Baltic for the spring and summer. In the fall, the *Pride* does a series of Canada/New England sailings and spends the rest of the year in the Caribbean and South America. *Seabourn Spirit* starts and ends the year in Southeast Asia. It spends spring, summer, and fall in the Mediterranean. *Seabourn Legend* starts off with Central American and Caribbean sailings before it heads to the Eastern Mediterranean for spring, summer, and fall. It returns to Central America and the Caribbean for the end of the year.

Outstanding features

The *Seabourn Legend, Pride,* and *Spirit* each have a teak-decked platform hidden in their hulls that, when lowered, provides a launching point for water sports — Sunfish sailboats, kayaks, snorkeling gear, high-speed banana boats, and water skis are available for use. The ships also have a metal mesh net that becomes a seawater swimming pool. The cruise fare includes tips, wine and spirits (and even premium champagne), and mini-massages (given on deck). Each cruise includes a complimentary shore-side experience such as a private visit to a museum after closing hours, a trip to a concert, or a visit to the home of a dignitary. Adventure Collection shore excursions (for which you pay extra) are designed for active travelers and include hiking, biking, snorkeling, fishing, horseback riding, and kayaking outings. The line doubled the size of the gym on each ship in 2003 to accommodate new classes such as yoga, Pilates, and Cardio Ki-Bo.

Super deals

Seabourn offers up to 50 percent off for booking early and savings of an extra 10 percent for combining two cruises. Special savings are available on select cruises for repeat passengers. Single travelers can get run-of-the-ship discounts, whereby Seabourn picks your cabin based on availability, and you save big bucks. The line offers occasional deals with free airfares. Table 15-7 shows more Seabourn rates.

Table 15-7	Seabourn Rates		
Ship	*Inside*	*Outside*	*Suite*
Seabourn Legend	N/A	N/A	$4,495–$14,295
Seabourn Pride [a]	N/A	N/A	$5,995–$15,795
Seabourn Spirit [b]	N/A	N/A	$5,975–$15,795

[a] For 7-day New England and Canada sailings
[b] For 7-day Eastern Mediterranean sailings

Fleet facts

All the cabins on the *Legend, Pride,* and *Spirit* are suites with 5-foot-wide picture windows; 36 suites on each of the ships have French doors that open onto a balcony offering sea views and breezes (although you don't have enough room to sit). All suites also have new *Bose* Wave radio/CD players (a library of music and book CDs is available onboard). The cabins offer complimentary bar setups, luxurious bathrooms, quality bath amenities from **Molton Brown** of London, and walk-in closets, among many other amenities. A couple of owner's suites on each ship are very large and offer private verandas. Table 15-8 shows current fleet specifications.

Table 15-8		**Seabourn Fleet Specifications**				
Ship	*Year Built*	*Passengers*	*Crew*	*Total Cabins*	*Tonnage*	*Length in Feet*
Seabourn Legend	1992	208	160	104	10,000	439
Seabourn Pride	1988	208	160	104	10,000	439
Seabourn Spirit	1989	208	160	104	10,000	439

SeaDream Yacht Club

2601 South Bayshore Dr., Penthouse 1B, Coconut Grove, FL 33133; ☎ *800-707-4911;* www.seadreamyachtclub.com

  ✔ **Type of Cruise:** Luxury (country club chic), romantic

  ✔ **Ship size/style:** Small, yacht-like

Size does matter. And in the case of the two ships, *SeaDream I* and *SeaDream II* (shown in Figure 15-5), from SeaDream Yacht Club, smaller is decidedly better. When the owners of SeaDream, Atle Brynestad and Larry Pimentel, the founder and former president of Seabourn Cruise Line, respectively, took over the former Sea Goddess ships from Cunard (operated most recently as part of the Seabourn brand), they promised "an extraordinary, ultra-luxury, mega-yachting experience not currently available." Whether you call their two vessels big yachts or small cruise ships, the experience is truly luxurious. Excellent service and fine dining are the hallmarks. With each ship carrying 110 guests in 55 suites, they sail small by any standards and offer an intimate, personalized trip.

The ships were built in the 1980s, and the space ratio is smallish by today's standards. Cruisers don't have much inside public space. And the ships have no cabins with verandas. To help make up for this, SeaDream has refitted the ships to provide plenty of excellent outside space, including the addition of an extra deck. The ships provide lounge chairs between the upper sitting decks (with some nifty dividers for privacy) and the aft pool area on deck three. You can also tan on 11 super-comfy Balinese Sun Beds on Deck 6 (umbrellas provide shade for people who don't want too much sun).

(Photo: SeaDream Yacht Club)

Figure 15-5: The *SeaDream II*

The passengers are mostly couples who have cruised before on other luxury ships, especially the smaller ones; most are in their mid-40s to 60s. SeaDream isn't a cruise line for the swinging young crowd; it favors travelers who like a refined, quiet trip where wonderful dining and great service, relaxation and conversation, and visits to interesting places are important. The largest number of guests, wherever the ship sails, are from the United States. Mediterranean cruises carry a decent number of Europeans. The atmosphere onboard is country club chic; over the top outfits and tuxes are not necessary in any way. Entertainment is usually a piano player before and after dinner; the activities director offers brief previews of each upcoming port. Other than that, the ships leave guests to their own devices when it comes to entertainment on board. Meals become a major focus of the day. Breakfasts and lunches are served either in the **Dining Salon** or outside at the **Topside Restaurant** (weather permitting). An expertly prepared and presented dinner is the evening's main entertainment. All meals are open seating and the Dining Salon is large enough to seat all passengers at one time. The Maitre d' tries to make sure that everyone sits with whom, and at the size table, they want. Champagne and caviar are plentiful, offered poolside and waterside at some ports.

The ships pay special attention to your well-being. SeaDream operates its own Asian-influenced spa and gym with a mind-and-body component. A golf simulator offers pretend play at 50 championship courses.

Itineraries

Both ships include the Caribbean, the Mediterranean, the Greek Islands, and the Croatian Coast in their itineraries. *SeaDream I* does 7-day Caribbean cruises (from St. Thomas, Antigua, and St. Martin) in winter and spring, 4- and 5-day cruises (from San Juan) in the winter, 4- to 7-day western Mediterranean cruises in the spring, and 7-day western Mediterranean and 7-day eastern Mediterranean cruises in the summer and fall. *SeaDream II* sails basically the same itineraries, but it sticks to the western Mediterranean in summer and fall.

Note: Many of the SeaDream sailings are privately chartered, so you may have to be flexible with your travel dates.

Outstanding features

The top feature is the ships themselves; at only 344 feet long, they can get into ports that other ships cannot and dock in very special places, such as curbside in Monte Carlo. The ships overnight in key ports (in St. Barts or St. Tropez, for instance), allowing extra time for you to wander. An activities director leads personalized (and complimentary) walking tours in certain ports, such as to the local market in St. Tropez. With a crew of 89 looking after just 110 guests on board, the service is fantastic. Smoking is allowed only on certain open decks.

Super deals

You can get early-bird savings (called "Book Now and Save" rates) of up to 65 percent and other specials that may create even more discounts off of the brochure rates we list in Table 15-9. SeaDream's Web site and brochures spell them out. Also, for comparison purposes, rates include all gratuities, virtually all beverages including wine with lunch and dinner and spirits anytime, and use of all water toys and select shore outings.

Table 15-9	SeaDream Rates		
Ship	*Inside*	*Outside*	*Suite*
SeaDream I*	N/A	$3,900–$6,900	$7,800–$17,250
SeaDream II*	N/A	$4,900–$6,900	$9,800–$17,250

Rates don't include port charges.

Fleet facts

Most cabins measure 195 square feet. Sixteen are convertible to a double-sized room — called a Commodore Club Stateroom — by booking two connecting rooms (essentially creating a suite with two bathrooms and a living room). At 490 square feet, the one Owner's Suite is extremely luxurious. All the rooms have ocean views and were refurbished as part of the conversion to the SeaDream brand. The linens are Belgian and very comfy. The bathrooms are efficient for their size (the floor to ceiling showers are excellent), and the toiletries are by *Bulgari* (exemplifying the luxury provided). And all the cabins come with a nice audio/video setup including a DVD player. Table 15-10 shows current fleet specifications.

Table 15-10	SeaDream Fleet Specifications					
Ship	Year Built	Passengers	Crew	Total Cabins	Tonnage	Length in Feet
SeaDream I	1984	110	89	55	4,260	344
SeaDream II	1985	110	89	55	4,260	344

Silversea Cruises

110 E. Broward Blvd., Fort Lauderdale, FL 33301; ☎ *800-722-9055;* www.silversea.com

 ✔ **Type of cruise:** Gourmet, luxury, romantic

 ✔ **Ship size/style:** Modern, smallish luxury ships

Luxurious sister ships *Silver Cloud* and *Silver Wind* carry just 296 guests each, but they carry those lucky few in true splendor. All the cabins are outside suites; more space is allotted to each passenger than aboard almost any other ship; and the ships employ a larger crew, a staff ready to cater to your every desire on a 24-hour basis. The fine accoutrements that complement all this luxury include Limoges china, Christofle silverware, fine Irish bed linens by Hilden, and wonderfully soft down pillows.

The newer *Silver Shadow* and *Silver Whisper* (see Figure 15-6) are slightly bigger at 25,000 tons, carrying 396 passengers. These all-suite vessels add such features as more private verandas (85 percent as opposed to 75 percent on the older ships), poolside dining venues, a larger spa facility, a computer center, a wine and champagne bar designed by Moët & Chandon, and a cigar lounge designed by renowned cigar purveyor Davidoff in the style of an English smoking club.

(P)Photo: Silversea Cruises)

Figure 15-6: The *Silver Whisper*

The atmosphere aboard all the Silversea ships is elegant in a low-key, sociable way. Activity offerings include bridge and other games, aerobics, dance lessons, wine tastings, lectures, and bingo and quiz shows. Nighttime entertainment includes small production shows, dancing, a piano bar, a small casino, and visiting performers from whatever region the ship sails through.

All the ships offer open-seating, five-star cuisine with new menus and expanded room service. The service is extraordinary — just ask and you shall receive.

Silversea's pricing is all-inclusive: The cruise fare covers tips, wines, spirits, champagne, a free mini-bar setup in your cabin, free shuttles from ports to city centers, and more. Select cruises also include a shore-side cultural event (such as a performance by a local dance troupe).

Passengers on these ships are generally well traveled and well heeled (and not necessarily American). Most are in the over-50 age group. Silversea doesn't design its ships for kids (although you may occasionally see a few on board).

Itineraries

When upscale cruisers look at Silversea's itinerary lineup for 2005, their wide eyes light up with glee. You can't find a major cruising area in the world that Silversea's four ships don't plan to reach. And, in a wonderfully innovative way, they have cruises from 6 to 18 nights and every length in between; they cover the world's top destinations and plan to reach over 30 new ports for the first time. The Silversea ships sail to and in the Africa/Indian Ocean (*Cloud, Shadow,* and *Wind*), Alaska/Pacific Coast (*Shadow*), Caribbean (*Whisper*), Far East/South Pacific (*Cloud* and

Shadow), Canada/New England/Colonial Coast (*Whisper*), and South America/Amazon (*Cloud, Shadow,* and *Whisper*). But for an incredible choice, all four ships sail in the Mediterranean during the key months and *Cloud* and *Whisper* sail in Northern Europe when the days feature long hours of daylight. The 2-night call in St. Petersburg — part of the July 5th cruise — is exceptional in that it allows for a full day's excursion to Moscow.

Outstanding features

Silversea has installed a new specialty restaurant on each of the four ships (**Saletta** on *Wind* and *Cloud* and **Le Champagne** on *Shadow* and *Whisper*). The restaurant is a new Relais & Chateaux (a guide that rates the top restaurants and hotels around the world) venture overseen by world-famous chef Joachim Koeper. The line includes this dining in the cruise price — only the vintage wines are added to the bill. Culinary cruises with Relais & Chateaux feature guest chefs from gourmet restaurants, and a new wine series features well-known vintners. Silversea offers lectures by noted journalists and photographers. You can e-mail from all ships, and all ships have Bloomberg Professional Service terminals that guests can use (for free) to check the latest stock market and financial news. Cabins have VCRs, and you can borrow tapes from the movie library.

Super deals

The line's early-booking savings program lists specific savings that go up as high as 50 percent. A most noteworthy program is Silversea's new and unique Personalized Voyages, which allows passengers to create their own itineraries and get on and off at select ports (you pay a daily rate, with a 5-night minimum stay required). If you pay at least six months in advance, you get an additional 5 percent off. Members of the line's Venetian Society Repeat Guest program save 5 to 15 percent on select cruises, combinable with other discounts. Special deals are available for singles. The new pre/post-cruise program, "Silver sights," offers more hotel and add-on land options in more cities. You can find more Silversea rates in Table 15-11.

Table 15-11	Silversea Rates*		
Ship	*Inside*	*Outside*	*Suite*
Silver Cloud	N/A	N/A	$3,951–$6,195
Silver Shadow	N/A	N/A	$3,395–$6,595
Silver Whisper	N/A	N/A	$2,047–$4,795
Silver Wind	N/A	N/A	$3,391–$6,095

*All Silversea rates are cruise-only.

Fleet facts

The all-suite cabins on Silversea ships have walk-in closets, marble bathrooms, and all-around fantastic upper-end amenities. The line adds duvets, clocks, and binoculars in each suite. Nearly 75 percent of the cabins come with private verandas. On the newer ships, the *Silver Shadow* and *Silver Whisper,* 85 percent of the cabins feature private verandas. The biggest suites are apartment-sized and come with extras like free laundry service. Table 15-12 shows current fleet specifications.

Table 15-12		Silversea Fleet Specifications				
Ship	Year Built	Passengers	Crew	Total Cabins	Tonnage	Length in Feet
Silver Cloud	1994	296	210	148	16,800	514
Silver Shadow	2000	388	295	194	25,000	597
Silver Whisper	2001	388	295	194	25,000	597
Silver Wind	1994	296	210	148	16,800	514

Chapter 16

Alternative and Sailing Ships

*N*ot the Vegas or giant resort type? Usually stay in a Bed & Breakfast rather than the Hyatt? Prefer a quiet read in the shade to a game of pool volleyball? Small ships may be your thing.

What these alternative ships offer is a casual, crowd-free cruise experience that gives passengers a chance to get up-close and personal with the natural surroundings of the destinations they visit. Thanks to their smaller size and shallow *drafts* (the amount of hull below the water), these ships can go places where larger ships can't. They tend to stop at ports on a daily basis, whether slipping into quiet coves or visiting sparsely inhabited islands and nature areas, including smaller ports that tend to cater to yachts. They may also visit some larger, popular ports along with their bigger peers (gawking at the larger ship anchored nearby is a classic small-ship experience). The itineraries of small ships are often structured more loosely than those of big ships, allowing them the flexibility to change plans as great opportunities arise — to follow a whale or, in the case of the sailing ships, to follow the wind.

In contrast to the megaships, which can carry 2,000 to 3,000 passengers (and sometimes even more), the ships in this chapter carry only 12 to 400 guests who share the ships' few public areas, dine together at open, invariably family-style seating in the dining rooms, and generally enjoy the much less formal and structured atmosphere, fostering camaraderie you don't normally find on a megaliner.

 Because most small/alternative lines operate in niche markets, they don't generally play the same constant discounting game as the big lines. Often, the prices they list in their brochures are exactly what you end up paying, although the lines do usually offer early-booking and other special discounts, some of which we detail in the "Super deals" section of each review.

What Alternative Ships Have

Small ships are, by definition, small, so with rare exceptions your cabin isn't overly spacious. Some small ships offer suites or deluxe cabins if you have a yen for yardage (and the bucks to pay for it), but most cabins on small ships are of comparable size. Cabins on the alternative ships often don't come equipped with televisions and telephones, and bathrooms are almost uniformly tiny and the amenities scant (no terry cloth robes, fancy shampoos, and the like.) Although cabins on Windstar come with everything.

Activity-wise, these ships may offer a deck power walk or an opportunity to swim off the side of the ship rather than the aerobics and pool games of the big ships. Conversely, alternative ships are more likely to feature expert lecturers who come aboard to explain the natural environment and the history of the regions you visit.

You don't need a tux on any of these ships — the dress is consistently casual, and sometimes *very* casual — and you can't find any fancy Las Vegas-type showrooms or casinos, either. Only on the most upscale of these small ships do you find a swimming pool, gym, or spa — and you can bet on it being small!

Tipping

Tipping on small ships is a little different from tipping on big ships. Gratuities are often pooled among the crew and may not add up to the same amounts as on big ships. Here we provide a rundown of suggested tips. Keep in mind that these tips are just suggestions (tipping is always at your own discretion).

Suggested tips per passenger, per day:

- **American Safari Cruises:** 5 to 10 percent of the cost of the cruise, pooled
- **American West Steamboat Company:** $12 to $14 a day, pooled
- **Clipper:** $10, pooled, plus tips to bartenders at your discretion
- **Cruise West:** $10 to $12, pooled
- **Glacier Bay Cruiseline:** $10 to $15, pooled
- **Lindblad Expeditions:** $8 to $14 (depending on the ship), pooled
- **Star Clippers:** $8 to $10, pooled
- **Windjammer:** $60 (per week), pooled
- **Windstar:** The line has a tipping-not-required policy, but the crew gratefully accepts tips

When the ships anchor, you may have the opportunity to enjoy water sports such as snorkeling, scuba diving, kayaking, and water-skiing, using equipment carried on board. Sometimes, the ships may spend the night in a port or depart late, allowing you to sample the local nightlife.

 Most small ships have no stabilizers, and their drafts are generally shallow, so the ride can be bumpy in rough weather. And because most ships don't have elevators, passage is difficult for travelers with disabilities. And the alternative-ship lines don't offer activities or facilities for children, although you may find a few families on some vessels.

American Safari Cruises

19101 36th Ave. West, Suite 201, Lynnwood, WA 98036; ☎ *888-862-8881;* www. amsafari.com

> ✔ **Type of cruise:** Adventure/educational, gourmet
>
> ✔ **Ship size/style:** Small, luxurious yachts

American Safari Cruises only started operations in Alaska and the San Juan Islands of the Pacific Northwest in 1997, but already it has expanded its range of cruises to include the Columbia/Snake Rivers of Oregon and Idaho, the California Wine Country, Baja/Sea of Cortez in Mexico, and most recently Costa Rica. It offers sailings for just 12 and 22 passengers on small, intimate, luxury yachts that visit the out-of-the-way reaches of the Inside Passage in Alaska, such as small cannery towns and Tlingit Native villages — one stop is at Meyers Chuck, population 35. For up-close experiences, each vessel carries a naturalist who leads passengers via *Zodiacs* (inflatable vessels) or kayaks (carried aboard ship) to view black bears or otters along the shoreline or to navigate fjords packed with ice floes and lolling seals.

Most passengers are well heeled (this line is not cheap) and range in age from about 45 to 65. Crewmembers cheerfully fuss over you, adjusting lunchtime dishes and making elaborate cocktails from the free open bar (they may even call ahead to the next port for your favorite beer), and the chef indulges guests with multiple-course meals (cuisine is finer than you may expect to find on small ships) and clever snacks when he isn't bartering with a fishing boat for the catch of the day. Speaking of fishing, you can sometimes troll right from the yacht.

Public spaces aboard the ships are intimate, homey, and luxurious, with four or five prime vantages for spotting wildlife — one great spot on the *Safari Quest* (see Figure 16-1) is a top deck hot tub. You have as little or as much privacy as you desire.

Figure 16-1: The *Safari Quest*

Unlike most other lines, American Safari Cruises ships anchor at night, making for quieter sleep time. This also allows guests to take in the local nightlife — on a crew-led pub crawl, for instance.

Itineraries

Safari Quest sails a 7-day route in spring and summer between Juneau and Sitka (and one 14-day cruise between Seattle and Juneau at the beginning and end of the season), 4- and 5-day California Wine Country cruises in the fall, and 8-day Sea of Cortez (including one pre-cruise hotel night) and Costa Rica voyages in the winter. The *Quest* also offers 11-day Pacific Northwest cruises in the fall that feature travel on the Columbia and Snake rivers. *Safari Escape* sails 9-day Alaskan cruises between Juneau, Sitka, and Prince Rupert, British Columbia in the spring and summer. You can also book the Escape for a 15-day voyage between Seattle and Juneau at the start and end of the season or 8-day Pacific Northwest cruises in the fall. The vessel hibernates for the winter. Rates cover beverages (including alcohol), shore excursions, kayaking, and transfers.

Outstanding features

The boats carry mountain bikes that you can borrow. Each ship has a resident naturalist trained in a field such as geology, marine biology, or oceanography. The main salons boast 50-inch televisions for movie viewing (or take one of the hundreds of selections from the video library back to your cabin). In Mexico and Costa Rica, you can enjoy complimentary windsurfing, snorkeling, sailing, and water skiing. Shore excursions are included in the price.

Super deals

The line offers sporadic specials; see Table 16-1 for rates. Some of the rates on the line's repositioning cruises between Seattle and Juneau in May and September represent the lowest per diems the company offers. If you can get together a group of 12 or 22 family members, friends, and/or business associates, you can charter the ships alone because of their small stature. The price? A mere $119,995 gets you and your group the *Quest* for a couple of weeks.

Table 16-1	American Safari Rates		
Ship	**Inside**	**Outside**	**Suite**
Safari Escape [a]	N/A	$2,795–$4,795	N/A
Safari Escape [b]	N/A	$3,895–$5,895	N/A
Safari Quest [c]	N/A	$3,995–$4,995	N/A
Safari Quest [d]	N/A	$1,695–$1,895	N/A
Safari Quest [e]	N/A	$4,995–$5,995	N/A

[a] For 8-day Pacific Northwest sailings
[b] For 9-day Alaska sailings
[c] For 8-day Alaska sailings
[d] For 4-day California Wine Country sailings
[e] For 11-day Columbia/Snake Rivers sailings

Fleet facts

American Safari vessels resemble private yachts more than cruise ships, and they have the cabins to match (see Table 16-2), with televisions, VCRs, and showers (but no tubs). All cabins have windows, but those on the lower deck are elevated, meaning sunlight comes in but you have no view. The Admiral's Cabins have a large picture window and small sitting area.

Table 16-2	American Safari Fleet Specifications					
Ship	**Year Built**	**Passengers**	**Crew**	**Total Cabins**	**Tonnage**	**Length in Feet**
Safari Escape	1983	12	6	6	*	112
Safari Quest	1992	22	9	11	*	120

*Tonnage statistics are unavailable, but suffice to say the ships are really small, although roomy enough for the number of passengers they carry.

American West Steamboat Company

2102 Fourth Ave., Suite 1150, Seattle, WA 98121; ☎ *800-434-1232;* www.columbia
rivercruise.com

> ✔ **Type of Cruise:** Soft adventure/nostalgia
>
> ✔ **Ship size/style:** Two small, beautifully-designed sternwheelers,
> built in the fashion of the ships of the 1800s and early 1900s

To sail on the *Empress of the North* (See Figure 16-2), in Alaska or on the
Columbia/Snake Rivers, or on the *Queen of the West*, which is in
Columbia/Snake River service year round, is to take a step back in time.
Feel the rush of the Alaskan Gold Rush days, the history of Mark Twain
and the great paddlewheelers on the Mississippi and other great
American-heartland waterways, and the age of riverside minstrel shows
and steam whistle–
powered calliopes.

The company began sailing the Columbia/Snake Rivers route a decade
ago with the *Queen* and followed that up with another sternwheel-
propelled vessel, the *Empress,* just a couple of years ago. Both vessels
offer a glimpse into the golden past of riverboat travel. The accommodations are plush and the atmosphere one of festive nostalgia. The artwork
on each ship is appealing and completely fitting, which is to say it has a
western-theme — paintings and artifacts of the Lewis and Clark expedition, cowboy bronzes, silver buckles and ornate spurs, chaps, and other
such period items.

American West Steamboat Company is committed to the Pacific Northwest, and it puts its money where its mouth is. Don't expect to see the
Queen or *Empress* sail in any other area. Their bow-landing capability
makes them ideal for poking around in the sometimes tight spaces of the
islands and inlets of the Inland Passage and the coves of the Oregon and
Idaho rivers.

Food on board is served family-style and is palatable enough, although
hardly gourmet. Our only criticism of either ship is that, with a full complement of passengers at dinner, the dining room becomes a little tight
for space — not seating space, of course: The crew provides plenty of
places for everybody. But, with every table full, the servers have difficulty delivering plates. ("Would you mind passing this on?" is a question
the servers ask often at mealtimes.) And woe betide you if you should sit
on the inside seat in one of the booths built for six and you need to leave
the room for whatever reason during a meal service.

The crew is enthusiastic and helpful. Most are young, but some of
them — the bartenders, for instance — tend to be more mature and
quite accomplished. Unlike the kids who work the dining rooms, these
guys have had many years of experience in their craft.

Because of the ships' size, organized activities are somewhat limited. The ships have no spa, no casino, and no movie theatre *per se* (the ships have occasional movie showings in the main lounge). A guest lecturer comes on board to talk about the history and culture of the area through which the ships pass, and his/her talks from the main lounge are available in the cabin by radio feed. The cabins have no television or telephone.

(Photo: American West Steamboat Company)

Figure 16-2: The *Empress of the North*

You don't find many kids on board, and those that do sail this line must find their own amusement.

Itineraries

The *Queen of the West* spends the entire year in the Columbia/Snake River pattern — 7 days out of Portland, Oregon. The *Empress of the North* sails in the same area, also a 7-day service, in the spring, fall, and winter and in 7- and 11-day Alaska service out of Juneau in the summer months. The *Empress* also has an 11-day Seattle-Juneau positioning cruise on tap at the start of the summer season, with a reverse voyage followed by one 4-day San Juan Islands cruise scheduled at the end.

Outstanding features

The nostalgia makes these ships outstanding. All the cabins have a river (or ocean) view, and one of the most attractive public rooms at sea is the **Paddlewheel Lounge,** where you can sit and sip a cocktail with a snack (supplied free before dinner) to the accompaniment of the thrum, thrum of the huge propulsion wheel visible through the room-wide window at the back.

Super deals

American West Steamboat Company doesn't routinely offer an early booking incentive. It does, however, juice up its sales chances by discounting an occasional cruise during the season, depending entirely on demand. Discounts tend to run in the 25 percent per person range and — this is a big incentive — sometimes come with free air, which the line doesn't offer on all purchases. Table 16-3 shows the typical rates.

Table 16-3   American West Steamboat Company Rates

Ship	Inside	Outside	Suite
Queen of the West [a]	N/A	$1,239–$3,279	$3539–$3,669
Empress of the North [b]	N/A	$1,799–$3,129	$3,409–$3,884
Empress of the North [c]	N/A	$2,999–$4,549	$4,799–$5,299
Empress of the North [d]	N/A	$4,349–$6,099	$6,529–$7,229

[a] For 7-day Columbia/Snake Rivers sailings
[b] For 7-day Columbia/Snake Rivers sailings
[c] For 7-day Alaska sailings
[d] For 11-day Alaska sailings

Fleet facts

Queen of the West, the smaller of the line's two ships, was built in 1995 and has operated in the Columbia and Snake Rivers ever since. Its bigger sister, the *Empress of the North*, debuted both there and in Alaska in 2003. The ships are more spacious than you may think at first glance from the shore. The public rooms on each evoke thoughts of a bygone era, and the bow landing ramp lets passengers walk easily on and off the vessel in some secluded spots that bigger ships can't reach. See the full fleet specifications in Table 16-4.

Table 16-4   American West Fleet Specifications

Ship	Year Built	Passengers	Crew	Total Cabins	Tonnage	Length in Feet
Queen of the West	1995	136	60	71	1,308	212
Empress of the North	2003	235	84	112	3,388	360

Clipper Cruise Line

Intrav Building, 11969 Westline Dr., St. Louis, MO 63146-3220; ☎ ***800-325-0010;*** www.clippercruise.com

> ✔ **Type of cruise:** Adventure/educational
>
> ✔ **Ship size/style:** Small, well-designed vessels (like a Princess ship shrunk down)

Passengers on Clipper ships get to explore rivers, sparsely inhabited islands, and fjords, yet these cruises are hardly about roughing it. They represent low-fuss vacations for people who want to find out about the places they visit.

Most of the passengers are relatively affluent, older, retired folks — seasoned travelers who don't demand too much. The average age is 69. They tend to be both adventurous and intellectually curious, and they want a comfortable, hassle-free cruise experience without sequins, glitz, or crowds. Clipper's approach to activities and excursions is unregimented. Rather than entertainers, the Clipper line features *enlighteners*: naturalists, historians, and other experts who offer informal lectures and lead expeditions to sites of interest. Stops at ports of call may include a hike in a wildlife preserve, a museum visit, swimming, snorkeling, or other options, including shore excursions similar to those the mainstream lines offer (see Part V for more shore excursion info). Occasional nights spent at port give passengers a chance to mingle with the locals. A young and personable staff delivers the service.

Itineraries

Nantucket Clipper sails 8- and 13-day U.S. southern cruises in spring, cruises between 8 and 13 days in the Northeast and Canada, 7- and 11-day East Coast and Inland Waterways cruises (including the Chesapeake Bay and Hudson River) in summer and fall, and Florida/Caribbean cruises in winter. *Yorktown Clipper* (see Figure 16-3) sails 7-day Caribbean and 8-day Costa Rican/Panama Canal itineraries in winter, 7-day Baja cruises in fall and early spring, 6-day voyages in the California Wine Country in late spring, and 7- and 11-day Alaskan cruises in summer. The line's newest ship, the *Clipper Odyssey,* spends winter in Australia/New Zealand, spring in Asia, and summer in Alaska, offering 13-day sailings (you can also sail one unique cruise from Russia's Kamchatka Peninsula to Alaska's Kenai Peninsula) before heading back to the South Pacific in the fall. The line's expedition ship, the *Clipper Adventurer,* spends the winter in Antarctica and South America and the spring and summer in Europe. The ship also spends time in a Greenland/Iceland pattern before heading down through Canada and Florida to South America, offering a variety of itineraries, including a 10-day western Caribbean/Central America sailing, along the way.

Figure 16-3: The *Yorktown Clipper*

(Photo: Clipper Cruise Line)

Outstanding features

Clipper sends extensive reference materials to passengers before each cruise, and onboard naturalists and historians add immeasurably to the discovery experience. You can sometimes swim and snorkel directly off the sides of the ships. The *Clipper Odyssey* has an elevator as well as a small swimming pool and jogging track. You can send and receive e-mail from all the vessels.

Super deals

Clipper provides special offers and discounts for repeat-passengers, as well as special rates for third passengers who share a cabin with two full-fare passengers. Table 16-5 includes more rates for Clipper.

Table 16-5	Clipper Cruise Line Rates		
Ship	*Inside*	*Outside*	*Suite*
Clipper Adventurer [a]	N/A	$6,920–$9,030	$9,990–$10,490
Clipper Odyssey [b]	N/A	$4,470–$6,490	$6,990
Nantucket Clipper [c]	N/A	$2,100–$3,670	N/A
Yorktown Clipper [d]	N/A	$2,450–$3,730	N/A

[a] For 12-day Antarctic/South America sailings
[b] For 14-day Australia/New Zealand sailings
[c] For 8-day Antebellum South sailings
[d] For 7-day Alaska sailings

Fleet facts

The *Nantucket Clipper* and *Yorktown Clipper* are both simple ships with simple amenities: one large lounge that can accommodate all guests, a single dining room, and several outside deck areas for sunning and relaxing. All the well-designed, smallish cabins are outside and most have picture windows and good amounts of storage space. Some have doors that open to the promenade deck rather than to an inside corridor. The two ships are very similar in design, although the *Yorktown Clipper* is slightly larger.

The *Clipper Adventurer* has an ice-hardened hull that allows it to sail exotic itineraries in the Arctic and Antarctica. It's an extremely comfortable and well-designed vessel, with several public rooms and plenty of deck space, allowing you more room to spread out than most small ships do. The *Clipper Odyssey* offers two lounges, a dining room, a library, a small pool, and even a jogging track. All cabins offer sitting areas with sofas, and eight deluxe cabins and one suite boast private verandas. The ship also has an elevator. See Table 16-6 for fleet specifications.

Table 16-6 Clipper Cruise Line Fleet Specifications

Ship	Year Built	Passengers	Crew	Total Cabins	Tonnage	Length in Feet
Clipper Adventurer	1975	122	15	61	4,364	330
Clipper Odyssey	1989	128	72	64	5,218	338
Nantucket Clipper	1984	102	32	51	1,471	207
Yorktown Clipper	1988	138	40	69	2,354	257

Cruise West

2401 Fourth Ave., Suite 700, Seattle, WA 98121; ☎ *800-888-9378;* www.cruise west.com

- ✔ **Type of cruise:** Soft adventure/educational
- ✔ **Ship size/style:** Small vessels, some plain and some fancy

Alaskan legend Charles B. "Chuck" West, a pioneer in Alaskan tourism who first created Westours, a firm he sold to Holland America in the early 1970s, founded Cruise West. In creating this cruise line, West wanted to present a genuine and close-up view of Alaska, so the company's small vessels, operating on imaginative itineraries, do just that. The company has extended its reach into other, equally imaginative areas as well — Mexico, Costa Rica, Panama, California, and the rivers of Oregon and Idaho. The West family still owns Cruise West.

Passengers on the line's vessels tend to be older, well educated, and independent-minded, and they appreciate the casual and relaxed onboard atmosphere, with no luxurious accouterments or white-gloved service.

Because these ships are small, they can navigate tight areas (Alaska's **Misty Fjords** and **Resolution Sound,** Costa Rica's **Manuel Antonio National Park,** and **Los Islotes & Isla Partida** in the Sea of Cortez, to name but a few) and call at lesser-visited ports (Metlakatla, Petersburg, Nome, and Dutch Harbor in Alaska, for instance.) They can scoot close to wildlife, sometimes following aquatic creatures on their journeys (subject to Federal law, of course; following creatures too closely, or too long, is an offense). They can idle in midstream to offer passengers better viewing as bears frolic on the banks of the river. Passengers usually find that each vessel's open bow area or windowed forward lounge presents the best vantage point. The ships provide binoculars for guest use, and the staff announces wildlife sightings over the intercom system.

As with most small-ship cruise lines, the young, friendly, and energetic crewmembers do multiple tasks; the same person may carry your bags, serve you at dinner, and make your bed. Each ship carries a naturalist guide who possesses knowledge of the region's history and lore. Forest Service rangers, local fishermen, and local natives often come aboard to share their knowledge of the sailing area as well. On select voyages, Kodak Ambassador photography experts are aboard to discuss — you guessed it — photography. Otherwise, do-it-yourself entertainment is provided by the crew or by your fellow passengers. If you want a workout, exercise machines are available on each ship.

All Cruise West ships offer two public areas: a **Grand Salon Lounge** and a dining room (the *Spirit of Oceanus,* the line's flagship, also boasts a second lounge, a library, a game room, a pool, and a hot tub). Home-style, American meals are served in one open seating, using fresh products purchased at the ports along the way.

Itineraries

Although all Cruise West ships spend most of spring through the summer in Alaska, cruising from ports including Juneau, Ketchikan, Valdez, Whittier, Seattle, and Vancouver, the line has broadened its scope to include the Pacific Northwest (the Columbia and Snake rivers), British Columbia, California's Wine Country, Central America, and Baja, Mexico at other times of the year. The Alaskan sailings have also expanded in recent years to include a number of 14-day sailings to the Bering Sea (touching on Russia).

Spirit of '98 (see Figure 16-4) sails 8-day Alaskan cruises in early spring and summer and 7-day Pacific Northwest cruises (Columbia and Snake rivers) in the fall. *Spirit of Alaska* sails 8-day Alaskan cruises in summer and 7-day Pacific Northwest cruises (Columbia and Snake Rivers) in spring and fall. *Spirit of Columbia* sails 3-, 4-, and 10-day Alaskan cruises in spring and summer and 7-day British Columbian cruises in spring and fall. *Spirit of Discovery* sails 8-day Alaskan cruises in spring and summer and 7-day Pacific Northwest cruises (Columbia and Snake rivers) in fall. *Spirit of Endeavor* sails 8-day Alaskan cruises in the summer, 3- and 4-day California cruises in the fall, and 7-day Baja cruises in winter and spring. *Spirit of Oceanus* sails 12-day Alaskan and 13-day Bering Sea cruises (between Anchorage and Nome; visiting Russia) in the summer. All but the 3-day cruises include one pre-or post-cruise hotel overnight. The only ship in the Cruise West brochure not known as the "Spirit of . . ." something-or-other is the *Pacific Explorer,* a Costa Rican-owned, 100-passenger vessel that the company charters to operate Costa Rica/Panama cruises throughout much of the year. Some of the smaller Cruise West ships are laid up in the winter for maintenance work.

Figure 16-4: The *Spirit of '98*

(Photo: Cruise West)

Outstanding features

The *Spirit of '98* and *Spirit of Oceanus* have elevators, and *the Spirit of '98* also has completely wheelchair-accessible cabins; the other ships in this fleet have neither. All the ships' bridges are usually open for visits. Some of the ships have movies to borrow for in-room viewing. Some Alaskan itineraries feature a stop at the **Tsimshian village of Metlakatla**, the only federal reservation for Native Alaskans in the state. In Alaska, the line offers pre- and post-cruise tours to such places as **Denali National Park**, Fairbanks, and Anchorage; in Baja, a series that includes Mexico's **Copper Canyon**; and on Columbia and Snake Rivers, daily excursions to the likes of **Mount St. Helens** and points of interest on the **Lewis & Clark Trail**. You can send and receive e-mails from the *Spirit of Oceanus* only. Select itineraries feature Kodak representatives offering photography tips and expertise.

Super deals

Cruise West offers early-booking discounts of $400 to $800 per couple, depending on the cruise you select. If you make your final payment early, you save $100 per couple. The line sells most cruises in Alaska as packages that include a night in a hotel (see Table 16-7).

Table 16-7	Cruise West Rates*		
Ship	*Inside*	*Outside*	*Suite*
Pacific Explorer [a]	N/A	$3,499–$4,649	N/A
Spirit of '98 [b]	N/A	$2,299–$2,899	$3,299–$4,499
Spirit of Alaska [c]	$2,899	$3,049–$4,949	N/A
Spirit of Columbia [d]	$1,449–$1,549	$2,049–$3,049	N/A
Spirit of Discovery [b]	N/A	$2,049–$3,099	N/A
Spirit of Endeavor [e]	N/A	$2,249–$3,599	N/A
Spirit of Oceanus [f]	N/A	N/A	$5,599–$8,399

[a] For 10-day Costa Rica/Panama sailings
[b] For 7-day Columbia/Snake River sailings
[c] For 10-day Alaska sailings
[d] For 7-day British Columbia sailings
[e] For 8-day Sea of Cortez sailings
[f] For 14-day Alaska/Bering Sea sailings
*Rates include shore excursions in each port.

Fleet facts

The impressive *Spirit of '98* (see Table 16-8 for this ship's and others' specifications) is a replica of a 19th-century steamship decorated in a Victorian style that carries through to its comfortable cabins. You even see a player piano in the lounge. Want a quick look at the ship? One of the final scenes in the Kevin Costner movie *Wyatt Earp* takes place on board.

The *Spirit of Endeavor* boasts large cabins and picture windows and is very similar to Clipper's *Nantucket Clipper* and *Yorktown Clipper* (refer to the section "Clipper Cruise Line" in this chapter for more info). The *Spirit of Discovery* has a similar feel (although not quite as fancy) with a streamlined, modern appearance. Cabins are snug but comfortable. American Canadian Caribbean Line built both the *Spirit of Columbia* and *Spirit of Alaska*; the two vessels feature ACCL's patented bow ramp that allows passengers to disembark directly onto a dockless shoreline, whereas the other ships use a gangplank-like bow ladder for disembarkation. The *Columbia* is a slightly smaller ship than the *Discovery* and offers seven suites among its cabins, including a large owner's suite with picture windows overlooking the bow. The *Alaska* is almost identical to the *Spirit of Columbia* but without the suites. All cabins are suites with outside views on the *Spirit of Oceanus,* which previously operated as Renaissance Cruises' *Renaissance V,* and 12 of the suites boast private verandas. The *Pacific Explorer* offers comfortable cabins and carries a fleet of Zodiacs, kayaks, snorkel gear, and banana boats.

The line's cabin-less yacht, *Sheltered Seas,* also offers cruisetours, sailing during the day and putting passengers up in hotels on shore at night — like a road trip, but without the road.

Table 16-8	Cruise West Fleet Specifications					
Ship	Year Built	Passengers	Crew	Total Cabins	Tonnage	Length in Feet
Pacific Explorer	1995	100	25	46	102	185
Spirit of '98	1984	98	23	49	96	192
Spirit of Alaska	1980	82	21	39	97	143
Spirit of Columbia	1979	78	21	39	98	143
Spirit of Discovery	1971	84	21	43	97	125
Spirit of Endeavor	1983	102	30	51	100	207
Spirit of Oceanus	1991	114	59	57	150	295

Glacier Bay Cruiseline

107 W. Denny Way, Suite 303, Seattle, WA 98119; ☎ *800-451-5952;* www.glacier baycruiseline.com

> ✔ **Type of cruise:** Adventure/educational
>
> ✔ **Ship size/style:** Small, expedition-style ships (and one fancier model)

Glacier Bay Cruiseline, under new management since the middle of last year, operates three small ships (dubbed Sport Utility Vessels for the adventure cruise experiences they provide). Along with the three ships, the line offers three different types of cruise experiences: low, medium, and high adventure. Medium adventure cruisers come aboard the 78-passenger *Wilderness Adventurer,* and high adventure cruisers hop on the tiny, 36-passenger *Wilderness Explorer.* Neither ship visits traditional ports; these vessels give passengers an opportunity to walk through lush forests, stroll on beachcomb on secluded shores, and go sea kayaking (no experience is required) in remote areas of Alaska's Inside Passage (the amount of time you spend doing active stuff like kayaking and hiking is much more intense on the *Wilderness Explorer,* and for that reason the ship tends to appeal to the younger set). The line offers medium adventure cruises that spend time in remote, wilderness areas but also visit some popular Alaskan ports on the 94-passenger *Wilderness Discoverer,* which is also outfitted with a fleet of kayaks. All the ships have Zodiac landing craft for going ashore in places without port facilities and carry a flotilla of stable, two-person sea kayaks that allow quiet and unobtrusive observation in wildlife areas. Onboard naturalists lead shore excursions and share information on the region's wildlife and history. *Wilderness Explorer* cruises also include one hotel night in Glacier Bay. The low-adventure cruises are on the *Wilderness Adventurer* in May and September as it travels between Seattle and Juneau.

All the ships offer a comfortable and casual environment, with meals served family-style, at one seating on an unassigned basis. The vessels' windowed observation lounges and large observation decks serve as the main gathering places. The line provides binoculars for guest use.

The adventure cruises attract younger guests. The passenger list includes as many couples in their 40s and 50s as in their 60s and 70s, although cruises that visit ports tend to attract a slightly older crowd.

Itineraries

Glacier Bay has three ships in Alaska from May to September. The line continues 6-day cruises of the Pacific Northwest's San Juan Islands (introduced in 2003) on the *Wilderness Explorer* in spring and fall.

The *Wilderness Adventurer* (see Figure 16-5) sails 7-day Alaskan medium-adventure and cultural-focused itineraries roundtrip between Juneau and Ketchikan in spring, summer, and fall. The *Wilderness Discoverer* sails 7-day combo medium-adventure and port-to-port itineraries between Juneau and Sitka in spring, summer, and fall. The *Wilderness Explorer* sails 5-day Alaskan high-adventure itineraries in spring and summer from Glacier Bay (fares for this itinerary include a roundtrip flight from Juneau and an overnight at the **Glacier Bay Lodge**), offering extensive hiking, kayaking, and wildlife-watching opportunities in the bay and other natural areas.

(Photo: Glacier Bay Cruiseline)

Figure 16-5: The *Wilderness Adventurer*

Outstanding features

All cruises include a day in the park; the line also offers special pre- or post-cruise packages to **Glacier Bay Lodge.** The *Wilderness Adventurer* and *Wilderness Discoverer* have bow-ramps that allow passengers to disembark right onto shore even when no dock is available. Cruise fares include shore excursions at the ports and/or exploration of wilderness areas. The *Wilderness Explorer* itineraries include a pre-cruise hotel night.

Super deals

Early-booking discounts are available, as well as special offers for singles in May and September. Occasionally you can get free airfare offers. Check out the cabins and rates in Table 16-9.

Table 16-9	Glacier Bay Rates		
Ship	*Inside*	*Outside*	*Suite*
Wilderness Adventurer [a]	$2,520	$2,735–$3,190	N/A
Wilderness Discoverer [a]	$2,640	$2,900–$3,770	N/A
Wilderness Explorer [b]	N/A	$1,780–$2,290	N/A

[a] For 7-day Alaska sailings
[b] For 5-day Alaska sailings

Fleet facts

Glacier Bay gussied up the *Wilderness Adventurer* with an extensive renovation in 1999. Cabins are small but comfortable in a summer camp kind of way. Bathrooms are small and not very comfortable, but you can consider that part of the adventure. Standard cabins and bathrooms are likewise small on the *Wilderness Discoverer*, but a $2.5 million renovation in 2001 added something the other vessels don't have — suites (four of them on board). The line calls the smaller *Wilderness Explorer* its "cruising base camp," which is another way of saying you can't really kick back and relax for hours on end. Its cabins are *tiny*, with upper and lower berths (bunk beds), but they do the trick, offering a cozy place to crash after a busy day of kayaking, hiking, and exploring. Table 16-10 offers the fleet's specifications.

Table 16-10		Glacier Bay Fleet Specifications				
Ship	*Year Built*	*Passengers*	*Crew*	*Total Cabins*	*Tonnage*	*Length in Feet*
Wilderness Adventurer	1983	74	24	35	89	157
Wilderness Discoverer	1993	94	24	43	95	169
Wilderness Explorer	1969	36	13	17	98	112

Lindblad Expeditions

720 Fifth Ave., New York, NY 10019; ☎ *800-762-0003;* www.expeditions.com

   ✔ **Type of cruise:** Adventure/educational

   ✔ **Ship size/style:** Small, well-designed vessels

Lindblad Expeditions specializes in environmentally sensitive soft-adventure cruises, offering a casual learning experience. Second-generation adventure travel pro Sven-Olof Lindblad, whose father, Lars-Eric Lindblad, pioneered the field, founded the line. The line's cruises are exploratory in nature; passengers tend to be physically active as well as intellectually curious and are generally in the over-55 age range, although the line does attract some families on its Costa Rican, Baja, Alaskan, and Galapagos programs. The ships, however, have no organized onboard children's programs.

Like the other small ships we review in this chapter (except for Windstar), these vessels don't have casinos or discos, and in this case, even televisions. You spend days finding out about and exploring the great outdoors with the help of experienced expedition leaders and naturalists trained in fields such as botany, anthropology, biology, and geology. The company, by the way, calls these people *expeditionists*, not tour guides. Bring your cameras and binoculars! Shore excursions are included in the cruise fare, and you can attend a recap lecture each evening to discuss what you saw that day.

Meals offer simple, hearty fare at open seatings. Pretty much every passenger on these ships goes to bed early to be ready for the next day's adventures.

Itineraries

Endeavour sails in South America and Antarctica in winter and spring and to Mediterranean/Europe in the summer and fall. *Sea Bird* and *Sea Lion* sail 8-day cruises in Baja California in winter and spring, 7- and 10-day Alaskan tours (from Juneau, Sitka, and Seattle) in summer, and 6-day Columbia River cruises in fall. The *Sea Voyager* sails 8- to 15-day Costa Rica/Panama Canal cruises in winter, spring, and fall and 7-day Costa Rica cruises (geared towards families) in summer. A fourth ship, *Polaris*, sails in 10- to 20-day patterns in the Galapagos Islands year-round.

Outstanding features

You can catch a nightly lecture/recap led by expedition leaders and naturalists, along with occasional film and slide presentations. Each ship has a small reference library. You use Zodiac crafts for shore excursions, and the ships have inflatable kayaks and snorkeling equipment on board for guest use. Special expeditions are designed for families in Costa Rica and Galapagos.

Super deals

 Early-booking and children's discount fares are available, as is free airfare on select sailings. You may also receive a discount of $500 on select itineraries for people with flexible travel dates (you choose a month rather than a specific day of travel). See Table 16-11 for Lindblad rates.

Table 16-11	Lindblad Expeditions Rates		
Ship	*Inside*	*Outside*	*Suite*
Endeavour [a]	N/A	$7,990–$10,540	$14,790
Polaris [b]	N/A	$3,480–$5,980	N/A
Sea Bird [c]	N/A	$2,390–$3,750	N/A
Sea Lion [d]	N/A	$2,290–$3,650	N/A
Sea Voyager [e]	N/A	$3,590–$4,980	N/A

[a] For 15-day Antarctica sailings
[b] For 7-day Columbia River sailings
[c] For 8-day Baja California sailings
[d] For 8-day Costa Rica/Panama sailings
[e] For 10-day Galapagos sailings

Fleet facts

The *Sea Lion* (see Figure 16-6) and *Sea Bird* are identical right down to their casual decor and furnishings (see Table 16-12 for fleet specifications). The cabins are tiny with minuscule bathrooms. (The toilet and shower are together in one space, an arrangement you also see on Glacier Bay vessels and on some of Cruise West's.) All cabins are outside and have picture windows that open to let in breezes and fresh air. Both ships have two public rooms: the observation lounge/bar and the dining room. Lindblad acquired and extensively renovated the *Sea Voyager* in 2001. The cabins, dining room, and lounge area are almost plush by expedition standards, and you even have a small fitness room. *Endeavour* is the biggest of the ships — at just over 3,100 tons and a capacity for 110 passengers — boasting a small swimming pool, fitness center, sauna, and hair salon. It underwent a major refurbishment in 1998. Cabins have windows or portholes, although the ship's two suites may be more enticing.

(Photo: Lindblad Expeditions)

Figure 16-6: The *Sea Lion*

Table 16-12   Lindblad Expeditions Fleet Specifications

Ship	Year Built	Passengers	Crew	Total Cabins	Tonnage	Length in Feet
Endeavour	1966	110	65	62	3,132	295
Sea Bird	1982	70	22	37	100	152
Sea Lion	1981	70	22	37	100	152
Sea Voyager	1982	62	22	33	1,195	175

Star Clippers

4101 Salzedo St., Coral Gables, FL 33146; ☎ *800-442-0553;* www.starclippers.com

- ✔ **Type of cruise:** Adventure/educational, romantic
- ✔ **Ship size/style:** Classic-style sailing ships

The twins *Star Flyer* and *Star Clipper* (see Figure 16-7) are replicas of the big 19th-century clipper sailing ships (or *barkentines*) that once circled the globe. Their tall masts carry enormous sails, are glorious to look at, and provide a particular thrill for history buffs. Unlike the sails on the much larger Windstar vessels, these sails are not just window-dressing: The *Star Clipper* and *Star Flyer* were constructed by using information from original drawings and the specifications of a leading 19th-century naval architect, and they have been updated with modern touches so that today they sail as the tallest and among the fastest clipper ships ever built, reaching speeds of more than 19 knots.

The *Royal Clipper* is the largest true sailing ship afloat. The 228-passenger, 5-mast vessel (with 42 sails) is also the line's plushest ship.

The atmosphere on board any of the line's vessels is akin to being on a private yacht rather than a cruise ship. The cruising experience is friendly and casual in an L.L. Bean sort of way — somewhere between the barefoot ambience of sailing competitor Windjammer and the more upscale ambience of Windstar. Activities on the ships lean toward the nautical, such as visiting the bridge, watching the crew handle the sails, and taking classes in skills such as knot tying. Sometimes, in the right weather conditions, boating-trained passengers are allowed to climb to the top of the masts to assist with the sails — wearing the correct safety harness, of course.

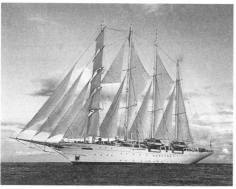

(Photo: Star Clippers/Harvey Lloyd)

Figure 16-7: The *Star Clipper*

The ships normally stop at ports of call in the late morning. In port, you can enjoy water sports such as scuba diving and snorkeling before a sunset sail to the next locale. Local entertainers sometimes come aboard at night, and the ships also have a piano player and a makeshift disco in the **Tropical Bar.** Movies are piped into passenger cabins.

Passengers range from ages 25 to 70 and average in the 40s. Many own their own sailboats and a good number are European. Star Clipper cruises are also appropriate for older kids (in fact, because the ships afford a chance to relive maritime history, they can be downright educational).

Itineraries

The *Royal Clipper* offers 7-day southern Caribbean cruises round-trip from Barbados in winter and fall and spends spring and summer in Europe doing 7-, 10-, and 11-day western Mediterranean itineraries from Rome. *Star Clipper* sails 7-day southern Caribbean cruises round-trip from St. Maarten in winter and 7-day France and Italy itineraries from Cannes in spring and summer. *Star Flyer* sails 7-day Greek Isles itineraries in spring and summer (roundtrip from Piraeus) and spends fall and winter in the Far East, sailing from Phuket, Thailand.

Outstanding features

Snorkeling equipment is free. For an extra fee, the ships offer PADI-approved scuba diving, including instruction. Additional water activities include waterskiing, banana boats, and Sunfish sail boats. Select Caribbean sailings are themed to jazz and blues, health and well-being, and indigenous Caribbean cultures and feature guest speakers, special activities, and entertainment.

Super deals

Star Clippers offers early-bird discounts of up to 50 percent on select sailings for bookings 120 days out, as well as repeat-passenger discounts and sometimes free hotel nights and heavily discounted or free airfare. Discounts are available if you book two 7-day cruises back-to-back. Some third-passenger rates are available, although few cabins can accommodate three people. Children ages 2 to 18, accompanying two full-fare paying adults, pay third passenger fares; if one child occupies a separate cabin, you pay no single supplement. See Table 16-13 for more rates.

Table 16-13	Star Clippers Rates*		
Ship	*Inside*	*Outside*	*Suite*
Royal Clipper [a]	$1,825	$1,925–$2,845	$3,845–$4,845
Star Clipper [b]	$1,395–$1,925	$2,145–$4,075	$5,675
Star Flyer [c]	$1,345–$1,545	$1,765–$2,465	$3,485

[a] For 7-day W. Mediterranean sailings
[b] For 7-day Caribbean sailings
[c] For 7-day Thailand sailings
*Port charges are extra: $155 in the Caribbean, $175 in Europe, and $145 in Thailand

Fleet facts

Decor on Star Clippers ships is conservative, with touches of mahogany and brass. Public rooms on the *Star Clipper* and *Star Flyer* are comfortable and almost cushy (see Table 16-14 for fleet specifications). Cabins are small (but okay for a ship of this size), and the teak sun deck space gives you much more room to spread out and enjoy the sea breeze than what you can usually find on small ships. The *Royal Clipper's* cabins include 14 veranda suites, and the vessel boasts a neat lounge that offers underwater viewing while the ship is at anchor.

Table 16-14	Star Clippers Fleet Specifications					
Ship	*Year Built*	*Passengers*	*Crew*	*Total Cabins*	*Tonnage*	*Length in Feet*
Royal Clipper	2000	228	100	114	5,000	439
Star Clipper	1992	172	70	84	2,298	360
Star Flyer	1991	172	70	84	2,298	360

 Despite stabilizers, Star Clipper ships can get knocked around in rough seas, which may be troublesome to those who get seasick. This problem is common to small ships in general.

Windjammer Barefoot Cruises

P.O. Box 190120, Miami Beach, FL 33119-0120; ☎ *800-327-2601* or *305-672-6453*; www.windjammer.com

> ✔ **Type of cruise:** Adventure/educational, family, party
>
> ✔ **Ship size/style:** Old-style sailing ships

With a fleet made up almost entirely of genuine old-time sailing vessels, Windjammer provides a completely different experience from what you find on a megaship, and the line is very proud of that fact. These ships are about sailing, making friends, experiencing a sense of adventure, and having barefoot fun — you don't need to pack much more than T-shirts, shorts, and a bathing suit or two. On a typical Windjammer cruise, passengers visit an island every day and have plenty of time to take in the beach scene, snorkel and swim, try out the local cuisine, or go hiking, biking, or jungle trekking on an organized excursion before the ship sets sail in late afternoon or evening. Because the ships are small, they can anchor in out-of-the-way Caribbean harbors, and their laid-back schedules allow them to stay late in some ports so passengers can explore legendary nightlife hotspots like **Foxy's** bar in the British Virgin Islands. Amenities aboard ship are minimal — think tight cabins, average food, and almost no organized activities — but cruise prices are sometimes ridiculously low, as are drink prices at the ships' bars.

Captain Mike Burke, the line's founder, built his company by buying up somewhat weathered vessels and restoring them to their former glory. Each has its own interesting history: E. F. Hutton once owned the *Mandalay*, and Gloria Vanderbilt asked Burke to take extra care of the *Yankee Clipper* (see Figure 16-8), which had once been her family's private yacht. The *Polynesia,* built in Holland in 1938, was the subject of Allen Villers's book *The Quest of the Schooner Argus,* and the line's newest vessel, the *Legacy,* was a French government research vessel in a former life. The line's only non-sailing ship, the *Amazing Grace,* is a former North Sea supply vessel that the British royal family occasionally pressed into service.

(Photo: Windjammer Barefoot Cruises)

Figure 16-8: The *Yankee Clipper*

Windjammer has a reputation for attracting party-hearty types, who run the gamut from college kids to leathery-skinned 70-somethings, all looking for the same kind of casual, unstructured, and way-unstuffy experience. With that said, some cruises are more sedate than others, although you can sail occasional nudist, singles, swingers, or gay cruises and the occasional "Pirates Week" (a full-on, adults-only party scene) to turn up the heat. Windjammer used to advertise in magazines such as *Forum, Screw,* and *Hustler,* but the line has gone much more mainstream under the leadership of Burke's daughter, Susan, who is now president. Sure, plenty of the passengers relish the free Bloody Marys served at breakfast, plow right on through the free rum swizzles that come out before dinner, and keep going on their own tab well into the night, but the ships still carry plenty of quieter types. Just don't expect to find many quiet hideaways curling up with a good book.

Kids over age 6 are welcome on the ships these days, with special programs for children 6 to 12 (Junior Jammers) and teens 13 to 17 offered aboard the *Legacy* and *Polynesia* from June through August. Some cruises can see as many as 40 kids aboard — a full third of the ships' passenger capacity. The ships shift their itineraries every other year so families that sail annually can experience different ports. Young children are kept busy with typical summer-camp-style activities such as sailing classes, snorkeling, ice cream parties, board games and movie nights, and even supervised island tours and beach Olympics. Activities for teens focus on sailing-related skills, kayaking, snorkeling, playing volleyball against the crew, taking island dance classes, going on four-wheel-drive safaris and island tours, and learning diving basics in a Junior Discover scuba program. When possible, both kids and teens can participate in a cultural-exchange program where they can hang with local youths on the islands.

Aside from goofy ship-and-shore activities like crab races and tugs of war, adult activities are almost nil, leaving passengers free to mix, mingle, and sun themselves on deck. If you want a little more structure, you can also opt for the less swingin' theme cruises the line offers, including some focused on island cuisine (with guest chefs, usually from the Caribbean), island beer and rum, painting and photography, murder mystery games, spa activities (with masseuses and yoga instructors on board), golf, bird-watching, or jazz.

Despite such mainstreaming, the line still has an anything-goes ambience aboard its ships. Relaxing, checking out the gorgeous scenery, and telling stories are the favorite pastimes. If you want, you can help hoist the sails, and if the captain okays it, you can even hang out in the netting strung from the ships' bowsprits while the sea rushes by below you. The attitude on the ships is that everyone is part of a big happy family; exactly what Cap'n Mike wanted when he started the line — for passengers to leave at the end of their vacation with tears in their eyes and immediately start thinking about their next trip. The line has an impressive 40 percent repeat rate, with very frequent passengers known as *jammers.* One guy, who goes by GOC (Good Old Cliffy), has been onboard some 100 times, and scores of regulars have sailed with the line upwards of 30 times.

Itineraries

Because Windjammer's ships tend to rely as much on their engines as their sails for propulsion, they stick to schedules that pure sailing vessels have a hard time keeping. That said, weather conditions and island events do play a part in determining where the ships go in any given week, with the captains choosing stops from a selection of islands. Itineraries, therefore, are far less set in stone than on mainstream ships and may change from week to week, with one exception: Cruises on the *Amazing Grace,* which does 12-day eastern Caribbean itineraries year-round from Freeport, the Bahamas, and Trinidad, carries passengers as well as supplies for the other Windjammer ships it meets at various ports. The ships embark from ports including St. Thomas, Saint Maarten, St. Lucia, Aruba, Antigua, Grenada, and Tortola. *Polynesia* and *Yankee Clipper* sail 5-day eastern Caribbean itineraries year-round. *Legacy* sails 3-, 4-, and 7-day Bahamas itineraries and 5-day eastern Caribbean cruises. *Mandalay* sails 12-day eastern Caribbean itineraries in winter and spring and 5-day southern Caribbean cruises in summer.

Outstanding features

Theme cruises include trips for singles and gays, photography, culinary, painting, and murder mystery cruises. Nudist and swinger groups sometimes charter the ships. In summers, the line offers kids and teens programs on the *Legacy* and *Polynesia.*

Super deals

You can stow away on the ship in port the night before your sailing for $55; much less than the cost of a hotel room, plus you also get dinner and free rum swizzles. If you book back-to-back cruises, you can sleep on board the night before your second sailing for free. Check out special fares for children ages 6 to 12. You can see the latest special deals and theme cruises at www.windjammer.com. And see Table 16-15 for more rates.

Table 16-15   Windjammer Barefoot Cruises Rates

Ship	Inside	Outside	Suite
Amazing Grace [a]	N/A	$1,300–$1,575	$2,875–$2,975
Legacy [b]	N/A	$700–$1,200	$1,200–$1,600
Mandalay [b]	N/A	$900–$1,200	$1,300–$1,400
Polynesia [b]	$900–$1,000	N/A	$1,200–$1,400
Yankee Clipper [b]	N/A	$900–$1,200	$1,300–$1,400

[a] For 12-day sailings, port charges are an additional $150

[b] For 5-day sailings, port charges are an additional $65 to $90

Fleet facts

The ships in the fleet (see Table 16-16) are tall, with the exception of the motorized *Amazing Grace,* which carries passengers as well as supplies for the other Windjammer ships (cargo areas of this ship are off-limits to passengers). The *Grace* tends to attract an older clientele.

Table 16-16   Windjammer Barefoot Cruises Fleet Specifications

Ship	Year Built	Passengers	Crew	Total Cabins	Tonnage	Length in Feet
Amazing Grace	1955	92	40	46	1,525	254
Legacy	1959	122	43	61	1,165	294
Mandalay	1923	72	28	36	420	236
Polynesia	1938	112	45	53	430	248
Yankee Clipper	1927	64	29	32	327	197

The sailing ships are all very tight and very "woody" — all polished rails, brass trimmings, and well-trod teak decks. Inside spaces are tight, with some tiny circular staircases. Each ship has a single dining room that functions on an open-seating basis, but all other onboard activities are out on the open decks and the open-air bars. Cabins on the ships are tiny and offer no frills; many have bunk-style beds (the *Polynesia* and *Legacy* even have some four-passenger dorm-style cabins). Some cabins on the *Amazing Grace* don't have private shower and toilet facilities, requiring that passengers share with neighboring cabins; the other ships provide individual showers in the cabins. The *Legacy,* which is much larger and more modern than the other ships, has somewhat larger cabins and bathrooms, wider corridors, and a small television room/library that gets little use.

Like other smaller ships without stabilizers, Windjammer sailing ships can get tossed around a bit in rough seas and aren't an ideal choice for people who get seasick easily.

Windstar Cruises

300 Elliott Ave. West, Seattle, WA 98119; ☎ *800-258-7245;* www.windstar
cruises.com

> ✔ **Type of cruise:** Adventure, gourmet, romantic
>
> ✔ **Ship size/style:** Modern, smallish ships with sails (and engines, too)

The Windstar ships may look like sailing vessels of yore, but they really
float along like upscale resorts, complete with all the amenities. These
ships are pretty enough to be in the movies (you feel proud when you
sail in or out of a port with the sails attracting attention) and luxurious
enough to host movie stars or plain folks in laid-back splendor. We're
talking top-notch service, incredible cuisine, fun and casual ambience
(no ties or gowns necessary), and virtually no set regimen outside of the
endless pampering. A watersports platform at the stern provides for a
variety of activities when the ships are in port. Nighttime entertainment
is low-key, with a pianist and sometimes a vocalist. Local entertainment
is sometimes brought aboard at ports of call. The ships also have small
casinos.

Cuisine on all the ships is excellent, right up there with what you find on
the luxury megaliners. Joachim Splichal — the renowned Los Angeles
chef/restaurateur — oversees the food preparation. Light cuisine expert
Jeanne Jones helped develop the healthy *Sail Light* menu (items available at every meal). The reservations-only Bistro alternative restaurant
on the *Wind Surf* offers a more intimate option to the dining room at no
extra charge.

Most of the passengers are sophisticated couples, ranging in age from
30 to 70, who are perfectly happy entertaining themselves.

Itineraries

Windstar itineraries in 2005 include Caribbean, Mayan Riviera, Central
American, and Mediterranean cruises. Sailings are mostly 7, 10, 11, or
14 nights. Windstar starts and ends the year with Central American sailings concentrating on Costa Rica; during the spring, summer, and fall,
the ship does a series of 7-night voyages all along the Mediterranean.
Wind Spirit (see Figure 16-9) winters in the Caribbean, sailing roundtrip
out of St. Thomas. From April through November, the vessel is in the
Mediterranean for 7-night sailings. *Wind Surf* starts the year with a series
of Mayan Riviera 7-night sailings, roundtrip from Cozumel. From late
April through mid-November, the ship is in the Mediterranean. Wind Surf
ends the year with Caribbean sailings, primarily roundtrip from
Barbados.

Figure 16-9: The *Wind Spirit*

(Photo: Windstar Cruises)

Outstanding features

You can visit the bridge whenever you please to see the sophisticated computer technology that controls the sails. During a recent fleet-wide renovation, Windstar added LCD flat screen televisions with DVD and CD players to all cabins with an impressive selection of DVDs and CDs available from each ship's library. Internet access is available at the Internet center on the *Wind Surf* (from the other ship you can only send and receive e-mail). Water sports (with the exception of diving) are complimentary. Wedding packages are available. Tipping is not required (but the staff accepts tips if you offer).

Super deals

Windstar offers low add-on (and sometimes free) airfares. Pre- and post-cruise tour offerings are also available. Table 16-17 has brochure rates, but advanced booking discounts up to 55 percent are always available.

Table 16-17	Windstar Cruises Rates		
Ship	*Inside*	*Outside*	*Suite*
Wind Spirit	N/A	$2,655–$3,475*	N/A
Wind Surf	N/A	$2,655–$3,475*	$4,203–$5,723

*Category B

Fleet facts

Although Windstar ships have tens of thousands of square feet of
Dacron flying from their masts, they operate as smoothly as the very
best modern yachts, owing to the million-dollar computers that control
the sails and stabilizers. The *Wind Spirit* and *Wind Star* are identical, with
all outside cabins (featuring large portholes) and impressive teakwood-
decked, recently refurbished bathrooms. The *Wind Surf* (formerly the
Club Med I) was built at the same shipyard and has the same sail-ship
concept as the other ships, but it has 31 suites, a whopping 10,000-
square-foot spa (bigger than on many much larger ships), and plenty of
excellent outside sitting and walking areas, making it bigger than the
other ships. Table 16-18 shows the current fleet specifications.

Table 16-18   Windstar Cruises Fleet Specifications

Ship	Year Built	Passengers	Crew	Total Cabins	Tonnage	Length in Feet
Wind Star/Spirit	1986/88	148	88	74	5,350	440
Wind Surf	1990	308	163	154	14,745	614

Part V

Landing at the Ports of Call

In this part . . .

Although shipboard life is a dreamy experience unto itself, the cruise experience is also about visiting places. In the Caribbean, you can check out popular and remote islands and even get to places accessible only by ship, such as the private islands in the Bahamas that some cruise lines operate. In Alaska, port calls may include Juneau, the only U.S. state capital that you can't reach by car. And in the Mediterranean, the ships visit big cities such as Rome and Barcelona, as well as small islands such as Elba and Mykonos.

The ports of call offer something for everyone. You can discover interesting facts about the destination's culture and history, try exotic foods, view and explore the location's natural beauty, enjoy sports activities, and, of course, shop!

Chapter 17

Seeing the Sights: Your Port of Call

*H*alf the fun of a cruise is the cruise itself, but the other half is touring the places you came so far to see. You may touch land as little or as much as you like, depending on the cruise you choose, but all cruises offer unique opportunities ashore.

Starting from your port of embarkation and including the ports of call along the way, you can explore on your own or join the cruise line's shore excursions (and, before or after your cruise, its add-on programs). This chapter describes how to make the most of your time in port.

Getting a Head Start: Beginning Your Vacation Before You Embark

The main ports of embarkation for Caribbean, Alaskan, and Mediterranean cruises are all tourist destinations unto themselves. Most lines offer a pre-cruise hotel package (often two to four days) and a post-cruise hotel package for cruisers who want to stretch their vacation. In Alaska and the Mediterranean, cruise lines offer escorted bus or train tours to sights away from the coastal areas, packaging these excursions with hotel accommodations and transfers.

If you want to make your own hotel arrangements, we suggest properties in the main embarkation cities in the port chapters of Part V.

Most ships don't start boarding until the afternoon and don't depart until after 4 p.m., so you may be able to fit in a half-day's sightseeing on your first day. (You can normally leave your luggage at the pier.)

For Shore: Touring Solo

Whenever your ship reaches port, you may choose to join the ship's organized shore excursions, to strike out on your own, or to take it easy and remain on the ship. Shore excursions — which we preview throughout Part V — are a social, convenient, efficient, and sometimes economical way for you to see the main sights at the ports of call. However, be aware that the cruise line runs these gigs as profit-making ventures. You usually pay for each excursion on top of your cruise fare, and these side jaunts can take a bite out of your vacation budget. On the other hand, in certain locales, the cost of going it alone can be prohibitive. Choosing to take a prearranged sightseeing trip is a matter of both personal preference and pocketbook concerns.

Consider these questions when you decide whether you want to go on your own or book a shore excursion:

- Do you enjoy the boisterous camaraderie of a group (even on a crowded bus) and a perky tour guide, or do you prefer exploring quietly by yourself (even if you get lost sometimes)?
- What's within walking distance of the ship and what's not?
- How easy is it to find a cab, bus, or rental car to tour on your own, and how reliable is that transportation?
- Does the tour include all the things you definitely want to see and do? If not, do you have time to see or do them before or after the tour?
- How much do the attractions cost?
- Does the activity you want to do require advance reservations (such as tee times for golf)?
- Can you get back to the ship on time if you go it alone?

In the ports chapters that follow, we provide more detailed information to help you answer these questions.

Of course, your ship doesn't require you to get off at every port of call. The restaurants remain open (so even if you do get off, you can come back to eat), activities are offered (but usually on a somewhat limited basis), ship spas typically offer discounts on spas and more during days in port, and you always have the option of just sitting and relaxing (you have more space to spread out on the ship with most others ashore).

What do shore excursions include?

Shore excursions usually mean piling people into tour buses, although, depending on the location, you may also take some other mode of transportation — minivan, jet boat, kayak, horse cart, or your own two feet. The cost of the excursion includes admission to all the attractions and sometimes a meal, a dance, or a musical performance. However, many tours make at least one stop at a souvenir stand, so you may want to bring some cash for impulse shopping. An enthusiastic guide always provides running commentary — mostly informative and occasionally corny. Guides expect tips, although the amount is entirely up to you — around 5 percent of the excursion cost is about right if you enjoy the tour.

Which shore excursions make sense?

In some ports where you can best reach sights by foot, beating your own path is often less expensive and more exciting. However, in locales where most attractions are far from the docks — and taxis or other local modes of transportation are scarce or expensive — you may be better off going with the flow and booking an organized excursion.

The other areas in which shore excursions are really worth the money are sports and adventure offerings, such as kayaking, biking, golfing, fishing, snorkeling, scuba diving, and flightseeing tours. Because these expeditions take smaller groups of passengers at a time, you feel like part of the team rather than part of the herd. Also, booking through the cruise line saves you the hassle of making your own advance reservations (such offerings are also popular with land-based tourists and can sell out) and finding reliable vendors. Having assurance that the cruise line screens the quality of the hang-gliding instructors is, in our opinion, definitely worth any higher costs.

How much do shore excursions cost?

Costs for prearranged shore excursions vary widely: You may pay $300 or more for a flightseeing trip via helicopter or plane and just $29 for a short bus or walking tour. During a longer port visit, you may fit in several organized expeditions, or you may opt for a short tour that still leaves time to shop or explore by yourself. You may also like to mix and match: Follow your own path at one port and hook up with the group next time.

How do I sign up for an excursion?

Until recently, you couldn't book shore excursions in advance of your cruise. Several lines have now introduced that option (you can even book your shore excursions at the lines' Web sites); otherwise, you book after you board. Signing up after departure works to both sides' advantage: The ship's tour staff has a chance to pitch you their spiel, and you have a chance to ask questions.

If you decide to go try a shore excursion, you need to sign up on an order form, usually available in your cabin on arrival, at the purser's desk, or at the first day's lecture on shore excursions. To reserve your tour, fill out the shore-excursion order form by marking the appropriate boxes, noting your cabin number, and signing the form. Return it as directed to the shore-excursion or purser's office. The staff charges your account and delivers the tickets to your cabin before your first scheduled tour. Look over the information on the tickets carefully: They should note the time and place for departure, and if you don't arrive on time, you may be left behind.

 Popular excursions sell out quickly! Book your priority shore excursions on the first day of your cruise. For this same reason, if your line accepts reservations in advance, make them early.

 Make sure that you really want to take all the tours you sign up for. Because the cruise lines almost universally use outside concessionaires to run the tours and have to arrange for a certain number of vehicles and guides days ahead of time, you can't change your mind the day before. (Naturally, you can opt not to go, but in most cases the line still charges you.)

Ship to Shore: All About Disembarking

You can't start sashaying down the gangplank as soon as the boat ties up to the dock. Nope. You have to wait for local authorities to stamp all kinds of paperwork before you can come and go. Because this may take up to two hours, you may as well put your feet up and study your city guide until the public address system gives you the all-clear announcement.

What if the ship anchors off shore?

When a ship comes to port, it either docks at the pier or anchors off shore, depending on the size of the ship and the port's facilities. Sometimes a ship needs to anchor slightly off shore because the ship is too big or the port is too crowded for docking. A small boat, called a *launch* or *tender,* shuttles passengers to dry land. The boat ride only takes a few minutes, but preparations take much longer.

Disembarkation works like this: Everyone who wants to ride the launch gathers in a public lounge and receives a boarding number. Shore-excursion parties disembark first. If you're not taking an excursion, you may get an earlier tender assignment by being first in line at the lounge, but you may face a long wait. We recommend that you spend that hour of waiting having some fun on board and leave the ship on a later launch.

Crewmembers are always ready to help passengers board the launch. Sometimes choppy waves sway the small boat, so you may need to jump a bit to get on board. If you have a disability and require special assistance getting in and out of the tender, alert the crew in advance so that they can better prepare to assist you.

 The ride to shore, although quite short, can be rather rough. If you suffer from seasickness, try to sit near an open area on the tender.

The tenders shuttle back and forth all day, so you can return to the ship at any time (including, if you choose, for lunch). Because tenders from several anchored ships may hang out around the dock, when you board a tender for your return, make sure that you pick the one for *your* ship.

What should I bring ashore?

Be sure to tote the following essentials when you disembark:

- ✔ **Ship boarding pass and/or shipboard identification:** Without them, you have trouble getting back on board.

- ✔ **Cash:** Although your ship expenses go on credit, and you can use credit cards at many stores and restaurants, you still need cash ashore to get around and buy keepsakes and postcards. (Chapter 4 has the details on how to get the appropriate currency for the country you visit in cases where merchants don't accept the U.S. dollar.) Don't bring too much cash, however, because pickpockets can spot tourists pretty easily.

- ✔ **Beach towels:** You can normally borrow towels from the ship as you prepare to disembark for a beach.

- ✔ **Bottled water:** You may want to buy a bottle on board, especially if you plan to visit places with low-quality drinking water.

Sightseeing on Your Own

If you want to explore on your own, remember the following tips:

- ✔ **Prioritize:** Create a "must see" list and calculate how much time and money you need to spend to get there (you can ask the ship's shore excursions staff for assistance in this regard).

- ✔ **Book adventures ahead of time:** Even if you don't want to book a shore excursion through the cruise line, you may want to consult with the shore-excursion staff for activities such as horseback riding, diving, tennis, and golf. They can tell you if you need a reservation and can recommend reliable operators. Keep in mind that facilities and operators ashore may get overrun not only with other cruise passengers but also with land-based vacationers.

- ✔ **Reserve a table:** If you want to dine at a particular restaurant (especially one popular in the guidebooks), make a reservation.

- ✔ **Ride only in marked taxis:** The unofficial cabdriver may be charming and offer a nice tour at a very nice price, but don't leave your common sense about safety behind on the boat.

- ✔ **Eat (and drink) smart:** Instead of snacking from street vendors' carts, sample the local cuisine at restaurants to minimize the risk of an upset stomach from exotic foods. Likewise, drink bottled water rather than tap water and ask the staff to make other drinks without ice.

- ✔ **Keep your cabbie:** If you find a reliable cab driver that gets you where you want to go, arrange for the same driver to pick you up when the time arrives to go back to the ship. This is especially important if you head to an out-of-the-way beach area (you may not find cabs waiting when you're ready to go).

- ✔ **Consider cost-sharing:** Share the cost of a cab with a couple of cruisemates (even if you all want to split up when you get to your destinations). And when you negotiate the cost, make sure you and the cab driver talk the same currency.

- ✔ **Don't dawdle:** Report to the dock in time to return to the ship.

Don't Miss the Boat!

 Cruise lines are very strict about sailing times. The staff posts schedules both in the daily bulletin delivered to your cabin and at the gangway. You must be back at the dock at least a half hour before the ship's scheduled departure — otherwise you may miss the boat. Shore excursions provide an exception to this rule. If they run late, the ship accepts responsibility and doesn't leave without you. If you travel on your own, however, you could get stuck.

If you do miss the boat, contact the cruise line representative at the port immediately. You can catch your ship at the next port of call, but you have to pay your own way there.

Chapter 18

Landing in the Caribbean

· ·

In This Chapter

▶ Exploring the ports of embarkation

▶ Finding the very best at the Caribbean ports of call

▶ Enjoying the best shore excursions in each port

· ·

*W*hen most people think "cruise," they automatically think "Caribbean," whether they mean to or not. But how can they help it? All those cruisey notions of white-sand beaches, swaying palms, clear turquoise waters, and colorful tropical birds (as well as rain forests, waterfalls, rivers, mountains, lush gardens, and even volcanoes) just scream Caribbean — no wonder it ranks as the number-one cruise destination in the world. Not only do you get all that perfect scenery, but you also get the region's plentiful marine life, rich culture, and great food. To top it all off, the islands are so close together that you can easily visit three, four, five, and even six different paradises in the course of a one-week itinerary. The multicultural history of the region creates an intriguing blend of attractions. You find marks of Spanish, French, Dutch, Swedish, British, and American influence in their respective former and current colonies or affiliates, as well as traces of pre-Columbian cultures. Native peoples, European explorers, pirates, and shipwrecked sailors contributed to the stories behind numerous ancient ruins, forts, churches, synagogues, historic homes, and museums.

Whether shopping in fancy showrooms for fine jewelry or quaint markets for local handicrafts, you have plenty of opportunities in the Caribbean to spend the greenbacks (or take out the charge cards), including duty-free bargains. If you prefer golfing, you can play on world-class courses as part of shore excursions organized through your cruise line.

Taking a Look Around

On many of the islands, you can visit the major sightseeing attractions pretty easily on your own. This chapter also offers transportation suggestions to help you get out of town and back to nature when you want to escape the tourist scene around the ports.

The Gulf of Mexico & the Caribbean

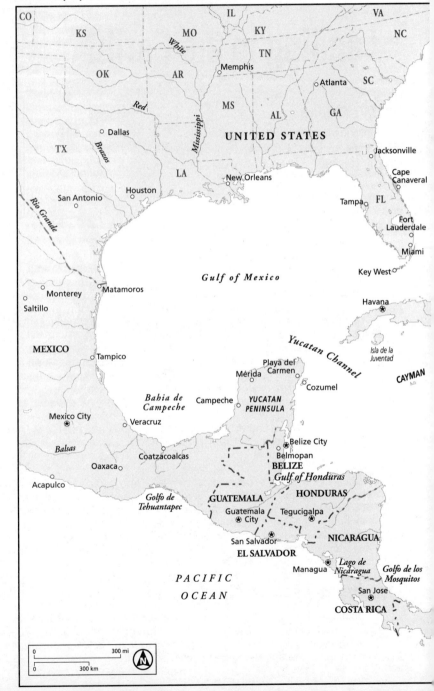

CO
KS
MO
IL
KY
VA
NC
OK
AR
White
TN
Memphis
Atlanta
SC
Red
MS
AL
GA
Dallas
Mississippi
UNITED STATES
Jacksonville
TX
Brazos
LA
Houston
New Orleans
Cape
Canaveral
San Antonio
Tampa
FL
Rio Grande
Fort
Lauderdale
Miami
Monterey
Matamoros
Gulf of Mexico
Key West
Saltillo
Havana
Isla de la
Juventad
Yucatan Channel
CAYMAN
MEXICO
Tampico
Playa del
Carmen
Mérida
*Bahia de
Campeche*
Campeche
YUCATAN
PENINSULA
Cozumel
Mexico City
Balsas
Veracruz
Belize City
Coatzacoalcas
Belmopan
Oaxaca
BELIZE
Acapulco
Gulf of Honduras
*Golfo de
Tehuantapec*
GUATEMALA
HONDURAS
Guatemala
City
Tegucigalpa
San Salvador
NICARAGUA
EL SALVADOR
Managua
*Lago de
Nicaragua*
*Golfo de los
Mosquitos*
PACIFIC
OCEAN
San Jose
COSTA RICA

0   300 mi
0   300 km
N

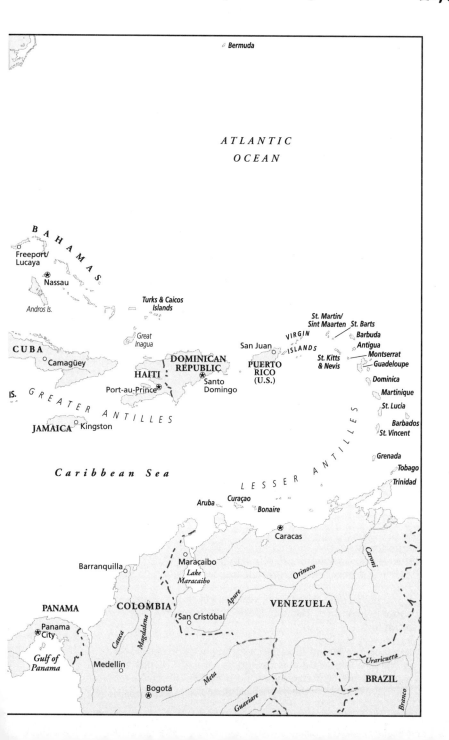

On the other hand, some of the cruise lines' shore excursions are really worthwhile, especially if you want to engage in hard-to-book activities such as tennis, golf, or sport-fishing or if you want to try your fins at snorkeling or scuba diving. Booking through the cruise line ensures that you deal with a reputable vendor and get a space at a convenient time for the cruise schedule.

The prices listed in this chapter are based on 2004 rates and may change slightly for 2005.

Boarding Ship for the Caribbean

The main port cities for Caribbean cruises — Miami, Fort Lauderdale/ Port Everglades, Cape Canaveral/Port Canaveral, Tampa, and New Orleans — are all tourist destinations unto themselves, so you may want to arrive a night or two early or stay a night or two after your cruise to enjoy the fun. The cruise lines offer pre- and post-cruise packages for hotels, sometimes including a rental car, admission to local attractions, and/or organized tours. We also cover San Juan, Puerto Rico — a port of embarkation *and* a popular port of call — in the ports of call section.

On Caribbean cruises, you usually board in the afternoon, and the ship departs after 4 p.m. So, if you fly in that morning, you may want to plan out a half-day of sightseeing to start your vacation right away. You should be able to leave your luggage at the pier or with a friendly hotel concierge.

The Ports of Embarkation

This section provides the lowdown on the five primary ports of embarkation for Caribbean cruises: Miami, Fort Lauderdale/Port Everglades, Cape Canaveral/Port Canaveral, Tampa, and New Orleans.

Miami

A five-lane bridge from the downtown district of Miami provides access to the number-one cruise port in the world, the **Port of Miami** (1015 N. America Way). For information, call ☎ **305-371-PORT.** To accommodate the enormous amount of cruise traffic, a dozen bi-level terminals offer easy car access and customs clearance (for when you get back).

If you have some time to kill, you can get to the nearby restaurant and shopping complex, **Bayside Marketplace,** by crossing a bridge in a cab or on foot.

If you fly into **Miami International Airport,** you can take a cab to the Port of Miami (about eight miles away) for around $21 (plus tip) or use the less expensive public **Metrobus** service (☎ **305-770-3131**). A better choice if you have luggage is the **SuperShuttle** service (☎ **305-871-2000**), which

Miami at a Glance

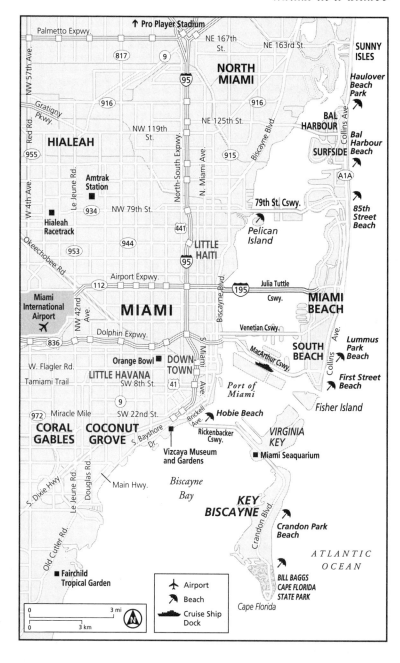

↑ Pro Player Stadium

Palmetto Expwy.

NE 167th St.

NE 163rd St.

SUNNY ISLES

817   9

NW 57th Ave.

NORTH MIAMI

95

Haulover Beach Park

Gratigny Pkwy.

916

916

BAL HARBOUR

Collins Ave.

Red Rd.

NW 119th St.

NE 125th St.

HIALEAH

955

Bal Harbour Beach

915

SURFSIDE

North-South Expwy.

N. Miami Ave.

Biscayne Blvd.

A1A

W. 4th Ave.

Le Jeune Rd.

Amtrak Station ■

79th St. Cswy.

85th Street Beach

934   NW 79th St.

441

Pelican Island

■ **Hialeah Racetrack**

Okeechobee Rd.

953

944

LITTLE HAITI

95

Airport Expwy.

Julia Tuttle Cswy.

112

195

Miami International Airport ✈

NW 42nd Ave.

MIAMI

Biscayne Blvd.

MIAMI BEACH

Dolphin Expwy.

Venetian Cswy.

836

SOUTH BEACH

Lummus Park Beach

W. Flagler Rd.

Orange Bowl ■ **DOWN-TOWN**

Collins Ave.

Tamiami Trail

LITTLE HAVANA

SW 8th St.   41

MacArthur Cswy.

First Street Beach

972   Miracle Mile

9

SW 22nd St.

S. Miami Ave.

Port of Miami

Fisher Island

CORAL GABLES

COCONUT GROVE

S. Bayshore Dr.

Brickell Ave. ↗ *Hobie Beach*

Rickenbacker Cswy.

VIRGINIA KEY

S. Dixie Hwy.

Le Jeune Rd.

Douglas Rd.

Main Hwy.

Vizcaya Museum and Gardens

■ Miami Seaquarium

Biscayne Bay

KEY BISCAYNE

Crandon Blvd.

↗ Crandon Park Beach

Old Cutler Rd.

ATLANTIC OCEAN

■ **Fairchild Tropical Garden**

✈ Airport

↗ Beach

BILL BAGGS CAPE FLORIDA STATE PARK

Cape Florida

🚢 Cruise Ship Dock

0   3 mi

0   3 km

Florida Home Ports

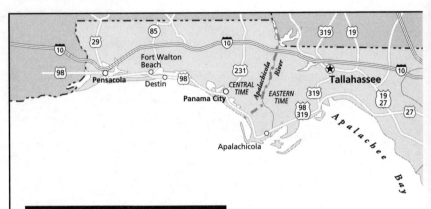

CRUISE LINE HOME PORTS

MIAMI	Carnival
	Norwegian
	Oceania
	Royal Caribbean
	Windjammer
FORT LAUDERDALE	Carnival
	Celebrity
	Costa
	Crystal
	Cunard
	Holland America
	Princess
	Royal Caribbean
	Seabourn
	Seven Seas
	Silversea
	Windstar
CAPE CANAVERAL	Carnival
	Disney
	Holland America
	Royal Caribbean
TAMPA	Carnival
	Celebrity
	Holland America
	Royal Caribbean
	Seven Seas

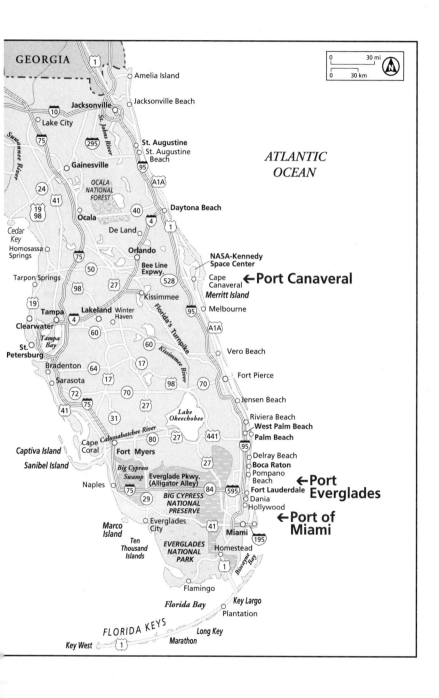

runs 24 hours a day, costs $9 to $12 per person, and includes two pieces of luggage. If you drive into town from the northwest, use I-75 or U.S. 27; if you come from the north, use I-95 or the Florida Turnpike (a toll road). The port provides long-term parking for $8 a day.

Cruising into port

Carnival, Norwegian Cruise Line, Oceania, Royal Caribbean, and Wind-jammer cumulatively have many, many ships that begin their itineraries here.

Exploring on your own

Go to the beach! You can beachcomb along ten miles of glorious sand and surf between the south of **Miami Beach** and **Haulover Beach Park** at the north end. Check out South Beach's renowned **Art Deco district.** True romantics can stroll hand-in-hand on a genuine wooden boardwalk between 21st and 46th streets for 1½ miles or so.

If oil paintings turn you on more than tanning oil, visit the **Bass Museum of Art** (2121 Park Ave.; ☎ 305-673-7530), which houses old masters and then some. Along similar lines, you can visit 34 rooms of art in the 70-room Italian Renaissance-style villa, **Vizcaya Museum and Gardens** (3251 S. Miami Ave., Coconut Grove; ☎ 305-250-9133).

Take the kids to the new 56,500-square-foot **Miami Children's Museum** (980 MacArthur Causeway; ☎ 305-373-KIDS), which is open from 10 a.m. to 6 p.m. Tickets are $8 for adults and kids over 12 months. Or head to **Parrot Jungle Island** (1111 Parrot Jungle Trail; ☎ 305-2-Jungle), which houses the world's largest crocodile. Tickets are $23.95 for adults and $18.95 for kids.

To see sea critters in action, watch a shark feeding or killer whale and dolphin shows at the **Miami Seaquarium** (4400 Rickenbacker Causeway, Key Biscayne; ☎ 305-361-5705).

Port Everglades

More upper-end and luxury ships make their home at **Port Everglades** than in any other port in the world, making it nearly as busy as the Port of Miami (some days even busier). Unlike Miami, Port Everglades doesn't offer much nearby activity while you wait in the comfortable cruise terminals — but you can find snack bars, seating areas, and plenty of pay phones. Port Everglades (☎ 954-523-3404) is located on State Road 84, east of U.S. 1, about a two-mile/five-minute drive from the **Fort Lauderdale/ Hollywood International Airport.** From the airport, take a cab to the cruise port for less than $10 or all the way into the city for about $12. When you drive to Port Everglades, you enter via Spangler Boulevard, Eisenhower Boulevard, or Eller Drive. The port provides long-term parking for about $12 a day.

Fort Lauderdale at a Glance

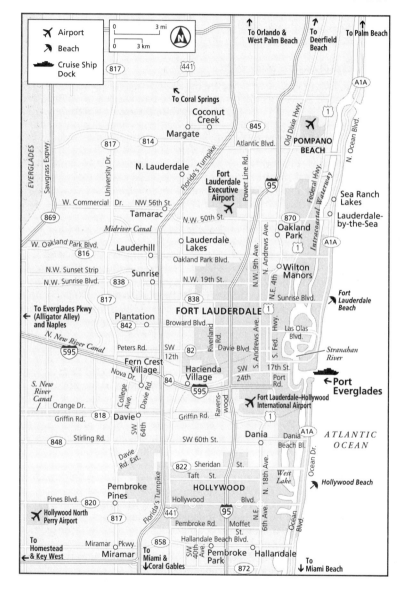

Cruising into port

Carnival, Celebrity, Costa, Crystal, Cunard, Holland America, Princess, Royal Caribbean, Seabourn, Seven Seas, Silversea, and Windstar all have ships that sail out of this port.

Exploring on your own

No longer considered Spring Break Central, **Fort Lauderdale Beach** has shooed partying college kids away to become a more family-friendly resort beach. On the **Fort Lauderdale Beach Promenade,** you can go rollerblading or biking (whether you're in college or not) when you get tired of lying around on the beach.

Sometimes called "the Venice of the Americas," Fort Lauderdale's 300 miles of navigable waterways and artificial canals make it a great place for riding a water-taxi, sightseeing by small boat, or enjoying a sunset dinner cruise.

Aside from the beach and water scenes, you can visit some fascinating area museums. Interact with cool science exhibits at the **Museum of Discovery and Science** (401 SW Second St.; ☎ **954-467-6637**), which also shows IMAX movies; ponder modern art at the **Museum of Art** (1 Las Olas Blvd.; ☎ **954-763-6464**); or fritter away your time among the *fritillaries* (fancy butterflies) at **Butterfly World** (3600 W. Sample Rd., Coconut Creek; ☎ **954-977-4400**), where 150 different varieties of the colorful insects perform butterfly ballet all summer long.

Cape Canaveral/Port Canaveral

Joining Miami and Port Everglades, **Port Canaveral** (200 George King Blvd.; ☎ **321-783-7831**) is among the busiest cruise ports in the world. And at the private **Disney terminal,** the Disney line's *Disney Magic* and *Disney Wonder* contribute an enchanted allure and a little bit of pixie dust (sprinkled over boarding passengers) to the port's atmosphere. Whichever line you sail, you have your choice of restaurants and bars near the port's modern, tasteful terminal facilities.

Orlando International Airport is the nearest flight center, about 45 minutes from Port Canaveral via Highway 528. Because no public buses run between the airport and the cruise port, the cruise lines offer passengers a van or bus service; if possible, arrange this service when you book. If these options aren't convenient for you, for approximately $20 per person each way (children under 12 are half price) the **Cocoa Beach Shuttle** (☎ **800-633-0427** or **321-784-3831**) provides shuttle service between the airport and the ship port.

You can drive to Port Canaveral and Cocoa Beach on Route 1 or I-95 or from Orlando along Highway 528 (also known as the Bee Line Expressway). The port offers long-term parking for $10 per day.

Cape Canaveral at a Glance

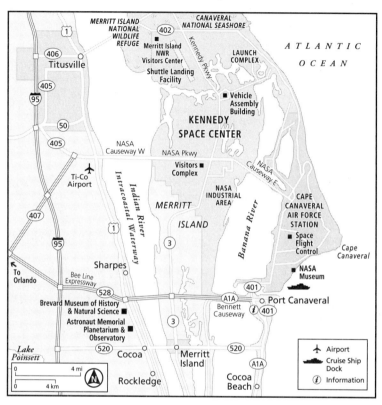

Cruising into port

Carnival, Disney, Holland America, and Royal Caribbean all have ships that sail out of Port Canaveral. And Carnival and Norwegian Cruise Line visit Port Canaveral as a port of call on cruises that depart from New York and other East Coast cities.

Exploring on your own

Although some folks prefer to dash over to Disney World or Universal Studios, you can lift off to exciting adventures here on the "Space Coast."

Ever since humankind's first trip to the moon in 1968 through the current space shuttle missions, the **John F. Kennedy Space Center Visitor Complex** (State Road 405 E., Titusville; ☎ 321-449-4322) has been the launch point for all U.S.-manned space missions. You can easily spend a whole day here, taking a bus tour past space shuttle launch pads — sometimes with an actual space shuttle in place — and viewing the special interactive exhibits, IMAX movies, and an actual Apollo/Saturn V moon rocket. Six miles west of the Kennedy Space Center, you find the **U.S. Astronaut Hall of Fame** (State Road 405, 6225 Vectorspace Blvd.; ☎ 321-269-6100), which displays Space Age memorabilia (if that's not too great an oxymoron).

The Space Coast also has its share of beautiful beaches, including the popular **Jetty Park** (400 E. Jetty Rd.); the quieter **Cherie Down Park** (8492 Ridgewood Ave.); the kid-friendly **Lori Wilson Park** (1500 N. Atlantic Ave.), complete with playground; and surfers' heaven **Robert P. Murkshe Memorial Park** (State Road A1A and 16th Street) in Cocoa Beach.

Tampa

Tampa is one of the fastest-growing port cities, and you see why upon arriving at the modern **Seaport Street Terminal** (13th and Platt Streets). The terminal anchors a 30-acre complex of shops, restaurants, and entertainment called the **Garrison Seaport Center,** which also includes a multiplex cinema, IMAX theatre, and the Florida Aquarium. For port information, call ☎ 813-905-5044.

If you fly into **Tampa International Airport** (approximately five miles from downtown), you can take a minivan service, operated by **Central Florida Limo** (☎ 813-396-3730), to the pier for $17.50 a person or a 15-minute taxi ride for around $10 to $15. You can drive into Tampa via a number of main roads, such as I-275, I-75, I-4, U.S. 41, U.S. 92, and U.S. 301, and then park at the port for $10 a day.

Cruising into port

Carnival, Celebrity, Holland America, Royal Caribbean, and Seven Seas all have ships that sail out of Tampa.

Exploring on your own

One of the top zoos in the United States, **Busch Gardens and Adventure Island** (☎ 888-800-5447 or 813-987-5171), offers an African-style setting for viewing animals, screaming on thrill rides, and enjoying games, shops, restaurants, and live entertainment. Admission prices run $53.95 for adults, $44.95 for children, and free for those two and under.

You can also visit the **Florida Aquarium** (701 Channelside Dr.; ☎ 813-273-4000), which displays more than 4,350 native Floridian marine animals and plants.

In addition to the animal attractions, you can find several interesting museums in Tampa and St. Petersburg. Replete with 13 silver minarets, **The Henry B. Plant Museum** (401 W. Kennedy Blvd.; ☎ 813-254-1891) is a replica of the Alhambra in Spain. A seven-acre riverfront park with sculpture garden enhances the **Tampa Museum of Art** (600 N. Ashley Dr.; ☎ 813-274-8130) with eight galleries of rotating exhibits. Or enter a

Tampa at a Glance

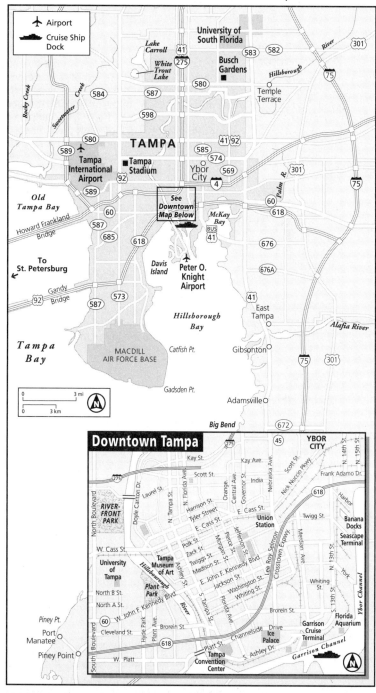

truly surreal world at the **Salvador Dalí Museum** (1000 Third St. S., St. Petersburg; ☎ 727-823-3767), which contains the world's largest collection of Dalí's work.

New Orleans

Cruise ships account for just a fraction of the hubbub at the port of New Orleans, one of the most active ports in the nation for commercial shipping. You usually board at the recently updated **Julia Street Cruise Ship Terminal** — originally developed as part of the 1984 Louisiana World Exposition — only about five minutes on foot from the **French Quarter.** Alternatively, many paddlewheel boats for upriver cruises and some southbound cruise ships depart from the **Robin Street Wharves.** (For port information for the Julia Street Terminal or the Robin Street Wharves, call ☎ 504-522-2551.)

The port is around ten miles southeast of **Louis Armstrong New Orleans International Airport.** You can ride a van from the **Airport Shuttle** service (☎ 504- 592-0555) at $10 per passenger each way (children under age 6 are free), or you can take a 20-minute taxi ride for around $28. If you choose to drive into town, take I-10, U.S. 90, U.S. 61, or Louisiana 25 (the Lake Pontchartrain Causeway). You can park at the port for $10 a day.

Cruising into port

Carnival, Norwegian, and Royal Caribbean have ships that sail out of New Orleans. Carnival and Silversea have ships that visit here as a port of call.

Exploring on your own

You can occupy yourself for hours in the ever-popular, historic, and slightly risqué **French Quarter** (including the world-famous **Bourbon Street**), which offers scrumptious Cajun cuisine, world-famous jazz clubs, shops, museums, and wonderful examples of 18th- and 19th-century architecture. For some theatrical fun, try a guided voodoo walking tour from the **New Orleans Historic Voodoo Museum** (724 Dumaine St.; ☎ 504-523-7685), daily from 10 a.m. A million gallons of marine fun await just outside the Quarter at the **Aquarium of the Americas** (1 Canal St., at the Mississippi River; ☎ 504-861-2537), which features an ever-popular penguin exhibit, an underwater tunnel, and an IMAX theater.

When you're ready to head out of the French Quarter, take the classic **St. Charles Avenue streetcar** at the corner of Canal and Carondelet Streets to ride to the **Garden District,** a mostly residential area that offers impressive homes and great restaurants.

The **Lower Garden District** and the **Warehouse District** along the Mississippi are hip areas for shops, art galleries, and historic sites.

Take the kids to the **Louisiana Children's Museum** (420 Julia St.; ☎ 504-523-1357); it offers a First Adventures exhibit for toddlers.

New Orleans's French Quarter

The Ports of Call

This section details most of the Caribbean islands visited by cruise ships, as well as some ports in the Bahamas, on Mexico's Yucatan Peninsula, and in the Florida Keys that make it onto many ships' itineraries.

The cruise lines' private islands

Several cruise lines have spent millions to operate and maintain their own fantasy islands or private beaches where you can relax and play away from crowds of local folks and non-cruise vacationers — although you may have to contend with big crowds of your fellow cruise passengers.

You normally get a whole day to take advantage of these fancy facilities and participate in the swinging mega-beach party atmosphere. Chefs barbecue, calypso bands play, and bartenders shake things up while guests sample all kinds of activities — from beach games to shopping for tropical beach goods to water sports (for a fee) such as snorkeling, water-skiing, sailing, paddleboat rides, and even parasailing. Children's activities may involve playground facilities, beach walks, and games. On some islands, you can also opt for a walk or tram ride (in a railcar) to a quieter beach to sun and wade in turquoise waters.

Among the most frequented private islands/beaches are the following *cays* (pronounced *keys*):

- **Great Stirrup Cay:** Norwegian Cruise Line purchased this small, uninhabited tropical island (about 120 nautical miles east of Fort Lauderdale) in 1977.

- **CocoCay:** Royal Caribbean has a private beach on this Bahamian island, the former Little Stirrup Cay. In addition, the line created a private retreat in Labadee on Haiti's secluded north coast, encompassing five beaches and 260 acres.

- **Princess Cays:** Princess set up this private beach in 1992 on the southwest coast of Eleuthera in the Bahamas.

- **Half Moon Cay:** Holland America has developed only 45 acres of this 2,400-acre island and maintains the rest as a wild-bird reserve on behalf of the Bahamian National Trust. You can explore a network of hiking trails while keeping an eye out for all sorts of birds, including terns, shearwaters, and Bahamian pintails. Activities the line offers include horseback riding, a WaveRunner Park, beach massages, and a stingray adventure program. (Carnival ships also visit here on some itineraries.)

- **Castaway Cay:** Disney runs this 1,000-acre Bahamian island, with separate beach areas for families, teens, and adults. At the family beach, you can snorkel to see real fish and fake Disney treasure; at the adults-only beach, you can get a massage for a fee in a private cabana. This is the only private island where the line's ships can dock right at a pier on the cay.

- **Dominican Republic government beaches:** Costa and Celebrity both offer a private-beach experience at government-owned beach facilities designated for cruise ships.

Because most lines anchor off shore and use small tender boats to take passengers to these remote islands, you may experience some difficulty getting ashore if you have a physical disability. Make sure to alert the crew if you require special assistance or a little extra "tender" care.

Antigua

Antigua (an-*tee*-gah) provides plenty of powder-white-sand beaches for those in quest of the perfect tan. For those in search of fascinating local history, **Nelson's Dockyard Park** (known as the Williamsburg of the Caribbean) awaits at English Harbour, the anchoring point for smaller cruise ships. About 11 miles from English Harbour, larger cruise ships drop passengers at **Deep Water Harbour Terminal,** under a mile from quiet St. John's, the island capital.

The Eastern Caribbean dollar (EC$) is the official currency here, but prices are nearly always quoted in U.S. dollars; check the price tag or ask the salesperson. US $1 = EC $2.67 (EC $1 = US 37¢). The official language is English.

Cruising into port

American Canadian Caribbean, SeaDream, and Windjammer have ships that begin their itineraries in Antigua. American Canadian Caribbean, Carnival, Celebrity, Crystal, Norwegian, Oceania, Princess, Royal Caribbean, Seabourn, Seven Seas, Star Clippers, and Windjammer have ships that make port calls here.

Seeking out the best shore excursions

On the **Antigua Island and Historical** tour, visit Nelson's Dockyard, English Harbor, the Admiral's House and Inn, and Shirley Heights, as well as some of the island's lush countryside. (3 hours, $42)

Exploring on your own

Antigua now docks cruise ships in its inner harbor thanks to the recent completion of **Nevis Street Pier.** Some ships continue to berth at the parallel **Heritage Quay,** which was also expanded. You can get around Antigua easily, especially if you join a shore excursion or take a cab rather than rent a car. Taxi drivers are qualified tour guides, and they fix fares for sightseeing trips at around $20 per hour for up to four people. Although buses are cheap (about $1), they serve locals better than tourists. You can find the **Antigua and Barbuda Department of Tourism** at Nevis Street and Friendly Alley in St. John's. The department also has an office in New York (☎ **888-268-4227**).

Within Walking Distance: Apart from duty-free shopping close to the docks at Heritage Quay and Redcliffe Quay, St. John's itself is a little rusty. On Saturday mornings you can get a taste of the local lifestyle at the market at the lower end of Market Street, where residents barter goods and gossip.

St. John's also offers a handful of intriguing historical attractions near the main dock. The old 1750s Court House building now houses the **Museum of Antigua and Barbuda** (Long and Market Streets), which

Antigua

Map legend:
- ✈ Airport
- 🏖 Beach
- ⚓ Cruise Ship Dock
- ⛰ Mountain

offers brochures for a self-guided walking tour past the historic build-
ings along **Redcliffe Cay.** You can top off the tour with a rum punch at
Redcliffe Tavern. Tour brochures cost $1. You can also visit the 1681
Anglican church, **St. John's Cathedral** (between Long and Newgate
Streets at Church Street), which has endured two tragic earthquakes.

Beyond Walking Distance: From St. John's, take a taxi to the popular
Nelson's Dockyard National Park, headquarters to British Admiral
Horatio Nelson (1784 to 1787). At the heart of this landmark is the
Dockyard Museum, where you discover the dockyard's links to famous
18th-century sea battles and pirates. Other components of the park
include sandy beaches, tropical vegetation, nature trails, and archeological sites that date back to well before the Christian era. Tours of the
dockyard can last 15 to 20 minutes, but an excursion along the trails can
last anywhere from 30 minutes to 5 hours. Admission to the park is
about $4.88 per person; children under 12 are admitted free.

At **Dow's Hill Interpretation Center** (about 2½ miles east of English Harbour), a multimedia presentation explains Antigua's history, from the British military occupation to the island's role in the slave trade. Admission is $5 for adults and free for children under 12.

For a scenic 20-mile circular route across Antigua's main mountain range, take a taxi along the steep (and sometimes rutted) **Fig Tree Drive** (fare negotiable). In the local lingo *fig tree* actually means *banana tree.* Either way, you get fantastic views of tropical forests and fishing villages.

Seek out the partially restored 19th-century plantation house and sugar mill **Harmony Hall** in Brown's Bay Mill, near Freetown, for Caribbean arts and crafts and local delicacies such as Green Island lobster. The 40-minute cab ride from St. John's generally costs about $25. Harmony Hall is open from the first week of November through the middle of May.

You can reach the best beaches by taxi, but remember to arrange for your driver to pick you up later so that you don't get stranded. For the full resort experience, head to **Dickenson Bay** and **Runaway Bay.** On the southeast coast, you can find great snorkeling at **Pigeon Point** and beautiful pink sand at **Half Moon Bay.**

Rendezvous Bay is the ideal stretch for couples looking to share a secluded moment. (See the "Antigua" map for locations.) All beaches in Antigua are public, and the tourism department claims that the island has a grand total of 365 — one for each day of the year. However, sticking to populated beach areas is advisable.

Discover the best daiquiri in town at **Hemingway's** on St. Mary's Street. People-watch from the cafe's upper veranda as you sip the house specialty — a pineapple daiquiri made from local rum and the famous Antigua black pineapple.

Aruba

Whether you want casino games, a romantic honeymoon spot, or just a great tan, sun-drenched Aruba (annual rainfall only 17 inches!) obliges. Because it doesn't stand in the usual Caribbean hurricane path, this island, part of the Kingdom of the Netherlands, is a popular getaway. The casinos get crowded, but the seven miles of sparkling beaches on the West Coast are delightfully free of pesky vendors. All beaches are open to the public. Downtown Oranjestad, noted for its unique Spanish- and Dutch-influenced architecture, offers plenty of shops within walking distance of the Aruba Port Authority.

The official currency is the Aruba guilder (AWG): US $1 = 1.79AWG (1AWG = US 56¢). Dollars are widely accepted, however. The official language is Dutch, but nearly everybody speaks English. You also hear Spanish and Papiamento, a regional dialect that combines Dutch, Spanish, and English with Amerindian and African words.

Aruba

Airport
Beach
Cruise Ship Dock
Lighthouse

California Point
California
Lighthouse

Malmok Beach

Hadicurari
(Fishermen's Huts)

2A
2B

Palm Beach

Alto Vista
Chapel

Noord

Caribbean
Sea

Eagle Beach

3B
3A

Manchebo
Beach

Druif Beach

2A
2B

4B
4A

6B
6A

Bushiribana

Natural Bridge

Oranjestad

7B
7A

Hooiberg

Santa Cruz

7B
7A

Queen
Beatrix
Airport

1A
1B

ARIKOK

Caves of
Canashito

NATIONAL

Boca Prins
Sand Dunes

Jamanota

Fontein
Cave

Spanish
Lagoon

PARK

Quadirikiri
Cave

Caribbean
Sea

Savaneta

1B
1A

7A
7B

San Nicolas

Boca Grandi

Seroe Colorado

Rodger's Beach

Baby Beach

Colorado
Point

0   3 mi
0   3 km

Cruising into port

Windjammer has ships that begin itineraries in Aruba, and Carnival, Celebrity, Crystal, Cunard, Holland America, Norwegian, Princess, Royal Caribbean, Seabourn, and Silversea all have ships that make port calls here.

Seeking out the best shore excursions

In addition to the trips we list here, most lines also offer an **Island Tour** (3 hours; $34), but in all honesty the tour is usually pretty dull.

De Palm Island Snorkeling Adventure: See the sights via a 20-minute ride in an air-conditioned bus, followed by a five-minute ferry ride to the island's best snorkeling destination. Snacks and gear are included. (4 hours; $42)

Aruba Off-Road Adventure: If you like the idea of exploring the island from behind the wheel but don't want to go it alone, this tour puts you in a convoy of other like-minded drivers. The program includes a four-wheel-drive vehicle, a guide, and itinerary; the group sets off caravan-style. Tours also feature sightseeing, lunch, and a swim or snorkel. (7½ hours; $98)

Exploring on your own

From the Aruba Port Authority facility, walk about five minutes up **Lloyd G. Smith Boulevard,** the main road that runs from Queen Beatrix Airport along the waterfront up to Palm Beach, to start your shopping spree. For an even wider array of goods, cross the street to **Caya G. F. Betico Croes** for quality items such as French perfume, Swiss watches, German and Japanese cameras, and English bone china. Delft blue pottery and Edam and Gouda cheeses from Holland are especially good buys.

Buses can conveniently stop across the street from the cruise terminal and take you to the casinos, hotel resorts, and beaches on the West Coast. Fares are inexpensive (about $2 round-trip).

Taxis are unmetered in Aruba, so figure out the fixed rate for your destination and settle in advance. A typical ride from the cruise terminal to most beach resorts is around $10 to $16 plus tip for a maximum of five passengers. Remember: If you take a taxi to a remote part of the island, arrange for the driver to pick you up again at a certain time. Most drivers have participated in the government's Tourism Awareness Program, and some are excellent tour guides. For about $35, you can book a one-hour taxi tour for up to four people at the dispatch office (☎ 297-8-22116) in Oranjestad on Sands Street between the bowling alley and Taco Bell.

Because Aruba's roads are generally good, many people get around on mopeds that rent for about $30 to $40 a day. You can get further information on renting mopeds at the cruise terminal or at the bike shops on Lloyd G. Smith Boulevard. You can also easily rent a car or four-wheel-drive vehicle from Hertz, Budget, Avis, or one of the other rental-car companies.

 Keep safety in mind when you drive here: The roads get very slippery when even slightly wet or when sand blows across them. You drive on the right.

Within Walking Distance: One of your first welcoming sights is the row of colorful boats docked at **Schooner Harbor,** where locals set up open stalls to display their goods. Up the beach, you can buy fresh seafood right off the boat. **Wilhelmina Park,** with a statue honoring Queen Wilhelmina of the Netherlands, shows the island's Dutch influences and includes a tropical garden.

Beyond Walking Distance: On a clear day, you can see Venezuela from the top of **Hooiberg** (also known as "The Haystack"), a prominent 541-foot peak. It stands about 15 miles southeast of Oranjestad in the center of the island and only requires 600 steps to the top.

To the northeast, **Ayo** and **Casibari** feature diorite boulders the size of buildings. The rocks at Ayo show Amerindian drawings, whereas the rocks at Casibari, shaped by winds and rains, resemble prehistoric birds and animals (open daily 9 a.m. to 5 p.m.). *Photo Op:* On the northern coast is **Natural Bridge,** a coral rock formation that measures over 100 feet long and 25 feet above sea level. Centuries of crashing surf and whipping wind formed the bridge. Farther east on the northern coast are caves, including the **Tunnel of Love,** covered with ancient paintings. Rent flashlights for $6 apiece and watch out for bats.

You can see caves decorated with **Arawak artwork** — the oldest traces of human existence on the island — in Savaneta, on the east side of the island about 25 minutes from Oranjestad by taxi. The area was also a 19th-century industrial center for phosphate mining; later, the town of San Nicolas was developed. Until 1985, an Exxon oil subsidiary refinery operated here. San Nicolas is home to **Charlie's Bar and Restaurant** (Main Street; ☎ **297-8-45086**), serving two-fisted drinks and decent food since 1941 in a nostalgic setting crammed with pennants, banners, trophies, and other memorabilia. **Boonoonoonoos,** (Wilheminastraat 18 ☎ **297-8-31888**), serves up Caribbean dishes in an old-fashioned Aruban house.

Sun worshipers adore the **Turquoise Coast** on the western and southern shores. You can reach two of the best beaches on the island, **Palm Beach** and **Eagle Beach,** via taxi from the cruise terminal for $8. In general, the northern coast is a bit wild and less hospitable to beachcombers.

Barbados

In Barbados, a former British colony, cricket is the national pastime, fish-and-chips appears on local menus, and, of course, you drive on the left. Bajans, as locals are known, refer to their island as "an England in the tropics" — only with much better weather. Barbados is home to fine dining, pink-and-white sandy beaches, small cottages with well-kept gardens, and historic parish churches. The northeast part of the island is hilly, with a morning mist that helped it earn the nickname "The Scotland District."

Unfortunately, the shopping area near your disembarkation point, **Bridgetown,** has noisy crowds of people and cars honking their horns. On Barbados, you're best off making a beeline for the beach. You find calmer waters at the beaches on the **Gold Coast** (the island's western side, dotted with luxury resorts), as opposed to the pounding surf on the Atlantic side of the island, which is better for windsurfing.

The Barbados Dollar (BD$) is the official currency, although most stores take U.S. dollars: US $1 = BD $2.02 (BD $1 = US 49¢). The official language is English.

Barbados

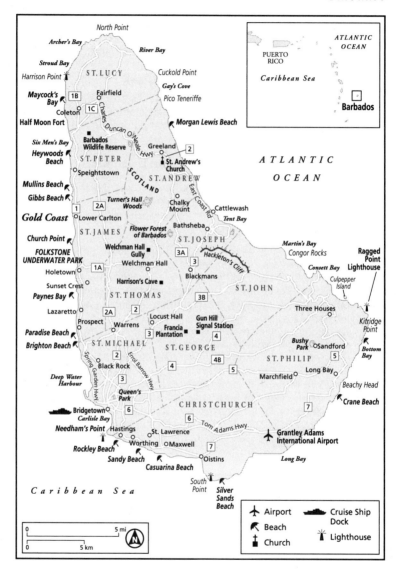

North Point

Archer's Bay

River Bay

Stroud Bay

ST. LUCY

Cuckold Point

Harrison Point

Gay's Cove

Maycock's Bay

1B

Fairfield

Pico Teneriffe

Coleton

1C

Half Moon Fort

Morgan Lewis Beach

Six Men's Bay

Barbados Wildlife Reserve

Greeland

2

Heywoods Beach

ST. PETER

St. Andrew's Church

Speightstown

ST. ANDREW

Mullins Beach

Gibbs Beach

Turner's Hall Woods

Chalky Mount

Cattlewash

Gold Coast

1

2A

Lower Carlton

Tent Bay

Flower Forest of Barbados

Bathsheba

Church Point

ST. JAMES

ST. JOSEPH

Martin's Bay

Congor Rocks

Ragged Point Lighthouse

FOLKSTONE UNDERWATER PARK

Welchman Hall Gully

3A

3

Hackleton's Cliff

Consett Bay

Holetown

1A

Welchman Hall

Blackmans

Culpepper Island

Sunset Crest

Harrison's Cave

ST. JOHN

Paynes Bay

ST. THOMAS

3B

Kitridge Point

Lazaretto

2A

2

Locust Hall

Gun Hill Signal Station

Three Houses

Prospect

Warrens

Francia Plantation

Bottom Bay

Paradise Beach

3

4

Bushy Park

Sandford

5

Brighton Beach

ST. MICHAEL

ST. GEORGE

ST. PHILIP

Black Rock

2

4

4B

Long Bay

5

Deep Water Harbour

3

4

5

Marchfield

Beachy Head

Queen's Park

6

Crane Beach

Bridgetown

CHRISTCHURCH

7

Carlisle Bay

6

Needham's Point

Hastings

Tom Adams Hwy.

Rockley Beach

Worthing

St. Lawrence

Maxwell

7

Grantley Adams International Airport

Sandy Beach

Oistins

Long Bay

Casuarina Beach

South Point

Silver Sands Beach

Caribbean Sea

0   5 mi
0   5 km

ATLANTIC OCEAN

PUERTO RICO

Caribbean Sea

Barbados

ATLANTIC

OCEAN

✈ Airport   🚢 Cruise Ship Dock
🏹 Beach   ☼ Lighthouse
✝ Church

Cruising into port

Seabourn, SeaDream, Silversea, Star Clippers, and Windstar all have ships that begin their itineraries in Barbados. Carnival, Celebrity, Crystal, Cunard, Holland America, Norwegian, Princess, Royal Caribbean, Seven Seas, Silversea, and Star Clippers make port calls here.

Seeking out the best shore excursions

The **Atlantis Submarine Adventure** takes you aboard an air-conditioned submersible to view underwater life, including tropical fish, plants, and an intact shipwreck. (2½ hours; $89 for adults and $54 for children 12 and under)

Swim with **Turtles, Shipwrecks, Snorkel and Beach Snorkel** off a catamaran at Turtle Bay, aptly named for the turtles that swim in its waters, followed by snorkeling at the shipwrecks site. (4¼ hours; $45 for adults; $36 for children 5 to 12)

Exploring on your own

A $25 million megapier — designed to attract larger cruise ships and offer passengers more amenities at the dock — began construction at the end of 2004 and will be completed in 2006. Meanwhile, the **Cruise Passenger Terminal** at the Bridgetown Port offers plenty of shopping opportunities and services. If you want to head into Bridgetown, spring for the $4 taxi ride. But the beautiful scenery outside the city remains the island's real attraction. Taxi service and car, motor scooter, or bike rentals are all available at the cruise terminal; just remember that you drive on the left. Although buses are frequent and inexpensive (the fare is about 75¢), they may get crowded at rush hour. As an alternative, look for a van with a "ZR" license plate: These licensed minibuses run around the island picking up tourists and locals for about the same rate as the bus. However, be forewarned that the minivans stop frequently and abruptly, and drivers tend to speed along in order to pick up the maximum number of passengers in the shortest amount of time — a mode of transport not for the faint of heart.

Within Walking Distance: You don't find much within walking distance from the terminal besides shopping. The cruise facility itself has 20 duty-free shops that sell everything from jewelry, watches, and electronic goods to fine china, crystal, cosmetics, and perfumes. Smaller vendors and 13 local retailers sell art and handicrafts. Goods made on Barbados, including rum, liquors, and jewelry, are duty-free. You also can take care of some business at the terminal's communications center, which provides postal, banking, and phone services such as cellular phone rentals.

Beyond Walking Distance: Visit the **Synagogue** (Synagogue Lane, Bridgetown), one of the oldest Jewish houses of worship in the western hemisphere. Brazilian Jews built the first temple on this site in 1654; the current building dates to 1833. A $4 taxi ride gets you here from the cruise terminal.

You can take a bus to reach the lush, tropical garden known as **Welchman Hall Gully,** about eight miles from the terminal. Some of the plant specimens date back to 1627, when English settlers first arrived. For example, they say the ancient breadfruit trees grew from seedlings brought over by Captain Bligh (of *Mutiny on the Bounty* fame). Admission is $6 for adults and $3 for children (kids under 5 get in free).

The most popular tourist attraction on the island is **Harrison's Cave** (Welchman Hall, St. Thomas), about a $20 cab ride from the cruise terminal, where you take an electric tram and trailer to view an underground world of stalactites and stalagmites. Admission is $13 for adults and $5 for children.

An old sugar plantation, **Flower Forest** (12 miles from the cruise terminal), is one of the most scenic sites on Barbados. It lies on the western edge of The Scotland District, and cab fare is $15 one way. Admission is $7 for adults and $3.50 for children.

You get a wonderful panoramic view of the island from **Gun Hill Signal Station** (12 miles from the port), one of a chain of early 1800s signal stations that British troops built while stationed here. A taxi ride to the highland of St. George, where the station is located, costs about $17.50. Admission is $9.20 for adults and $4.60 for children under 14.

Visiting **Francia Plantation,** St. George, is worth the 20-mile ride (and $20 cab fare) from the terminal. Located on a wooded hillside overlooking the St. George Valley, the house features antique maps and prints, including a West Indies map printed in 1522. Descendants of the original owner still own and live in this house. Admission is $5.

All beaches in Barbados are open to the public. Two popular beach options within an $8 cab ride of the terminal are **Paynes Bay** on the West Coast (a.k.a. Platinum Coast) if you want to snorkel and the family-friendly **Sandy Beach** on the South Coast. The waters are calmer on the South and West Coasts. **Crane Beach** is another popular beach on the Southeast Coast, known for its big ocean waves. If surfing is your thing, head to **Bathsheba** on the East Coast.

Angry Annie's Bar & Restaurant (1st Street) at Holetown, St. James offers lively entrees such as Limbo Lamb, Jump-up Ribs, and Rasta Pasta. If you're in the mood for Bajan flying fish, a local specialty, stop by the waterfront **Rusty Pelican** in downtown Bridgetown.

The British Virgin Islands

Once upon a time, the British Virgin Islands served as a haven for pirates, but today they're a haven for sun-seekers. Most of the 40-some islands that make up the island group are quite small; the largest three are **Tortola, Virgin Gorda** (or "Fat Virgin" — so called because the island's mountain resembled a protruding stomach to Christopher Columbus), and the less-frequented **Jost Van Dyke.**

The British Virgin Islands

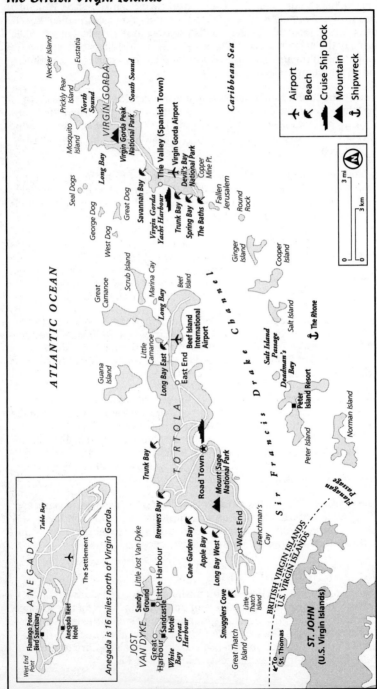

Treasure Island fans get a kick out of **Norman Island,** said to be the setting for Robert Louis Stevenson's classic tale. Legend holds that the notorious pirate Blackbeard stashed a bottle of rum and marooned 15 men at Deadman Bay on neighboring **Peter Island,** inspiring the famous "yo, ho, ho and a bottle of rum" ditty.

Although their official name is the *British* Virgin Islands, the U.S. dollar is the official currency. English is the official language.

Cruising into port

Windjammer Barefoot Cruises has ships that begin their itineraries in Tortola. American Canadian Caribbean, Carnival, Crystal, Norwegian, Oceania, Princess, Royal Caribbean, Seabourn, SeaDream, Seven Seas, Silversea, Windjammer, and Windstar make port calls at Tortola and/or Virgin Gorda.

Seeking out the best shore excursions

Take the **Virgin Gorda and the Baths Tour** and zip off in a launch from your ship along Sir Francis Drake Channel to Spanish Town, and then board open-air buses that take you to The Baths for sunning, swimming, and snorkeling amid mammoth boulders and sea caves. Includes a Caribbean-style buffet lunch. (4 hours; $59 for adults and $47 for children)

Exploring on your own in Tortola

Your launch boat usually lets you off at **Road Town,** the capital of Tortola; a 5-minute walk takes you from the pier to Main Street. Alternatively, you can take one of the taxis lined up to meet the cruise ship (fares are fixed) to get around. Tortola's bus service is inconvenient for tourists, so you may want to rent a car to explore the island, even though the roads are bad and you need to adjust to driving on the left (this is a British colony, after all). Budget, Hertz, and Avis all have offices on Tortola. Reservations may be required (see "Car-Rental Agencies" in the Appendix for reservation numbers).

Within Walking Distance: You can walk from the pier to Tortola's **Main Street,** which has a relatively quiet shopping area by Caribbean standards, although you can get some good bargains on duty-free British goods such as English china.

Across from the dock on the waterfront is **Pusser's Road Town Pub,** the place for tasty pizzas and the infamous Pusser's Rum drinks.

Beyond Walking Distance: Take a taxi to **Mount Sage National Park,** on Tortola, where the island's mountain soars to a magnificent 1,780 feet. You can experience a lush tropical rain forest setting in the 92-acre park while you hike the Rain Forest Trail and the Mahogany Forest Trail. (You can pick up a trail map at the tourist office in the center of Road Town near the dock just south of **Wickam's Cay** 1.)

If you're in the mood to party, check out the bar scene near the West End at **Bomba's Surfside Shack** at **Cappoon's Bay.** Day-Glo graffiti covers this junk palace along with plenty of other intermingled stuff. For suntanning, the beach within easiest reach of the dock is **Cane Garden Bay** on the northwest shore. Consequently, this spot is the most popular beach on the island. If you want to snorkel, the best beaches on Tortola are **Smugglers Cove,** on the western tip, and **Brewer's Bay,** on the northwest side. **Apple Bay,** also northwest, is popular with surfers. You can take a 20-minute cab ride from the cruise terminal to any of the beaches for about $15 each way. Remember to arrange to have the cab pick you up to get back to the ship.

Exploring on your own in Virgin Gorda

Instead of heading for Tortola, some smaller ships anchor outside of Virgin Gorda and bring visitors ashore by tender. You have to take a taxi to get there, but **The Baths** is the most popular beach destination on the island. Huge boulders fell on each other over the years to form saltwater grottoes for exploring and pools for swimming. Look out below!

Follow a path away from the Baths for about 15 minutes through boulders and dry coastal vegetation to **Devil's Bay National Park.** You can enjoy good snorkeling at nearby **Spring Bay,** one of the island's best beaches, and glorious white sand at **Trunk Bay.**

Cozumel and Playa del Carmen, Mexico

A stop at the island of Cozumel affords cruise passengers a chance to visit the Mayan ruins on the mainland, at **Tulum** and **Chichén-Itzá.** Also luring legions of vacationers here are the island's alabaster beaches and turquoise waters, which are ideal for snorkeling and scuba diving. Some ships spend a day in Cozumel and then the next in nearby Playa del Carmen, which is on the Yucatán Peninsula and closer to the ruins.

Cozumel has only one town, **San Miguel,** which has, unfortunately, lost much of its quaintness to an invasion of entirely too familiar fast-food and chain restaurants such as the Hard Rock Cafe. You can still sample a handful of Mexican eateries and, of course, plenty of shops. Outside of town, you can explore deserted beaches and observe plenty of wildlife, such as tropical birds, lizards, and armadillos.

The Mexican nuevo peso is the official currency, although most vendors accept U.S. dollars. You can exchange money at several banks clustered near the docks. The exchange rate is $11 pesos to every US $1 ($1 peso = US 9¢). Spanish is the official language, but English is spoken in most places frequented by tourists.

Cruising into port

Carnival, Celebrity, Costa, Crystal, Cunard, Disney, Holland America, Norwegian, Princess, Royal Caribbean, Seven Seas, Star Clippers, and Windstar make port calls at Cozumel and/or Playa del Carmen.

Cozumel/Playa del Carmen Area

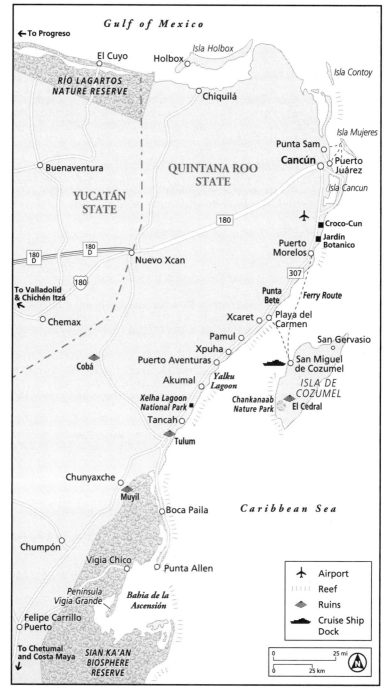

To Progreso

Gulf of Mexico

El Cuyo
Holbox
Isla Holbox
Isla Contoy

RÍO LAGARTOS
NATURE RESERVE

Chiquilá

Isla Mujeres

Punta Sam
Cancún
Puerto
Juárez

Buenaventura

QUINTANA ROO
STATE

Isla Cancun

YUCATÁN
STATE

180

Croco-Cun

Jardín
Botanico

Puerto
Morelos

180
D
180
D
180
D
Nuevo Xcan

307

To Valladolid
& Chichén Itzá

180

Punta
Bete
Ferry Route

Chemax

Xcaret
Playa del
Carmen

San Gervasio

Pamul

Cobá

Xpuha
Puerto Aventuras

San Miguel
de Cozumel

Akumal
Yalku
Lagoon

ISLA DE
COZUMEL

Xelha Lagoon
National Park

Chankanaab
Nature Park
El Cedral

Tancah

Tulum

Chunyaxche

Muyil

Caribbean Sea

Boca Paila

Chumpón

Vigia Chíco
Punta Allen

Peninsula
Vigia Grande
Bahia de la
Ascensión

Felipe Carrillo
Puerto

To Chetumal
and Costa Maya

SIAN KA'AN
BIOSPHERE
RESERVE

✈	Airport
‖‖‖	Reef
◈	Ruins
⛴	Cruise Ship Dock

0   25 mi
0   25 km

Seeking out the best shore excursions

Tulum Mayan Ruins/Xel-Ha: Considered the ruin to see, Tulum boasts a pyramid and a number of other ruins. Cool off afterward with a snorkel break in the caves of Xel-Ha. (8 hours from Playa del Carmen; $99 to $75, including snacks and beverages.) In Mexico, you can expect to pay a fee of $8 to $10 for using a video camera at the ruins.

Passion Island Escape: Hop on a motorized tender or a four-person canoe to a private beach on Passion Island, where you can relax on the beach, enjoy water sports, and feast on a traditional Mexican grilled lunch. (5 hours; $69 to $35)

Xcaret: From Cozumel, you transfer by ferry to Playa del Carmen and get about 3½ hours to enjoy this unique eco-archaeological theme park, whose name is pronounced ish-car-ET. See "Beyond Walking Distance" in the Playa del Carmen section for more details. (8 hours; $66 to $88)

Exploring on your own in Cozumel

Ships either dock at the international pier, very close to Cozumel's beaches and only four miles from San Miguel, or take you by tender to the Muelle Fiscal pier in the center of San Miguel. Inexpensive taxis are always available at both locations; the typical fare from San Miguel to most resorts and beaches is about $8, whereas trips to more remote locations may cost $12 and up. Be sure to settle on the fare before you start out, however, because drivers sometimes overcharge cruise passengers.

For an alternative mode of transportation, consider a moped for around $25 to $30 per day, but watch out for heavy traffic, hidden stop signs, and potholes. If you prefer to rent a car, choose a vehicle with four-wheel-drive because the roads leading to ruins and remote beaches are rough.

You can also take a ferry between Cozumel and Playa del Carmen. The crossing takes approximately 45 minutes and a one-way fare costs around $4 to $5 per person.

Within Walking Distance: You can easily get around the small town of San Miguel on foot. You can find a nice selection of restaurants and shops on Avenida Rafael Melgar (the main street, running along the waterfront) and Plaza del Sol, both close to the downtown pier.

Three blocks from the downtown pier is **Museo de la Isla de Cozumel** (on Rafael Melgar between Calles 4 and 6 North), in what was once Cozumel's first luxury hotel. The building houses two floors of historical exhibits, from pre-Hispanic times to the present, which include swords and nautical artifacts. Admission is $3.

Beyond Walking Distance: You don't want to miss **Chankanaab Nature Park,** well worth a ten-minute, $12 (or less) taxi ride from the downtown pier. Enjoy strolling through an archaeological park, botanical garden, and wildlife sanctuary; swimming in a saltwater lagoon with a beautiful powder-white beach; and snorkeling or scuba diving among fish-filled offshore reefs (equipment rentals are available). Even young children can take part in a dolphin or sea lion encounter under the watchful eye of a trainer. The park also provides some small shops, a restaurant, and a snack bar. Admission is $10 (free for children 9 and under).

Right near the international pier is Cozumel's best beach — the three-mile stretch of **Playa San Francisco** on the southwestern coast. From downtown, you can get to the beach by taxi for around $10. One of the more popular and crowded beaches, **Playa del Sol,** is about a mile south, or you can take a taxi or car to **Playa Bonita** (also called Punta Chiqueros) on the east (windward) side of the island. Getting to the remote site is tough but worth it if you really want to avoid the crowds.

Exploring on your own in Playa del Carmen

Some ships bring passengers over by tender from Cozumel, but many dock at the Puerto Calica Cruise Pier, eight miles south of the town. Waiting taxis at the pier can take you downtown quickly. From the tender pier, you can easily walk to the heart of town, the beach, and major shops.

Within Walking Distance: Playa del Carmen is small and easy to explore on foot. Even though the white-sand beach gets crowded, you can enjoy excellent snorkeling and turtle-watching. For shopping, stroll the **Rincon del Sol,** a tree-lined Mexican colonial-style courtyard with some appealing local handicrafts stores.

Beyond Walking Distance: Your first choice when the ship docks in Playa del Carmen is most likely to take an organized shore excursion to the ruins at **Tulum.** Alternatively, you can laze around on the beach or visit **Xcaret,** a 250-acre ecological theme park only four miles south of Playa del Carmen. Enjoy the park's blue lagoons, sandy beaches, lazy rivers, and botanical gardens at your leisure or expand your horizons at the aviary, aquarium, cultural performances, or archaeological sites. The highlight of this visit is the underground river snorkel tour, which involves donning a floaty vest and letting a gentle current carry you along a crystal river in an underground cave. The tour is even suitable for children. ***Note:*** The use of commercial sunscreens is prohibited here for ecological reasons, but park officials pass out a more earth-friendly version free of charge. Buses go regularly to the park from Playa del Carmen or you can take a taxi for around $5, one-way. Admission is $49 for adults, $25 for children 5 to 11, and free for children 4 and under.

Join your fellow cruise passengers and quench your thirst with a yard-long glass of beer at **Carlos 'n Charlie's,** Avenida Rafael Melgar 11. Check out the happening party on Friday nights.

Curaçao, Netherlands Antilles

Upon entering Willemstad's harbor, you watch a floating bridge swing aside and invite your ship into a narrow channel, where rows of pastel-colored Dutch-colonial homes create a fairy-tale effect. According to local lore, the sun reflecting off the white houses caused horrible headaches for one of the first governors of Curaçao, and to ease his eyes, all the homes were painted with vibrant colors. Contrasting with this quaint and colorful architecture, the rest of the island's landscape may remind you of the desert-like southwestern United States.

The official currency is the Netherlands Antillean florin (NAf), also called a guilder: US $1 = 1.78 NAf (1 NAf = US 56¢). Most places accept U.S. dollars for purchases. People here speak Dutch, Spanish, and English, along with Papiamento, a regional dialect that combines these three major tongues with Amerindian and African dialects.

Cruising into port

Crystal, Holland America, Princess, Royal Caribbean, Seven Seas, and Windjammer all make port calls here.

Seeking out the best shore excursions

Animal Encounter Scuba Adventure: Explore a natural tidal pool at the edge of a colorful reef where you may see sharks and stingrays. If you aren't a certified diver, you can experience this scuba-diving excursion by receiving PADI (Professional Association of Diving Instructors) intro training. Open to adults and children 12 and up. (4 hours; $89)

Discover Curaçao: Visit the city of **Willemstad,** the countryside, the **Hato Caves,** and the **Petroglyph Trail.** (3½ hours; $40)

Willemstad Trolley Tour: Take in the quaint Dutch architecture aboard a guided trolley tour that brings passengers by such attractions in the city as the **Pietermaai Cathedral, Emmanuel Synagogue,** and **Queen Wilhelmina Park.** (1½ hours; $35)

Exploring on your own

You can tour Willemstad on your own in about two or three hours, leaving plenty of time for sunbathing and swimming.

Just outside the harbor entrance is a $9 million megapier. It has a tourist information booth, car rental agencies, and workshop space for local artists. The new pier deposits you near the city center. The new **Queen Emma** pontoon bridge, which connects the pier and the city's principal shopping and business areas, makes walking downtown fairly simple. Taxis are also available; they have no meters here, but fares are fixed. Agree on your fare with the driver before you start out. A taxi tour can be had for about $30 an hour. Tipping, although not required, is suggested at 10 percent of the fare.

Curaçao

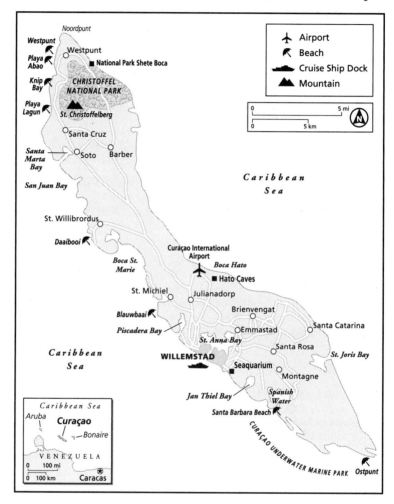

Noordpunt

Westpunt
Westpunt
Playa Abao
National Park Shete Boca
Knip Bay
CHRISTOFFEL NATIONAL PARK
Playa Lagun
St. Christoffelberg
Santa Cruz
Santa Marta Bay
Soto
Barber
San Juan Bay

Caribbean Sea

Airport
Beach
Cruise Ship Dock
Mountain

0   5 mi
0   5 km

St. Willibrordus
Daaibooi
Boca St. Marie
Curaçao International Airport
Boca Hato
Hato Caves
St. Michiel
Julianadorp
Brienvengat
Blauwbaai
Santa Catarina
Piscadera Bay
Emmastad
Santa Rosa
St. Joris Bay
St. Anna Bay
WILLEMSTAD
Santa Barbara Beach
Seaquarium
Montagne
Jan Thiel Bay
Spanish Water

Caribbean Sea

CURAÇAO UNDERWATER MARINE PARK
Ostpunt

Caribbean Sea
Aruba
Curaçao
Bonaire
VENEZUELA
0   100 mi
0   100 km
Caracas

You can also get around the island by two kinds of buses. Take either a van (called a *bus* — easily recognizable by the BUS on the license plate) or one of the yellow or blue buses called *konvoi.* Yellow buses run from **Wilhelmina Plein** (near the shopping center) to most parts of the island. Fares for all buses are 50¢ to $1.

Within Walking Distance: Schooners from Venezuela, Colombia, and other areas dock alongside the canal at the **Floating Market,** a short walk from the Queen Emma pontoon bridge. Here, amid a bustling crowd, vendors sell fresh fish, tropical fruits, and spices. Nearby, you can trace the island's history through the exhibits at the **Curaçao Maritime Museum** (Van den Brandhof Street), a recently renovated former bordello. Admission is about $5.50 for adults and $3.30 for children.

The oldest Jewish congregation in the New World gathers in the 1651 **Mikve Israel Emanuel Synagogue** (at the corner of Columbusstraat and Hanchi Snog). White sand covers the floor, symbolic of the desert that the early Israelites roamed. Next door, the **Jewish Cultural Historical Museum** displays ritual, ceremonial, and cultural objects, many dating back to the 17th and 18th centuries. Admission is $2 for adults and $1 for children.

If you enjoy paintings, objets d'art, or antique furniture, visit the **Curaçao Museum** (Van Leeuwenhoekstraat). Admission is about $3 for adults and $1.50 for children.

Museum Kura Hulanda is a $6 million cultural center dedicated to African history. You reach this new museum by small boats that cross the harbor to the site of a former slave yard and prison. Admission is about $5.50 for adults and $2.75 for children.

Beyond Walking Distance: If you like to swim up close and personal with the sea critters, the **Curaçao Seaquarium** (off Dr. Martin Luther King Boulevard) displays more than 400 species of fish and plant life and offers divers, snorkelers, and experienced swimmers a chance to feed, film, and photograph sharks, stingrays, lobsters, and other marine life in a controlled environment. If you don't swim, a 46-foot semi-submersible observatory enables you to watch the underwater action. The Seaquarium also maintains the island's only full-facility, palm-shaded, sugar-white beach. The facility is about a 10-minute, $8 cab ride from Queen Emma pontoon bridge. Admission is $15 for adults and $7.50 for children under 14.

A 40-minute taxi ride from Willemstad, **Mount Christoffelberg** rises 1,230 feet from the desert-like landscape in **Christoffel National Park,** a 4,500-acre preserve abundant with flora and fauna. Hiking along several trails to the top of the mountain, you find Arawak paintings and **Piedra di Monton,** a rock formation created by the slaves who cleared this former plantation. Admission is $13.50.

Next to Christoffel National Park, you can check out the **National Park Shete Boka** (Seven Bays), a turtle sanctuary. Admission is $1.50.

If you want to explore the island's deeper side, head to **Hato Caves,** replete with stalagmites, stalactites, and underground pools. Runaway slaves used these haunting caverns as a hiding place. Admission is $7.25 for adults, $5.75 for children ages 4 to11, and free for kids 3 and under.

Honeymooners and other couples can snuggle on a blanket at one of Curaçao's 38 beautiful beaches. The better ones are **Santa Barbara Beach, Playa Abao,** and **Blauwbaai** (Blue Bay). **Knip Bay** boasts live music and dancing on the weekends. You can negotiate the fare for a taxi and make arrangements with the driver to pick you up at a specific time.

Beware of stepping on the sea urchins that lurk in these waters. If you do, a local remedy says to apply vinegar or lime juice to ease the pain.

Dominica

Tiny Dominica, sandwiched between Guadeloupe and Martinique, calls itself "the nature island of the Caribbean."

Unlike most other Caribbean spots, Dominica (pronounced dome-ee-*nee*-ka) doesn't have much in the way of sugar-white beaches. However, the island is blessed with virgin coral reefs, lush rain forests, spectacular waterfalls, and untamed rivers.

Bear in mind that Dominica is a bit rough around the edges when it comes to tourism. You can't find casinos or much else in the way of nightlife. The island's natural treasures are the real draw, plus the historical sites of interest including **Cabrits National Park,** built around the ruins of Fort Shirley (an 18th-century garrison constructed of volcanic stone). The island also is home to 3,500 Carib Indians who, along with the Arawaks, were the island's original inhabitants.

The Eastern Caribbean dollar (EC$) is the official currency here, but merchants accept the U.S. dollar virtually everywhere. U.S. $1 = EC $2.67. The official language is English, but most people also speak Creole.

Cruising into port

American Canadian Caribbean, Carnival, Clipper, Crystal, Cunard, Holland America, Norwegian, Oceania, Princess, Seabourn, Seven Seas, Star Clippers, Windjammer, and Windstar all visit Dominica as a port of call.

Seeking out the best shore excursions

Trafalgar Falls and Sulphur Tour: Take a short walk to Trafalgar Falls, followed by a moderate walk through the rain forest to the Wotton Waven sulphur springs. (3½ hours; $45)

Wacky Rollers 4WD Adventure: Drive to **Roseau** aboard a four-wheeler, enjoy the views at **Morne Bruce,** and drive into the **Morne Trois Pitons National Park** to swim in the Titou Gorge. (3½ hours; $69)

Exploring on your own

Ships typically drop anchor at Roseau, the island's capital and the largest port. Or they head to the northwestern town of Portsmouth, which gives instant access to Cabrits National Park and Fort Shirley.

Taxis and minivans are designated by HA or H on the license plate. Drivers double as tour guides, and cabs can be pricey (expect to pay $60, for instance, to get from Roseau to the northern beaches or **Emerald Pool**). The vehicles are not metered, so make sure to negotiate a rate before you go. Generally, prices are $18 an hour for up to four people.

Dominica

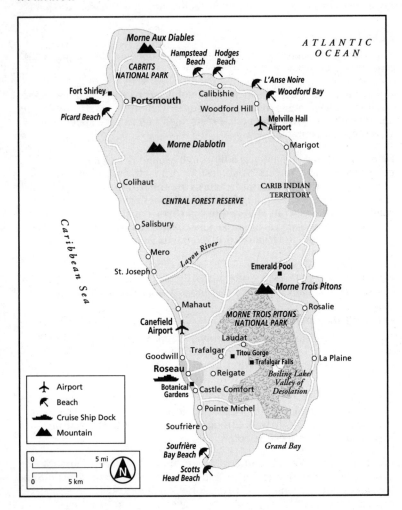

Renting a car is another option. You need a valid driver's license and Dominican Driver's Permit, which costs $12. Daily rental car rates range from $35 to $75. You drive on the left, and many of the main roads can be narrow, winding, and mountainous. In Roseau, call **Island Car Rentals** (☎ 767-448-20738) or **Valley Rent a Car** (☎ 767-448-3233).

Within Walking Distance (Roseau Port): On the bay front at the dock in Roseau is the **Dominica Museum,** located in an old market house dating from 1810. Here you can find out about the island's geology, history, archeology, economy, and culture from the permanent exhibit. The museum is open Monday through Friday from 9 a.m. to 4 p.m. and Saturday from 9 a.m. to noon. Admission is $2.

Behind the museum is **Old Market Square,** where merchants have gathered for centuries. At one time, it was also the site for executions, slave auctions, and political rallies. Now, you find Dominican crafts and souvenirs for sale. The **Public Market Place,** at the mouth of the Roseau River and to your left as you leave the ship, is the town's commercial hub. Expect it to be especially jumping on Saturday mornings when farmers and countryside vendors display fruits, vegetables, and flowers.

On the eastern edge of Roseau, also within walking distance of the docks, are the **Botanical Gardens,** located at the base of Morne Bruce. The gardens were established at the end of the 19th century, and about 150 of the 500 original species of trees and shrubs remain. Keep your eyes out for the Carib Wood tree, whose red blossom is the island's national flower (in bloom March to May).

Within Walking Distance (Portsmouth Port): The cruise-ship dock at Portsmouth leads directly to the 260-acre **Cabrits National Park,** which boasts dazzling mountain scenery, tropical forests, swamplands, volcanic sand beaches, coral reefs, and an 18th-century garrison. You can still see several cannons from the days of Fort Shirley scattered among the trails. Previous visitors to the area have included Christopher Columbus, Sir Francis Drake, Admiral Horatio Nelson, and John Smith, who stopped here on his way to Virginia to found Jamestown. You can spend a whole day touring the park, so wear good walking shoes.

To get to Cabrits National Park from the Roseau cruise-ship dock is about a 45-minute to one-hour drive (or a $60 cab ride).

Beyond Walking Distance: About 15 to 20 minutes by cab from Roseau is **Trafalgar Falls,** two separate cascades that tumble side by side. A short trail from the road brings you to a viewing platform where you see the two falls converge into rocky pools. You can take a dip in the brisk water at the base of the falls, but be careful, the rocks are slippery.

Emerald Pool is located deep in the rain forest, not far from the center of the island. Expect about a 40-minute drive from Roseau. After you walk 15 minutes along a flat trail shaded by magnificent trees, you reach a 50-foot waterfall that crashes into the pool named for the moss-covered boulders that enclose it. You can splash around in the grotto's crystal-clear waters.

Another swimming spot that beckons visitors is **Titou Gorge,** near the village of Laudat. The water-filled canyon snakes along to the base of a waterfall. The flow is quite strong, and at times, you may feel like a salmon swimming upstream. A hot mineral cascade at the canyon's mouth relieves sore muscles. From Roseau to Laudat is about a 30-minute drive.

Beaches — featuring plenty of rocks and dark, volcanic sand — are not Dominica's strong point, but the island's top choices are on the northern coast, about 20 minutes from Roseau. The best stretches are **Woodford Bay, L'Ance Tortue, Pointe Baptiste,** and **Hampstead Beach.** All have white sand, palm trees, and sky-blue waters.

Dominican Republic

Rich in colonial history and renowned for its natural treasures — including sugar-white beaches, mountain peaks, and lush landscapes — the Dominican Republic is one of the fastest-growing destinations in the Caribbean. During his first voyage to the New World, Columbus supposedly exclaimed, "There is no more beautiful island in the world." Issues such as poverty, crime, and political instability, including Rafael Trujillo's infamous reign (1930 to 1961) and the civil wars that followed, have kept many American tourists away, but that trend is changing. Travelers from the United States are discovering the Dominican Republic, whose Latin flavor provides a distinct contrast with its British- and French-influenced neighbors. Locals are friendly and share a love for baseball.

The official currency is the Dominican peso (DOP), although cab drivers and some shopkeepers accept U.S. dollars: US $1 = 50 DOP (1 DOP = US 2¢). Spanish is the official language, but you hear some English spoken in tourist areas. Knowing some key Spanish phrases comes in handy.

Cruising into port

Carnival, Costa, Celebrity, Holland America, Royal Caribbean, Seabourn, and Windjammer have ships that visit the Dominican Republic as a port of call.

Seeking out the best shore excursions

Maravillas Caves & Romana Panoramic: Tour the recently opened Maravillas Caves — complete with hieroglyphics dating from the Taino Indians — followed by a shopping expedition to **Columbus Plaza.** (3½ hours; $42)

Columbus Lighthouse, Amber Museum, and Cathedral Tour: Explore the lighthouse, stop to see some of the most precious amber in the world, and visit the cathedral where Columbus was originally buried. ($20; 3 hours)

Juan Dolio Beach Tour: Spend the day at the resort's beach, with access to a pool, snorkeling equipment, and clubhouse facilities. The tour includes a buffet lunch and drinks. ($40; 6 hours)

Exploring on your own

In Santo Domingo, ships dock at San Souci, about three miles from downtown. You can find a tourist information stand, telephones, a bank, and some shops at the terminal. The quickest and easiest way to get downtown is by taxi. A cab ride from the port to the Colonial City costs about $10, and the average fare within Santo Domingo is $6. Taxis aren't

Dominican Republic

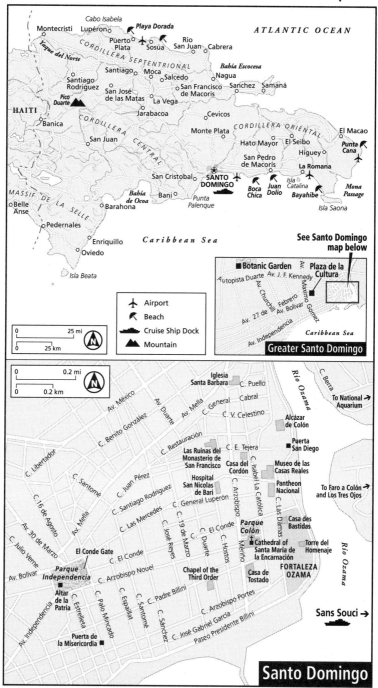

ATLANTIC OCEAN

Cabo Isabela
Playa Dorada
Montecristi Lupérón
Puerto
Plata Sosúa Rio
San Juan Cabrera
CORDILLERA SEPTENTRIONAL
Yaque del Norte
Bahía Escocesa
Santiago Moca Salcedo Nagua
Santiago
Rodríguez
San José San Francisco Sánchez Samaná
de las Matas de Macoris
Pico La Vega
Duarte
HAITI
Jarabacoa
Banica Cevicos
CORDILLERA Monte Plata CORDILLERA ORIENTAL El Macao
San Juan Hato Mayor El Seibo
CENTRAL Higuey Punta
San Pedro Cana
de Macoris La Romana
San Cristobal SANTO Isla
DOMINGO Boca Juan Catalina Mona
Chica Dolio Bayahibe Passage
MASSIF DE LA SELLE
Belle Bahía Bani
Anse de Ocoa Punta Isla Saona
Barahona Palenque
Pedernales
Enriquillo Caribbean Sea See Santo Domingo
map below
Oviedo
Botanic Garden Plaza de la
Isla Beata Cultura
Autopista Duarte Av. J. F. Kennedy

✈ Airport
🏖 Beach
🚢 Cruise Ship Dock
▲ Mountain

0   25 mi
0   25 km

Av. Churchill
Av. 27 de Febrero
Av. Bolivar
Av. Independencia
Caribbean Sea
Greater Santo Domingo

0   0.2 mi
0   0.2 km

Iglesia
Santa Barbara C. Puello
Rio Ozama
Av. México C. Berra
Av. Duarte Av. Mella C. General Cabral To National →
C. Benito Gonzalez C. V. Celestino Aquarium
Alcázar
C. Restauración de Colón
C. Libertador Las Ruinas del C. E. Tejera Puerta
Monasterio de Casa del San Diego
San Francisco Cordón Museo de las
C. Juan Pérez Hospital Casas Reales
C. Santomé San Nicolas C. Isabel La Católica Pantheon To Faro a Colón →
de Bari C. Arzobispo Nacional and Los Tres Ojos
C. Santiago Rodríguez C. General Luperón
C. 16 de Agosto C. Las Mercedes Casa des
Av. 30 de Marzo C. José Reyes C. El Conde Parque Bastidas
Av. Mella C. 19 de Marzo Colón C. Las Damas
Av. Julio Verne El Conde Gate C. Duarte Cathedral of Torre del Rio Ozama
C. El Conde C. Hostos Santa María de Homenaje
Parque C. Meriño la Encarnación
Independencia C. Arzobispo Nouel Chapel of the FORTALEZA
Av. Bolivar Third Order Casa de OZAMA
Altar C. Espaillat Tostado
de la C. Estrelleta C. Padre Billini
Patria C. Palo Mincado C. Arzobispo Portes
Av. Independencia C. Santomé C. Sánchez Sans Souci →
C. José Gabriel García
Puerta de Paseo Presidente Billini
la Misericordia

Santo Domingo

metered, so make sure you agree with your driver on the fare before-
hand. Another option for getting around is taking the cheaper *moto con-
chos,* or motorcycle taxis. Buses are another alternative, and private
companies such as **Caribe Tours** (☎ 809-221-4422) and **Metro Expreso**
(☎ 809-566-7126) operate scheduled service in air-conditioned buses for
inexpensive fares (ranging from $3 to $6). Public buses, called *guaguas,*
are cheap (about $1), but the service is erratic. We don't recommend
renting a car because the country's secondary roads are particularly difficult to drive on and routes are poorly marked.

Ships also anchor at Catalina Island in La Romana, home to the famous
Casa de Campo, an upscale resort that offers water sports, golf, horseback riding, and nice restaurants. You can get there by taxi for about $13
each way. Cruise lines also offer excursions to the resort and its environs,
including **Altos de Chavon,** a replica of a 16th-century Mediterranean village complete with cobblestone streets, artisans' workshops, and sweeping views of the green mountains and blue waters.

Within Walking Distance: You don't find much near the cruise terminal, so your best bet is to take a taxi to the beach or to Santo Domingo's
Colonial City (Zona Colonial), home to an historic cathedral, monastery,
and university in the New World. **Calle Las Damas** is the oldest street in
the New World, and in colonial times it served as the promenade for the
ladies of the viceroy's court. The main shopping area is along **Calle El
Conde.** The Colonial City is best explored on foot.

Alcazar de Colon (Columbus' Palace), on Calle Las Damas, was built for
Columbus' son Diego in 1510. Diego was the first viceroy of the Indies,
and the palace served as the center of the Spanish court. Inside you see
furnishings and paintings from that era. Admission is $1.

The Cathedral of Santa Maria de la Encarnacion, on Calle Arzobispo
Merino, was built between 1510 and 1540, although the bell tower was
never finished. Pope Paul III declared it the first cathedral in the New
World in 1542. A mausoleum inside held the remains of Christopher
Columbus until they were transferred to the Columbus Lighthouse
Memorial just outside the Colonial City in 1992. Admission is free. Next
to the cathedral is **Parque Colon** (Columbus Square), which features a
larger-than-life bronze statue of the discoverer.

Las Ruinas del Monasterio de San Francisco (The Ruins of the San
Francisco Monastery), between Calle Hostos and Calle Emiliano Tejera,
has managed to survive despite hurricanes, earthquakes, the French
artillery, and a pillaging by Sir Francis Drake. Constructed in the early
16th century, this is the oldest monastery in the New World.

Fortaleza Ozama, on Calle Las Damas, overlooks the Ozama River and is
considered the earliest military building in the New World. You can also
peek inside **La Torre del Homenaje** (The Tower of Homage), a former
prison and fortress within the larger fort. Admission is $1.

Pate Palo Brasserie (La Atarazana; ☎ 809-687-8089) claims to be the oldest pub in the New World. The menu is international, and the waiters are friendly. You can find country-style cooking at **El Conuco,** (Casimiro de Moya; ☎ 809-221-3231). The restaurant looks like a hut on a Dominican farm.

Beyond Walking Distance: At the **National Aquarium,** on Avenida Espana, check out the salt-water and fresh-water marine life, including turtles and sharks.

Just outside the Colonial City and commemorating the 500th anniversary of Christopher Columbus' arrival in the Americas in 1492 is **Faro a Colon** (Columbus's Lighthouse) on Boulevar al Faro. The monument is one of many claiming to house the discoverer's remains. Admission is $2.

You can explore three subterranean lagoons surrounded by stalagmites and lush greenery at **Los Tres Ojos** (The Three Eyes), on Avenida Las Americas. Expect about a 15-minute ride from Santo Domingo.

Die-hard baseball fans know about **San Pedro de Macoris,** the home-town of such players as Sammy Sosa and Pedro Martinez. The town is about a 45-minute drive from Santo Domingo. If you're lucky, you may catch a game at the local stadium and spot some future major leaguers.

Although the Dominican Republic is known for its great beaches, most are some distance from Santo Domingo. You need to take a taxi (about $25 to $30 one way) to reach even the closest ones: **Boca Chica** (about 35 minutes away) and **Juan Dolio** (about 45 minutes away). Both resorts have white-sand beaches, calm waters for swimming, hotels, restaurants, bars, and even a few of your favorite pesky vendors.

If you are in Boca Chica, stop by **Neptuno's Club** (Avenida Duarte; ☎ 809-523-4703) for a bite to eat. The open-air restaurant is known for great seafood dishes.

Freeport/Lucaya, Bahamas

A renaissance has taken place on Grand Bahama Island during the past few years, with new hotels and renovated attractions leading the initiative. You can while away the day at nearly 100 shops at the International Bazaar, swim with dolphins, golf at a championship course, suck down a Bahama Mama, or sample conch (pronounced konk) in a surprising variety of preparations, including salad, chowder, and fritters. If you feel green, stroll through one of the island's parks and gardens; if you feel like spending some green, visit some of the Caribbean's best shopping and casinos. The Bahamian dollar has equal value with the U.S. dollar. For orientation's sake, note that Freeport is technically the landlocked section of town, and Lucaya lies right next door, along the waterfront. Although originally intended to be two separate developments, they've grown together over the years.

Freeport/Lucaya

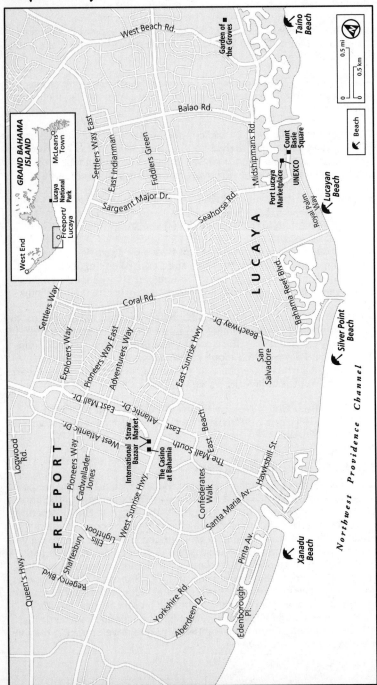

Cruising into port

Carnival, Disney, Holland America, and Norwegian make port calls here.

Seeking out the best shore excursions

Swim with Dolphins: Unlike some dolphin encounters, you actually swim with the animals during this session, in groups of six, under the supervision of a trainer. (2½ hours; $169)

Snorkel Adventure: Get an underwater view of colorful coral and fish during an outing suitable for both adults and kids. Equipment and how-tos are included. (3 hours; $36)

Exploring on your own

When you disembark at the west end of Grand Bahama Island, you're actually in the middle of nowhere. Head to **Lucaya, Freeport,** and the **International Bazaar,** the center of most action on the island; a taxi for two costs about $10. Taxis are metered, and the rates are fixed by law. The meter starts at $2.20, and you incur a 30¢ charge for each ¼ mile for one or two passengers (additional passengers pay $3 per person).

Buses run from the International Bazaar to downtown Freeport and from the Pub on the Mall to the Lucaya area. You need exact change for the 75¢ fare. Other ways to explore the island include renting a car ($50 to $75 a day), moped ($40 a day), or bicycle ($12 for a half day or $20 for a full day).

Within Walking Distance: Unfortunately, the island provides nothing of interest within walking distance of the pier.

Beyond Walking Distance **(Freeport/Lucaya):** Named in honor of a great jazz musician who used to reside on the island, **Count Basie Square** (in the center of the waterfront area of Port Lucaya) showcases the best live music on the island nightly. For more shopping and dining options, visit the **Port Lucaya Marina and Marketplace** (across the street from the Lucayan Beach), which also offers daily entertainment, such as strolling musicians and steel-drum bands.

A truly unique shopping experience in the Bahamas is the theme-park-like **International Bazaar** (East Mall Drive and East Sunrise Highway). You can find just about any souvenir or gift your heart desires in the nearly 100 shops. For specifically Bahamian items, visit the Bazaar at the **Straw Market** located next door.

The main attraction of the island is **Garden of the Groves** (at the intersection of Midshipman Road and Magellan Drive on the East End, seven miles east of the International Bazaar). This scenic 11-acre garden — accessible by taxi from Port Lucaya for about $13 — honors Wallace Groves, the founder of Freeport/Lucaya. Here you find waterfalls, flowering shrubs, and some 10,000 trees that attract all kinds of tropical birds. Admission is $9.95 for adults and $6.95 for children 3 to 10 (children under 3 free).

You can also explore the lovely **Lucayan National Park** (on Sunrise Highway, also on the East End of Grand Bahama Island, about 12 miles from Lucaya), a 40-acre park filled with palm, mangrove, and pine trees. Follow a winding wooden path through the woods to caves and freshwater springs. The park is home to one of the most secluded beaches on Grand Bahama. Admission is $3; kids under 12 get in free.

Junior explorers enjoy the 100-acre **Rand Nature Centre,** run by the Bahamas National Trust. Armed with binoculars and a trail map, kids can easily spot coral-colored flamingos, families of turtles, and even a re-created Lucayan village. Admission is $5; $3 for children 5 to 12; and children under 5 get in free.

If you prefer gaming, try your luck in the **Casino at Bahamia** at the Mall on West Sunrise Highway, adjacent to the International Bazaar.

For a wonderful adventure, the Underwater Explorers Society (UNEXSO) created the **Dolphin Experience.** You can get up close and personal with the dolphins for $69 — great for younger children — or actually swim with them in protected waters for $159. UNEXSO also offers daily snorkeling excursions, reef trips, shark dives, and wreck dives. Call ☎ **888-365-3483** in the United States. (Reservations are essential.)

You find most of the beaches on Grand Bahama Island in Lucaya, near the major resort hotels, but you may want to go to Freeport to check out the popular mile-long **Xanadu Beach** at the Xanadu Beach Resort. A favorite picnic place is **Gold Rock Beach,** about 20 minutes by car or cab east of Lucaya. **Taino, Churchill,** and **Fortune Beach** also offer sandy escapes.

Grand Bahama is also good for golfers — all courses stay open to the public year-round. The courses are within 1.7 miles of each other, so you generally don't have to wait to play. You can rent clubs at the pro shops.

For savory conch chowder and yummy carrot cake, head to **The Pepper Pot,** East Sunrise Highway at Coral Road.

Grand Cayman, Cayman Islands

The largest of the Cayman Islands, Grand Cayman is one place where you can literally go to Hell and back (see "Beyond Walking Distance" in this section) and still have time to snorkel or go diving. You probably have more to see underwater than on land, but even so, championship shopping lines the streets around the port in George Town, the island's capital. Cruise ships ferry passengers into George Town to a pier along **Harbour Drive,** conveniently located in the center of the shopping district.

Grand Cayman

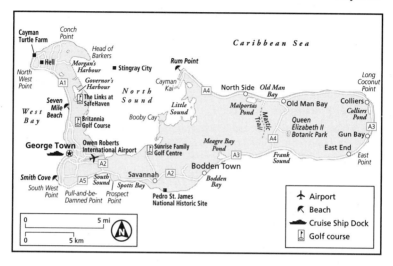

The area was first home to shipwrecked sailors and buccaneers in the 16th and 17th centuries. The real British connection occurred later, however, when Scottish fishermen arrived, setting the slow pace of local life. Columbus referred to the islands as Las Tortugas, or The Turtles, because of the large number of green sea turtles in the surrounding waters. Those turtles are now an endangered species. The Cayman Islands received attention in the late 1990s when it denied access to a gay cruise charter. The public outcry that ensued apparently didn't do its work, because the island later prohibited cruise lines from making port calls on Sundays, Christmas, and Good Friday. These moves were apparently the work of island church leaders.

Grand Cayman has more than 500 tax-advantaged offshore banks for the financially secure. The official currency is the Cayman Islands dollar (C.I.). Merchants accept Canadian, U.S., and British currencies, but you can save money if you exchange your U.S. dollars for Cayman Islands dollars: US $1 = C.I. 82¢ (C.I. 1 = US $1.22). Many restaurants and shops quote prices in Cayman Islands dollars. English is the official language.

Cruising into port

Carnival, Celebrity, Costa, Disney, Holland America, Norwegian, Princess, Royal Caribbean, Seven Seas, and Silversea all make port calls here.

Seeking out the best shore excursions

Stingray City Sandbar: This popular destination for snorkelers and scuba divers gives visitors the chance to swim among 30 to 50 relatively tame stingrays. And you get to touch and feed them, too (if you're brave enough). Don't worry: Despite their alien looks, stingrays are very friendly. Just don't step on them. This is a good excursion for families; sharp-eyed youngsters may even see a nurse shark or giant turtle in the waters nearby. (2½ to 3½ hours; $45)

Reef Runner Jungle Tour: Glide through the mangroves in your own boat — no kids under 7 allowed — and then snorkel in the **Living Coral Gardens.** Departs from **Blue Water Sports** complex. (3 hours; $64)

Exploring on your own

You can easily get around Grand Cayman by car after you adjust to driving on the left. Car rentals are available through several franchise agencies, including Avis, Budget, and Hertz. Expect to pay between $40 and $70 a day. Bicycles and motorcycles are a nice alternative given the flat roads; scooters rent for about $30 a day and bikes about $15. Taxi fares are fixed. The average hourly rate for an island tour for four people is $37.50. Privately owned and operated minibuses also offer service along the main roads in and out of George Town.

You can find duty-free shopping right across the street from the pier. Stores offer a variety of quality goods, from a variety of turtle products to Irish linens, British woolens, silver, and china.

Be forewarned that you can't bring turtle products for sale on Grand Cayman (and elsewhere in the Caribbean) back to the United States.

Within Walking Distance: Located in the island's former courthouse, the **Cayman Islands National Museum** on Harbour Drive displays a variety of Caymanian artifacts from the 1930s. Admission is $4 for adults and $2 for students and seniors.

Beyond Walking Distance: The **Cayman Turtle Farm** at Northwest Point is the world's only green-sea-turtle farm. Its aim is to supply quality turtle meat to the local market and also to help replenish the turtle population in local waters. Visitors have an opportunity to view turtles from eggs to 600-pound adults. Young children can even handle the smaller turtles in a special petting pool. Admission is $6 for adults and $3 for children 6 to 12 (kids under 6 get in free).

The tiny mail outpost called **Hell,** at Northwest Point, includes a coral formation that looks like a Dalí interpretation of the outpost's namesake. The signposts pointing toward the area make for a nifty snapshot, but that's about the extent of its draw.

The **Queen Elizabeth II Botanic Park,** off Frank Sound Road, North Side, allows you a one-hour walk through wooded land, wetlands, swamp, and mahogany trees. Good news: Footsore travelers can find plenty of rest stations. Admission is about $7.30 for adults and about $4.25 for children over 5 (children under 5 get in free).

At the **Mastic Trail** west of Frank Sound Road, a 45-minute drive from George Town, a restored 200-year-old footpath takes you through a woodland area in the center of the island that experts estimate to be 2 million years old. You can easily get lost touring on your own; the 3-hour tours offered are a better bet and cost $45 per person. Reservations are required; bring cash or travelers checks. (☎ **345-949-1996** or **345-945-6588**).

Wear comfortable walking shoes and bring bug repellant and water.

Pedro St. James National Historic Site in Savannah is the country's first national landmark. The centerpiece of the attraction is **Pedro Castle,** a restored great house and estate that was built in 1780. At the visitors' center, a multimedia show details the history of the island. Admission is $8 for adults and $4 for children 6 to 12 (children under 6 get in free).

Seven Mile Beach, which begins north of George Town, offers sugar-white sands with a backdrop of Australian pines. You may recognize this beach from the Tom Cruise movie *Cocktail.* The water temperature averages a balmy 80 degrees. Watersports equipment is available. You can also go horseback riding, letting your hair blow in the salty breeze. Check with local operators — the **Equestrian Center, Honey Suckle Trail Rides, and Nicki's Beach Rides** — for options. The beach is a short cab ride from the cruise dock.

You can find the island's best seafood at **Cracked Conch by the Sea,** West Bay Road, near Turtle Bay Farm. Indulge your sweet tooth with a slice of Tortuga Rum Cake at **Café Tortuga** at Galleria Plaza.

Grenada

Remember the time in the early '80s when the news reported that the U.S. military had invaded a place called Grenada and everybody said, "Where?" Well, a lot of time has passed, and today the likelihood of a superpower invading this little spice island is pretty darn low — heck, it hasn't even been overrun by tourists. Today, Grenada (pronounced gre-NAY-da) remains an unspoiled Caribbean gem, where natural attractions take precedence over duty-free stores, fast-food outlets, and high-rise hotels. You can discover national parks, waterfalls, and sparkling stretches of beach, including the island's famous two-mile-long **Grand Anse Beach** (considered one of the best in the Caribbean). You can also hike through rain forests dense with palm and banana trees, bougainvillea, hibiscus, and ferns.

Locally grown spices make Grenada as fragrant as it is sublime. Among the spices you can buy at the waterfront market in St. George's are cinnamon, cocoa, clove, mace, and nutmeg. Situated in a dead volcano crater, St. George's, the capital, is flanked by several old forts. Georgian colonial buildings line narrow, steep streets that lead down to **The Carenage,** the main street, on the waterfront. The official currency is the Eastern Caribbean dollar (EC$). Generally, US $1 = EC $2.67. English is the official language.

Grenada

Cruising into port

American Canadian Caribbean, Clipper, and Windjammer have ships that begin their itineraries in Grenada. Celebrity, Cunard, Princess, Seabourn, SeaDream, Silversea, Star Clippers, Windjammer, and Windstar vessels make port calls here.

Seeking out the best shore excursions

Grenada Highlights: You can enjoy Grand Anse Beach along with part of the rain forest and the interior and coastal regions. In addition, you can visit a sugar factory that produces rum and check out charming villages along the way. (3 hours; $46)

Hike to Seven Sisters Waterfalls: Visit the **Grand Etang** rain forest, where after about a mile's hike along a muddy path you come to waterfalls and natural pools where you can swim. (4 hours; $59)

New Waves/Grenada Discover Scuba Diving: Scuba wannabes can take the plunge in this introductory course that includes instruction in a swimming pool followed by a reef dive. Check out the colorful sponges, fish, and pillar coral. (4 hours; $99)

Exploring on your own

Some ships dock at the horseshoe-shaped harbor in St. George's, and others bring their passengers ashore by tender. (A new multi-million dollar port with two big berths is also under construction on the western side of St. George's.) If you can handle the steep inclines, you can see St. George's on foot, but you can also take advantage of a variety of other transportation options. Probably the most scenic way to get around town is by water taxi ($4 to Grand Anse Beach). The cheapest way to get from one end of the island to the other is by minivans ($2), which act as minibuses, making frequent stops to pick up other passengers. You can find taxi drivers who offer guide services for about $20 an hour, but be sure to work out the price ahead of time. You can rent a car for between $50 and $60 a day, but getting around on the narrow streets isn't particularly easy. You drive on the left, and you must have a local driving permit you obtain at the time of rental. The permit costs about $37. Avis, Budget, and Dollar have facilities on the island.

Within Walking Distance: You can walk to the main street, the **Carenage,** from the pier for shopping and connection through the Sendall Tunnel to the **Esplanade** on the Outer Harbour, a scenic market area. The foundation of a 1704 French barracks and prison at Young and Monckton streets holds the **Grenada National Museum,** which contains items such as a marble bathtub used by Josephine Bonaparte. Admission is $2.

Beyond Walking Distance: Two miles of sugar-white sands give **Grand Anse Beach** a deserved reputation as one of the best beaches in the Caribbean. The beach is a ten-minute drive from the pier, and once there you can walk to some of the island's best resorts.

A quick taxi ride gets you to **Fort George,** which overlooks the harbor and offers a major photo op. You can enjoy spectacular views of St. George's tile-roofed architecture and its skyline. The Fort, which is open for sightseeing, was built in 1706 and now serves as the headquarters for the Royal Grenada Police Force.

Fifteen minutes from St. George's on the outskirts of Willis lies **Annandale Falls,** where you can stroll through a forest featuring elephant ear plants and liana vines. Share a picnic here with the 50-foot-high cascade as your backdrop and then take a dip. Another choice spot to take a dip is **Seven Sisters,** about one hour from St. George's.

Take a bus, taxi, or water taxi 15 miles from St. George's to **Levera National Park** and bask on its white beaches. You can also go snorkeling amid seagrass beds and coral reefs. The surf can be rough, so take care. You can also hike through a mangrove swamp and bird sanctuary.

Also worth the trek is a visit to **Grand Etang National Park,** home to a large crater lake surrounded by mountains that are often obscured by clouds. Flora and fauna — most notably monkeys and colorful birds — flourish here. Admission is $1.

Get your fill of traditional island dishes such as callaloo soup, curried chicken, yam-and-sweet-potato casserole, and pepperpot stew, whose ingredients include pork and oxtail, at **Morne Fendue Plantation House** (also known as **Betty's**). This early 20th-century plantation house at St. Patrick's is about 25 miles north of St. George's. (☎ 473-442-9330) **Nutmeg,** located on the Carenage in St. George's, is a good lunch spot that serves up West Indian specialties like roti. (☎ 473-440-2539)

Guadeloupe

The configurations of the islands that comprise the country of Guadeloupe make it look like butterfly wings. The island's "wings" are connected by the Riviere Salee, a channel that flows between them. The eastern island, **Grande-Terre,** boasts sugar plantations and rolling hills. The western island, **Basse-Terre,** is mountainous, with an active 4,800-foot volcano, **La Soufrière,** towering above its rain forest and waterfalls.

The capital, **Pointe-à-Pitre** on Grande-Terre, is a great place to spend a day doing some leisurely shopping at the open-air markets. But the crowds disappear when the shops close at sunset. Francophiles enjoy a strong French influence here, with plenty of great cuisine and a sophisticated ambience.

The official currency is the euro (€), and restaurants generally post prices in that currency, but tourist shops often quote prices in U.S. dollars. The exchange rate is usually lower than the official rate. At press time, the euro exchange rate was US $1 = .83€ (1€ = US $1.22). You may be able to communicate in English in shops, but elsewhere you hear French, the official language, as well as Creole.

Cruising into port

Crystal, Cunard, Seabourn, SeaDream, and Windjammer all make port calls here.

Seeking out the best shore excursions

Your ship mostly likely offers an excursion to Grande-Terre (3 hours; $30 to $40) and may throw in a visit to Basse-Terre also.

A **Carbet Falls Tour** includes visits to rain forests and banana plantations, followed by a 30-minute hike to the falls and a refreshing swim. Comfortable shoes are a must. (4 hours; $40)

Exploring on your own

You can find a bank, telephones, and both duty-free and open-air shopping right at the pier at Pointe-à-Pitre on Grande-Terre.

Guadeloupe

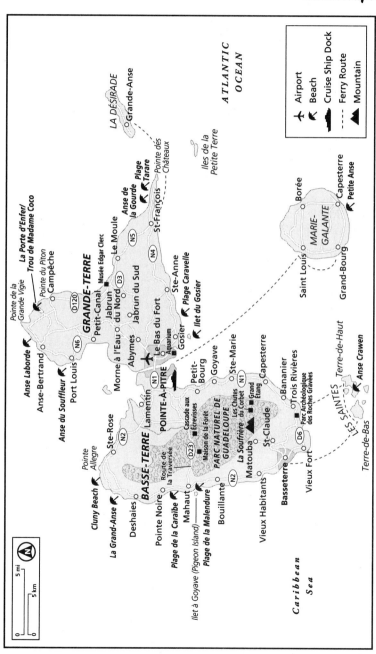

Legend:
- Airport
- Beach
- Cruise Ship Dock
- Ferry Route
- Mountain

ATLANTIC OCEAN

LA DÉSIRADE
Grande-Anse

Îles de la Petite Terre

Pointe des Châteaux

Plage Tarare

Anse de la Gourde
St-François

Le Moule
Musée Edgar Clerc

N5

N4

GRANDE-TERRE

La Porte d'Enfer/
Trou de Madame Coco

Pointe du Piton
Campêche

Pointe de la Grande Vigie

D120

Petit-Canal
Jabrun du Nord
D3
Jabrun du Sud

Ste-Anne
Plage Caravelle
Îlet du Gosier

N6

Anse Laborde
Anse-Bertrand

Anse du Souffleur
Port Louis

Morne à l'Eau
Abymes
Le Bas du Fort
Aquarium
Gosier

Goyave
Ste-Marie

Capesterre

MARIE-GALANTE

Borée

Capesterre
Petite Anse

Saint Louis

Grand-Bourg

Ste-Rose
Lamentin
POINTE-À-PITRE
N1
Petit-Bourg

N1

Bananier
Trois Rivières
Parc Archéologique des Roches Gravées

Terre-de-Haut
Anse Crawen

LES SAINTES

Pointe Allègre

BASSE-TERRE

Cascade aux Écrevisses
Maison de la forêt
PARC NATUREL DE GUADELOUPE
Les Chutes du Carbet
Grand Étang

D23
Route de la Traversée

Deshaies

Cluny Beach
La Grand-Anse

Pointe Noire

La Soufrière
Matouba
St-Claude

D6

Mahaut

Îlet à Goyave (Pigeon Island)
Plage de la Caraïbe
Plage de la Malendure

Bouillante

Vieux Habitants

Basseterre

Vieux Fort

Terre-de-Bas

Caribbean Sea

5 mi
5 km

Taking a taxi is the most popular way to get around the islands, but fares are expensive, especially on Sundays and holidays. Negotiate your price before you get in the cab. The government supposedly regulates fares, but drivers tend to ignore the regulations. You can also take the bus or rent a car. To visit Basse-Terre, taking a car or taxi is the way to go.

Within Walking Distance: The corner of rue Frebault and rue Thiers is home to a bustling covered market. You can find local wares in the back streets and good prices on French goods in the more mainstream shops. If you want to relax, stroll over to the shade of the palm trees and poincianas lining the park in the town center, **Place de la Victoire.**

Beyond Walking Distance: The primary resort on Grande-Terre is **Gosier,** with its five miles of beachfront. **Fort Fleur d'Epee,** an 18th-century site, affords spectacular views over the bay.

The **Edgar Clerc Archaeological Museum,** at Parc de la Rosette, Le Moule, devotes its exhibits to the civilizations of the Arawak and Carib Indians. Admission is $1.65.

The tourist complex of **Bas du Fort,** two miles east of Pointe-à-Pitre, off the main highway near Gosier, boasts the **Aquarium de la Guadeloupe,** one of the largest and most modern aquariums in the Caribbean. It houses marine life such as tropical fish, coral, and massive sharks. Admission is about $7.90 for adults, $4.25 for children 6 to 12, and free for kids 5 and under.

Nature-lovers can enjoy the forest at **Parc Naturel de Guadeloupe.** Covering almost a fifth of the island's acreage, the forest is home to the island's mascot, the titi (raccoon), plus tame birds and other wildlife. Exhibits highlight the island's volcano, as well as coffee, sugarcane, and rum.

Some of the island's best beaches are on Grande-Terre, including **Caravelle Beach,** known for great snorkeling. If you're looking for nude sunbathing, head to **Ilet du Gosier,** a tiny island opposite the seafront in the town of Gosier. You can take a fishing boat to the island, a 10-minute jaunt, for about $2.50 round-trip.

Stunning spots on Basse-Terre are **La Grande Anse** and **Cluny Beach.** Climbing **La Soufrière** is an exhilarating experience. You can drive to a parking area at La Savane a Mulets, and then hike the final 1,500 feet right to the mouth of the volcano. The two-hour trek is worth it, but make sure to go with an experienced guide.

For heavenly ice cream, head to **Chez Monia** at 4 Rue Victor Hugues, off of Rue Nozieres in Pointe-à-Pitre. Flavors include pear, lemon, and kiwi.

Jamaica

Jamaica's lush foliage, sparkling white beaches, and relaxed attitude make it a justly famed vacation destination. The port at **Ocho Rios** on the northern coast is where most ships dock, but your ship may drop anchor at **Montego Bay** (Mo Bay). The two cities offer very similar experiences, so you get the feel of Jamaica wherever you dock. Kingston, a major port in the 1600s, may once again become an active harbor if efforts to revive it are successful.

If you choose to sightsee via taxi, look for a government-licensed cab with Public Passenger Vehicle (PPV) plates (don't take an unregistered cab), and make sure that the price you negotiate with the driver is for your entire party, not per person.

The official currency is the Jamaican dollar (J$), but merchants accept the U.S. dollar in most places. Make sure you know whether the price they quote you is in U.S. or Jamaican dollars. US $1 = J $60 (J $1 = US $.017). English is the official language, but most Jamaicans speak a rich local dialect.

Cruise lines cooperate with the Jamaican government's efforts to prevent and reduce crime against tourists, which has been a problem in recent years. Follow their advice not to explore on your own: Opt for organized excursions or hire a taxi — don't go on foot.

Cruising into port

Carnival, Celebrity, Costa, Cunard, Holland America, Princess, Royal Caribbean, and Seven Seas all make port calls here.

Seeking out the best shore excursions

The excursions we detail are generally offered from both Montego Bay and Ocho Rios. In addition to these excursions, you can raft aboard 30-foot, 2-seat bamboo boats on the **Martha Brae River** (five hours for about $50). But frankly, these rafting trips aren't the best experience you can have.

Dunn's River Falls Jeep Safari: Travel by a four-wheel-drive or safari bus to **Fern Gully,** which has over 200 species of ferns. You can explore small villages and climb the 600-foot **Dunn's River Falls.** (5½ hours; $65)

Helmet Diving: Even children and non-swimmers can experience this unique way of exploring marine life under the sea: in a helmet that feeds you fresh air. (3 hours; $89 for adults and $75 for children)

Exploring on your own: Ocho Rios

The port at Ocho Rios is just a mile away from the major shopping area, **Ocean Village Shopping Centre.**

Jamaica

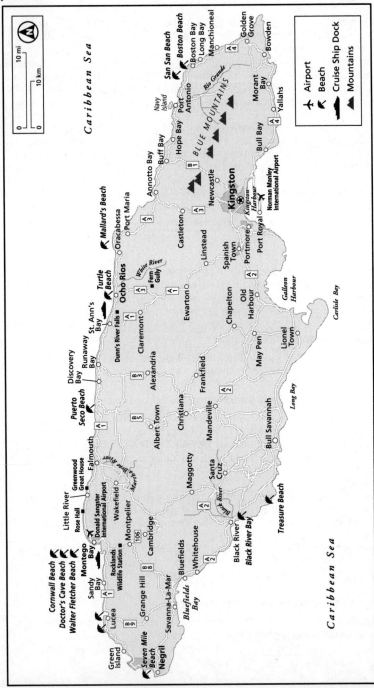

Within Walking Distance: Shopping opportunities are plentiful, but not for the timid: Street merchants can be very persistent. And don't let them tempt you to buy some *ganja* — local marijuana. Despite its prevalence, the drug is illegal.

Beyond Walking Distance: Shore excursions are the best way to see popular sights such as **Dunn's River Falls** (see "Seeking out the best shore excursions" earlier in this section).

We don't recommend renting a car in Jamaica. You have to arrange one in advance, make a deposit, and then deal with bad drivers while driving on the left.

You can check out a canoe made from a single piece of cottonwood and other attractions at the **Columbus Park Museum,** located at Discovery Bay. Admission is free.

Playwright Sir Noël Coward and his companion, Graham Payn, lived at **Firefly,** about 20 miles east of Ocho Rios. You can visit Coward's gravesite while touring the house and grounds. Admission is $10.

Mallards Beach is the most popular of Jamaica's spectacular beaches, but you can opt for a less crowded environment at **Turtle Beach.**

For a bite to eat, head to DaCosta Drive and feast on jerk pork and chicken at the **Ocho Rios Jerk Centre.** Try other Jamaican-style treats at the **Parkway Restaurant,** also on DaCosta Drive.

Exploring on your own in Montego Bay

Ships dock at Montego Bay's modern cruise facility, which has duty-free shops, telephones, and tourist information. To get into the center of "Mo Bay," however, you have to take a $5 taxi ride.

Within Walking Distance: Shopping options include duty-free stores at **City Centre,** the **Holiday Village Shopping Centre, Montego Freeport** near the pier, and arts and crafts goods at **Old Fort Craft Park** and the **Crafts Market.**

Beyond Walking Distance: The **Rose Hall Beach Club,** about 11 miles east of the city, has a restaurant, two beach bars, a covered pavilion, an open-air dance area, showers, restrooms, and changing areas. Along with enjoying water sports, you can play beach volleyball and check out live entertainment. Admission is $8 for adults and $5 for children 12 and under.

Rose Hall Great House is a restored home steeped in history and notoriety. John Palmer built it in 1780, but it was the second mistress of the house who made it a legend. "Infamous Annie" Palmer, wife of the builder's grandnephew, supposedly experimented with witchcraft and took slaves as her lovers, killing them after she grew bored with them. Admission is $15 adults and $10 children under 12. On the ground floor is **Annie's Pub.**

The Georgian-design **Greenwood Great House** formerly belonged to the Barrett family — relatives of poet Elizabeth Barrett Browning. Located about 14 miles east of Montego Bay, the house displays custom-made Wedgwood china, paintings of family members, musical instruments, and antique furniture. Admission is $12 adults and $6 children under 12.

At the **Rocklands Wildlife Station,** you can hand-feed finches and small doves and possibly get up close and personal with a Jamaican doctor bird. The station is about a mile from Anchovy, on the road from Montego Bay. Admission is $8.55.

You can find the best jerk chicken at the open-air **Pork Pit** (27 Gloucester Ave.) near Walter Fletcher Beach.

Key West, Florida

Home to a colorful cast of characters over the years (including Ernest "Papa" Hemingway), eclectic attractions, legendary sunsets, and hopping nightlife, Key West is a fun port of call for all ages. No other city in the United States truly evokes the spirit of the Caribbean — no doubt because Key West is the final link in a chain of islands extending 103 miles from the Florida mainland. The island beckons visitors to have a good time, although your ship may leave too early for you to enjoy the famous sunset hour. Don't fret: In Key West, nightlife begins at about noon, especially when a ship is in and people head to the famous bars.

If you have limited time here, skip the crowds at the cruise docks or touristy Duval Street and explore less-frequented byways such as Olivia or William Streets. You also find great opportunities to golf, snorkel, or scuba dive at this port.

Ships dock at Mallory Square or at nearby Truman Annex, and almost everything (shopping, bars, restaurants, and attractions) is either right there or a short ride away.

You're in Florida, so the U.S. dollar is the official currency and English is the language.

Cruising into port

Carnival, Celebrity, Costa, Disney, Crystal, Holland America, Norwegian, Royal Caribbean, Seven Seas, and Silversea make port calls here.

Seeking out the best shore excursions

The entire island is so readily accessible that we recommend saving your time and money at Key West by creating your own expedition rather than signing up for a shore excursion.

Wildlife Rescue Center of the Florida Keys: Great White Herons, Eastern Brown Pelicans, and Red-shouldered Hawks are among the birds you see at this rescue center. Follow your observatory walk with a stroll through the six-acre park. (1½ hours; $24)

Key West

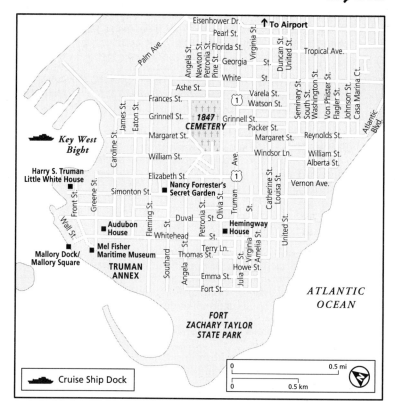

Key West Nature Kayak Tour: Hop in one- or two-person kayaks for a moderately strenuous but rewarding guided tour through the mangroves of the inner coastal waterways. Guides point out water creatures and birds along the way, and if you're very lucky, you may even spot a manatee. (2½ hours; $44)

Exploring on your own

Because Key West is only two miles wide and four miles long, everything is within walking distance and you can easily explore it on your own. You can ride around the island in about an hour on the bus quite cheaply (75¢ for adults, 35¢ for seniors and children 6 years to 12 and free for kids 5 years and under). You can even take public transportation to go to the beaches on the Atlantic side. We don't recommend renting a car.

For something a bit more organized, you can take a 90-minute narrated **Conch Tour Train** trolley tour past the local sites (fare for adults is $20, $10 for children 4 to 12, and free for kids under age 4). Alternatively, **Old**

Town Trolley lets you get off and on at top attractions. Tours cost $20 for adults, $10 for children ages 4 to 12, and are free for kids under age 4.

Island taxis operate 24 hours a day. If you use a taxi service to go to the beach, arrange a time for the cab to pick you up. Taxi rates are uniform; the meter starts at $1.75, with an additional 45¢ for every ¼ mile.

With most streets fairly traffic-free (apart from main roads), biking is another popular way to get around the island. You can rent a bicycle for $6 a day. A 3-hour motor-scooter rental costs $15; all day is $22.

A typical introduction to Key West may involve a pub crawl, starting at **Sloppy Joe's** (201 Duval St.), wandering on to **Captain Tony's Saloon** (428 Green St.), and finishing up at **Jimmy Buffett's Margaritaville** (500 Duval St.). All three fun spots offer fantastic margaritas, fast food, and some local Hemingway gossip.

If you want the real scoop on "Papa" Hemingway, stop by **Hemingway House** (907 Whitehead St.), where the Pulitzer Prize-winner lived with his second wife, Pauline, and wrote *For Whom the Bell Tolls* and *A Farewell to Arms.* Not only do you see some original furnishings of the estate, but you can also check out the descendants of Hemingway's cats — some 50 of them roam the grounds. Count their toes — many of them are *polydactyl* (meaning they have extra toes)! Admission is $10 for adults and $6 for children ages 6 to 12 (children under 6 get in free).

President Truman's former vacation residence, the **Harry S. Truman Little White House** (111 Front St.), is part of the 103-acre Truman Annex and has a museum inside. Admission is $7.50. *Note:* Lines at both Truman's house and Hemingway's house can get long, so pick the place you really want to see as your starting point.

Although ornithologist John James Audubon never lived at the **Audubon House** (205 Whitehead St.), the site is devoted to the renowned naturalist's engravings. Surrounded by lush tropical gardens, the three-story home gives you an idea of how rich sailors lived on the island in the 19th century. And a recent addition is the **John Malcolm Brinnin Commemorative Butterfly Garden.** Brinnin, a poet and biographer, was a Key West resident. Admission (to the house and garden) is $9 for adults and $5 for children 5 to 12 (children under 5 free).

Jessie Porter Newton (Miss Jessie to friends) was the grande dame of Key West and hosted many celebrities at her home. **Jessie Porter's Heritage House and Robert Frost Cottage** (410 Caroline St.) gives you a glimpse into her intriguing lifestyle. As a friend of the family, Robert Frost often stayed in the cottage out back that now bears his name. Other guests included Gloria Swanson (a childhood friend) and Tennessee Williams. The main house is filled with funky antiques and various interesting items the Porter family accumulated over six generations. Admission for a self-guided tour is $15.

Another off-beat attraction is the 21-acre **Key West Cemetery,** where you can find gravestones inscribed with such memorable phrases as "I Told You I Was Sick" and "At Least I Know Where He Is Sleeping Tonight." The main entrance is located at Margaret Street and Passover Lane.

At the **Mel Fisher Maritime Museum** (200 Greene St.) you can view treasures from shipwrecked Spanish galleons — jewelry, doubloons, and silver and gold bullion — recovered by the late treasure-hunter, Mel Fisher. Admission is $10 for adults and $5 for children.

Enjoy a perfect picnic lunch at one of the tables in **Nancy Forrester's Secret Garden** (1 Free School Lane, off Simonton between Southard and Fleming Streets). More than 150 species of palms, palmettos, climbing vines, and ground covers surround you. Admission is $6.

If your ship leaves late enough, you can partake in one of Key West's most celebrated rituals: watching the sunset from **Mallory Dock** while imbibing the carnival-like atmosphere of fire-swallowers and acrobats.

Beaches are not a big attraction here — they're mostly manmade with sand brought in from the Bahamas or mainland Florida. Close to the docks, **Fort Zachary Taylor State Beach** is fine for sunbathing but not great for swimming due to rocks. Other choices include **Higgs Memorial Beach** and **Smathers Beach.**

No visit to Key West is complete without a slice of Key lime pie at **Camille's,** located at 703½ Duval St. between Angela and Petronia Streets. The oldest eatery in the Florida Keys (established in 1909) is **Pepe's Café & Steak House** at 806 Caroline St. between William and Margaret Streets. Try the famous steak sandwich.

Martinique

Need a chance to brush up on your French? You got it. This lovely island is actually *part* of France (officially, a *département*), even if a couple thousand miles separate Martinique from Paris. Under French influence more or less continuously since 1635, it figures often in French history. Louis XIV's mistress, Madame de Maintenon, lived for a time in the fishing village Le Precheur. Empress Josephine, the wife of Napoleon, was born on the island in 1763.

The main town, **Fort-de-France,** has a New Orleans/French Riviera feel, with flower-covered, iron-balconied houses lining narrow, steep streets. Those same flowers cover much of the island. Martinique also offers white-sand beaches south of Fort-de-France and gray-sand beaches to the north, five bays and coves, top-drawer shopping, Creole cuisine, and **Mount Pelée,** which rises to 4,656 feet in the rain forest to the north.

The euro (€) is the official currency. At press time, the euro exchange rate was US $1 = .83€ (1€ = US $1.21). Almost everyone here speaks French, the official language. You hear English spoken occasionally in the major tourist areas.

Martinique

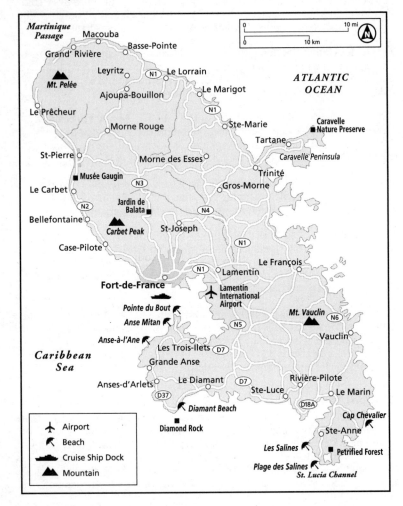

Martinique Passage

Macouba

Grand' Rivière

Basse-Pointe

Leyritz

N1

Le Lorrain

Mt. Pelée

Ajoupa-Bouillon

Le Marigot

ATLANTIC OCEAN

Le Prêcheur

N1

Morne Rouge

Ste-Marie

Caravelle Nature Preserve

St-Pierre

Tartane

Morne des Esses

Caravelle Peninsula

Musée Gaugin

N3

Trinité

Le Carbet

Gros-Morne

Jardin de Balata

N4

Bellefontaine

Carbet Peak

St-Joseph

Case-Pilote

N1

Le François

N1

Lamentin

Fort-de-France

Lamentin International Airport

Pointe du Bout

Anse Mitan

Mt. Vauclin

N6

Anse-à-l'Ane

N5

Vauclin

Les Trois-Ilets

D7

Grande Anse

Caribbean Sea

Anses-d'Arlets

Le Diamant

D7

Rivière-Pilote

Ste-Luce

Le Marin

D37

Diamant Beach

D18A

Cap Chevalier

Diamond Rock

Ste-Anne

Les Salines

Petrified Forest

Plage des Salines

St. Lucia Channel

0   10 mi
0   10 km

Airport

Beach

Cruise Ship Dock

Mountain

Cruising into port

American Canadian Caribbean, Carnival, Cunard, Holland America, Norwegian, Princess, Seven Seas, Silversea, Star Clippers, Windjammer, and Windstar all make port calls here.

Seeking out the best shore excursions

One of the most intriguing outings in the Caribbean is a trip through the green countryside to St. Pierre, formerly the cultural and economic capital of Martinique. Mount Pelée devastated the city on May 7, 1902, when the volcano erupted with fire and lava, killing 30,000 people and giving rise to the nickname The Pompeii of Martinique. The **Musée Volcanologique** offers pictures and relics excavated from the debris, including a clock that stopped at the exact moment the lava hit. (2½ to 3½ hours; $47 to $64)

Exploring on your own

Cruise ships dock at the **International Pier** in Fort-de-France, which has docking quays for two large-sized vessels. Because Martinique is a very popular port of call, ships also dock at the main harbor, located on the north side of the bay, a few minutes' drive from the center of Fort-de-France. Of the two, the International Pier is more convenient because it's adjacent to **La Savane,** the heart of Fort-de-France and the downtown area. The pier's proximity to La Savane enables passengers to walk to the area quickly and avoid a $10 (or more) cab ride or long, hot walk from the main harbor. Smaller vessels may anchor in the **Baie des Flamands** and transport passengers to the heart of Fort-de-France via tender.

Taxis are the best, but priciest, way to get around — make sure that you and the driver settle on a fare before the ride. If you want to take an island tour via taxi, you may want to get a group of four or five people together to minimize the expense. A five-hour tour ranges from $120 to $145. Bear in mind that most drivers do not speak English.

You have access to two kinds of bus service: *Grand buses* go anywhere within Fort-de-France for 85¢ to $1.35, whereas *taxis collectifs* (privately owned minivans) travel outside the city for about $5 one-way. Both options are usually crowded and uncomfortable.

You can rent a car from Avis, Budget, or Hertz for around $70 per day. Consider getting a collision-damage waiver as protection against the island's hordes of reckless drivers. You can generally get cheaper rates when you reserve a car from North America at least two business days before your arrival.

The cheapest way to get between **quai d'Esnambuc** in Fort-de-France and **Pointe-du-Bout,** the main tourist zone, is by a 15-minute ferry ride; one-way fare is $6.

Within Walking Distance: In the center of Fort-de-France lies **La Savane,** a garden of palms and mangoes with a headless statue of Napoleon's Josephine turned toward her birthplace in Trois-Ilets. Some years ago, angry citizens removed the head after they discovered that Josephine had been instrumental in bringing slavery back to Martinique.

The island's religious centerpiece, **St. Louis Roman Catholic Cathedral** (rue Victor-Schoelcher), dates from 1875. Its iron facade makes it look more like a railroad station than a church.

Even older history is on display at the **Musée Departemental de la Martinique** (9 rue de la Liberté), which contains relics from the island's early residents, the Arawaks and Caribs. Admission is $3.30 for adults, $2.20 for students, and $1 for kids 3 to 12 (kids under 3 get in free).

Beyond Walking Distance: Jean-Phillippe Thoze built **Jardin de Balata** (just north of the capital along Route N3) as a tropical botanical park on former jungle land that threatened to overgrow his grandmother's Creole house. The house has been restored and furnished with antiques and etchings. Admission is $8 for adults and $4 for children.

Le Carbet was the landing point of Columbus in 1502 and of the first French settlers in 1635, and the beach still looks much as it did when Paul Gauguin painted it in his *Bord de Mer.* Gauguin lived here in 1887 before he traveled to Tahiti to paint his most famous works. Books, prints, and other items linked to Gauguin's brief stay in Le Carbet are on display at the **Centre d'Art Musée Paul-Gauguin** (Anse Turin). Admission is $3.30.

Marie-Josephe-Rose Tasher de la Pagerie (who later wed Napoleon I and became empress of France) was born at **Trois-Ilets** (pronounced TWAHZ-ee-lay) in 1763. Take a 20-minute taxi ride south of Fort-de-France to visit a small museum devoted to Josephine in La Pagerie.

For the best beaches, try the white sands of **Pointe du Bout,** near the major hotels, and **Plage des Salines** and **Anse Mitan** in the south.

Think seafood when you come to this island, because fish is king. Dine on French-cum-Creole cooking in Fort-de-France at **Le Blénac,** a small, inexpensive restaurant at 3 rue Blénac, just off La Savane. This is a good venue to sample two staples of Creole cuisine: *crabes farcis,* a combination of land crabs and bread crumbs, highly seasoned and baked in the shell, and *blaff,* a tasty broth made of fish poached in wine and spiced with lime, garlic, cloves, onion, bay rum berries, thyme, and peppers. The story goes that blaff got its name for the sound the fish makes when first plopped into simmering water.

Nassau, Bahamas

The capital city of the Bahamas, Nassau (on New Providence Island) retains British colonial charm and also beckons with duty-free shopping, great entertainment, and sugar-white beaches. Get ready for company, however: Thanks to millions of government development dollars, 11 cruise ships can dock at Nassau's port simultaneously, bringing with them a veritable army of visitors. The official currency is the Bahamian dollar (B$1), equal in value to the U.S. dollar; merchants accept both currencies. English is the official language.

Cruising into port

American Canadian Caribbean has itineraries that begin in Nassau, and Carnival, Celebrity, Costa, Crystal, Disney, Holland America, Norwegian, Royal Caribbean, Seven Seas, and Windjammer all make port calls here.

Nassau

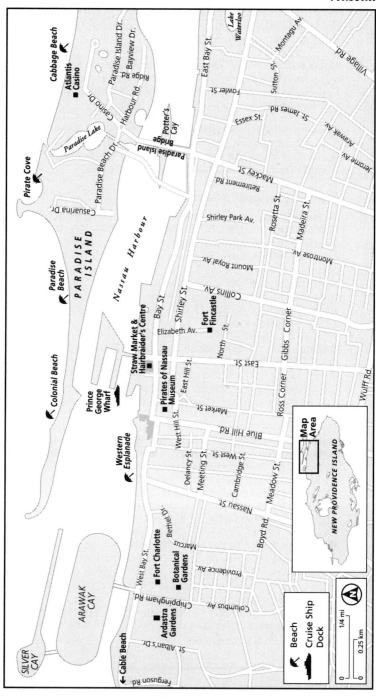

Lake Waterloo

Paradise Island Dr.
Bayview Dr.
Ridge Rd.
Harbour Rd.
Casino Dr.
Paradise Beach Dr.
Casuarina Dr.

Cabbage Beach
Atlantis Casino
Potter's Cay
Paradise Island Bridge
Pirate Cove
Paradise Lake
Paradise Beach
Colonial Beach

PARADISE ISLAND

Nassau Harbour

Prince George Wharf
Straw Market & Hairbraider's Centre
Western Esplanade

SILVER CAY
ARAWAK CAY

Cable Beach
West Bay St.
St. Alban's Dr.
Ferguson Rd.
Chippingham Rd.
Columbus Av.
Bethel Dr.
Marcus

Ardastra Gardens
Fort Charlotte
Botanical Gardens
Providence Av.
Boyd Rd.

Delancy St.
Meeting St.
West St.
Cambridge St.
Nassau St.
Meadow St.
Blue Hill Rd.
West Hill St.
East Hill St.
Market St.

Pirates of Nassau Museum
Bay St.
Shirley St.
Elizabeth Av.
North St.
East St.
Collins Av.
Fort Fincastle

Ross Corner
Gibbs Corner
Wulff Rd.

Mount Royal Av.
Montrose Av.
Shirley Park Av.
Rosetta St.
Madeira St.
Retirement Rd.
Mackey St.

East Bay St.
Fowler St.
Essex St.
St. James Rd.
Sutton St.
Montagu Av.
Jerome Av.
Arawak Av.
Village Rd.

NEW PROVIDENCE ISLAND
Map Area

Beach
Cruise Ship Dock

1/4 mi
0.25 km
0

Seeking out the best shore excursions

Because Nassau is highly accessible, you really don't need to join a shore excursion to explore downtown.

Sights and Pirates of Nassau Tour: Relive Nassau's past with the kids on this tour, which begins with a pirate meeting you at the gangway. Explore **Fort Fincastle,** experience the **Pirates of Nassau** museum, and finish with a 15-minute stroll back to the ship. (2 hours; $29)

Discover Atlantis and Historical Harbor Tour: Explore the sights of Nassau from the water, and then walk through **The Dig,** a mythical re-creation of the lost city of Atlantis (and a walk-through aquarium), at **Atlantis** resort on **Paradise Island.** (3 hours; $59)

Exploring on your own

Cruise ships anchor near **Rawson Square,** the heart of the city and its main shopping district. With many stores and attractions within walking distance, you can easily explore Nassau on foot. If you want public transportation, the cheapest method on the island is the *jitneys* (buses). You need exact change for the 75¢ fare (50¢ for kids). For more distant island destinations, taxis are a reasonable option. The taxis are metered, and fares start at $3 and increase 40¢ per ¼ mile for the first two passengers; additional passengers pay $3. For about $45 an hour, you can hire taxis for a sightseeing tour.

You may prefer to see Nassau from an old-fashioned horse-drawn carriage, starting at Rawson Square. Each carriage takes a maximum of three passengers, and the average fare is $5 to $10 per person; be sure to settle on a fare before the ride. The carriages operate daily from 9:00 a.m. to 4:30 p.m. (although drivers may give their horses a break during the heat of the afternoon).

Another travel option is to tool around by ferry or moped. The ferries (which can get very crowded) run from **Paradise Island** (where the famous **Atlantis Resort** is located) to downtown Nassau at a cost of $3 for a one-way trip (they run every 20 minutes or so). Mopeds cost $30 per hour, $40 for 2 hours, $40 for a half day, and $60 for a full day, plus $4 for insurance. A $10 deposit is required. As always, exercise caution when you drive a moped.

Within Walking Distance: The **Straw Market** near Rawson Square makes a fun, if somewhat touristy, stop. Merchants expect you to bargain at the market, so don't pay the first price they offer you (in the shops, on the other hand, the price is set). A short walk along the waterfront takes you to the native market where Bahamian fishers unload fish and produce. For another view of daily life, you can watch *sloops* (single-masted sailing vessels) bringing in the daily catch, including conch, under the **Paradise Island Bridge** at Potter's Cay.

You can climb the 66 steps of the **Queen's Staircase,** a landmark named for Queen Victoria, to **Fort Fincastle** (on Elizabeth Avenue), which the royal governor, Lord Dunmore, constructed in 1793. At the fort, you can take an elevator to the top for great views (or you can walk up more steps, if you still have the energy).

Kids who loved the recent hit movie *Pirates of the Caribbean* don't want to miss the **Pirates of Nassau Museum.** Located at the corner of Marlborough and George Streets, the museum brings the "golden age" of piracy back to life. Climb aboard the pirate ship *Revenge* and hear tales about notorious marauders such as Blackbeard and Captain Kidd. You can put your head and hands in the wooden slots of the outdoor stocks for a great photo opportunity. Admission is $12 for adults; $6 for children 2 to 18; and free for kids under 2.

You can have your hair braided and beaded in the island fashion at the government-sponsored **Hairbraider's Centre,** which is close to the ship pier. As with any hair-braiding venue, be aware that the process takes a long time and can be uncomfortable for younger children. (By the way, the hairdressers expect you to try negotiating the price down a little, rather than paying what they post on the board.)

Beyond Walking Distance: You don't want to miss the Marching Flamingos at the 5-acre **Ardastra Gardens,** about a mile west of Nassau. These pink flamingos are trained to walk in formation and do so daily at 11:10 a.m., 2:10 p.m., and 4:10 p.m. You can also see boa constrictors, macaws, monkeys, a crocodile, and various waterfowl.

If you prefer gamblin' to ramblin', check out the huge **Paradise Island Casino** (in the **Atlantis Resort,** Casino Drive, on Paradise Island), with 1,000 slot machines, 60 blackjack tables, 10 roulette wheels, 12 tables for craps, 3 for baccarat, and 1 for big six. Near the casino, you can stroll by the bars, restaurants, and cabarets along **Bird Cage Walk.** Consider buying a guest pass to **Atlantis Resort** — $25 for adults and $19 for children 3 to 12 (children under 3, free), subject to availability — a 14-acre waterscape of aquariums, waterfalls, lagoons, and underground grottos. You can visit the grounds without the pass, but the resort requires it if you want to use the pools or water slides. Well-known **Cable Beach** stretches for four miles (about two miles from the port and accessible by bus or taxi). Be careful when you swim, however: One day the water may be quite tranquil, and the next it may become rough. Shops, casinos, nightlife, and restaurants are all close to the beach, and you can pick from plenty of watersports.

Just a 10-minute walk from the cruise pier is **Western Esplanade,** a nice free beach with changing facilities and a snack stand. Alternatively, you can drive across the bridge or take a ferry to gorgeous **Paradise Beach,** on Paradise Island, another popular locale for sunbathers. (Admission is $3 for adults and $1 for children, which includes the use of a shower and locker.)

Conch Fritters Bar & Grill, Marlborough Street, across from the **British Colonial Hilton,** serves Bahamian and American specialties, tropical drinks, and, of course, "the best conch fritters in town." You can also feast on conch at **Arawak Cay,** a small manmade island across West Bay Street. Watch the staff crack the conch before your eyes and try it with some hot sauce.

Puerto Rico

San Juan offers a wide array of history compared to other Caribbean destinations, from ruins dating to the Spanish empire to modern high rises. At the same time, you find casinos, a glitzy beach strip, and other touristy diversions. San Juan is also the busiest cruise port in the West Indies: More than 700 cruise ships bring approximately 850,000 vacationers to the island per year, so you can expect crowds.

Because Puerto Rico is a commonwealth of the United States, the U.S. dollar is the official currency. Spanish is the native tongue, but most people involved in the tourist industry speak English.

Cruising into port

Carnival, Celebrity, Norwegian, Princess, Royal Caribbean, Seabourn, SeaDream, Seven Seas, and Silversea all have ships that begin and/or end their itineraries here. Most of these lines, as well as Costa, Cunard, and Holland America, also have vessels that visit San Juan as a port of call.

Seeking out the best shore excursions

Old San Juan's top tourist sites are within walking distance, so you don't need to take an organized tour of the area. The following two tours take you outside the historic area.

Old San Juan Walking Tour: Explore at the military fortifications at **San Felipe El Morro,** the **Casa Blanca Museum & Gardens,** the **Ballaja Barracks,** and **Quincentennial Square.** (3 hours; $38)

El Yunque Rain Forest Tour: See lush vegetation and enchanting waterfalls. You can also climb an observation tower for sweeping views of the coast. (4½ hours; $30)

Exploring on your own

Cruise ships normally dock at one of eight piers on the south shore of Old San Juan, which the Spanish first settled in the early 1500s. A walkway connects the piers to the cobblestone streets of the city's historic district and to some great shopping. Some piers are right near shops and others are a ten-minute walk away. On weekends, ships may use alternate docks, such as **Frontier Pier** near the beach at Condado or the **Pan American Dock** in Isla Grande across San Antonio Channel, and then you need to take a taxi or van to reach Old San Juan.

Puerto Rico

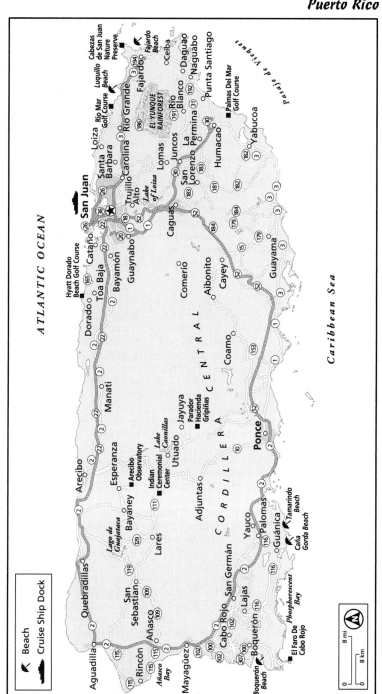

ATLANTIC OCEAN

Caribbean Sea

Pasaje de Vieques

Beach
Cruise Ship Dock

Cabezas de San Juan Nature Preserve
Fajardo Beach
Luquillo Beach
Río Mar Golf Course
Ceiba
Daguao
Naguabo
Punta Santiago
Palmas Del Mar Golf Course
Fajardo
Río Grande
Río Blanco
EL YUNQUE RAINFOREST
La Permina
Humacao
Yabucoa
San Juan
Santa Barbara
Loíza
Carolina
Trujillo Alto
Lomas
Juncos
San Lorenzo
Lake of Loíza
Caguas
Guaynabo
Cataño
Bayamón
Comerío
Aibonito
Cayey
Guayama
Hyatt Dorado Beach Golf Course
Dorado
Toa Baja
Manatí
CORDILLERA CENTRAL
Jayuya
Parador Hacienda Gripiñas
Coamo
Ponce
Arecibo
Esperanza
Arecibo Observatory
Indian Ceremonial Center
Lake Caonillas
Utuado
Adjuntas
Lago de Guajataca
Bayaney
Lares
Quebradillas
San Sebastián
Añasco
Añasco Bay
Rincón
Aguadilla
Mayagüez
San Germán
Cabo Rojo
Lajas
Yauco
Palomas
Guánica
Tamarindo Beach
Caña Gorda Beach
Phosphorescent Bay
Boquerón
Boquerón Beach
El Faro De Cabo Rojo

8 mi
8 km

Renting a car is not worth the hassle because San Juan is a congested urban area. You can hop on and off a free trolley in Old Town as often as you like. Or you can ride the city bus for 50¢ or less. Taxis are inexpensive (about $1 per mile) and charge a minimum fare of $3.

The Agua Expresso ferry links Old San Juan to **Hato Rey** and **Catano** across the bay. The one-way fare is 75¢ to Hato Rey and 50¢ to Catano.

Within Walking Distance: Walking the cobblestone streets of the historic landmark area of Old San Juan, you sense five centuries of history as you pass many of Puerto Rico's top historical attractions. You also find shops and cafes on any walking tour.

One must-see attraction is **El Morro** (Castillo de San Felipe del Morro) — indeed, you can't miss it as it sits at the top of a hill at the tip of the city. Its walls are part of a network of defenses that made San Juan a walled city, and for centuries, the fortress was considered impregnable. Here Spanish Puerto Rico defended itself against the navies of Great Britain, France, and Holland, as well as against hundreds of pirate ships. The National Park Service maintains both El Morro and **Fort San Cristobal,** located a little under a mile east along the north coast.

Other varied and interesting sites include **La Fortaleza and Mansion Ejecutiva,** the centuries-old residence of the Puerto Rican governor; **Plaza de Armas,** the most beautiful of the squares in Old Town, flanked by the neoclassic **Intendencia,** which houses offices of the State Department and San Juan's historic City Hall; **La Casa Blanca,** which the son-in-law of Juan Ponce de León built as the great explorer's island home (although he never lived there); and **La Princesa,** once the most-feared prison in the Caribbean. The *Puerto Rican Academy of Fine Arts* is at the **Antiguo Monicomio Insular** (originally built in 1854 as an insane asylum). The nearby **Asilo de Beneficencia,** or "Home for the Poor," is a stately neoclassical building dating to the 1840s.

In the **Plaza de San José,** the statue of explorer Juan Ponce de León was cast from an English cannon captured during a naval battle in 1797. Dominicans established the **Iglesia de San José,** the church for which the plaza is named, in 1523. Several other historic buildings surround the plaza, including the **Museo de Pablo Casals,** which honors the Spanish-born cellist who lived his final years in Puerto Rico, and a former 17th-century convent, **El Convento,** which has been converted into one of the few hotels within the Old City. The **Catedral de San Juan,** Puerto Rico's most famous church, is across the street. You can also visit **Capilla de Cristo** (calle del Cristo), a tiny chapel with a silver altar dedicated to the Christ of Miracles. Also not far from the plaza, the **Cuartel de Ballaja** houses the **Museum of the Americas** on its second floor.

Beyond Walking Distance: Among the better casinos in San Juan is the one at the **Caribe Hilton.** The largest, at 18,500 square feet, is at the **Ritz-Carlton** (6961 State Rd.). Most **casinos** in Puerto Rico are open from noon to 4 p.m. and again from 8 p.m. to 4 a.m.

Old San Juan

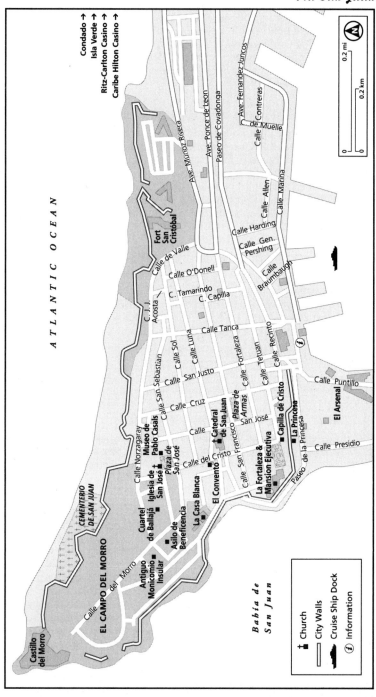

Condado →
Isla Verde →
Ritz-Carlton Casino →
Caribe Hilton Casino →

ATLANTIC OCEAN

Ave. Muñoz Rivera

Ave. Ponce de Leon

Paseo de Covadonga

Ave. Fernandez-Juncos

Calle de Muelle

Calle Contreras

Calle Marina

Calle Allen

Calle Harding

Calle Harding

Calle Gen. Pershing

Fort San Cristóbal

Calle de Valle

Calle O'Donell

Calle Braumbaugh

C. Tamarindo

C.J.J. Acosta

C. Capilla

Calle Tanca

Calle Sol

Calle Luna

Calle Recinto

Calle San Sebastian

Calle San Justo

Calle Fortaleza

Calle Tetuan

Calle Puntillo

Calle Cruz

Plaza de Armas

San José

El Arsenal

Calle

Catedral de San Juan

Capilla de Cristo

La Princesa

Calle Norzagaray

Museo de Pablo Casals

Calle San Francisco

La Fortaleza & Mansion Ejecutiva

Calle Presidio

Iglesia de San José

Plaza de San José

Calle del Cristo

El Convento

Paseo de la Princesa

CEMENTERIO DE SAN JUAN

Cuartel de Ballajá

La Casa Blanca

EL CAMPO DEL MORRO

Asilo de Beneficiencia

Antiguo Monicomio Insular

Calle del Morro

Castillo del Morro

Bahia de San Juan

0.2 mi
0.2 km

Church
City Walls
Cruise Ship Dock
Information

Although all beaches are open to the public, you pay a fee for facilities such as lockers and showers. Public beaches are closed on Mondays (unless a holiday falls on Monday, in which case they stay open that day and close on Tuesday that week). You can enjoy good snorkeling and watersports at the two most popular beach areas, **Condado** and **Isla Verde.** Both are east of Old San Juan and offer rental equipment for water sports.

St. Barthélemy (St. Barts)

Christopher Columbus found his way to St. Barthélemy (the full name of St. Barts) in 1493; however, its present-day residents are descended from Breton and Norman fishermen, with a dash of Swedish thrown in — the capital city Gustavia is named after a Swedish king. However, St. Barts has been part of France since 1878. The island experience here is a little different from other Caribbean destinations, with a touch of Normandy and Sweden influencing the food, language, and lifestyle. Make the most of your time at this port by relaxing on the beach — forget about historical sites and watersports for a while anyway. If you're lucky, you may see a Hollywood star or noted public figure — this place is a favorite of celebrities.

The official currency is the euro (€), but most stores and restaurants prefer payment in U.S. dollars. At press time, the euro exchange rate was US $1 = .83€ (1€ = US 1.21). The official language is French, but nearly everyone speaks English too.

Cruising into port

American Canadian Caribbean, Crystal, Oceania, Seabourn, SeaDream, Seven Seas, Windjammer, and Windstar all make port stops here.

Seeking out the best shore excursions

The typical **Island Tour** that most cruise ships offer hits several of the island's 14 beaches and villages, such as **Corossol,** a tiny fishing village where the locals make straw products from lantana palms. (1½ hours; $25)

Exploring on your own

Small cruise ships are the only ones that visit St. Barts, anchoring off Gustavia and ferrying passengers to town. Expect a short walk into the center of Gustavia and its restaurant and shopping district. Taxis are plentiful and cheap for travelers coming ashore, and although cabs aren't metered, the government does set rates (the fare is about $4 for the first five minutes; each additional three minutes costs about $3.20). Getting around in rented open-sided Mini-Mokes and Suzuki Samurais, which are in plentiful and colorful supply, is another option. Rental cars are available from Budget, Hertz, and Avis, but these companies require reservations (allow a month in high season; see the Appendix for reservations phone numbers). Prices begin at about $40 a day. Motorbike and motor scooter rentals are available for about $30 a day. A $200 deposit is required.

St. Barthélemy (St. Barts)

Within Walking Distance: You may enjoy just walking around the capital city and browsing through the first-rate shops, some of which offer the lowest prices in the region on liquor and French perfume.

Beyond Walking Distance: In Gustavia, the best place for people-watching and celebrity-sighting is **Le Select** (rue de la France), a simple cafe that attracts the select set. (Ever hear of Jimmy Buffett? How about Mick Jagger? You can dream.)

The most famous beach is **St-Jean,** where you can enjoy watersports, beach restaurants, and a few hotels. If you want peace and privacy, however, St. Barts also has 14 beautiful secluded beaches. The best include **Marigot** and **Colombier** to the north, and **Saline** and **Gouverneur** to the south (which is very remote). Topless sunbathing is quite common (and at Saline, you may also see a lot of people in the altogether, even though nudity is officially forbidden).

St. Kitts

Ever heard the expression "sleepy Caribbean island"? That's St. Kitts in a nutshell. Although the island is increasing its position as a tourist Mecca, the economy still relies on the sugar industry, which dates from the 17th century.

St. Kitts and its main town, **Basseterre,** retain plenty of their old West Indies character (and aren't totally overrun by the tourist trade, like many other ports in the Caribbean). But you have little to see here besides the amazing **Brimstone Hill** fortress and really pretty white beaches on the southeastern peninsula.

The official currency is the Eastern Caribbean dollar (EC$), although many shops and restaurants list prices in U.S. dollars: US $1 = EC $2.67 (EC $1 = US 37¢). English is the official language.

Cruising into port

American Canadian Caribbean, Celebrity, Cunard, Holland America, Oceania, Princess, Royal Caribbean, Seven Seas, Silversea, Star Clippers, and Windjammer all make port stops here.

Seeking out the best shore excursions

St. Kitts Scenic Rail Tour: Ride the antique narrow gauge railway — once used to deliver sugar cane from the fields to the mills in Basseterre — and kick back in the double-deck railcars. (4 hours; $104)

Catamaran Adventure & Nevis Beach Barbecue: Enjoy a 45-minute sail along the southern coast of St. Kitts and nearby Nevis, along with plenty of time for snorkeling, swimming, and a barbecue lunch. (6 hours; $114)

Exploring on your own

The main attraction in St. Kitts is **Brimstone Hill Fortress.** To get there, take a taxi from the dock in Basseterre. Most taxi drivers also act as tour guides, and a taxi is the most convenient way to putter around. Agree on a price before you hop in (taxis are not metered), and be sure you know whether you're agreeing on U.S. dollars or Eastern Caribbean dollars. A 3-hour island tour costs around $60. We don't recommend renting a car.

Within Walking Distance: The capital city of Basseterre, where the docks are located, has typical British colonial architecture and some quaint buildings, as well as shops and a market where the locals display fruits and flowers — but even this description may be overstating the place's appeal. Truth is, it's a very poor town, with few attractions aimed at visitors. **Independence Square,** a stone's throw from the docks along Bank Street, is pretty with its central fountain and old church; however, you have no good reason to linger unless you want to sit in the shade and toss back a bottle of Ting, a refreshing (if sweet) grapefruit-based soda made in Jamaica. **St. George's Anglican Church,** on Cayon Street

St. Kitts

St. Kitts map showing:
- Scale: 0–5 mi / 0–5 km, with compass rose (N)
- Dieppe Bay Town, Dieppe Bay
- St. Paul's, Sandy Bay, Sadlers
- Newton Ground
- ATLANTIC OCEAN
- Hermitage Bay, Ottley's
- Mount Liamuiga
- Sandy Point Town, Brimstone Hill Fortress, Cayon, Keys
- Half-Way Tree, Middle Island, Romney Gardens/ Carib Rock Drawings
- Old Road Town, St. Peter's, Conaree Bay
- Challengers
- Basseterre, North Frigate Bay
- North Friar's Bay
- Frigate Bay
- South Friar's Bay, Turtle Beach
- Sand Bank Bay
- Great Salt Pond, St. Anthony's Peak
- White House Bay, Cockleshell Bay
- Caribbean Sea
- Nag's Head, Banana Bay
- to Nevis

Legend:
- ✈ Airport
- 🏖 Beach
- 🚢 Cruise Ship Dock
- ---- Ferry Route
- ⛰ Mountain

(walk straight up Church Street or Fort Street from the dock), is the oldest church in town and is worth a look.

Beyond Walking Distance: The must-see attraction on St. Kitts, **Brimstone Hill Fortress,** is one of the Caribbean's largest and best-preserved landmarks. Once known as "The Gibraltar of the West Indies," the citadel is nine miles west of Basseterre. The British built Brimstone Hill Fortress in the 17th century. When the French invaded in 1782, it was the focus for one of the largest military conflicts in Caribbean history. After the British recaptured the island the following year, they enlarged the fort, and it now contains a series of bastions, barracks, and other structures cleverly grafted to the top and upper slopes of a steep, 800-foot hill. Today, the place has been restored and made part of a national park. It features nature trails and plenty of plants and wildlife, including the green vervet monkey. On a clear day, you can glimpse six neighboring islands. You can take a self-guided tour of the complex and visit the gift shop on its grounds. Admission is $5 for adults and $2.50 for children.

If you enjoy hiking, head to **Mount Liamuiga,** an inactive volcano since 1962. Clouds usually obscure the peak, but along the way up and back you can get your fill of tropical wildflowers, colorful birds and butterflies, and maybe glimpse a green vervet monkey. A round-trip hike to the peak takes about four hours and generally starts from the Belmont Estate on the north end of St. Kitts.

Find the best sugar-white beaches on the narrow peninsula in the southeast, near St. Kitts's salt ponds. **Conaree,** about three miles from Basseterre, is a good spot for swimming. Other fine choices include **Frigate Bay** and **Friar's Bay.**

If you want a respite from the island's alabaster stretches, head to the northern end of St. Kitts for **gray volcanic sand beaches.** All beaches are open to the public, but you must get permission and pay a fee if you want to use a resort's beach facilities.

To experience the sweeter side of St. Kitts, try a stalk of sugar cane. Buy one from any farmer, peel it, and chew the inner reeds to enjoy the sweet juice. Try it with ice and a splash of rum.

In Basseterre's most colorful intersection, the Circus, near the cruise dock, is **Ballahoo Restaurant,** which offers some of the best chili and baby-back ribs around.

St. Lucia

Of all the islands in the Caribbean, St. Lucia is most likely to make you think you're in the South Pacific, with its green mountains, the peaks of **Petit Piton** and **Gros Piton,** and the brilliant white sandy beaches along the northwest coast.

The island's capital, **Castries,** built around an extinct volcanic crater, looks more modern than other regional capitals because fires destroyed many of the original French colonial and Victorian buildings typical of the region's architecture. But at its heart, Castries is still very traditional. Women from the countryside wear traditional headdresses, with the number of knotted points on top indicating their marital status. (See them for yourself at the Saturday market on Jeremie Street.)

The official currency is the Eastern Caribbean dollar (EC$). Many shops and restaurants quote prices in U.S. dollars: US $1 = EC $2.67 (EC $1 = US 37¢). English is the official language.

Cruising into port

Some Windjammer ships begin their cruises here. American Canadian Caribbean, Carnival, Celebrity, Clipper, Cunard, Crystal, Holland America, Norwegian, Oceania, Princess, Royal Caribbean, Seabourn, SeaDream, Silversea, Star Clippers, Windjammer, and Windstar ships make port stops here.

St. Lucia

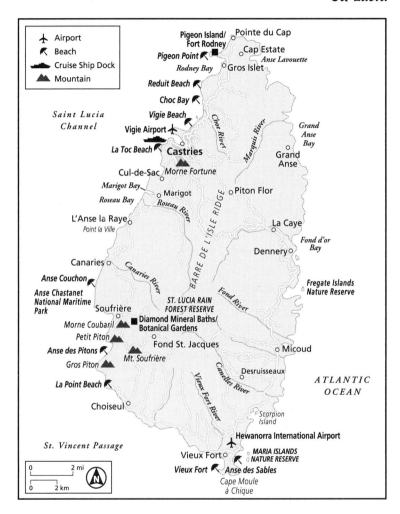

- ✈ Airport
- ⬏ Beach
- ⬅ Cruise Ship Dock
- ▲ Mountain

Pigeon Island/ Pointe du Cap
Fort Rodney
Pigeon Point ⬏ Cap Estate
Rodney Bay Anse Lavouette
Reduit Beach ⬏ Gros Islet

Choc Bay ⬏

Saint Lucia Channel Vigie Beach
Vigie Airport ✈
La Toc Beach ⬏ Castries

Cul-de-Sac Morne Fortune
Marigot Bay Marigot Piton Flor
Roseau Bay Roseau River

L'Anse la Raye
Point la Ville

Canaries

Anse Couchon ⬏
Anse Chastanet
National Maritime
Park Soufrière
Morne Coubaril ▲ Diamond Mineral Baths/
Botanical Gardens
Petit Piton ▲
Anse des Pitons ⬏ Fond St. Jacques
Gros Piton ▲ Mt. Soufrière
La Point Beach ⬏
Choiseul

St. Vincent Passage

Choc River
Marquis River
Grand Anse Bay
Grand Anse
BARRE DE L'ISLE RIDGE
La Caye
Fond d'or Bay
Dennery
Fregate Islands
Nature Reserve
ST. LUCIA RAIN
FOREST RESERVE
Fond River
Micoud
Canelles River
Desruisseaux
ATLANTIC OCEAN
Vieux Fort River
Scorpion Island
Hewanorra International Airport ✈
Vieux Fort MARIA ISLANDS
NATURE RESERVE
Vieux Fort ⬏ Anse des Sables
Cape Moule à Chique

0 2 mi
0 2 km

Seeking out the best shore excursions

Pigeon Island Sea Kayaking: Explore Pigeon Island National Park on calm waters in a two-person kayak. Enjoy the beach, swim, and visit a local museum. (3 hours; $64)

Jungle Biking: Explore the 12 miles of scenic trails, stop for a buffet lunch, and cool off with a swim or snorkel in the marine park. (7½ hours; $118)

Exploring on your own

You can find everything from great shopping to information at a small visitor information bureau, the pier at **Pointe Seraphine.** The pier is a short cab ride from the center of Castries. Your ship may also dock at the **Elizabeth II** pier, a short walk to the center of Castries. Smaller ships may anchor off Soufrière and tender to shore.

Taxi drivers are trained to serve as guides, and the rates are government-regulated. A sightseeing trip around the island (for up to four people) goes for about $20 an hour. Make sure you know whether your driver quotes a rate in U.S. or E.C. dollars.

If you want to rent a car, you need to get a St. Lucia driver's license for about $15. Budget, Hertz, and Avis all have offices here. If you drive, watch out for the hilly, narrow switchbacks outside Castries.

Within Walking Distance: The main streets are William Peter Boulevard and Bridge Street. Up Morne Fortune (Hill of Good Luck) is the barracks of **Fort Charlotte.** The fort features the Four Apostles Battery — four muzzle-loaded cannons, a panoramic view of Castries harbor, and a small museum.

Beyond Walking Distance: The Caribbean and the Atlantic lie on either side of **Pigeon Island National Landmark,** a national park, and a causeway joins the island with the mainland. A peg-legged pirate named Jambe de Bois ("Leg of Wood") once used the island as a hideout. The climb to the hilltop fort isn't too much for most people, and the view is magnificent. The **Interpretation Centre** contains a number of artifacts, including some dating back 1,000 years to the Amerindians. Stop by the **Captain's Cellar** pub in the basement, with seating out on the lawn just beyond the spray from the Atlantic waves. *Note:* If you take a taxi here, be sure to arrange for a return trip in time to get back to your ship.

St. Lucia's leading export is bananas, and you can visit its plantations: The three biggest are **Roseau Estate,** south of Marigot Bay; the **Cul-de-Sac,** north of Marigot Bay; and **La Caye,** in Dennery on the east coast.

If you choose to visit the beach, try **Vigie Beach,** north of Castries Harbour; **Pigeon Island,** off the island's northern shore; or the one at **Anse Chastanet,** a resort north of Soufrière, where the snorkeling is fantastic. All beaches are open to the public. The West Coast beaches have calmer waters than those on the Atlantic side of the island, where swimming can be dangerous.

Sample the local cuisine at the **Green Parrot** (Red Tape Lane, Morne Fortune), about 1.5 miles east of the town center. The emphasis is on home-grown foods, including christophine au gratin (a Caribbean squash with cheese) and Creole soup made with callaloo and pumpkin. For fresh fish and Creole cooking, head to **Jimmie's,** at Vigie Cove Marina.

Sint Maarten and St. Martin

Two former colonial powers, the French and the Dutch, peacefully coexist on this 37-square-mile island. Local legend says that to arrange this agreement, a wine-drinking Frenchman and a gin-guzzling Dutchman walked around the island in 1648 to see how much territory they could claim. The Frenchman got the most territory, but the Dutchman got the better real estate.

St. Martin is the French region, and Sint Maarten is the Dutch side. On the Dutch side, **Philipsburg** bustles with energy from the hordes of tourists exploring its shops and casinos. On the French side, **Marigot** feels more cosmopolitan, with the latest French fashions in its shops and fresh croissants and pastries in its charming bistros. But the only real way to tell that you have crossed from one side to the other is by the "Bienvenue Francaise" signs at the border.

The island is known as a duty-free shopping haven. The official currency in Dutch Sint Maarten is the euro, but merchants accept U.S. dollars as well. French St. Martin uses the euro. At press time, the euro exchange rate was US $1 = .83€ (1€ = US $1.21). The official languages are Dutch and French on their respective sides of the island, but most people also speak English.

Cruising into port

American Canadian Caribbean, SeaDream, and Windjammer all have ships that begin their itineraries here, and Carnival, Celebrity, Crystal, Cunard, Disney, Holland America, Norwegian, Princess, Royal Caribbean, Seabourn, SeaDream, Seven Seas, Silversea, Windjammer, and Windstar ships make port calls on the island.

Seeking out the best shore excursions

Don't feel compelled to do the usual sightseeing tour while on St. Martin/ Sint Maarten; the island's most notable attractions are its beaches.

America's Cup Regatta: A sailing adventure aboard one of the yachts that competes in the America's Cup races. (3 hours; $84)

Pinel Island Snorkeling Tour: Offered on the French side. (3½ hours; $37) Take a scenic bus ride to the French side and catch a boat to this small offshore islet for some of St. Martin's best snorkeling.

Exploring on your own in Sint Maarten

Taxis are unmetered, but Dutch Sint Maarten law requires taxi drivers to list fares to major island destinations. The minimum rate is usually $4 for two passengers with an additional charge of $4 for each additional passenger. A cab from Philipsburg to Marigot on the French side is about $12 each way for two. Buses are a crowded but fairly cheap way to get around the Dutch side of the island. Fares range from 85¢ to $2, and buses generally follow a specified route. Renting a car is a practical way to get around the island and costs about $50 a day.

Sint Maarten & St. Martin

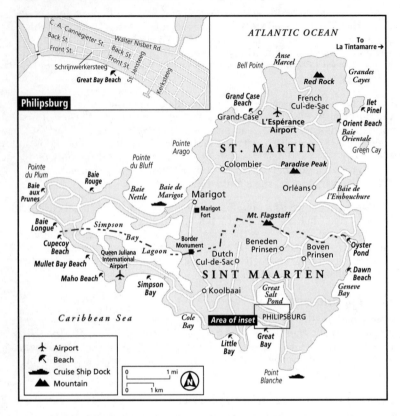

Within Walking Distance: Smaller vessels can dock at Marigot's harbor (on the French side), but most ships head to Philipsburg (on the Dutch side) and dock at the modern, $15 million **Great Bay Port.** At the welcome terminal, you can find a Tourist Information Center, ATM machines, restrooms, taxis, and telephones. The new $40 million **Harbor Point Village** waterside complex at the port offers a host of shopping and entertainment venues housed in old West Indies-style architecture.

You can catch a ferry from the dock to the tender pier, located at **Captain Hodge's Wharf** in Wathey Square, steps away from the duty-free shopping area of Front Street. Or take a taxi or bus into town (you can also walk, but it takes about 20 minutes and is rather dull). The main shopping area is in the heart of Philipsburg, along Front and Back Streets. At No. 8 Front Street is the **Guavaberry Shop,** which stocks the island's traditional guavaberry liqueur — a mix of rum, sugar, spices, and locally grown berries that are harvested at Christmas time.

If you want to check out the gaming action, visit the **Coliseum Casino** on Front Street. The Roman-themed gaming center has the highest table limits at $1,000.

From the center of town, you can check out **Great Bay Beach** and hike (part of the 20-minute or so walk is uphill) or taxi to **Little Bay Beach,** known for great snorkeling.

Beyond Walking Distance: The island is renowned for its powder-white beaches — 37 between the French and Dutch sides. The topless or *au naturel* beaches are on the French side; the Dutch side is more modest. However, **Cupecoy Beach,** on the Dutch side near the border of St. Martin, has strong surf and a clothing-optional section.

Simpson Bay Beach offers a secluded seashore. Both **Mullet Bay Beach** and **Maho Beach,** near the airport, are popular with swimmers.

Tourists have reported robberies at some isolated beach locations. Avoid bringing valuables to the beach.

Food is generally better on the French side, but **Cheri's Café** (45 Cinnamon Grove, Shopping Centre, Maho Beach) is an island hot spot known for its grilled fish, 16-ounce steaks, juicy burgers, and killer drinks.

Exploring on your own in St. Martin

Taxis are the most common means of transportation and may also offer two-hour sightseeing tours. Cabs are unmetered, so settle on a fare before you get in. Buses on the French side (actually minivans operated by local drivers) typically cost $2 and depart from Marigot every hour to the Dutch side.

Within Walking Distance: Marigot bustles with energy in the mornings at the harbor, where vendors present fruits, spices, and handicrafts at an **open-air market.** A wide selection of European merchandise awaits day-trippers to Marigot. Salespeople commonly quote prices in U.S. dollars, and they speak English. Another busy center of activity is **Port La Royale,** the largest shopping arcade on the French side.

Beyond Walking Distance: Top-rated beaches on the French side are **Baie Longue, Baie Rouge, Grand Case Beach,** and **Pinel Island.** If you want a stripped-down adventure, visit the famous clothes-optional **Orient Beach.**

Petit Club is the oldest restaurant in Marigot, serving Creole and French specialties such as spicy conch stew and fresh fish.

St. Thomas and St. John, U.S. Virgin Islands

St. Thomas is the shopping capital of the Caribbean and one of its busiest ports, often hosting more than ten cruise ships a day during the peak winter season. The island's capital, **Charlotte Amalie,** merges the charming and the tacky with its masses of shops, restaurants, bars, resorts, and of course, throngs of tourists. All this business (and U.S. government programs) has raised the standard of living here to one of the highest in the Caribbean and made the island, 12 miles long and 3 miles wide, the most developed of the U.S. Virgins. Condominium apartments have grown up over the debris of bulldozed shacks.

For a calmer respite, try the perfect arcs of gleaming white beaches on St. John. The **Virgin Islands National Park** comprises more than half of the island, with hiking trails providing ample opportunities for bird and animal sightings. The trails also lead you past the ruins of 18th-century Danish plantations and offer breathtaking views.

Most vessels dock in Charlotte Amalie on St. Thomas, but some anchor off St. John. Most of the lines offer excursions to St. John, but even if yours doesn't, you can easily find your way there by boat.

The U.S. dollar is the official currency, and English is the official language.

Cruising into port

American Canadian Caribbean, Seabourn, SeaDream, Windjammer, and Windstar all have ships that begin their itineraries here. Carnival, Celebrity, Costa, Crystal, Cunard, Disney, Holland America, Norwegian, Princess, Royal Caribbean, Seven Seas, and Silversea all have ships that visit the islands as a port of call.

Seeking out the best shore excursions

Expect to snooze through the St. Thomas sightseeing trips that most ships offer. Here are a few better bets:

St. John Trunk Bay Beach & Snorkel: Find out why **Trunk Bay** is world famous for its clear green water and white, sandy beaches. Instructors provide equipment and lessons. Or relax on the prow of the boat or on the beach, which offers a snack bar and amenities. (4½ hours; $48)

St. Thomas Helicopter Tour: Enjoy a bird's eye view of St. Thomas and scenic St. John on this 20-minute flight — plus transfers — complete with guided narration. (1 hour; $99)

Exploring on your own in St. Thomas

Most ships make port at **Havensight Mall,** 1½ miles from the eastern end of the Charlotte Amalie harbor. There you find a tourist booth, restaurants, duty-free shopping, a bank, a U.S. postal van, phones, and a bookstore. If Havensight is congested with other ships, your vessel may dock at **Crown Point Marina,** west of Charlotte Amalie.

St. Thomas

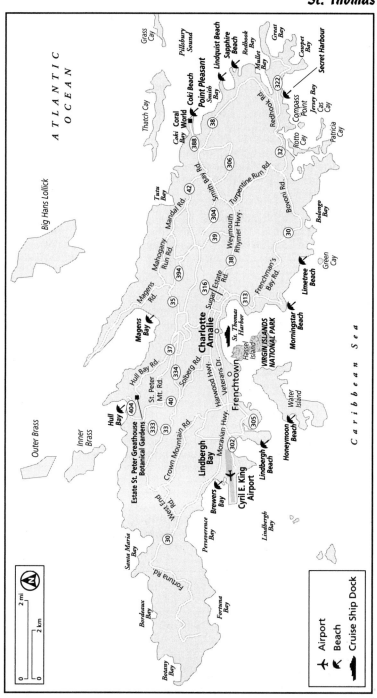

ATLANTIC OCEAN

Grass Cay

Thatch Cay

Big Hans Lollick

Outer Brass

Inner Brass

Pillsbury Sound

Lindquist Beach

Sapphire Beach

Great Bay

Coupet Bay

Secret Harbour

Coki Beach

Point Pleasant

Smith Bay

Mullet Bay

Redhook Bay

322

Coral Coki World Bay

Compass Point

Jersey Bay

Cas Cay

388

38

Redhook Rd.

Rotto Cay

32

Patricia Cay

Tutu Bay

306

Mandal Rd.

42

Smith Bay Rd.

Bovoni Rd.

Bolongo Bay

Mahogany Run Rd.

304

39

Weymouth Rhymer Hwy.

Turpentine Run Rd.

30

Green Cay

394

38

Frenchman's Bay Rd.

Limetree Beach

35

316

Sugar Estate Rd.

313

Magens Rd.

37

Charlotte Amalie

Morningstar Beach

Magens Bay

St. Thomas Harbor

334

Solberg Rd.

Hassel Island

Hull Bay Rd.

St. Peter Mt. Rd.

Harwood Hwy.

Veterans Dr.

VIRGIN ISLANDS NATIONAL PARK

40

Frenchtown

Water Island

Hull Bay

404

Moravian Hwy.

Honeymoon Beach

Estate St. Peter Greathouse Botanical Gardens

333

305

Crown Mountain Rd.

Lindbergh Bay

Lindbergh Beach

33

302

West End Rd.

Brewers Bay

Cyril E. King Airport

Lindbergh Bay

30

Santa Maria Bay

Perseverance Bay

Fortuna Rd.

Fortuna Bay

Bordeaux Bay

Botany Bay

Caribbean Sea

2 mi

2 km

✈ Airport

Beach

Cruise Ship Dock

The preferred mode of transport is the taxi. Taxis are unmetered, so agree on a rate before you get in. Traveling from Crown Point Marina to the town center costs about $4. Two passengers taking a 2-hour sightseeing trip in a cab officially costs $30. Each additional passenger pays another $12. Up to 12 people can share a van to see multiple attractions.

You can also ride the air-conditioned Vitran buses, which serve Charlotte Amalie and even go to **Red Hook,** a jumping-off point for St. John. Within Charlotte Amalie, the fare is 75¢; to Red Hook, $3; and to other districts, $1. Taxi vans, a fleet of privately owned vans or minibuses, cost the same as Vitran buses. The vans are usually less comfortable, however, and the service is inconsistent. We don't recommend renting a car — you have to deal with a lot of hairpin turns, which is extra tricky if you aren't used to driving on the left. No worries, though. You won't have any problem finding a taxi.

Within Walking Distance: Shopping is a main attraction in St. Thomas, and **Main Street** is the main shopping street. To the north is the fully stocked **Back Street.** The **Waterfront Highway** also sports stores, and you can always check out the side streets, alleys, and walkways between these principal streets.

St. Thomas isn't all shopping, though. Squeeze in visits to some key historical buildings, including the so-called **Grand Hotel,** near Emancipation Park, which houses a visitors center and some shops, and the **St. Thomas Synagogue,** which has a sand floor and dates to 1833.

Dating back to 1672 and dominating the center of town, **Fort Christian** was named after the Danish monarch Christian V and has served as everything from a governor's residence to a prison. Some of the cells have become part of the **Virgin Islands Museum.** Historical artifacts are on display at the small facility.

Beyond Walking Distance: The number-one attraction on the island is **Coral World Marine Park and Underwater Observatory,** a 20-minute drive from downtown. The trip from the port costs $7 by taxi and $1 by bus. Visitors can view local marine life from an underwater observatory or try the new Sea Trekkin' adventure, where you don a bathing suit and helmet for a walk along the ocean floor near coral beds teeming with colorful fish. Sea Trekkin' is available for adults and children ages 8 and up who weigh at least 80 pounds. Admission to the park and observatory is $18 for adults and $9 for children; Sea Trekkin' is an additional $50 per person. Visitors also have access to **Coki Beach,** adjacent to the park.

On the **Paradise Point Tramway,** the lift takes you from the Havensight area to **Paradise Point,** a 697-foot peak that affords breathtaking views of Charlotte Amalie harbor. A restaurant, bar, shops, and hiking trails are located at Paradise Point. The ride lasts only 3½ minutes at a whopping $15 per person, $7.50 for kids, round-trip.

St. John

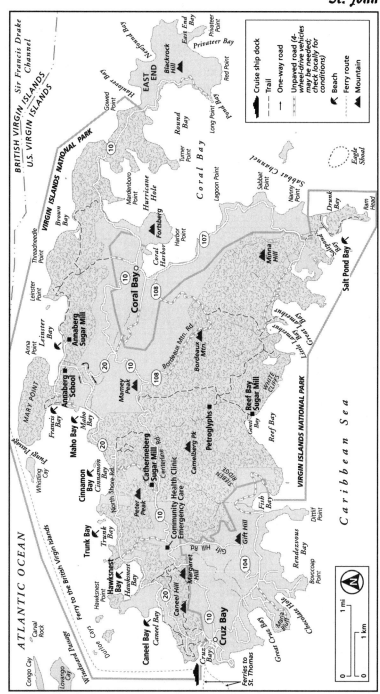

Legend:
- Cruise ship dock
- Trail
- One-way road
- Unpaved road (4-wheel-drive vehicles may be needed; check locally for conditions)
- Beach
- Ferry route
- Mountain

ATLANTIC OCEAN

BRITISH VIRGIN ISLANDS
U.S. VIRGIN ISLANDS

Sir Francis Drake Channel

Carval Rock
Congo Cay
Lovango Cay
Durloe Cays
Whistling Cay
Fungi Passage
Windward Passage
Ferry to the British Virgin Islands

Ferries to St. Thomas

VIRGIN ISLANDS NATIONAL PARK

Navigand Bay
East End Bay
Privateer Point
Privateer Bay
Blackrock Hill
Red Point
EAST END
Gowed Point
Haulover Bay
Round Bay
Turner Point
Long Point
Pond Bay
Coral Bay
Lagoon Point
Sabbat Point
Sabbat Channel
Nanny Point
Drunk Bay
Ram Head
Eagle Shoal

Brown Bay
Threadneedle Point
Mardenboro Point
Hurricane Hole
Fortsberg
Harbor Point
Coral Harbor
Minna Hill
Leinster Point
Leinster Bay
Anna Point
MARY POINT
Francis Bay
Maho Bay
Cinnamon Bay
Trunk Bay
Hawksnest Point
Hawksnest Bay
Caneel Bay

Annaberg Sugar Mill
Annaberg School
Catherineberg Sugar Mill
Centerline Rd
North Shore Rd
Peter Peak
Community Health Clinic Emergency Care
Margaret Hill
Caneel Hill
Cruz Bay

Mamey Peak
Bordeaux Mtn. Rd
Bordeaux Mtn.
Camelberg Pk
Petroglyphs
Reef Bay Sugar Mill
Genti Bay
Reef Bay
WHITE CLIFFS
Little Lameshur Bay
Great Lameshur Bay
Salt Pond Bay
Salt Pond Bay

VIRGIN ISLANDS NATIONAL PARK

Caribbean Sea

SIEBEN RIDGE
Fish Bay
Gift Hill
Gift Hill Rd
Dittif Point
Rendezvous Bay
Boyccap Point
Chocolate Hole
Great Cruz Bay
Moravia Pt

10
20
107
108
104

N

1 mi
1 km
0

If you're looking for a fun restaurant or bar, go west of Charlotte Amalie to **Frenchtown,** a quaint fishing village founded by some French-speaking people who were uprooted when Swedes invaded their homeland of St. Barts. Many of the residents are direct descendants of those settlers.

The **Estate St. Peter Greathouse Botanical Gardens** gives you the opportunity to wander among gardens boasting 200 different plants and trees, a rain forest, monkey habitat, waterfalls, and reflecting pools. The gardens are a 15-minute cab ride from Charlotte Amalie at St. Peter Mountain Road (route 40) and Barrett Hill Road. Admission is $8 for adults and $4 for children.

St. Thomas's excellent beaches are easily accessible by taxi and open to the public, but some charge a fee. The most well known (and most popular for windsurfing) is **Sapphire Beach** on the East End. Rent snorkeling gear or lounge chairs, or stretch out on its white-coral sand and take in the sun and the spectacular views of the bay.

Other worthwhile beaches are **Magens Bay, Coki Beach** (at the Marine Park), and the **Renaissance Grand Beach Resort,** located on the North side. **Morningstar, Limetree Beach, Brewer's Beach,** and **Lindbergh Beach,** all on the South side, are also worth visiting.

If you check out the beaches on St. Thomas, be sure to protect your belongings — pickpockets and thieves have been known to strike. Also, to ensure that you don't miss the boat, arrange for a cab to pick you up at a specific time.

Exploring on your own in St. John

Cruise ships can't dock at the two piers in St. John, so they either anchor off Cruz Bay and send passengers on tenders to the **National Park Services Dock,** or they dock in St. Thomas, from which passengers can reach St. John on shore excursions or on their own by ferry.

Ferries leave from the waterfront in Charlotte Amalie, St. Thomas, starting at 9 a.m. and running at one- to two-hour intervals until the final departure at around 5:30 p.m. Returning, the last boat leaves Cruz Bay for Charlotte Amalie at 3:45 p.m. The ride lasts about 45 minutes and costs $7 each way. Another ferry, running from the **Red Hook Pier** on St. Thomas's eastern tip, departs almost every half hour starting at 6:30 a.m. The ride to Cruz Bay takes almost 20 minutes, and the last ferry departs Cruz Bay at 11 p.m. The one-way fare is $3 for adults and $1 for children under age 11.

St. John's horse-and-carriage-style taxis are a great way to explore the island. Average fares from Cruz Bay are $9 to **Trunk Bay,** $11 to **Cinnamon Bay,** and $15 to **Maho Bay.** A 2-hour island tour by taxi costs about $30 for one or two people. The fare drops to about $12 per person when three or more people come along for the ride.

If you want to take off on your own, rent a four-wheel-drive vehicle. The island's roads are uncrowded, and the views are lovely. Hertz (☎ 800-654-3001, 340-693-7580) and Avis (☎ 800-331-1084, 340-776-6374) have offices here. Reservations are required; cars are sometimes in short supply, especially during the busy midwinter season.

Within Walking Distance: Shopping is a must-do experience on St. Thomas, but on St. John the shopping scene is more laid-back. For a low-key day, check out the sleepy port village of **Cruz Bay,** which boasts some nice bars, restaurants, boutiques, and pastel-painted homes. The public library contains the **Elaine Ione Sprauve Museum,** filled with local artifacts, for your daily shot of history.

Beyond Walking Distance: At the **Virgin Islands National Park,** head to the visitors center and then hit the trails and the **Annaberg Ruins,** a former Danish plantation and sugar mill that dates back to 1718. Park rangers give guided tours on certain days of the week. Admission is $4.

Trunk Bay is your best bet for the local beach experience, especially for snorkelers, who can rent gear and explore the underwater trail near the shore. Trunk Bay has amenities, such as showers, a snackshop, and lifeguards, but it also has crowds. Beware of pickpockets. **Hawksnest Beach, Cinnamon Bay, Maho Bay,** and **Salt Pond Bay** are all good beach choices.

Chapter 19

Arriving in Alaska

. . . .

In This Chapter

▶ Discovering which cruise lines go where

▶ Finding the best attractions and shopping at the major ports of call

▶ Exploring the best shore excursions

. . . .

*W*hy visit Alaska? Imagine these postcard images: glaciers, whales, icebergs, moose, bears, towering mountains, rain-forested fjords, tundra, bald eagles, ravens as big as pug dogs, ice-fields as big as cities, lumberjacks as big as . . . lumberjacks.

Alaska is one of the top cruise destinations in the world — nearly 730,000 passengers are expected to arrive this year to sail through calm waters and absorb the breathtaking scenery of this last "untouched" wilderness. But, alas, the cruise industry takes a toll on the region. Critics of Alaskan cruising argue — and not without some merit — that ships' guests swell pedestrian traffic on normally quiet city streets and that buses jam the roadways as they whisk shore excursionists away for the day.

To some extent, those criticisms are still valid, although much less so now than in previous years. Ship operators have recently taken steps to minimize the negative impact they have on the lives of local inhabitants by scheduling land tours differently and by using more efficient road equipment. Another charge frequently leveled at the cruise industry — also somewhat valid — is that smokestacks belch too many pollutants into the crystal clear air and that cruise ships are sometimes lax about their waste-discharge practices. Although some lines have received fines for offenses against the environment, the industry has become much more sensitive to public concerns.

Ship lines have instituted in-house and industry-wide monitoring and voluntary compliance rules, and they've contributed to cleanup and educational efforts. Citizens and legislators who worked hard to make the industry pay more have backed off a little, although they remain vigilant for signs of back-sliding by the cruise lines (see the sidebar in this chapter). The battle goes on, and the jury remains out.

Alaska Home Ports

ANCHORAGE (SEWARD)	Celebrity Clipper Cruise West Holland America Radisson Seven Seas Royal Caribbean
JUNEAU	American Safari American West Clipper Cruise West Glacier Bay Lindblad
KETCHIKAN	Cruise West Glacier Bay
PRINCE RUPERT	American Safari
SAN FRANCISCO	Celebrity Crystal Princess

SEATTLE	American West Clipper Cruise West Glacier Bay Holland America Lindblad Norwegian Princess
SITKA	American Safari Glacier Bay Lindblad
VANCOUVER	Carnival Celebrity Cruise West Holland America Norwegian Princess Radisson Seven Seas Royal Caribbean
WHITTIER	Carnival Princess

Chukchi Sea

RUSSIA

Little Diomede Island

Nome *Norton Sound*

St. Lawrence Island

Yukon Delta Nat'l Wildlife Refuge

Bethel
Yukon Delta Nat'l Wildlife Refuge

Nunivak Island

B e r i n g   S e a

Bristol Bay

Attu Island

Pribilof Islands

Cape St. Stephen   Rat Islands

Alaska Peninsula

Adak
Adak Island

Atka Island
Atka

Fort Glen

Dutch Harbor
Unimak Island

Cold Bay

Unimak
Unalaska

A l e u t i a n   I s l a n d s

P A C I F I C

0	100 mi
0	100 km

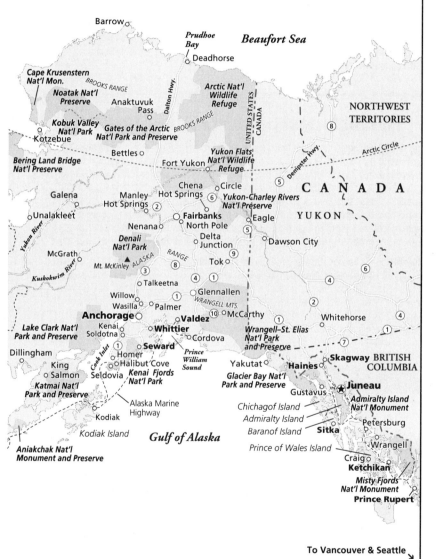

ARCTIC OCEAN

Barrow

Prudhoe
Bay
Deadhorse

Beaufort Sea

Cape Krusenstern
Nat'l Mon.
BROOKS RANGE
Noatak Nat'l
Preserve   Anaktuvuk
Pass

Arctic Nat'l
Wildlife
Refuge

NORTHWEST
TERRITORIES

Kobuk Valley
Nat'l Park   Gates of the Arctic   BROOKS RANGE
Kotzebue   Nat'l Park and Preserve

Dalton Hwy.

UNITED STATES
CANADA

Dempster Hwy.

⑧

Arctic Circle

Bering Land Bridge
Nat'l Preserve   Bettles   Yukon Flats
                Fort Yukon   Nat'l Wildlife
                             Refuge

Galena   Manley   Chena   Circle   CANADA
          Hot Springs   Hot Springs ⑥ Yukon-Charley Rivers
Unalakleet   ②   Nat'l Preserve   YUKON

⑤

Yukon River

Nenana   Fairbanks   Eagle
          North Pole   ⑤
Denali
Nat'l Park   Delta
          Junction   Dawson City
McGrath
Mt. McKinley ALASKA   RANGE
Kuskokwim River   ③   Tok   ⑨
                  ④ ①
          Talkeetna   ⑥
Willow   Glennallen   ②   ④
Wasilla   Palmer WRANGELL MTS.
Anchorage   ⑩ McCarthy   ①   Whitehorse   ④
          Kenai   ①
Lake Clark Nat'l   Soldotna   Valdez
Park and Preserve   Whittier
Dillingham   Seward   Cordova   Wrangell–St. Elias   ⑦
          Homer   Prince   Nat'l Park
King   Halibut Cove William   and Preserve
Salmon Seldovia   Kenai Fjords Sound   Yakutat   Haines   Skagway   BRITISH
Katmai Nat'l   Nat'l Park   Glacier Bay Nat'l   COLUMBIA
Park and Preserve   Park and Preserve   Gustavus   Juneau
          Alaska Marine   Admiralty Island
          Highway   Chichagof Island   Nat'l Monument
Kodiak   Admiralty Island   Petersburg
Kodiak Island   Gulf of Alaska   Baranof Island   Sitka
                         Prince of Wales Island   Wrangell
Aniakchak Nat'l   Craig
Monument and Preserve   Ketchikan
                                        Misty Fjords
                                        Nat'l Monument
                                        Prince Rupert

To Vancouver & Seattle

OCEAN

Despite the continuing conflict between local communities and inhabitants on the one side and the operators of passenger ships on the other, cruise visitors themselves are very much welcome when they visit Alaska. The bulk of the population still enjoys interacting with people from the "outside" (which a native's word for anything that isn't Alaska.)

The number of big ship entries into Glacier Bay is restricted because of environmental concerns. But, although Glacier Bay has enormous appeal, and deservedly so, don't be put off if the ship you want travels to Misty Fjord, Hubbard Glacier, or some other wilderness area. All these sites are incredibly beautiful.

The high cost of cruising in Alaska

Some years ago, several cruise lines were massively fined for offenses against the environment. As a result, in an image-mending program, the industry agreed to pay for waste monitoring, standby clean-up barges, educational programs, essential services used while in dock, and so on. But some citizens and lawmakers still insist that the industry doesn't pay enough. Their viewpoint no longer involves wanting the lines to pay for the damage they allegedly do to the fragile Alaska environment. Now these detractors seem to want to use the cruise business and passengers to help offset a huge budget shortfall caused by the state's declining oil output and revenue.

Former Alaska Governor Tony Knowles proposed charging a tax of $30 for every cruise passenger who arrives at Alaskan ports. The legislative body never adopted that proposal, but Knowles' successor as governor, Republican Frank Murkowski, put forward a somewhat broader, $15 a head "wildlife conservation" fee charged to all visitors of Alaska — both cruise passengers and people who travel by land. Others — legislators and citizen groups — talked about having fees as high as $50 a head imposed on cruise passengers. Naturally, the cruise and tour industries are against a head tax that increases the cost of visiting Alaska.

The lines feel victimized, of course. They point out that cruising generates close to $200 million in revenue for the ports of the Inside Passage alone, and that the city of Anchorage, which welcomes about half of the cruise passengers in the state each year, makes another $100 million-plus in direct cruise-visitor income. Why bite the hand that feeds you, they ask.

In fairness, constituents expect their Alaska state legislators to find new revenue sources and make the bite on residents as painless as possible. Hence, visitors become a prime target, and cruisers —— the bulk of the state's visitor intake — become the most inviting target of all.

Needless to say, every person involved in providing visitor services — cruise lines included — wants to "educate" legislators about the revenues tourists bring to Alaska. The legislators argue that travel operators should prepare to suffer some of the deficit-reducing pain. Stay tuned!

As in any region that relies heavily on the tourist industry, Alaskan summer vendors come into towns to sell imported souvenirs and go away at season's end. But you can steer clear of the clichéd art. The ports of call we cover in this chapter — most of them dotted along the protected waterway of Southeast Alaska known as the Inside Passage — maintain varying degrees of their rustic charm and remain unique places to discover the state's fascinating history, Native culture, geography, and wildlife.

Boarding Ship for Alaska

Most cruises to Alaska begin and/or end in Vancouver, British Columbia; Seattle; Seward, Alaska; or Whittier, Alaska, the ports nearest to Anchorage. (Cruises to the Inside Passage generally run round-trip from Vancouver or Seattle; Gulf of Alaska cruises generally run northbound or southbound between one of these ports and Vancouver or Seattle and either Seward/Anchorage or Whittier.) This year, as well, three ships will operate to Alaska roundtrip out of San Francisco. As with cruise ship departures in the Caribbean and Europe, ships typically start boarding passengers in the early afternoon on the first day and then depart in the early evening.

If possible, arrive a day or two before your sail date, especially if you have to travel a long distance to reach Alaska. You can use that extra day to recover from jet lag and explore your port of embarkation. And by scheduling extra pre-cruise time, you avoid that "What if I miss the boat?" anxiety if your airline delays your flight. You can also, of course, expand your trip with a day or two after the cruise.

If you prefer to book a package, consult your cruise line. Most cruise lines offer a variety of optional pre- or post-cruise hotel nights and tour programs.

Hitting the Town

In addition to the standard walking tours, bus tours, and even a few horse-drawn carriage tours, nearly all the cruise lines that sail in Alaska offer shore excursions for passengers who want to get active. You can choose among mountain-bike trips, salmon fishing expeditions, kayak voyages, and much more. You can also book these kinds of activities directly with vendors at the ports of call, possibly getting them cheaper that way, but when you book through the cruise line you know that you deal with a reputable vendor — no cruise line wants to risk the bad publicity that comes with a shipload of people that have a rotten day in port.

At the adventurous extreme of excursion offerings, flightseeing trips show you the vast and varied Alaskan landscape from the air. Tour operators offer these trips in both small planes and helicopters. Air tours are an expensive but exhilarating way to round out your Alaska experience — you may even land on a glacier and take a short walk around. How often do you get to do *that* at home?

Note: Shore excursion prices we list in this chapter are for 2004 and may increase slightly in 2005. In most ports (Sitka and Skagway, for instance), the downtown area is small enough to tour on your own by foot if you choose. Don't expect that luxury in some of the major ports of embarkation, such as Anchorage, Vancouver, Victoria, San Francisco, and Seattle. Even in some of the smaller Alaskan communities you may need a bus or taxi to get to some of the more important attractions — for example, the **Mendenhall Glacier** in Juneau, the **Saxman Totem Pole Park** in Ketchikan, or the **Raptor Rehabilitation Center** in Sitka. We provide information in each port write-up on which attractions you can walk to.

Choosing a Cruisetour

Unlike the Caribbean, where all the fascinating places are close to the water, Alaska hides some of its best tourist attractions inland. Go ashore to find the corridor from **Anchorage** alongside **Denali National Park** to **Fairbanks,** the historic mining towns of **Glennallen** and **Kennicott,** the **Kenai Peninsula,** or even locations north of the Arctic Circle. The cruise lines offer combination platters — cruises with land tours — called *cruisetours.* The tour costs typically include hotel stays, transportation (usually train and/or bus and sometimes a plane or ferry), and some meals.

Holland America, Princess (each with seven ships in the market), and Royal Caribbean Cruises (with its Royal Caribbean International and Celebrity Cruises brands, a total of five ships) are the bigwigs in the Alaskan cruisetour market. Each line owns its own transportation, including tour buses and trains (other cruise lines buy at least some of their cruisetour components from these lines). Holland America and Princess also own hotels and lodges.

The Ports of Embarkation

You have to start somewhere, and for an Alaskan cruise you likely start in Vancouver, Seattle, or Seward/Whittier (which serve Anchorage). Some small ships also sail itineraries that begin and/or end in Juneau and Ketchikan.

Anchorage

Anchorage is the usual northern port of embarkation/disembarkation on Gulf of Alaska cruises, at least in name. Ships don't actually sail there; they dock in Seward or, in the case of Princess and Carnival, in Whittier on the eastern side of the Kenai Peninsula. The ships bus passengers to and from Anchorage. This saves the long, slow slog around the peninsula

Downtown Anchorage

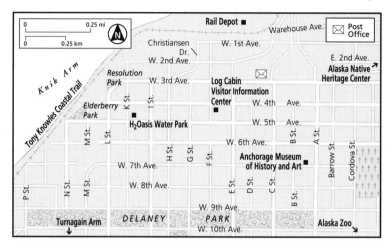

by ship, cutting almost a full day off your transportation time. This allows you to quickly get started with your cruise (if you fly into Anchorage) or to get to Anchorage and/or into the Alaskan Interior (if your cruise ends here and you plan to either fly home directly or take a land tour).

You generally don't spend much time in Seward because it only acts as a port of embarkation and disembarkation, although the **Alaska SeaLife Center** is worth seeing. And you certainly don't spend any time in Whittier, a dreary little place whose sole advantage to cruisers seems to be its close proximity to Anchorage, the place to be.

Cruising into port

The ports for Anchorage are Seward or Whittier.

Exploring on your own

Anchorage's downtown caters to tourists and maintains a pleasant approach. Visit the heritage museums or head out to the Chugach Mountains or along Turnagain Arm to feel like you're really in Alaska.

Within Walking Distance: If you visit town on a weekday from June to August, you can join one of the historic tours hosted by **Alaska Historic Properties** (☎ 907-274-3600). Meet in the lobby of the old City Hall (524 W. Fourth Ave.; next to the Log Cabin Visitor Information Center) at 1 p.m. The one-hour tours cover about two miles and cost $5 for adults, $4 for seniors, and $1 for children.

You can view contemporary Alaskan art in the galleries of the **Anchorage Museum of History and Art** (121 W. Seventh Ave.; ☎ 907-343-4326). The museum also features an Alaskan history and anthropology display.

Stretch your legs along the 11-mile paved **Tony Knowles Coastal Trail** that follows the water from the western end of Second Avenue to Kincaid Park. You can hop on the trail at several points, including **Elderberry Park** at the western end of Fifth Avenue. You can also rent a bike from **Downtown Bicycle Rental** (333 W. Fourth Ave.; ☎ 907 279-5293) for $15 for the first three hours and $2 for each hour thereafter, up to a total of $29 for a 24-hour rental. The company has mountain bikes, kids' bikes, tandems, and more.

Beyond Walking Distance: **The Alaska Native Heritage Center** (8800 Heritage Center Dr.; ☎ 800 315-6608 or 907-330-8000), which opened in 1999, is just a few minutes drive from downtown and features reconstructions of traditional Native dwellings, from the Tlingits of the southeast to the Yup'ic of the Far North. Native interpreters explain what life was like in traditional communities. The center also hosts regular storytelling and musical presentations. Admission is $20.95 for adults, $18.95 for seniors, and $15.95 for children 7 to 16 — kids 6 and under can attend for free.

Anchorage has another major attraction of the amusement park variety — **H2Oasis Water Park** (1520 O'Malley Rd.; ☎ 888-H2OASIS or 907-344-8610). A day pass for an adult (13 and older) costs $19.95; children under 13 pay $13.95. A lazy river ride circles the park, whose fun areas include a wave pool that generates 3-to-4-foot waves, a 150-foot long, 23-foot high enclosed body slide, a children's lagoon, a pirate's ship, and water cannons.

About six miles south of downtown, the **Alaska Zoo** (4731 O'Malley Rd.; ☎ 907-346-3242) affords you a closer look at many Alaskan animal species and some non-native varieties.

If you want to head out of town and into the wilderness, the **Alaska Public Lands Information Center** (605 W. Fourth Ave., Suite 105; ☎ 907-271-2737) can show you a good route to the easily accessible and scenic **Chugach Mountains.** Or you can take a drive along **Turnagain Arm,** which stretches roughly 50 miles south from the Seward Highway to Portage Glacier, providing breathtaking mountain views and a chance to see wildlife, such as moose and Dall sheep (and occasionally beluga whales), right from your car window. You can rent a car in Anchorage (see the appendix for toll-free numbers of rental firms) or take one of the seven-hour **Gray Line** bus tours (☎ 800-544-2206), offered twice daily in summer, which include a boat ride to the **Portage Glacier.**

Seward

Seward is the main northern embarkation/disembarkation port for most cruise ships on Gulf of Alaska itineraries. From here, cruise lines transport passengers by bus or train to their real northern destination — Anchorage. Ships also occasionally visit Seward as a port of call. Most vessels dock about a half-mile from downtown.

Seward

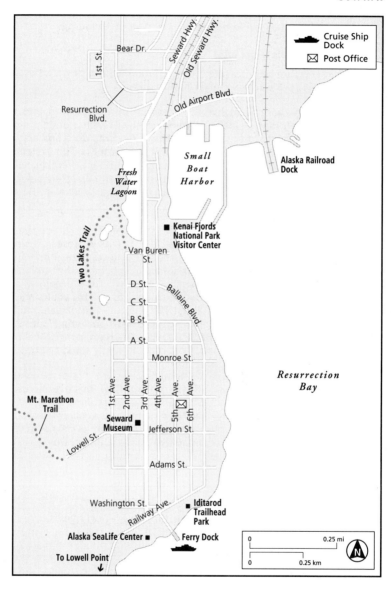

Cruise Ship Dock

⊠ Post Office

Bear Dr.

1st St.

Seward Hwy.

Old Seward Hwy.

Old Airport Blvd.

Resurrection Blvd.

Small Boat Harbor

Alaska Railroad Dock

Fresh Water Lagoon

Two Lakes Trail

■ Kenai Fjords National Park Visitor Center

Van Buren St.

D St.

Ballaine Blvd.

C St.

B St.

A St.

Monroe St.

1st Ave.

2nd Ave.

3rd Ave.

4th Ave.

5th Ave.

6th Ave.

Resurrection Bay

Mt. Marathon Trail

Lowell St.

⊠

Seward Museum ■

Jefferson St.

Adams St.

Washington St.

Railway Ave.

■ Iditarod Trailhead Park

Alaska SeaLife Center ■

Ferry Dock

To Lowell Point

0   0.25 mi

0   0.25 km

N

Cruising into port

Celebrity, Clipper, Holland America, Royal Caribbean, and Seven Seas all have ships that sail from Seward, the port of Anchorage.

Exploring on your own

Resurrection Bay, seagate to the rest of Alaska, is Seward's main attraction, along with **Kenai Fjords National Park.**

Within Walking Distance: To explore downtown Seward, pick up a walking-tour map available from one of the Chamber of Commerce visitor information kiosks, located at the cruise ship dock and also downtown in the old Alaska Railroad car at the corner of Third Avenue and Jefferson Street. Seward's surroundings also offer several excellent hiking trails. Visitors can get a complete list and directions at the **Kenai Fjords National Park Visitor Center,** on Fourth Avenue, at the small-boat harbor (☎ 907-224-3175).

In town, the **Alaska SeaLife Center** (1000 Rail Way, right on the waterfront; ☎ 800-224-2525 or **907-224-6300**) is a major research aquarium founded in 1998 with money from Exxon, following the infamous *Exxon Valdez* oil spill. Part of the aquarium is also open to the public, so you can view all kinds of sea critters, such as sea otters, sea lions, seals, porpoises, and many, many fish. Admission is $12.50 for adults and $10 for kids ages 7 to 12. A display about 18th-century Russian shipbuilding in Seward is one of the highlights of the **Seward Museum** (Third Avenue and Jefferson Street; ☎ 907-224-3902), which preserves local historical memorabilia. Admission is $2 for adults and $.50 for kids 5 to 12.

Beyond Walking Distance: Several firms offer tours of the **Resurrection Bay** fjords by boat. **Coastal Kayaking and Custom Adventures Worldwide** (☎ 800-288-2134 or **907-258-3866**) offers kayaking day trips in Resurrection Bay as well as longer trips into Kenai Fjords National Park. For a truly alternative transportation experience, ride a wheeled dogsled and see dogsled demonstrations at **Iditarod Dogsled Tours** (Old Exit Glacier Road, 3.7 miles out the Seward Highway; ☎ 800-478-3139 or **907-224-8607**).

Whittier

Whittier joins Seward as an important cruise port by virtue of the fact that both Princess, with its five Gulf of Alaska ships, and Carnival, with one, use it as their northernmost turnaround point. Although both lines used to operate their Gulf itineraries between Vancouver or Seattle and Seward, which became known as "the port for Anchorage," now they turn their ships around for the southbound voyages in Whittier.

The reason is fairly basic. Hauling passengers from Seward to Anchorage is a three-hour schlep. Shipping them from Whittier takes half that time because the Anton Anderson Memorial Tunnel, which runs from Bear Valley to Whittier, is now accessible to both road and rail traffic. In the past, the only way vehicle traffic could get through was by piggy-backing on the flat cars of the Alaska Railroad trains, a time-consuming and volume-inhibiting process. Although only 2 ½ miles long, that tunnel (named for the chief engineer of the project that brought rail travel to Whittier in 1919) is the most important thing to happen to the community in many a long year.

Whittier's only other claim to fame is its position as Anchorage's closest gateway to the wilderness splendor of **Prince William Sound.** Until the tunnel was widened and a roadbed laid, however, operators of wildlife sightseeing boats were forced to tailor the timing of their product to the schedule of the Alaska Railroad. Now they send their boats out with less regard to the arrival and departure times of the trains. The system isn't perfect; you still wait both coming and going. But the system is vastly better than it was.

In all honesty, Whittier is a bleak little place. It consists primarily of one major building, the 14-story **Begich Towers,** where practically all 185 inhabitants make their homes. It stands as a forbidding, fortress-like structure, housing the town's only grocery store and medical center. An underground walkway links it with the local school so the kids don't have to plough through the 14 feet of snow Whittier endures every year.

Whittier was built as an army town — and it retains much of its barracks-like ambiance.

Cruising into port
Princess and Carnival have ships that cruise out of Whittier.

Exploring on your own
Prince William Sound is the only attraction that you should consider exploring. But if you don't have the time to take one of the boats of **Phillips Cruises and Tours** (519 W. Fourth Ave., Anchorage; ☎ **800 544-0529** or **907-276-8023**) or **Major Marine Tours** (411 W. Fourth Ave., Anchorage; ☎ **800 764-7300** or **907 274-7300**) through the sound, spend five minutes and go look at the town. It doesn't take longer!

Vancouver, British Columbia
Most cruise ships that explore the Inside Passage and Gulf of Alaska use Vancouver as the main southern embarkation and disembarkation port. Here, they usually dock at the famous **Canada Place** pier terminal at the end of Burrard Street. A city landmark, this five-sail structure is built right into the harbor at the edge of the downtown district. The **Tourism Vancouver Infocentre** is near the piers, as are hotels, restaurants, and shops. You can easily walk to **Gastown** and **Robson Street** from here to find fashionable shopping. Some ships may dock at the **Ballantyne** cruise terminal, about five minutes away by taxi.

Downtown Vancouver

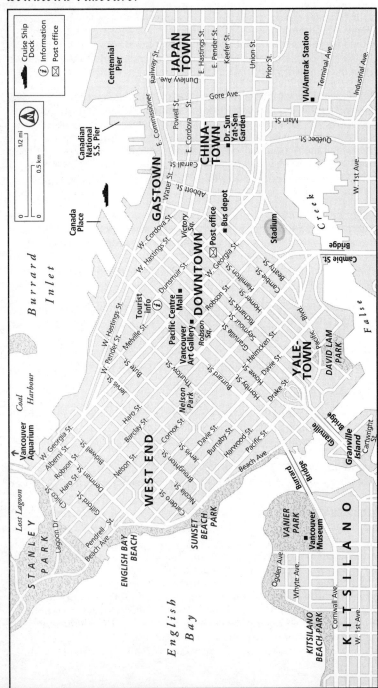

Cruising into port

Carnival, Celebrity, Cruise West, Holland America, Norwegian, Princess, Royal Caribbean, and Seven Seas all have ships that sail from Vancouver. In addition, Crystal and American West Steamboat Company visit here as a port of call.

Exploring on your own

Within Walking Distance: So close to the ship pier, you can't miss it: **Gastown** is an absolutely charming area of historic buildings, cobblestone streets, and, of course, gaslights (although the name comes from a 19th-century saloon-owner, "Gassy" Jack Deighton). Tourists enjoy the Bohemian atmosphere, complete with street musicians and plenty of antique and art shops, boutiques, cafes, and clubs.

Besides featuring delicious Asian cuisine and shops selling Chinese goods, Vancouver's **Chinatown** (one of the largest in North America) is also a historic district. You can see fine examples of Chinese architecture at the **Dr. Sun Yat-sen Garden** (578 Carrall St.; ☎ 604-689-7133). Check out **Robson Street** and the **Pacific Centre Mall** for trendy fashions and bargains — when you compare prices, remember that the U.S. dollar is generally worth more than the Canadian dollar. Depending on the day-to-day currency fluctuations, the U.S. dollar can be valued at as much as CAN$1.30, so Canadian goods are easy on the U.S. pocketbook. We quote all prices in this section in U.S. dollars.

Cruise passengers may be particularly interested in visiting an exhibit of a 19th-century immigrant ship's steerage deck at the **Vancouver Museum** (1100 Chestnut St.; ☎ 604-736-4431), which covers the history of the city from prehistoric times to the present. Admission is $6.50 for adults and $3.75 for seniors and children. Or, for a wide-ranging collection of Canadian and international artwork, as well as a special children's gallery, visit the **Vancouver Art Gallery** (750 Hornby St.; ☎ 604-662-4719). Admission is $6.50 for adults, $5 for seniors, and children under 12 get in free.

Beyond Walking Distance: Beautifully wooded **Stanley Park** offers 1,000 acres just north of downtown, with gorgeous rose gardens, hiking trails, totem poles, a kids' water park, and the **Vancouver Aquarium** (☎ 604-659-3400) — the third-largest aquarium in North America. Admission rates are $9.50 for adults, $8 for seniors and students, and $6 for children between the ages of 4 and 12. Just 15 minutes from downtown across False Creek is **Granville Island,** a shoppers' paradise with art studios and a lively market.

Seattle, Washington

A longtime embarkation port for small ships, Seattle is now home base for some of the big ships of Norwegian Cruise Line, Holland America, and several smaller vessels of other companies. Similar to Fisherman's Wharf in San Francisco, the **Seattle Waterfront,** which runs along

Downtown Seattle

Alaskan Way from Yesler Way North to Bay Street and Myrtle Edwards Park, is both touristy and home to some great restaurants and shops. You also find the popular **Seattle Aquarium** here.

Cruising into port

American West, Clipper, Cruise West, Glacier Bay, Holland America, Lindblad Expeditions, Norwegian, and Princess all have ships that sail from Seattle.

Exploring on your own

Within Walking Distance: Built for the 1962 World's Fair, the 600-foot **Space Needle** (203 Sixth Ave. N.) has become a symbol of Seattle and still points to architectural trends in some Jetsonian future. You can enjoy breathtaking views from the observation deck (or sit in the indoor lounge if heights make you dizzy). You also have a choice of two equally expensive restaurants inside. Admission is $9 for adults, $8 for seniors, $4 for children 5 to 12, and free for kids under 5.

A National Historic District, **Pike Place Market** (between Pike and Pine streets at First Avenue) provides space for the creations of some 200 local artisans and fine artists, along with room for the countless street performers. Restaurants and literally hundreds of shops fill what was once a simple farmer's market. Only two blocks away from the market, the **Seattle Art Museum** (100 University St.) features an unparalleled collection of Northwest Coast Indian art and diverse exhibits ranging from Andy Warhol to African masks. Admission is $7 for adults, $5 for students and seniors, and free for kids under 12.

If the huge octopus at the **Seattle Aquarium** (1483 Alaskan Way, in Waterfront Park; ☎ 206-386-4300) doesn't pull you in, its well-designed exhibits about the sea life of **Puget Sound** will. Admission is $11.50 for adults (13 years and older), $7.50 for kids ages 6 to 12, and $5.25 for kids ages 3 to 5.

Beyond Walking Distance: Across Puget Sound on **Blake Island State Marine Park** is **Tillicum Village,** another surprising legacy (like the Space Needle) of the 1962 World's Fair. You arrive by boat across the shining waters of the Sound to this incredibly scenic spot where totem poles guard a traditional Northwest Coast Indian longhouse surrounded by forest. Tillicum isn't actually an entire village; inside, the longhouse is a large restaurant and performance hall where you can watch traditional masked dances while you enjoy an alder-smoked salmon dinner. **Tillicum Village Tours** (Pier 56; ☎ 206-933-8600) operates visits that include round-trip boat transportation to the village, an elegant dinner, and dance performance. The cost is $69 for adults, $59 for seniors, and $25 for kids ages 5 to 12.

The Ports of Call

Generally, a ship visits three or four ports of call during a 7-night Alaskan itinerary (plus the ports of embarkation and disembarkation), including some combination of the places in this section.

Haines

Surrounded by snowcapped mountains, Haines is the quintessential quiet, small town . . . a place where you may find the occasional moose wandering down Main Street, window-shopping. It could have been the prototype of the quirky little town of Cicely, the setting for the television show *Northern Exposure.* Of course, when a cruise ship comes to port, the atmosphere livens up a bit.

Downtown Haines has the usual assortment of shops and museums, but if you don't mind taking a short walk, you can visit a 1903 U.S. Army outpost, **Fort William Seward,** which was deactivated after World War II. Now the fort's nine-acre parade grounds contain a replica of a Tlingit clan house and an arts and cultural center that features a Native dance troupe and woodcarvers.

The Haines area also hosts incredible numbers of bald eagles (more than 3,000 in fall and winter). Unfortunately, their greatest concentration tends to take place before and after the cruise season.

Haines

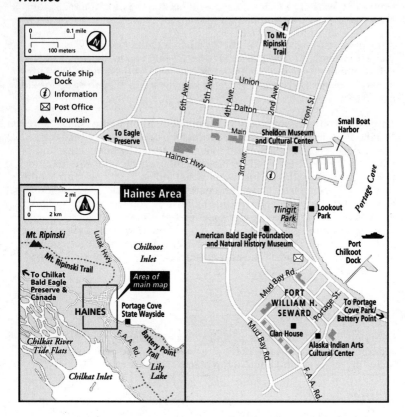

Cruising into port

Clipper, Cruise West, Glacier Bay, and Holland America make port calls here.

Seeking out the best shore excursions

Chilkat Dancers Evening of Dance and Story Telling: Performances Monday through Wednesday evenings in the **Totem Village Tribal House** at Fort William Seward. (1 hour; $10 adults, $5 children)

Chilkat Nature Hike: A guide tells you all about Alaskan rain forests as you hike this moderately difficult 4.8-mile trail. With any luck, you may catch a glimpse of a bald eagle. (4 hours; $59 to $67)

Chilkoot Bald Eagle Preserve Jet Boat Tour: View forests and awe-inspiring mountains as you cross lovely Chilkoot Lake on powerful jet boats in search of bald eagles and other wildlife. (4 hours; $90 to $99)

Chilkat Bicycle Adventure: Tour the Fort Seward area and then continue along the Chilkat River by bike. You may even spot a few eagles. Equipment is provided. (1½ hours; $49)

Exploring on your own

Large cruise ships usually take passengers ashore in a *tender* (launch), to a small boat harbor downtown or more often to **Port Chilkoot,** where small ships usually dock. Most ships provide shuttle service from the dock to Main Street, or you can walk down Front Street to Main Street, which is only about ¾ of a mile from port. Alternatively, head up Portage Street to Fort William Seward. If you want to follow your own path, pick up a map at the kiosk at the end of the Port Chilkoot dock.

Within Walking Distance: Just above the dock lies Fort William Seward, home of the **Alaska Indian Arts Cultural Center** (P.O. Box 271), with a small gallery, carver's workshop, and gift shop.

Two museums in the Main Street area may interest you. You can view an expansive woodland diorama at the **American Bald Eagle Foundation History Museum** (115 Haines Hwy.). Admission is free, but the museum accepts donations. For local history, check out the small **Sheldon Museum and Cultural Center** (11 Main St.), which also features Tlingit art and cultural artifacts. The Center requires a nominal donation for admission.

Beyond Walking Distance: Nothin' but fields and trees. Did we mention that Haines is a very small town?

Juneau

Juneau, Alaska's state capital and third-largest city (after Anchorage and Fairbanks), is surrounded by icefields on three sides and water on the fourth, which makes it the only U.S. state capital that you can't drive to. Although the hilly downtown looks relatively small, Juneau is the largest state capital in terms of mass, with 3,108 square miles (mostly icefield, wilderness, and water) within its city limits. In spite of its remote locale, Juneau is — certainly by Alaskan standards — a cosmopolitan city with a flourishing tourism industry. During cruise season, four or five cruise ships make port here virtually every day, adding up to about 450 port calls per summer.

As soon as you disembark, look up along the Mount Roberts Tramway to spot the ruins of the **Alaska-Juneau Mill** on the mountainside. This town has its foundations in the gold industry that began in 1880 — when Joe Juneau and Richard Harris struck it rich — and continued through the 1940s.

In town, you find tourist shops, a great museum, and wonderful historical architecture, including the **State Capitol Building** and a couple of genuine saloons. Various forest hiking trails and the blue-white **Mendenhall Glacier** stand a short jaunt away from town.

Juneau

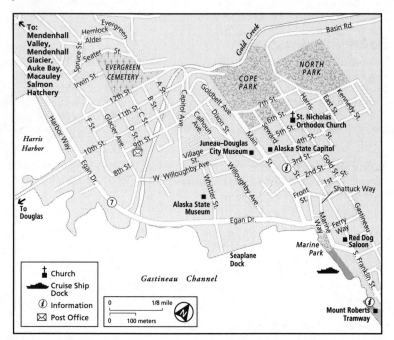

To: Mendenhall Valley, Mendenhall Glacier, Auke Bay, Macauley Salmon Hatchery

Evergreen
Hemlock
Alder
Seater St.
Spruce St.
Irwin St.

EVERGREEN CEMETERY

Gold Creek

Basin Rd.

NORTH PARK

COPE PARK

12th St.
11th St.
9th St.
10th St.
8th St.

F St.
Glacier Ave.
A St.
B St.
C St.
D St.
9th St.

Capitol Ave.
Goldbelt Ave.
Calhoun Ave.
Dixon St.

7th St.
6th St.
5th St.
4th St.
3rd St.
2nd St.
1st St.

Harris
East St.
Kennedy St.
Seward St.
Main St.
Gold St.

† St. Nicholas Orthodox Church

Harris Harbor

Harbor Way

Egan Dr.

Village St.
W. Willoughby Ave.

Juneau–Douglas City Museum ■

(i) ■ Alaska State Capitol

Whittier St.
Willoughby Ave.

To Douglas

⑦

■ Alaska State Museum

Egan Dr.

Front St.
Shattuck Way

Gastineau Ave.

Marine Way
Ferry Way

Seaplane Dock

Marine Park

■ Red Dog Saloon

S. Franklin St.

Gastineau Channel

† Church
Cruise Ship Dock
(i) Information
⊠ Post Office

0 ____ 1/8 mile
0 ____ 100 meters

(i)
Mount Roberts ■
Tramway

Cruising into port

American West, American Safari, Clipper, Cruise West, Glacier Bay, and Lindblad all have ships with itineraries that begin in Juneau. In addition, Carnival, Celebrity, Clipper, Crystal, Holland America, Norwegian, Princess, Royal Caribbean, and Seven Seas have ships that visit Juneau as a port of call.

Seeking out the best shore excursions

Glacier Helicopter Tour: For a terrific view of the jagged peaks, this heli-copter tour lands you right on either the **Norris** or the **Mendenhall Glacier,** where you can actually get out and walk around in ice boots to take in the breathtaking scenery. (2 to 4 hours; $176 to $310)

Gold History Tour: Looking for something to excite the kids? Here's a real gold mine. A guide explains all about the gold rush and shows you how to pan for gold near the ruins of an old mine. (1½ hours; $36 to $40)

Mendenhall Glacier Float Trip: An experienced rafter steers your ten-person raft across Mendenhall Lake and past icebergs until you get to the **Mendenhall River** and its beautiful scenery. The company provides special clothing so that you don't get too wet, although the rapids are only moderate. Where else are you going to get smoked salmon and reindeer sausage for a snack? (3 to 3½ hours; $85 to $105)

Mendenhall Glacier and City Highlights Tour: Travel by bus from downtown Juneau to the glacier and its **U.S. Forest Service Observatory.** There, as time allows, you can follow one of the nature trails or hike to within ½ mile of the glacier — which sounds far, but the ice face is so enormous that you think you stand within spitting distance. A visit to the **University of Alaska** campus and the **Gastineau Salmon Hatchery** round out your tour. (2 to 3 hours; $35 to $75)

Wilderness Lodge Flightseeing Adventure: This tour combines flightseeing over an icefield and glaciers with a salmon bake at the Taku Glacier Lodge. You also have some time to hike on nature trails. (3 hours; $184 to $210)

Exploring on your own

Ships usually dock along Franklin Street or, on busy days, anchor offshore and take you there by tender. You can take a shuttle bus, but downtown is only a short stroll up and to the left from the dock. A visitor information center at the wharf provides walking maps and visitors' guides; you can also pick them up at the **Davis Log Cabin Visitor Center,** a replica of the city's first schoolhouse on Seward Street (☎ 907-586-2201).

Within Walking Distance: The state's Russian and Native cultures are well represented at the **Alaska State Museum** (395 Whittier St.), which showcases Alaskan art and artifacts. Admission is $5 for adults and free for students and children 18 and under. You can take a free tour of the **Alaska State Capitol** (on 4th Street between Main and Seward; closed Saturday afternoon and Sunday), which has photomurals depicting the early days of Juneau.

Right by the docks, you can hop on board the **Mount Roberts Tramway** (490 S. Franklin St.) for a six-minute ride up Mt. Roberts, at the top of which you find an observation area, restaurant, shops, and a series of nature trails that offer great views of the Gastineau Channel below. Don't bother going if the sky looks overcast because you can't see anything, but if the sky is clear, slather on the mosquito repellent because the mountain is a buggy place! Tickets for a daylong pass are $21.95 for adults and $12.50 for children 7 to 12.

Take a peek at the octagonal chapel of **St. Nicholas Orthodox Church** (Fifth and Gold streets). Tlingits built the church in 1893 and it remains an active parish to this day. The church stays open daily during the tourist season. A small donation is requested.

Beyond Walking Distance: About three miles from downtown, you can visit the **Macauley Salmon Hatchery** (2697 Channel Dr.), where you get to see every step of the harvesting and fertilizing of salmon eggs. Admission is $3 for adults and $1 for kids ages 12 and under.

Mendenhall Glacier is the most visited glacier in the world due to its easy access — only 13 miles from downtown Juneau. Several hiking trails from the U.S. Forest Service visitor center allow you to get close to the glacier; one is an easy ½-mile nature trail. A video and rangers at the center can answer your questions about the glacier.

Specializing in children's programs, the small but engaging **Juneau-Douglas City Museum** (Fourth and Main streets) displays artifacts from the city's history and gold-mining past. Admission is $3 for adults and free for students and children 18 and under.

Ketchikan

Because Ketchikan is the southernmost port of call for Southeast Alaska, residents call it the "first city" — the first place ships from Vancouver or Seattle stop on northbound cruises. Although it comes in as Alaska's fourth-largest city, it likes to project a quaint if quirky image (complete with a quaint if quirky old-time red-light district, **Creek Street,** which was in full swing until the 1950s).

You may be able to find wetter places than Ketchikan, with its average rainfall of 13 feet per year, but at a certain point you become too damp to judge the difference. Suffice to say, it's wet.

To cater to tourists, Ketchikan offers plenty of shopping near the docks, but you can also hang out and watch salmon-fishing boats set out across the harbor. The city is unofficially known as the "Salmon Capital of the World," although commercial fishing is declining in importance to the local economy.

Because it has the largest concentration of Tlingit, Haida, and Tsimshian people in Alaska, Ketchikan is a wonderful place to gain an understanding of Native Alaskan culture — and see the world's largest collection of totem poles.

Cruising into port

American West, Carnival, Celebrity, Clipper, Cruise West, Crystal, Glacier Bay Cruise Line, Holland America, Norwegian, Princess, Royal Caribbean, and Seven Seas all make port calls here. Cruise West and Glacier Bay also have ships that use Ketchikan as their home port.

Seeking out the best shore excursions

Misty Fjords Flightseeing: Soar from rugged mountains to fjords, over forests and waterfalls; a floatplane takes you everywhere a taxi can't. You may even spot some wildlife from this eagle's-eye view. (2 hours; $189 to $199)

Saxman Native Village Tour: Not just another tourist attraction, this arts and cultural center is a real village where hundreds of Tlingit,

Ketchikan

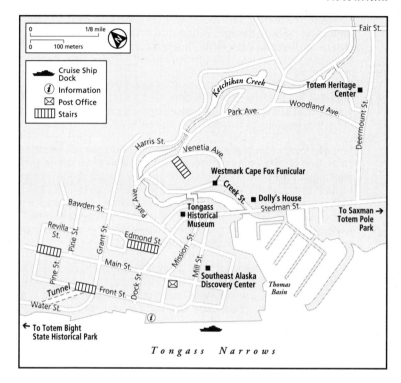

Tsimshian, and Haida people live. On this excursion, you tour the
grounds, see a Native performance, and listen to Native stories. You may
also watch artisans demonstrate totem carving. (2½ hours; $42 to $47)

Sportfishing: You may never get a better chance to catch salmon than
on a chartered fishing boat excursion in this region. The boat crew supplies your fishing gear, tackle, and bait; you catch the fish, and they ship
it home for you (for a fee). *Note:* You must purchase a $10 fishing license
and $10 king-salmon tag. (4 to 6 hours; $160 to $179)

Totem Bight Historical Park Tour: A bus takes you through the Tongass
National Forest to this historic Native fish camp, where you can view the
totem poles and a ceremonial clan house. Some tours also visit points of
interest in Ketchikan. (2 to 2½ hours; $30 to $40)

Exploring on your own

Pick up a walking-tour map at the **Ketchikan Visitor Information Center**
on the pier.

Within Walking Distance: Don't miss the **Southeast Alaska Discovery Center** (50 Main St., only a block from the pier; ☎ **907-228-6214**), which contains an amazing series of dioramas depicting local history, environment, and cultural themes. Admission is $4. On a smaller scale, the one-room **Tongass Historical Museum** (629 Dock St.; ☎ **907-225-5600**) focuses on the Native heritage and history of the city. Admission is $2.

Hello, **Dolly's House!** This home at 24 Creek Street — the former residence of Big Dolly Arthur — is now a museum. The beautifully board-walked and photogenic street once served as the red-light district and is still quite fetching to tourists. Admission is $4.

You can find totem poles all over town, but you can admire the biggest collection of 19th-century totem poles in the world indoors at the **Totem Heritage Center** (601 Deermount St.). The center's guides are very well trained in explaining the unique art form. Admission is $4. To see totem poles in a more natural setting, from Creek Street you can take the funicular (roundtrip fare is $2) 211 feet up the hill to the **Westmark Cape Fox Lodge,** which has a nice grouping of totem poles — and a bar that serves a great pint of Alaskan Amber ale!

Beyond Walking Distance: The Alaska Division of Parks maintains **Totem Bight State Historical Park,** about 10 miles outside of town on the North Tongass Highway (a short walk through the woods is involved), for the preservation of Tlingit artifacts, including totem poles and a clan house.

Visitors can also view Native artifacts at **Saxman Totem Pole Park,** located about 2½ miles south of Ketchikan on the South Tongass Highway in the Saxman Native Village. The 2-hour tour includes a slide show, dancing, and art demonstrations (such as carvers at work). *Note:* No interpretive material is available if you choose to tour on your own. Admission is $30 for adults and $15 for children 12 and under.

Sitka

Besides its natural beauty, Sitka offers many attractions connected with its unique blend of Tlingit, Russian, and American cultures and history. Here, the proud Tlingit people fought Russian invaders, although the Russians later built up the city until 1867 when the United States bought it.

Cruising into port

American Safari, Glacier Bay, and Lindblad have ships that depart from Sitka. And American West, Carnival, Celebrity, Clipper, Cruise West, Crystal, Glacier Bay, Holland America, Princess, Royal Caribbean, and Seven Seas all make port calls here.

Seeking out the best shore excursions

Sea Otter and Wildlife Quest: For a chance to spot wildlife ranging from otters to bears, visit **Salisbury Sound** with a naturalist who can explain the area's marine ecosystem and point out the critters along the way. A jet boat usually takes you on this 50-mile excursion. (3 hours; $94 to $102)

Sitka

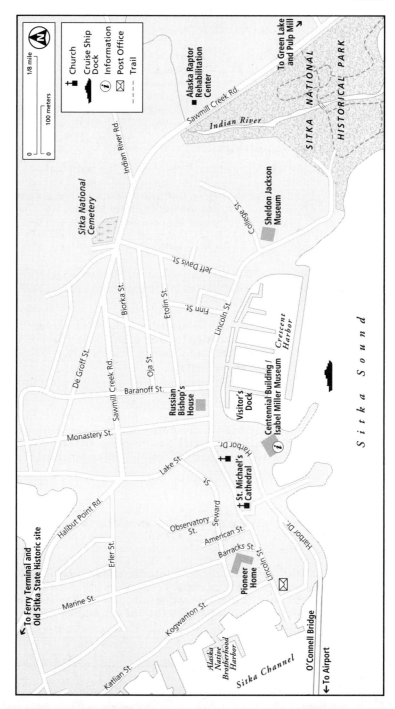

Silver Bay Nature Cruise: Take an excursion boat through the beautiful scenery of Silver Bay to visit a salmon hatchery and the ruins of the **Liberty Prospect Gold Mine.** (2 hours; $39 to $42)

Sitka Historical Tour: On this bus tour, you visit the city's main historical attractions, such as **Sitka's National Historical Park** and **St. Michael's Cathedral,** a fine example of Russian architecture. You also see the **New Archangel Dancers** perform traditional Russian dances. Some tours also stop to see the birds of prey at the **Alaska Raptor Rehabilitation Center** (expect to pay about $10 more). (3 hours; $40 to $45)

Exploring on your own

You usually take a tender into Sitka because the small harbor can't accommodate large ships. Maps are available at the Sitka Convention and Visitors Bureau, located at the visitors' dock in the **Centennial Building** (which also houses the **Isabel Miller Museum** and the auditorium where the New Archangel Dancers perform). You can take a free shuttle bus, one of the $3 cabs that greet cruisers at the docks, or you can easily walk downtown in a few minutes.

Within Walking Distance: The all-female **New Archangel Dancers** perform traditional Russian dances in the Centennial Building at the visitors' dock. Tickets are $6.

Although only a replica of the original church (which burned in 1966), **St. Michael's Cathedral** remains a town landmark (at Lincoln and Cathedral streets) and strikes a fine pose as one of Alaska's most photogenic buildings. Historic icons are on display.

The Russian Bishop's House is an 1842 Russian log cabin at Lincoln and Monastery streets. Tours are offered for $3.

The state-owned **Sheldon Jackson Museum** has a wonderful collection of Alaskan Native artifacts. You find it on the campus of **Sheldon Jackson College** at 104 College Dr. Admission is $3 (kids under 18 get in free).

Sitka National Historical Park (106 Metlakatla St.) is the site of a historic battle between the Tlingits and the Russians. Today, an interpretive center with Native artifacts offers films on the history of Sitka and demonstrations of Native weaving, silver etching, and totem carving. Phenomenally tall totem poles line the hiking trails. (*Note:* Expect a hearty 20-minute walk from the cruise ship pier.)

Beyond Walking Distance: At the **Alaska Raptor Rehabilitation Center** (1101 Sawmill Creek Blvd.), visitors can closely observe birds of prey, such as owls, hawks, and bald eagles, which the staff treats here for injuries. Admission is $10 for adults and $5 for children (you donate to a good cause).

Skagway

Skagway was once a rootin' tootin', six-gun-shootin' wild west town that played host to thousands of prospectors who wanted to get rich by hiking up the Chilkoot Trail or the White Pass into Canada and staking a gold claim in the Yukon. The boom eventually went bust, as booms do, but the people who remained had the good sense to recognize the historic value of their town and didn't knock it all down to "modernize." The National Park Service restored a historic district of older buildings downtown, but don't expect a pristine museum — many of the antique buildings house shops that sell kitschy T-shirts and one, the Mercantile Building, even has a sign that proclaims "We proudly serve Starbucks coffee."

Although the gold rush gave way to the tourism rush in Skagway, you can have plenty of fun while taking in a lot of history by riding the **White Pass and Yukon Route Railway** up 28 miles of narrow-gauge rails to Fraser on the Canadian border. The train ride costs $94, but you get your money's worth on a clear day, when the views are simply spectacular.

Cruising into port

Carnival, Celebrity, Cruise West, Crystal, Glacier Bay, Holland America, Norwegian, Princess, Royal Caribbean, and Seven Seas make port calls here.

Seeking out the best shore excursions

Chilkoot Pass and Glacier Flightseeing: Fly via helicopter over the Trail of '98 (the prospectors' path) and then to high mountain peaks where you can view glaciers and even land on one. (1½ hours; $189 to $269)

White Pass and Yukon Route Railway: From the dock, ride this famous narrow-gauge railway — complete with vintage parlor cars — past parts of the old prospectors' trail and stunning waterfalls to **White Pass Summit,** which marks the U.S./Canadian border. *Note:* If you run into foggy weather, don't bother spending the money on this excursion. (3 hours; $94)

Horseback Riding: See the scenic Dyea Valley and the remnants of **Dyea,** once a booming gold rush town, on horseback. On longer tours you take in the breathtaking views across the border in Canada. (3½ to 5½ hours; $120 to $139)

Skagway by Streetcar: This tour makes for an entertaining theater experience: Guides in period costume accompany you in 1930s sightseeing limos and tell stories about the good old days. This crazy ride gives you a chance to get a little farther outside town than you can if you explore on your own, including up to the old **Gold Rush Cemetery** and past another, more recent graveyard where propellers mark the resting places of pilots. One of the best shore excursions you can find anywhere. (2 hours; $36 to $40)

Skagway

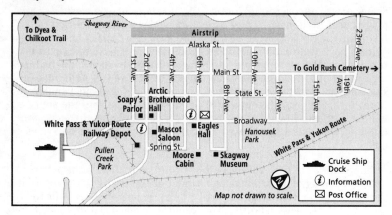

Exploring on your own

You can take a shuttle bus or walk pretty easily to downtown. You find everything on the main street, Broadway, or on branches just off it. Pick up a great walking-tour map, which details all the historical sites, at the **Skagway Convention and Visitors Bureau** (Broadway and Fifth Avenue).

Within Walking Distance: Although you can certainly explore any of the historic downtown buildings on your own, you may want to take one of the short tours from the **Klondike Gold Rush National Historic Park Visitor Center** (corner of Broadway and Second Avenue). Offered several times a day, these tours show you around the **White Pass & Yukon Railway Depot; Soapy's Parlor,** a preserved saloon once owned by the notorious badman Soapy Smith; the **Moore Cabin,** Skagway's original homestead; and the **Mascot Saloon,** a museum that simulates a real 19th-century tavern.

No wonder the **Arctic Brotherhood Hall** (on Broadway between Second and Third avenues) is one of the most photographed buildings in Alaska: More than 20,000 pieces of driftwood cover its facade! Formerly the headquarters of the **Trail of '98 Historical Museum,** this city-owned building now houses the Skagway Convention and Visitors Board. The museum (which features photos and artifacts and is worth a visit) is at Seventh and Spring streets and now goes by the name **Skagway Museum.**

You can catch Skagway's long-running *Days of '98* show at the **Eagles Hall** (Broadway and Sixth Avenue). Now in its 78th year, the show is a live melodrama that features dancing girls, ragtime music, a shootout, and more. The production offers daytime (10:30 a.m. and 2:30 p.m.) and evening (8 p.m.) performances. Admission is $12 during the day and $14 at night.

Back around 1898, the **Red Onion Saloon** (Broadway and Second) was a swinging dance hall, with a bar downstairs and a bordello upstairs. Today you can sit at the elegant original mahogany bar and order up a drink, but the upstairs services are no longer available.

Beyond Walking Distance: The townspeople used the **Gold Rush Cemetery** until 1908. You can visit the graves of Soapy Smith, the badman who ran Skagway back in its most raucous days, and Frank Reid, the surveyor hero who finally shot him. You only have to walk about 1½ miles from town up State Street. Skagway streetcar tours normally include a visit, and the White Pass and Yukon Route railway passes by the cemetery on its way into the mountains.

Valdez

Yep, this is the town that the *Exxon Valdez* tanker made famous in 1989, when the ship ran aground 23 miles from port and spilled its load of oil, poisoning the environment of Prince William Sound and the surrounding area. Yet oil remains the lifeblood of Valdez (pronounced val-DEEZ), and tankers still fill up here to take crude oil to the rest of the continental United States.

If oil gleams in your stock portfolio, gaze in awe at the huge oil storage tanks that receive the black stuff pumped down from Prudhoe Bay through the Alaska Pipeline. However, we highly recommend that you turn your back on those to gape up at the 5,000-foot peaks of the Chugach Mountains. Now you know why many consider this town the Switzerland of the Alaskan coast.

Because of the 9/11 terrorist attacks, tours of the pipeline terminal at which the tankers dock — once a popular shore excursion — are currently banned for security reasons.

Cruising into port

Carnival, Celebrity, and Cruise West make port calls here.

Seeking out the best shore excursions

Rafting in Keystone Canyon: These guided trips provide all the equipment you need to explore a fair piece of the Lowe River. The four-mile ride is hectic and the views of thundering waterfalls and sheer canyon walls on either side take your breath away. (1 hour; $35)

Valdez Sportfishing: It may sound odd with all that oil spilling and all, but Valdez is a great place to fish, especially for Coho salmon. This excursion, operated mid-July to early September only, offers opportunities for beginners and experienced anglers alike. (4 hours; $139)

Valdez

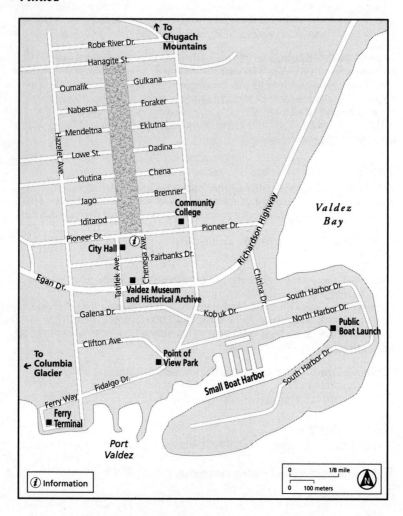

Exploring on your own

You don't have many options here. Take a shuttle bus from the pier to the Tourist Information Center for a map. You can then walk to the **Valdez Museum** (217 Egan Dr.), which presents the town's history, from early white exploration up to the oil spill. Admission is $3.

Victoria, British Columbia

Alaskan cruises that start in San Francisco or Seattle frequently call at Victoria, the capital of British Columbia, on Vancouver Island.

Victoria, not surprisingly, exudes a very Victorian atmosphere that stems from its British heritage. Beautiful 19th-century architecture prevails, accented with flowering gardens.

Cruising into port

American West, Clipper, Crystal, Holland America, and Princess all visit here.

Seeking out the best shore excursions

City Tour and Butchart Gardens: After a quick bus tour of the city sights, a short ride out to the Saanich Peninsula takes you to the world-renowned 130-acre **Butchart Gardens.** Stroll around for a couple of hours and make a promise to yourself to come back. (3½ to 4 hours; $44 to $58)

City Tour with High Tea and Castle Visit: To capture the British flavor of Victoria, try riding a double-decker bus with a tour guide who points out the main sights of the Inner Harbor, downtown, and the residential areas. These tours also stop for high tea or visit **Craigdarroch Castle.** (4 hours; $82)

Exploring on your own

Ogden Point is the normal cruise ship-docking terminal. Shuttles are available to the **Inner Harbor,** the center of Victoria. You can find walking maps right on the waterfront at the **Visitors Information Center** (812 Wharf St.).

Within Walking Distance: For afternoon tea, including perfect scones and genuine clotted cream (at a stiff $34 a head), visit the elegant **Empress Hotel** (721 Government St.). *Note:* The hotel enforces a dress code. For reservations, which the hotel recommends, call ☎ **250-384-8111.**

The **Royal British Columbia Museum** (675 Belleville) offers exhibits of historical interest. Behind the museum is **Thunderbird Park,** where native totem poles and a ceremonial house are on display. Admission is $6.50 for adults and $4.50 for youths 6 to 18.

One of the oldest houses in British Columbia is **Helmecken House** (10 Elliot St.), formerly a pioneer doctor's home, which displays some pioneering medical devices to remind you how painful life on the frontier could be.

Victoria, British Columbia

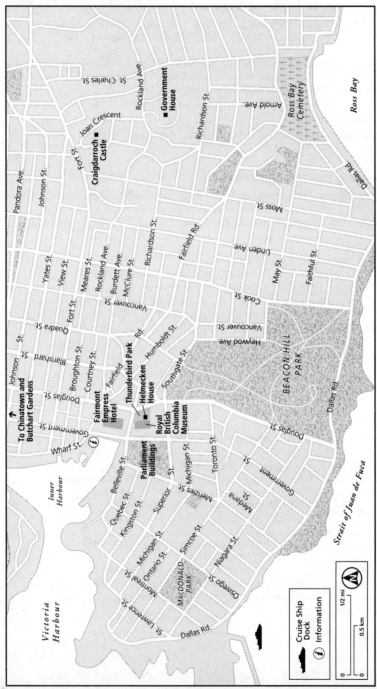

Ross Bay

Ross Bay Cemetery

St. Charles St.

Rockland Ave.

Government House

Richardson St.

Arnold Ave.

Dallas Rd.

Joan Crescent

Craigdarroch Castle

Fort St.

Johnson St.

Pandora Ave.

Moss St.

Fairfield Rd.

Richardson St.

Linden Ave.

May St.

Faithful St.

Yates St.

View St.

Meares St.

Rockland Ave.

Burdett Ave.

McClure St.

Vancouver St.

Cook St.

Fort St.

Quadra St.

Humboldt St.

Vancouver St.

Heywod Ave.

BEACON HILL PARK

Johnson St.

Blanshard St.

Broughton St.

Courtney St.

Fairfield Rd.

Thunderbird Park

Helmecken House

Southgate St.

Douglas St.

Fairmont Empress Hotel

Royal British Columbia Museum

Dallas Rd.

Douglas St.

To Chinatown and Butchart Gardens

Government St.

Wharf St.

i

Parliament Buildings

Menzies St.

Michigan St.

Toronto St.

Government St.

Inner Harbour

Belleville St.

Quebec St.

Kingston St.

Superior St.

Menzies St.

Medana St.

Strait of Juan de Fuca

Michigan St.

Ontario St.

Simcoe St.

Niagara St.

Oswego St.

Victoria Harbour

Montreal St.

St. Lawrence St.

MACDONALD PARK

Dallas Rd.

N

Cruise Ship Dock

i Information

1/2 mi

0.5 km

0

0

Beyond Walking Distance: Built by a millionaire coal-mining magnate, the 1890s-era **Craigdarroch Castle** (1050 Joan Crescent) is worth the 8-minute cab ride to peek inside. Admission is $6. You also need to take a taxi about 13 miles north of town to reach the internationally famous **Butchart Gardens** (800 Benvenuto Ave., in Brentwood Bay). Spend several hours exploring the stunning English, Italian, Japanese, water, and rose gardens of this 130-acre estate. Admission is $15 for adults, $6.25 for youths 13 to 17, and $1 for children 5 to 12.

A Whale Watching Introduction

Whale watching is possibly the number-one reason many people make a trip to Alaska in the first place. These large, graceful creatures fascinate Alaskan cruise passengers — and perhaps the whale's very elusiveness draws people to seek opportunities to get as close as possible.

When a captain or officer on watch on a large cruise ship spots a whale, he or she announces the sighting but doesn't stop the ship for photo ops. Many small ship lines, on the other hand, make whale watching an important focus of the cruise, so those ships often visit favorite whale hangouts and linger for an encounter or swing the ship around to follow up on whale sightings broadcast over marine-traffic radio. Most Alaskan cruises offer expert talks about whales at an appropriate point in the journey.

Chapter 20

Meandering in the Mediterranean

*T*he Mediterranean was looking hot, hot, hot as a cruise destination, with more big American ships heading across the Atlantic for the summer season than ever before. Then came September 11, 2001. As a result of the tragedy, the industry saw a general slowdown in international travel because of security concerns, and some lines decided to pull their ships out of the Mediterranean and move them to the Caribbean, Mexico, or Alaska.

But you still have plenty of cruise options in the region. And if world conditions are stable, you can expect European itineraries to be popular again in 2005. When you plan a Mediterranean cruise, however, keep up on current events and consult with your travel agent as to possible itinerary changes.

A Mediterranean cruise vacation appeals to people who want more than fun in the sun. Sure, you find glistening beaches with semi-nude bodies (in the French Riviera anyway) and such diversions as shopping and casinos (as in Monte Carlo). But in the Med, you also find incredible scenery, medieval ramparts, archaeological finds, and some of the best museums in the world. History lurks around every corner, and ancient sites such as Ephesus in Turkey can leave you drop-jawed. Cultural and culinary opportunities also abound; a lunch or dinner ashore is a must. The Mediterranean ports are close together, too, so you can generally visit several European countries — typically Spain, France, and Italy on a western itinerary and Greece, Turkey, and sometimes Italy on an eastern itinerary.

Mediterranean Ports

Norwegian
Sea

Bergen

NORWAY

NORTH ATLANTIC
OCEAN

Aberdeen

North
Sea

Glasgow

Belfast
Edinburgh

DENMARK

IRELAND

DINGLE
PENINSULA   Dublin
KERRY
COUNTY

Liverpool

U.K.
Oxford

THE
NETHERLANDS   Hamburg

Bath

Stonehenge   London
Salisbury

Amsterdam

BELGIUM

GERMANY

English Channel

Bruges

Brussels   Liège   Bonn

LUX.   Frankfurt

Le Havre

ATLANTIC
OCEAN

Paris

Strasbourg   Rothenburg
ob der Tauber
Augsburg

LOIRE VALLEY

Munich
BAVARIAN ALPS

FRANCE

Bern   Innsbruck
SWITZERLAND   LIECH.
BERNER
OBERLAND

Bay of Biscay

Bordeaux

Geneva

Milan

Bilbao

Arles   PROVENCE   MONACO

Porto

Marseille   Nice

ANDORRA

St-Tropez   Côte d'Azur   Florence
Cannes   TUSCANY

PORTUGAL

Madrid

Barcelona

CORSICA

Lisbon

SPAIN

Córdoba

ALGARVE

Seville   ANDALUSIA
Granada

Valencia

SARDINIA

MALLORCA

Cagliari

Málaga

Costa del Sol

Mediterranean Sea

0   150 mi
0   150 km

MOROCCO   ALGERIA   TUNISIA

CRUISE LINE HOME PORTS

ATHENS (PIRAEUS)
Crystal
Orient
Holland America
Oceania
Seabourn
SeaDream
Seven Seas
Silversea
Star Clippers
Windstar

BARCELONA
Celebrity
Holland America
Orient
Princess
Royal Caribbean
Seabourn
SeaDream
Seven Seas
Silversea
Windstar

CANNES
Star Clippers

ISTANBUL
Crystal
Orient
Seabourn
SeaDream
Seven Seas
Silversea
Star Clippers
Windstar

LISBON
Clipper
Holland America
Oceania
Seabourn
Silversea
Windstar

MONTE CARLO
SeaDream
Seven Seas
Silversea

NICE
Seabourn
SeaDream
Silversea
Windstar

ROME (CIVITAVECCHIA)
Celebrity
Clipper
Costa
Crystal
Holland America
Oceania
Orient
Norwegian
Princess
Seabourn
SeaDream
Seven Seas
Silversea
Star Clippers
Windstar

VENICE
Celebrity
Costa
Crystal
Holland America
Oceania
Orient
Princess
Seabourn
Seven Seas
Silversea
Star Clippers
Windstar

Hitting the Town

Shore excursions at Mediterranean ports usually focus on educating you about the region and involve buses with English-speaking guides. As in the Caribbean and Alaska, local contractors, rather than the cruise lines, conduct the tours. Some of the more upscale and educational lines have expert lecturers that accompany shore excursions. And some lines offer tours in limos and minivans rather than in big buses.

In some countries, including Greece and Turkey, the guides must be licensed and very knowledgeable about their subject matter. Elsewhere, we have been generally impressed with the quality of the tours offered, with a few notable exceptions. We had a guide from Monaco, for instance, who tried to entertain us on our way to St-Paul-de-Vence with a combination of inane commentary on the scenery ("Oh, look at the sea, isn't it blue?") and gossip about Monaco's royal family.

The prices we list for shore excursions are for 2004 and may go up slightly in 2005. We convert admission fees to U.S. dollars.

You can always go touring on your own, of course. In some ports, you can walk to the best sights from the docks, but in others the major attractions are some distance away. In most ports, renting a car on your own is both a hassle and expensive, so you're better off hiring a car and driver. By getting together a small group, you can split the price of the cab and save money. Your ship's tour office can usually offer recommendations. In some ports, public transportation, such as buses, subways, and trains, is also an option.

For touring, wear comfortable shoes (cobblestones and uneven surfaces are common in Europe) and bring along bottled water (available on the ship), a hat, and sunscreen, especially in the summer. Also, some churches, mosques, and other religious sites are more conservative than others, so both men and women should wear long pants or skirts (shorts and short skirts are a no-no) and avoid wearing sleeveless shirts.

Boarding Ship in Europe

As with cruise ship departures in the Caribbean, Alaska, and elsewhere, ships typically start boarding passengers in the early afternoon on the first day and then depart in the early evening. If you fly into the port of embarkation that day, however, the ship may allow you to board earlier — the cruise lines know people are generally exhausted after an overseas flight.

In Europe, the lines may require you to be on the ship a few hours before it actually sets sail.

Minding Your Money

If you want to buy something at the ports in the Mediterranean, you have to exchange your dollars for local currency (on the ship, at a bank, or at a currency exchange), get money from a local ATM, or use your charge card. In most cases in the Mediterranean, the official currency is now the euro (Turkey is the exception). Trust me, this new inter-Europe currency makes buying a whole lot easier, especially for cruise travelers, because you don't have to keep switching currency for each country you visit. At press time, the euro exchange rate was $1 = .83€ (1€ = $1.21); for Turkey it was $1 = 1,335,000 Turkish lire. However, because exchange rates fluctuate, you should check an international newspaper or an online currency converter to get the most up-to-date rates. Try the handy currency calculator at www.bloomberg.com.

The French Riviera

Cannes, Monte Carlo, Nice, St-Tropez, and Villefranche are all so close together geographically that they offer nearly the same shore excursions. The French Riviera is the place of dreams, the **Côte d'Azur** (meaning the part of the Riviera in France), where beautiful mountains and a very blue sea combine with yachts and high culture to create a playground for the rich and famous (and for us mortal folk, too). Artists once drawn to the landscape included Matisse, Cocteau, Picasso, Leger, Renoir, and Bonnard, and their legacy remains in a host of wonderful museums. Medieval cities are within easy reach, as are numerous shopping opportunities.

Cannes is a bustling commercial center, famous for the international **Cannes Film Festival** held there every year in mid-May. The city offers easily accessible beaches and plenty of shopping prospects. The 370-acre municipality of **Monaco** has symbolized glamour for centuries — the 1956 marriage of Prince Rainier and American actress Grace Kelly after their meeting at the Cannes film festival only enhanced that renown.

Nice is nice. It really is. What was once a Victorian playground for the aristocracy is now a big middle-class city with much to offer tourists, including great art museums (see the information in "Beyond Walking Distance" later in this section) and shopping opportunities. Actress Brigitte Bardot made **St-Tropez** famous, and fun-in-the-sun still thrives in this artist colony. Although residents and visitors proudly uphold its reputation for hedonism (topless and even bottomless sunbathers bask at beaches outside of town), you can find some quaint mixed in. **Villefranche** is a lovely little port town that houses artists and is home to the U.S. Sixth Fleet. The quiet mood definitely changes when the fleet's in town.

The official currency is the euro. At press time, US$1 = .83 €. French is the official language, although most store clerks speak English, too.

The French Riviera

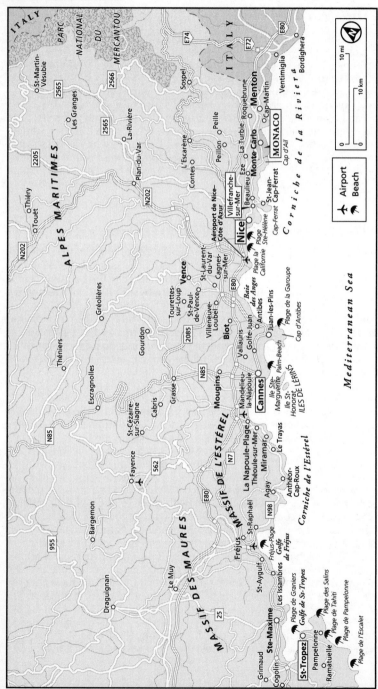

Cruising into port

Several lines call French Riviera ports home during the season. SeaDream, Seven Seas, and Silversea have ships that sail out of Monte Carlo; Star Clippers has ships out of Cannes; and Seabourn, SeaDream, Silversea, and Windstar have ships that sail out of Nice.

All the cities in this section serve as cruise ports, visited by the following lines (an asterisk (*) indicates that the line has ships that depart from the port):

- ✔ **Cannes:** Crystal, Orient, Princess, Seabourn, SeaDream, Seven Seas, Silversea, Star Clippers*, and Windstar

- ✔ **Monte Carlo, Monaco:** Clipper, Crystal, Holland America, Princess, Royal Caribbean, Seabourn, SeaDream*, Seven Seas*, Silversea*, Star Clippers, and Windstar

- ✔ **Nice:** Seabourn*, SeaDream*, Silversea*, and Windstar*

- ✔ **St-Tropez:** Holland America, Crystal, Seabourn, SeaDream, Seven Seas, and Windstar

- ✔ **Villefranche:** Celebrity, Crystal, and SeaDream

Seeking out the best shore excursions

The best way to explore the French Riviera ports is on your own. You needn't book an excursion unless you have problems with walking or you want to travel to a port other than the one your ship visits. But some outlying areas are worth exploring by tour, including the following:

St-Paul-de-Vence: This walled medieval city offers art galleries and shops, cobblestone streets, cafes, and gorgeous country views, as well as a world-renowned modern art museum, **Fondation Maeght.** (4 hours; $52 to $58)

Medieval Eze: The French medieval town of Eze literally clings to the rocks above the sea. A guided walk takes you on narrow streets past lovely restored houses with stunning ocean views. Tours also allot some time for you to check out boutiques and artists' studios. (3 to 4 hours; $45 to $68)

Exploring on your own

Taxis are available at all the piers, but they are expensive. (You may want to double up with other passengers if you plan to go any long distance.) You can walk from all the ports to many of the main local attractions. You can also take the great train service between cities on the Côte d'Azur, as well as the local bus service. In St-Tropez, you can rent bikes (for about $8 an hour) to get to the more daring beaches. The biggest bicycle outfitter is **Louis Mas** at 5 rue Josef-Quaranta.

Cannes, France

Within Walking Distance: The grand hotels you see on television during the annual Cannes Film Festival are located on the seafront, close to the ship pier. Also within walking distance of the pier are free public beaches, including **Plage du Midi,** where exhibitionism and voyeurism are likely both in full view, and private beach areas where you pay a fee ($11 and up) that includes the rental of a beach mattress and sun umbrella. You can shop near the pier at world-famous boutiques, including major Paris brands such as *Saint Laurent, Rykiel,* and *Hermès*, which you can find on **La Croisette,** the main drag facing the sea. More affordable but still quite fashionable shopping is a few blocks inland on **rue d'Antibes.**

Beyond Walking Distance: Across the bay from Cannes are the Lérins Islands, including **Ile Ste-Marguerite,** where the unlucky man immortalized in *The Man in the Iron Mask* was imprisoned. You can visit his cell. The island also boasts a maritime museum and nice family-run restaurants. The trip is about 15 minutes and the ferries depart every half hour. The roundtrip fare is $10 per person.

Monte Carlo, Monaco

Within Walking Distance: When exploring this city, you walk up some steep hills or use the municipality's rather bizarre system of public elevators to be lifted from the harbor to the casino area, for instance. Keep in mind that laws prohibit you from walking around town in swimsuits, bare-chested, or barefoot. And don't forget to check out the million-dollar yachts in the harbor.

The **Monte Carlo Casino** at Place du Casino lets you put on your finery and play James Bond. Built in 1878, the casino is wonderfully ornate but surprisingly small. Admission is $8.90 to $17 depending on where in the casino you go, and you must show your passport. The casino admits no one under 21. At night, men must wear a jacket and tie. To get a whiff of the Monte Carlo lifestyle, check out the gazillion-dollar cars parked outside the casino or just watch *Goldeneye* before you leave. The more casual, American-style **Salle Américaine** casino (where admission is free) is next door.

Beyond Walking Distance: You can walk from the harbor to the city's historic area, but because the uphill hike is only for the vigorous (although the elevators help), we put it in this section. Try taking a cab uphill, and then take a walk back down.

The **Place du Palais** is the Italianate home of the Grimaldis, the royal family of Monaco. Tours of **Les Grands Appartements du Palais** include the throne room and art collection and a combined admission to a separate museum with many Napoleonic items. Admission is $6.90 for adults, $3.45 for children 8 to 14, and free for children 7 and under. At 11:55 a.m., a 10-minute changing-of-the-guard ceremony takes place outside.

The **Oceanographic Museum,** on Av. St-Martin, fascinates visitors with over 90 fish tanks that exhibit many species new to North Americans. Admission is $12.65 for adults, $7.80 for children 6 to 18, and free for children 5 and under.

Nice, France

Within Walking Distance: You can walk from the harbor to old town, where colorful houses line narrow streets, and to the **Flower Market** area, full of outdoor cafes and great places for people-watching. (On Mondays, you can browse a wonderful antiques market here.) A few blocks inland, you find plenty of shopping opportunities for high fashion, Provencal wares, and more, especially on **rue Masséna, place Magenta,** and **rue Paradis.** You may also find it worth a trek uphill (you can use the elevator option, too) to the old graveyard of Nice in **Le Château Park,** where both great views and lavishly sculpted monuments delight you at the top (the park is also home to a Naval museum).

Also within walking distance of the ship pier is **promenade des Anglais,** a wide boulevard stretching several miles on the bay, with beaches (where teeny bikinis rule), cafes, and historic buildings, including Victorian hotels.

Beyond Walking Distance: Nice boasts so many great museums that you can hardly go wrong in choosing one. But a must-see for modern art fans is **Musée Matisse,** located in a lovely setting in Cimiez on a hill above Nice. Matisse and his heirs donated all the works in the museum, which include *Nude in an Armchair with a Green Plant* and other famous paintings along with practice sketches, designs, and items from the artist's own collection and home. Admission is $4.35 for adults and $2.65 for children. About a 15-minute walk away, also in Cimiez, the **Musée National Message Biblique Marc-Chagall** features a collection donated by Chagall and his wife that includes oils, gouaches, drawings, pastels, lithographs, and sculptures, as well as a mosaic and stained-glass windows. A brochure is available in English to help you understand the biblical themes the artworks depict. Admission is $6.35 for adults, $4.60 for students and seniors, and free for children (rates may be higher for special exhibitions).

St-Tropez, France

Within Walking Distance: Family beaches, including **Plage de la Bouillabaisse** and **Plage des Graniers,** are close to the center of town. You can find good shopping at a wealth of antique and art galleries in the city's old town. Celebrities visit here often, so keep your eyes peeled: You may bump into Oprah Winfrey or Sly Stallone. **L'Annonciade Musée St-Tropez,** at Place Georges-Grammont, is an art museum located in a former chapel with a renowned modern art collection. Admission is $5.20 for adults and $2.60 for children.

Beyond Walking Distance: The most daring beaches — **Plage des Salins, Plage de Pampellone,** and **Plage de Tahiti** — are located a few miles from town.

Villefranche, France

Within Walking Distance: This little town provides a nice setting for a walk, if you don't head into Nice (four miles away). Jean Cocteau left his legacy here in the form of frescoes on the 14th-century walls of the Romanesque **Chapelle St-Pierre** on Quai de al Douane/rue des Mariniéres. Admission is $2.60 (closed on Mondays).

Beyond Walking Distance: Head to nearby Nice, about four miles away. Check out the previous section on Nice for info on the sites.

Greece

Ancient sites and architectural treasures join forces with the sun, scenery, and food to make Greece one of the best vacation spots on Earth. Be ready for a feast for the mind and the senses, a place that is exotic but at the same time friendly and familiar, where something always reminds you of the past.

The official currency is the euro €. At press time, US$1 = .83€. Greek is the official language, but English and French are widely spoken also.

Athens

This fabled metropolis, home of the original and the 2004 Olympic Games, intersperses ancient monuments, tavernas, and neo-classical buildings with high-rises, fast-food outlets, and souvenir shops, especially at the **Pláka,** the oldest continuously inhabited section of the city. The **Parthenon** and the treasures on display at the **National Archaeological Museum** best reflect the image most of us have of ancient Greece. But in reality, modern Athens is crowded, teems with taxis and cars, and is a hard place to get around. The city is also polluted and very hot during the summer. An organized tour is a good bet here. If you do spend the day on your own, check out the **Acropolis,** have lunch in the Pláka, and accept that you don't have time to see everything, so pick the places most important to you.

Cruising into port

Crystal, Holland America, Oceania, SeaDream, Seven Seas, Silversea, Star Clippers, and Windstar all have ships that begin their itineraries in Athens (or rather, in its nearby port city Piraeus). Celebrity, Holland America, Orient, Princess, Royal Caribbean, and Seabourn have ships that visit Athens (Piraeus) as a port of call.

Seeking out the best shore excursions

Half-Day Athens City Tour: Includes a guided tour of the **Acropolis;** a drive past other Athens highlights, including **Constitution Square,** the **Parliament, the Temple of Zeus, Hadrian's Arch,** and **Olympic Stadium**; plus time for souvenir shopping. (3½ to 5 hours; $50 to $89)

Full-day Athens Tours: Full-day tours also include a visit to the National Archaeological Museum, time to shop in the Pláka, and lunch. (8 to 8½ hours; $95 to $109)

A Day Tour of Delphi: If you've visited Athens before or just aren't into big cities and crowds, you may want to opt for this day trip to one of the great sites of antiquity. The tour visits the ruins of the Temple of Apollo, located in a stunning setting on the slope of Mount Parnassus. Lunch is included. (9½ hours; $96 to $109)

Exploring on your own

Ships dock in **Piraeus;** the city is located about seven miles southwest of Athens, but the trip may seem much longer due to traffic. You can take a metro train or taxi into the city or hop the bus service that most cruise lines offer for a fee. We recommend the train, which you can walk to from the pier and ride for about $1.

If you want to take a taxi, the average meter fare from Piraeus to Syntagma Square in Athens should be around $10, but many drivers may quote a flat rate as high as $22. Try bargaining or find another taxi driver willing to turn on the meter.

 Greek taxi drivers don't always accept you as a fare. They usually ask where you want to go and are free to decline if they don't want to go your way; consequently, allow a fair amount of time to find a cab. Also, a driver may stop and pick up two or three different parties to fill the cab. If this happens, you're responsible only for your leg of the journey. Also, check for a meter and for your driver's photo ID (an increasing number of gypsy cabs have found their way into the city).

Within Walking Distance: Piraeus is a gritty port city without the kind of ancient attractions that you find in Athens. Ship aficionados may enjoy a walk around the huge dock area, but everyone else should head on into Athens.

 In the summer, start out as early as possible in the morning, when the sun isn't at its strongest and the crowds aren't as overwhelming.

Beyond Walking Distance: For many centuries, the **Acropolis** was the religious center of Athens. At various periods, it served as the seat of a king and the "home" of gods and goddesses. Because it rests on a hilltop, you can glimpse it from many parts of the city. The most striking structures are the **Parthenon** (the most recognized Greek monument; a temple dedicated to Athena), the **Propylaea** (the gateway to the Acropolis), the **Temple of Athena Nike** (built in the fifth century B.C. and restored in the 1930s), and the **Erechtheion** (the main temple, divided into two sections — one devoted to Athena and the other to Poseidon). You can't enter the Parthenon for preservation and restoration reasons. Admission to the Acropolis complex is $14 for adults, $6.90 for students, and free for kids under age 18 (includes same-day admission to the Acropolis Museum and the National Archeological Museum). Free on Sundays.

Athens

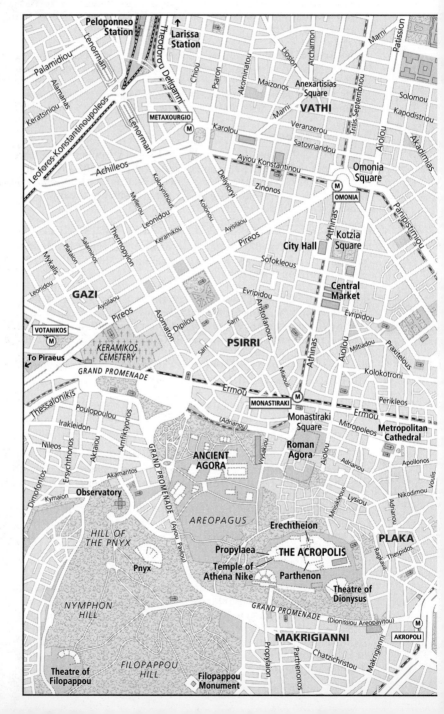

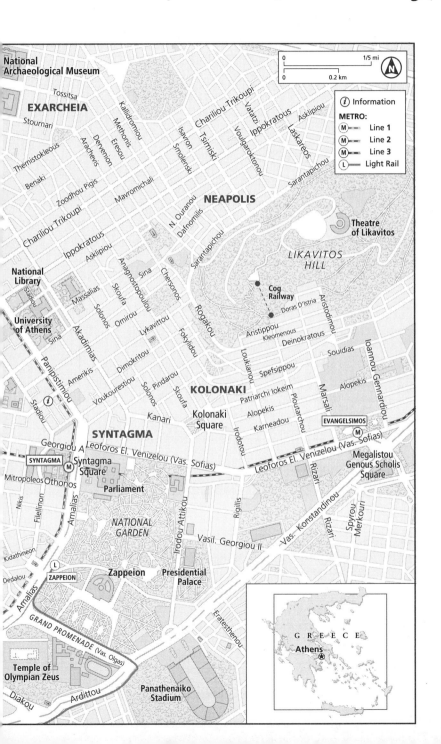

National
Archaeological Museum

0   1/5 mi
0   0.2 km

N

EXARCHEIA

Tossitsa
Stournari
Kallidromiou
Methonis
Eresou
Dervenion
Arachevis
Themistokleous
Benaki
Zoodhou Pigis
Chariliou Trikoupi
Ippokratous
Asklipiou
Mavromichali
Chariliou Trikoupi
Vatatzi
Ippokratous
Asklipiou
Isavron
Smolenski
Tsimiski
Voulgaroktonou
Laskareos
Sarantapichou
N. Ouranou
Dafnomilis

NEAPOLIS

Information

METRO:

M — Line **1**
M — Line **2**
M — Line **3**
L — Light Rail

Theatre
of Likavitos

*LIKAVITOS
HILL*

Sarantapichou

**National
Library**

**University
of Athens**

Anagnostopoulou
Sina
Skoufa
Massalias
Solonos
Omirou
Lykavittou
Chersonos
Rogakou
Fokylidou
Cog
Railway
Doras D'Istria
Aristippou
Kleomenous
Deinokratous
Aristodimou
Souidias
Ioannou Gennardiou

Stadiou
Sina
Panipistimiou
Akadimias
Amerikis
Dimokritou
Voukourestiou
Solonos
Pindarou
Skoufa

KOLONAKI

Loukianou
Spefsippou
Patriarchi Iokeim
Alopekis
Alopekis
Ploutarchou
Marsali
Alopekis

Stadiou
Kanari
**Kolonaki
Square**
Irodotou
Karneadou

EVANGELISMOS
M

SYNTAGMA

Georgiou A
Leoforos El. Venizelou (Vas. Sofias)
Leoforos El. Venizelou (Vas. Sofias)

SYNTAGMA
M
Syntagma
Square
Mitropoleos
Othonos

Megalistou
Genous Scholis
Square

Nikis
Filellinon
Amalias

Parliament

*NATIONAL
GARDEN*

Irodou Attikou
Vasil. Georgiou II
Rigillis
Vas. Konstandinou
Rizari
Spyrou
Merkouri
Rizari

Kidathineon
Dedalou

L
ZAPPEION

Zappeion

**Presidential
Palace**

Eratesthenou

Amalias

GRAND PROMENADE (Vas. Olgas)

**Temple of
Olympian Zeus**

Diakou
Ardittou

**Panathenaiko
Stadium**

G R E E C E
Athens
⊛

The Greek Isles

The National Archeological Museum has one of the richest collections of ancient Greek art in the world and was renovated for the 2004 Olympics. Admission is $6.90 for adults, $3.45 for students, and free for kids under age 18.

Mykonos

Think picture-postcard perfect. **Hora,** Mykonos's main town, dazzles with white-washed homes, their doors and window frames painted brightly, and a harbor lined with fishing boats. Pelicans, the mascots of Mykonos, greet you at the pier, and as you explore the cobblestone streets you encounter windmills, outdoor cafes, and small churches with blue domes, all within easy walking distance of the pier. A very quaint atmosphere, despite the large numbers of sun-seekers, the town's well-deserved party reputation (especially in July and August), and the inevitable souvenir shops.

Unlike other Greek islands that cruise ships visit, Mykonos has no ancient ruins. Passengers starving for sacred sites of note can catch a shore excursion to nearby **Delos,** the birthplace of Apollo.

Mykonos is the best place for diving in the Aegean, especially in September. The most well-established diving center is at **Psarou Beach** (☎ and fax **30-22890-24-808**).

Cruising into port

Celebrity, Costa, Crystal, Orient, Princess, Seabourn, SeaDream, Seven Seas, Silversea, Star Clippers, and Windstar have ships that visit Mykonos.

Seeking out the best shore excursions

Travel by small boat from Mykonos harbor to Delos for a two-hour guided walking tour of **Delos Apollo Sanctuary,** a tiny island that once served as the religious and commercial hub of the Aegean Sea. Now the sanctuary is home only to ancient ruins and their caretakers. Also visit the Archaeological Museum. (3 to 4½ hours; $37 to $63)

Exploring on your own

Your ship's tender delivers you to the main harbor area along the Esplanade in Hora. The central bus station is located off the left of the harbor, and the bus service is quite good, heading to all the beaches. Still, the best way to get around town is to walk. Or, you can choose from two types of taxis. The standard cab, which you can find at Taxi (Mavro) Square, can take you outside of town. A notice board at the square displays rates. Smaller scooter taxis with a cart for passengers also zip through the narrow streets of Hora — you find them at the pier.

Within Walking Distance: Hora is the main attraction here. The best activity is to simply wander. You can browse in plenty of art galleries and souvenir shops (some may say too many), and this is a great place to sit at a cafe and people-watch. You can also stop by the **Archaeological Museum** near the harbor to view finds from Delos. Admission is $2 for adults, $1 for students, and free for those under 18 and for all on Sunday.

Check out the local cuisine at **Edem** restaurant in Hora (follow the signposts off Matoyanni Street, near the Panahrandou church; ☎ **0289-22-855**). The food is tasty and the service is great.

Beyond Walking Distance: About four miles east of Hora lies Mykonos's second town, **Ano Mera,** which has a more traditional ambience and some religious sites of note. The **Monastery of Panayia Tourliani** dates to 1580 and has a handsomely carved steeple, as well as a small religious museum inside. You can also visit the 12th-century **Monastery of Paleokastro** nearby.

Mykonos Town

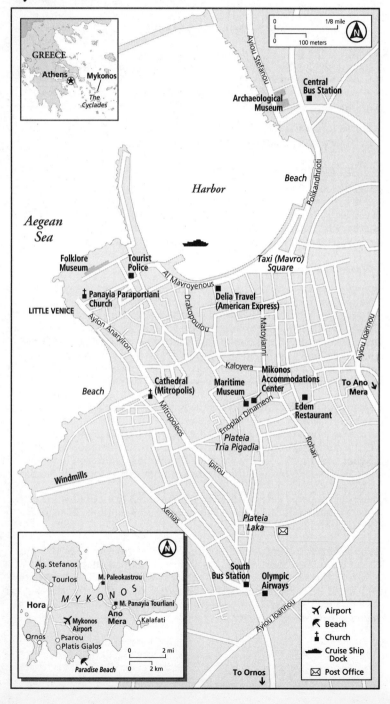

Rhodes

Rich in history, Rhodes is blessed with beautiful beaches, mountain villages, and fertile plains. The island's most famous inhabitants were the Knights of St. John, who came in 1291 after fleeing Jerusalem. They reigned for more than two centuries, and their treasures remain within the medieval walls of the old town of Rhodes (the city shares its name with the island). Lindos, a picturesque village about 50 minutes from Rhodes city, boasts the **Acropolis at Lindos,** which rises about 400 feet above a beautiful bay.

Cruising into port

Celebrity, Costa, Crystal, Holland America, Princess, Seabourn, SeaDream, Seven Seas, Silversea, Star Clippers, and Windstar all have ships that visit Rhodes.

Seeking out the best shore excursions

Rhodes and Lindos: Travel by bus through the scenic countryside to Lindos, a medieval walled city with a history that dates to ancient times. Walk or take a donkey up to the ancient Acropolis to see ruins and great views (you pass souvenir shops on the way). The trip may include a walking tour of old town Rhodes; a stop at a workshop selling Rhodian ceramics; and/or a visit to the ruins of ancient Rhodes, the Temple of Apollo, and Diagoras Stadium. (4 to 4½ hours; $49 to $65)

Lindos with lunch by the beach: Drive to Lindos and explore the city (see preceding section). Continue on to a secluded beach for some swimming and sunning. (Changing facilities, restrooms, and showers are available.) Also includes a brief city tour of Rhodes. The tour may stop at a ceramic workshop to observe the making of Rhodian ceramics. The tour includes lunch at a beachside restaurant. (8 hours; $79 to $109)

Exploring on your own

Ships dock at the commercial harbor, which is within walking distance of Rhodes's old section. The new town is also within walking distance, but the old town offers more sights of interest. The best way to explore either place is on foot. If you want to see other parts of the island, you can find taxis at the end of the pier. Negotiate fares with taxi drivers for sightseeing; the hourly rate is $32 to $45. Public buses are also available.

Within Walking Distance: The **old town of Rhodes** is the oldest medieval town in Europe and offers plenty of beauty, although be forewarned: You can easily get lost in the maze of streets (few of which have names). The 15th-century **Hospital of the Knights,** now home of the **Archaeological Museum,** features fine works from the Mycenaean and Roman eras. Admission is $3 for adults, $2 for students, and free for kids under 18. Stroll along the cobblestone **Street of the Knights** (called *Ippoton* on the maps) to see medieval inns that served as clubs and meeting places for the multinational Knights of St. John; their facades mirror the architecture of the various countries the knights came from.

Rhodes Town

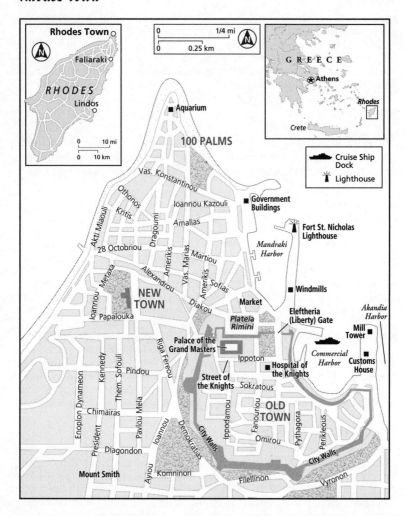

The famous **Colossus of Rhodes,** a 100-foot-tall bronze statue of the sun god Helios, considered one of the Seven Wonders of the Ancient World, was erected somewhere on **Mandraki Harbor** — legend says that it straddled the harbor. Nothing remains of the statue today.

You can find plenty of places to stop for a bite in old town and new town; seafood restaurants are your best bet. One of the best is **Alexis Taverna** (Odos Sokratous 18, in old town; ☎ **0241-29-347**; reservations recommended), where the likes of Winston Churchill and Jackie O once dined. Dinners run about $50 per person.

Beyond Walking Distance: In addition to its historical attractions, Rhodes is also known for its great beaches, many of which lie on the east coast. **Faliaraki,** about 20 minutes from Rhodes, is one of the most popular.

If you want to visit **Lindos,** you should book a shore excursion (Lindos is 50 minutes away from Rhodes, and the excursion guarantees that you get back in time).

Santoríni

Whitewashed homes, black-pebble beaches, rich vineyards, and ancient ruins dot one of the most breathtaking islands in the world: Santoríni. Approaching its volcanic cliffs by sea is a dramatic experience. Ships enter the *caldera,* a central crater formed when a volcano erupted in 1500 B.C. Ash fell on the remaining land, burying the ancient city of Akrotiri — an event that some believe may have sparked the legend of Atlantis.

Fira, the capital, perches about 1,000 feet above sea level. Along its winding streets, you find shops, cafes, and art galleries. **Ia,** about 10 to 15 minutes away by cab, is a quiet and picturesque artist colony.

Cruising into port

Celebrity, Costa, Crystal, Holland America, Princess, Royal Caribbean, SeaDream, Seven Seas, Silversea, Star Clippers, and Windstar all have ships that visit Santoríni.

Seeking out the best shore excursions

Akrotiri Excavations and Fira Town: This tour takes you to Akrotiri, an excavation site that dates back to the second millennium B.C. After the tour, you have time to explore Fira and make your own way back to the ship. (3 hours; $56 to $69)

Village of Ia and Winery: Walk on the picturesque narrow cobblestone streets of the small village of Ia, perched on a cliff. Stop at the **Boutari Winery** in the nearby village of Megalochoris for a tasting. The tour ends in Fira. (4 hours; $54)

Exploring on your own

The ship's tender takes you to the port of **Skala,** where you have three options to reach Fira: donkey, cable car, or foot. The donkey and cable car rides cost about $4 each way. The walk up the 587 steps is the same route the donkeys take. Word to the wise: Donkeys are fed at the bottom of the hill, so they tend to run down whether carrying someone or not. They also smell. Donkey rides take about 20 to 30 minutes depending on traffic and availability. Cable cars run every 20 minutes; walking takes about 30 minutes (depending on the individual).

Santoríni

You can easily explore the town of Fira on foot, and you can take taxis (not cheap and not always easy to find) or buses to other parts of the island. If you hike regularly, you may want to try the 6.2-mile pedestrian path from Fira to Ia that follows the edge of the caldera and offers stunning views. Along the way, you pass several churches and climb two substantial hills.

Within Walking Distance: Fira offers shops and art galleries. If your ship stays late enough in port, watch the sunset from a cafe for a classic Greek Isles experience. In addition, Fira has one of the best restaurants in Greece: **Selene,** located in the passageway between the **Atlantis** and **Aressana Hotels** (☎ **22860-22-249;** reservations suggested). Local produce is the star, with main courses ranging from $9 to $18. (The restaurant also offers cooking classes that start at 10:30 a.m. and conclude with lunch at 2 p.m.)

Beyond Walking Distance: Ia is quieter than Fira and offers charming homes and galleries that showcase modern and folk art and traditional handicrafts. To visit Ancient **Akrotiri,** located about five miles from Fira, we recommend that you take a shore excursion with a guide to get expert commentary.

 You want to explore the excavation at Akrotiri in the morning because its enclosing metal shed magnifies the afternoon heat.

Italy

If you ask ten people to name their favorite country in Europe, expect to hear at least eight say Italy — a beautiful and diverse country with an incredible cultural heritage. You can eat great food, talk to friendly people, shop for the latest fashions, see some of the ancient world's most famous ruins (such as the **Forum** in Rome and the ancient city of **Pompeii**), immerse yourself in the Renaissance in **Florence**, and be part of living history in **Venice**.

This is the land of Leonardo (da Vinci, not DiCaprio) and Michelangelo, of caesars, and of popes. And whether you feel drawn by the art, incredible architecture, religious significance, gorgeous scenery, wonderful pasta, or all of the above, Italy delivers your heart's desires.

The euro € is the official currency. At press time, US$1 = .83€. Italian is the official language, although many people speak English.

Civitavecchia and Rome

The name Civitavecchia probably has you shaking your head wondering *Civita-who?* But Civitavecchia has actually served as the port of Rome since A.D. 108. Cruise ships shuttle passengers from here to Rome, about an hour and a half away. Rome, of course, is Italy's largest city, where you find incomparable sights such as the **Vatican** and the **Forum**, as well as other cultural opportunities, diverse restaurants, and great shopping.

Cruising into port

Celebrity, Clipper, Costa, Crystal, Holland America, Oceania, Orient, Norwegian, Princess, Seabourn, SeaDream, Seven Seas, Silversea, Star Clippers, and Windstar all have ships that begin itineraries here (or specifically the nearby port of Civitavecchia). In addition, Celebrity, Cunard, Holland America, Princess, Royal Caribbean, Seabourn, Seven Seas, and Silversea all have ships that visit Rome (Civitavecchia) as a port of call.

Seeking out the best shore excursions

In addition to the following recommended excursion, most ships offer a bus transfer, for $56 to $69, allowing you easy transportation to explore Rome on your own. Some also offer the option of a half-day tour followed by a half-day on your own for $75 to $92.

Rome

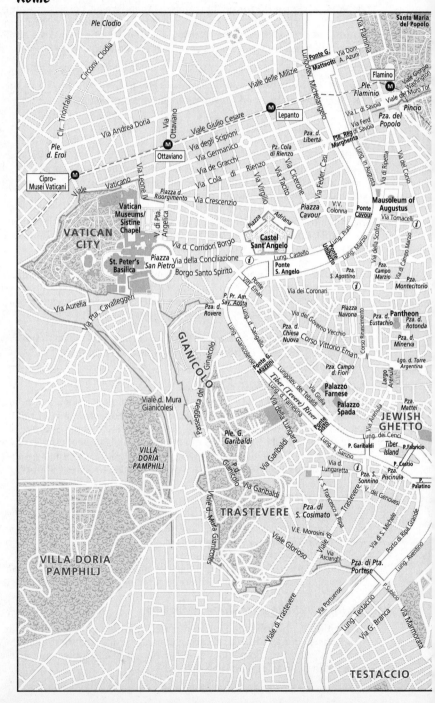

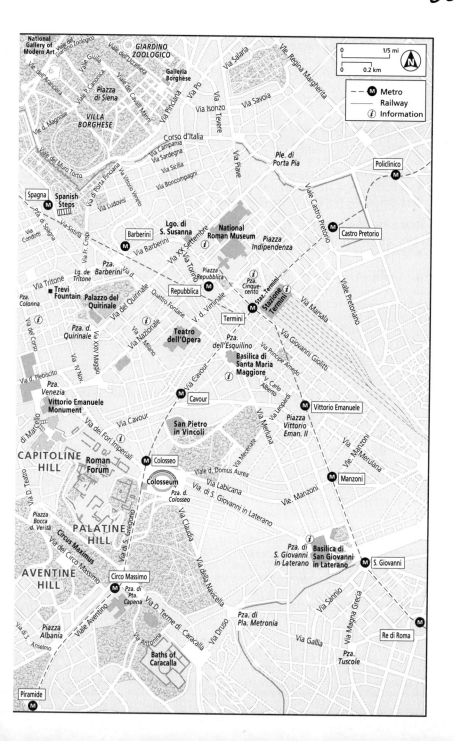

The comprehensive **Rome City Tour** includes a visit to the **Colosseum, St. Peter's Basilica**, the **Vatican Museum**, and the **Sistine Chapel**. The driver also passes such landmarks as the **Roman Forum, Trajan's Column**, the **Arch of Constantine**, and the **Circus Maximus**. The tour may also include a short walk to see **Trevi Fountain** and definitely includes lunch and time to shop for souvenirs. (9½ to 10½ hours; $135 to $182)

Exploring on your own

From the pier, you can take a 15-minute walk or 5-minute cab ride into the town of Civitavecchia. Taxis are usually available at the pier, and the ride to Rome is 90 minutes. A train service to Rome is also available. The train station is in town, and the ride takes about an hour (depending on the time of day, service is hourly or twice hourly).

Within Walking Distance: We highly recommend taking a shore excursion to Rome or going to Rome on your own because you can't see much in Civitavecchia.

Beyond Walking Distance: In Rome, the **Basilica di San Pietro** (St. Peter's Basilica), the earthly locus of the Roman Catholic Church, is amazing both inside and out and well worth a visit even if you're not Catholic. The church is magnificent and so is the square on which it stands. Admission is free to the basilica; stairs to the dome cost $4; an elevator to the dome is $4.50; and guided tours of St. Peter's Tomb (children under 15 aren't admitted) are about $8.

Women visiting the Vatican must wear pants or skirts that cover their knees. Men cannot wear shorts. No one is allowed to wear sleeveless tops.

American priests studying in Rome offer excellent, free tours of the Basilica. The tours last about two hours and are highly informative about the architecture and the religious significance of various parts of the area. Inquire at the Vatican Tourist Office (in the building to the left when you face the Basilica).

Nearby, the **Vatican Museum** and the **Sistine Chapel** are where the Vatican displays its gigantic collection of treasures. The museum is massive, so you need to choose a route based on four color-coded itineraries, which range from 1½ to 5 hours. All four itineraries culminate in the Sistine Chapel, where Michelangelo labored for four years (1509 to 1512) to paint the famous ceiling frescoes. Admission is normally $14.50 and free for everyone the last Sunday of each month (be ready for a crowd).

The best way to view the Sistine Chapel's ceiling is to bring along binoculars.

Rome boasts so many other must-see sights that choosing among them is hard, but you probably want to catch a glimpse of the **Roman Forum,** the **Colosseum,** and the **Pantheon.** A must-do stop for many is the **Trevi Fountain,** a lavish Baroque creation; according to legend, if you toss in a coin, you'll return to Rome (you may have to make your way through crowds to get close enough to drop your money, however). The famous **Spanish Steps** take their name from the Spanish Embassy, which used to be headquartered at the site. The steps are always packed with crowds of people browsing the carts of the flower and jewelry vendors or just people-watching. Shoppers also love the neighborhood, so check out the posh shops on **Via Borgognona** and **Via Condotti.** For a less-expensive alternative, head to **Via Sistina** and **Via Francesco Crispi.**

Venice

Built at the waterline, spectacular Venice rises straight out of the Gulf of Venice. Everywhere you look in this living museum you see something artistic or otherwise fascinating, including amazing numbers of Gothic and Renaissance structures and construction projects aimed at stopping buildings from sinking into the sea.

Be prepared to get lost exploring the city's maze of canals, side streets, and medieval bridges — scratching your head is part of the fun. But don't worry; you can't get too lost because yellow signs everywhere point you to major landmarks such as **St. Mark's Square** and the **Rialto Bridge.**

Getting out on the **Grand Canal,** a watery version of a main city boulevard, is a must-do, whether you take the touristy route of paying for a gondola (negotiate up front with the driver and expect to pay through the nose) or an equally overpriced water taxi. You can also do like the Venetians: ride a *vaporetto* (water bus). Any way you go, you pass historic buildings, ornate bridges, and waterfront palaces, and you share the waterway with ambulance boats, delivery barges, and other vessels reminding you that the canal is the byway for ordinary life in Venice — the city has no cars (or streets wide enough to drive on).

Venice also has a treasure trove of paintings, statues, and frescoes in its churches and palaces. Check out the cafes and shops, with their glassware and wonderful Italian design items (including designer clothes).

Cruising into port

Celebrity, Costa, Crystal, Holland America, Oceania, Orient, Princess, Seabourn, SeaDream, Seven Seas, Silversea, Star Clippers, and Windstar all have ships that begin their itineraries here. Crystal, Cunard, Seabourn, Seven Seas, and Silversea have ships that visit Venice as a port of call.

Searching out the best shore excursions

Venice City Sightseeing: Take a motor launch to St. Mark's Square for a guided walking tour of **St. Mark's Cathedral** and a visit to the **Doge's Palace,** the former residence of the Duke of Venice. The itinerary also includes the **Golden Staircase,** where you can enjoy the views of St. Mark's Basin. You also cross the famous **Bridge of Sighs** and stop at the small workshops of glass manufacturers. (3 hours; $50 to $99)

Venice

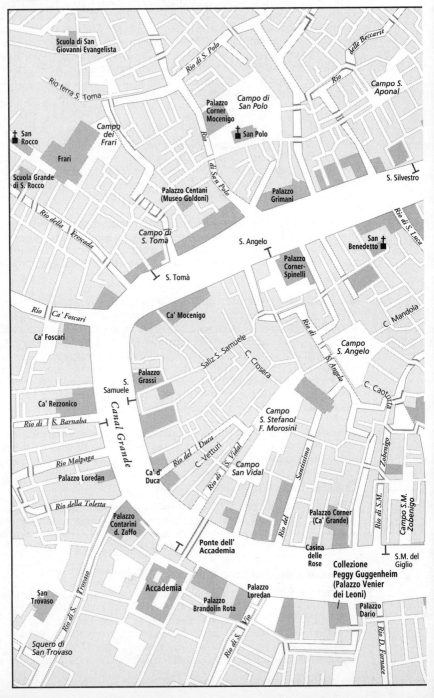

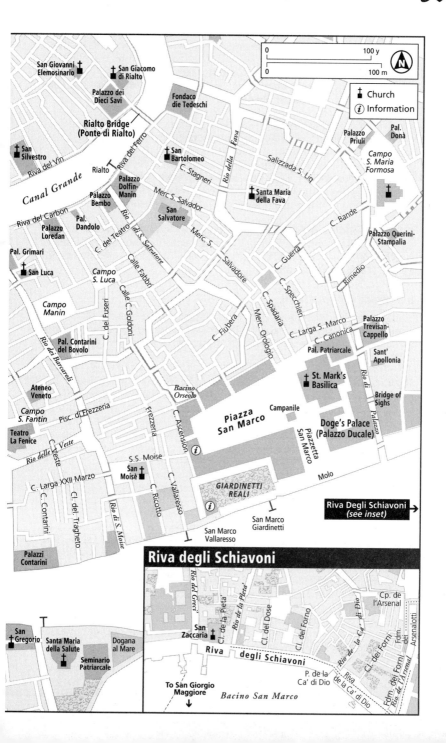

The Grand Canal and the Inside Canal: Travel by motorboat with a guide and 10 to 12 other people and see the way the city works — the police, fire brigade, even wedding and funeral processions travel by boat. From the water, you get a wonderful view of St. Mark's Square and other sights, including palaces and the **Guggenheim Museum.** You also go under the famous **Rialto Bridge.** (2½ hours; $83 to $118)

The Historic Jewish Ghetto: In the 16th century, the Jews of Venice were restricted to the Ghetto unless they were doctors. They had to wear distinctive clothing and couldn't own land. The Ghetto has been preserved and offers a fascinating glimpse of what life was like for the people who lived there and of the modern Jewish culture in Venice (several synagogues in the Ghetto still have active congregations). You take a motor launch to the entrance and tour on foot. (3½ hours; $59 to $72)

Evening Gondola Ride with Serenade: It may sound hokey, but we think you'll find something magical about exploring the canals of this romantic city on these black pointy vessels, with a gondolier singing in Italian. (2 hours, $87 to $89)

Exploring on your own

Ships generally dock about 15 to 20 minutes by boat from St. Mark's Square. Travel is on the water by the vessel of your choice: on the ship's arranged boats, a water taxi (which is pricey), or the public water buses called *vaporetti* (which are cheap).

Within Walking Distance: Take a boat to **St. Mark's Square.** From there, you can walk to the rest of the attractions that we list here. The square itself is the cultural hub of the city, and you can easily spend hours here watching people feed the pigeons, sitting with the fashionable in a cafe, visiting the **Basilica** and the **Doge's Palace,** and shopping. As a tourist hub, however, the square is very crowded during the day, particularly in the summer high season. To avoid the crowds, go in the early morning or in the evening. At night, you may catch free musical performances by chamber orchestras and other groups.

St. Mark's Basilica, located on the square, is nicknamed the "Church of Gold" and is one of the most elaborate churches in the world. You can see the Basilica's dome as your ship moves down the Grand Canal. The **Marciano Museum** contains the Triumphal Quadriga — four famous horse statues looted from Constantinople by Venetian crusaders in 1204. Admission to the Basilica is free, treasury $2.30, presbytery $1.75, and Marciano Museum $1.75.

Men and women are banned from wearing shorts or exposing bare arms or shoulders in the Basilica, and women may not wear skirts above the knee. Silence is required, and no photos are allowed.

For $6.90 for adults and $3.45 for students, you can climb to the top of the bell tower of St. Mark's, and you don't even have to brave a dark, steep, winding staircase to do it — just hop in the elevator. From the top you can get a bird's-eye view of the city and a nice view of the basilica's cupolas. Nearby, **Palazzo Ducale** (Doge's Palace) is Italy's grandest civic structure. Admission is $11 for adults, $5.90 for students, $3.55 for children 6 to 13, and free for kids under 5.

You can shop right on the square and on the streets between the square and the Rialto Bridge. A favorite shopping street is Salizzida San Moisé, where you find designer shops such as Prada. Generally, the farther away from St. Mark's you go, the more reasonable the prices.

Beyond Walking Distance: A must-see attraction for lovers of modern art is the **Collezione Peggy Guggenheim,** located in a waterfront palazzo on the other side of the canal from St. Mark's (you can get there by water taxi or water bus, or take a long walk, crossing at the Ponte dell' Accademia bridge). The impressive palazzo, which was art patron Mrs. Guggenheim's home, houses works by Pollock, Ernst, Picasso, Braque, Magritte, Duchamp, Chagall, Mondrian, Brancusi, Dalí, Giacometti, Moore, and others. Admission is $9.20 for adults and $5.75 for students and children 16 and under.

Nearer the Ponte dell' Accademia bridge is the **Galleria dell'Accademia,** a museum where the glory of old Venice lives on in a remarkable collection of paintings from the 14th to the 18th centuries. Admission is $7 for adults, $3.50 for students, and free for children 12 and under.

Portugal

First off, we know Portugal isn't on the Mediterranean. Even so, the country's capital city, **Lisbon,** is the starting point for some Mediterranean itineraries.

Although Lisbon is Europe's smallest capital, it still gives the impression of a cosmopolitan city, boasting seven hills and a pleasing combination of history, cultural arts, modern amenities, and visual treats. Some areas may remind visitors of Paris (with street painters and the like), others of hilly San Francisco, and still others — such as the old Moorish Alfama section — of life in a small, colorful town. Lisbon is a walking city, and you can easily get around, although the hills may prove challenging to some.

The euro € is the official currency: At press time, US$1 = .83€. Portuguese is the official language, but many young people may also speak Spanish, English, and/or German.

Cruising into port

Clipper, Crystal, Holland America, Oceania, Seabourn, Silversea, and Windstar all have ships on itineraries that begin in Lisbon. In addition, Costa, Crystal, Cunard, Holland America, Lindblad, Norwegian, Orient, SeaDream, and Seven Seas all have ships that visit as a port of call.

Lisbon

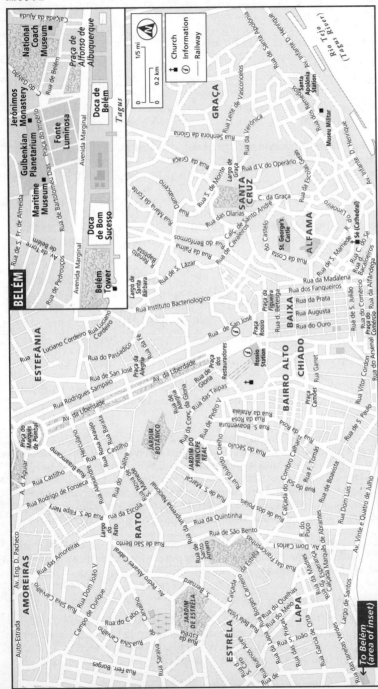

Seeking out the best shore excursions

Lisbon City Tour: Ride by bus around Lisbon to see a number of city highlights, including **Avenida da Liberdade,** with its mosaic-lined sidewalks and the magnificent views of the River Tagus at **Black Horse Square.** Tour the impressive **Jerónimos Monastery.** Also visit the **National Coach Museum** or the **Convent of Madre de Deus,** founded in 1509, which contains samples of religious architecture. (3½ hours; $44 to $61)

Sintra and Estoril: This tour along the famous and scenic Estoril coast includes such memorable highlights as **Sintra** — a serene historic resort nestled in the forested hills of Serra de Sintra and the summer residence of kings and nobility. Continue inland to **Queluz** to tour the magnificent 18th-century palace built in the style of Versailles. Some tours also include the well-known seaside resort of **Cascais.** (4 hours; $44 to $64)

Fatima and Batalha: Located 100 miles from Lisbon is the place known to Roman Catholics as the "Lourdes of Portugal." Here, at Fatima, according to legend, three young shepherds in 1917 claimed they saw the Virgin Mary in an oak tree. Lunch is served at a local restaurant or hotel. Afterwards, you continue on to Batalha for a visit to the impressive gothic church of **Santa Maria da Victoria.** (8 to 9 hours; $72 to $129)

Exploring on your own

Cruise ships dock at the Port of Lisbon, about 15 minutes by car from the city center. Taxis (usually diesel-engine Mercedes) are generally available outside the terminal building. The ride to the central sightseeing and shopping districts is between $7 and $11. Traffic can be congested, so give yourself extra time. The city also has a good bus and tram service, as well as a subway, to get around. A *funicular* (elevator) connects the **Baixa** area, where you find shopping (between the Rossio, which is the city's main square, and the River Tagus), with the **Bairro Alto,** where you find nightlife.

Within Walking Distance: You need to take a taxi to the Alfama, the Belém area, and other sights.

Beyond Walking Distance: Houses in the alleys of the old **Alfama** district are so close together that you can't stretch your arms fully in some places. Visit the 12th-century **Sé** (cathedral), check out the goods at the markets, and climb up to the **Castelo São Jorge** (St. George's Castle) to enjoy the views. The fortress predates the Romans, and the Moors erected many of the walls that still stand. On the grounds, you may encounter a swan or rare white peacock. Admission is free.

Belém, where the River Tagus meets the sea, is where Portuguese explorers such as Magellan launched their missions. **Belém Tower** is a 16th-century monument to Portugal's age of discovery and its famous seafarers. Admission is $3.45 for adults, $1.40 for children, and free for seniors. Nearby **Jerónimos Monastery,** built in 1502, stands as a masterpiece of

Manueline architecture. Admission to the church is free; admission to the secluded monastery is $3.45 adults, $1.40 students, and free for children and seniors. The **Maritime Museum,** located in the Jerónimos Monastery's west wing, is one of the most important of its kind in Europe. It contains hundreds of ship models, ranging from 15th-century sailing ships to 20th-century warships. Admission is $3.45 for adults, $1.75 for students, and free for seniors and children under 9.

Spain

Spain offers fascinating history, pretty beaches, Moorish palaces, quaint villages, and, of course, Picasso. But you also feel the beat of the country's modern-day vitality. Spain began to change with the death of Generalissimo Francisco Franco and the country's entry into the European Union; today the nation is undergoing a cultural renaissance. Visitors delight in the energy of newly prosperous cities such as **Barcelona.**

The official currency is the euro €: At press time, US$1 = .83€. You hear Spanish and Catalan spoken in Barcelona. Many young people also speak English and German.

The Romans developed Barcelona as a port, and it has long been a Mediterranean center of commerce. More recently, cruise lines, attracted by the city's prime location on the Iberian Peninsula, rediscovered its historical, cultural, and artistic treasures.

Once home to artists such as Picasso, Miró, Dalí, and Casals, Barcelona is renowned for its architecture, which mixes ancient Roman ruins and buildings from the 13th and 15th centuries with startlingly modern creations by Antoni Gaudí and I. M. Pei. You can find great museums, friendly people, pleasant cafes, and a very active nightlife. And Barcelona even has sandy beaches thanks to a recently reclaimed waterfront.

Cruising into port

Celebrity, Crystal, Oceania, Orient, Princess, Royal Caribbean, Seabourn, SeaDream, Seven Seas, Silversea, and Windstar all have ships that begin their itineraries here. In addition, Clipper, Costa, Crystal, Cunard, Holland America, Norwegian, Orient, Seabourn, SeaDream, Seven Seas, and Silversea have ships that visit as a port of call.

Seeking out the best shore excursions

City Highlights: This bus and walking tour includes the **Gothic Quarter,** a stop at **Montjuïc** for the views, the Olympic Stadium, **Gaudí's La Sagrada Familia, Les Ramblas,** and **Catalunya Square.** (3½ to 4 hours; $32 to $53)

Museums Tour: This tour visits the **Picasso Museum** and may include a drive to Montjuïc for the impressive views, the **Miró Foundation Museum,** and/or a drive past buildings created by Antoni Gaudí. (3½ to 4 hours; $48 to $62)

Pilgrimage to Montserrat: This trip heads 36 miles north of Barcelona to the sacred **Mountain of Montserrat,** one of Spain's natural wonders. Standing about halfway up the mountain, the Montserrat Monastery is famous for its shrine of the Virgin Mary, Our Lady of Montserrat. After you return to Barcelona, enjoy a brief tour of the city before you return to the ship. Lunch is included in the longer tours (5 to 7hours; $69 to $126)

Exploring on your own

We recommend taking a cab or the cruise line's shuttle service. **La Rambla** (the Rambles) — the place to be in Barcelona — is about 1 to 2 miles from the pier, depending on where your ship docks.

Taxis are available outside the terminal. The rate begins at $2.40, with a charge of about $1 per kilometer and an extra charge if the taxi goes into the pier area. The city also has a good Metro and bus system. During the summer, **Bus Turistic** operates, passing a dozen of the most popular sights. You can get on and off as you please, or you can ride the **Tibidabo funicular** and the **Montjuïc cable car and funicular** (both for panoramic city views) for the price of a single ticket (about $15 per day). Purchase tickets on the bus or at the transportation booth at Placa de Catalunya.

Within Walking Distance: Although the pier is within walking distance of the Barri Gótic or La Rambla — both good starting points for a walk — we recommend that you get a taxi or take the cruise line's shuttle to get there. Upon arrival you can easily reach many interesting sights on foot.

Beyond Walking Distance: In the **Barri Gótic** (Gothic Quarter), you can wander for hours — getting lost is part of the fun. Stop in at the **Gothic Cathedral de Barcelona** (admission to the church is free; the museum costs $1.20) and saunter the cobblestone streets past fountains, vintage stores, and cafes. Stroll **La Rambla** (the Rambles), which Victor Hugo called "the most beautiful street in the world." A tree-lined boulevard, the street runs from Placa de Catalunya to the sea and bustles with 24-hour performers, flower vendors, birds in cages, cafes, and shops.

Check the views from the **Montjuïc** or **Tibidabo** mountain parks, both of which you can access by funicular. Two Gothic palaces house the **Museu Picasso,** which boasts an impressive collection of the artist's work. Pablo Picasso himself donated some 2,500 of his paintings to the collection, including a piece he painted at the age of 9. Admission is $5.75 for adults, $2.85 for students, and free for kids 12 and under. A must-do is a glimpse at the fantastical work of Antoni Gaudí. The designer's creations in Barcelona include **La Sagrada Familia** (Church of the Holy Family), a truly bizarre architectural wonder. Admission is $6.90 for adults, $4.60 for students and seniors, and free for kids under 9.

Barcelona

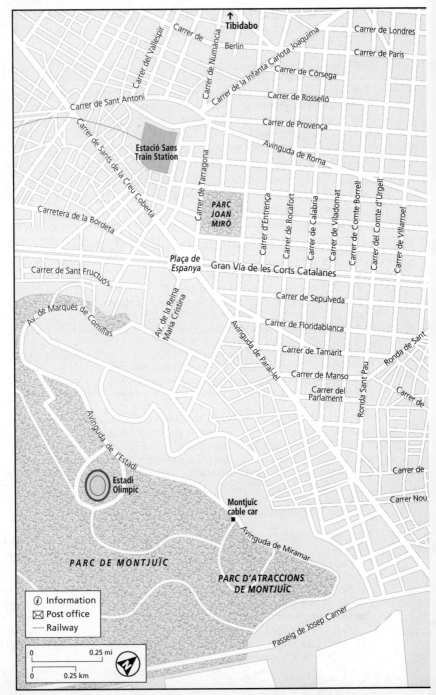

Carrer de Londres
Carrer de Paris
Carrer de
Tibidabo
Berlin
Carrer del Vallespir
Carrer de Numància
Carrer de la Infanta Carlota Joaquima
Carrer de Còrsega
Carrer de Sant Antoni
Carrer de Rosselló
Carrer de Sants de la Creu Coberta
Carrer de Provença
Avinguda de Roma
Estació Sans Train Station
Carrer de Tarragona
Carretera de la Bordeta
PARC JOAN MIRÓ
Carrer d'Entrença
Carrer de Rocafort
Carrer de Calàbria
Carrer de Viladomat
Carrer de Comte Borrell
Carrer del Comte d'Urgell
Carrer de Villarroel
Plaça de Espanya
Gran Vía de les Corts Catalanes
Carrer de Sant Fructuós
Av. de Marqués de Comillas
Av. de la Reina Maria Cristina
Carrer de Sepulveda
Carrer de Floridablanca
Avinguda de Paral·lel
Carrer de Tamarit
Ronda de Sant
Carrer de Manso
Ronda Sant Pau
Carrer de
Carrer del Parlament
Avinguda de l'Estadi
Estadi Olímpic
Carrer de
Montjuïc cable car
Carrer Nou
Avinguda de Miramar
PARC DE MONTJUÏC
PARC D'ATRACCIONS DE MONTJUÏC

ⓘ Information
⊠ Post office
— Railway

0   0.25 mi
0   0.25 km

Passeig de Josep Carner

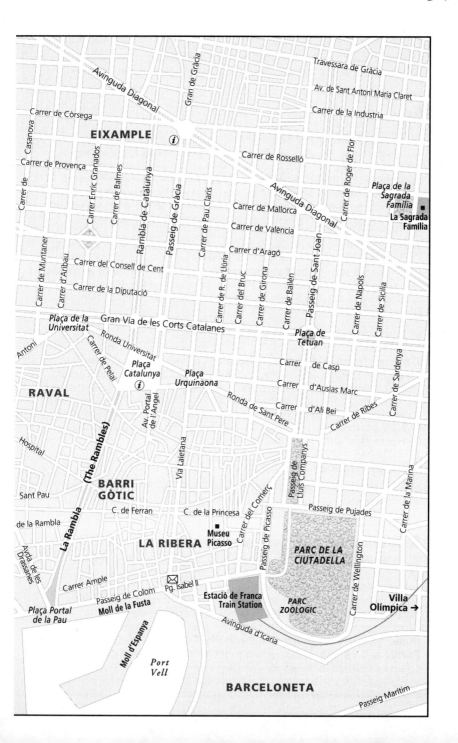

Watch out for pickpockets in the Barri Gótic at night.

Shoppers delight in the offerings on **Passeig de Gràcia,** the main shopping street, as well as on streets in the old quarter (including the Rambles).

Turkey

Turkey is literally where East meets West (Istanbul sits where Europe and Asia touch). Very likely, this imaginary gateway is the most exotic country you can visit on a Mediterranean cruise — a land of mosques and minarets, sultans' treasures, crowded bazaars, Greek and Roman archaeological sites, and holy Christian landmarks. Although its cities teem with the energy of a modern nation looking to the West, its villages remain much as they've been for the past several hundred years.

The Turkish lira is the official currency: At press time, US$1 = 1,335,000 Turkish lire. Because of the wide fluctuation of Turkish currency, only exchange the amount that you intend to spend. The rug shops and some other vendors often deal in U.S. dollars. Turkish and Kurdish are the official languages, although you commonly hear English, French, and German spoken as well.

Istanbul

The city where the continents of Asia and Europe meet is chaotic, congested, fascinating, and exciting. Cars careen (literally) past museums, churches, palaces, grand mosques, and other historic monuments that reveal a rich and ancient history. Among the many treats for your senses are the smells of a spice market, the sound of prayer, the taste of traditional Turkish dishes, the feel of a Turkish carpet, and the treasures left by rulers past.

Cruising into port

Crystal, Seabourn, SeaDream, Seven Seas, Silversea, Star Clippers, and Windstar all have ships that begin their itineraries here. Celebrity, Costa, Orient, Princess, and Seabourn also have ships that visit as a port of call.

Seeking out the best shore excursions

The **Highlights of Istanbul** tour typically includes the **Hippodrome,** once the largest chariot race grounds of the Byzantine Empire; the **Sultan Ahmet Mosque,** also known as the Blue Mosque for its 21,000 blue Iznik tiles; the famous **St. Sophia,** once the largest church of the Christian world; and **Topkapi Palace,** the official residence of the Ottoman Sultans and home to treasures that include **Spoonmaker's Diamond,** one of the biggest in the world. The tour also visits the **Grand Bazaar** and its 4,000 shops. Some tours bring you back to the ship for lunch and others include lunch in a first-class restaurant. You can also take shorter tours that include some of the features of the full tour. (7 to 9 hours; $89 to $109)

Old Istanbul

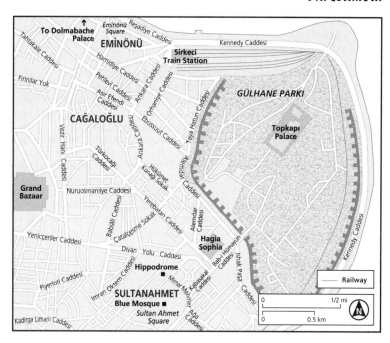

To Dolmabache Palace

Eminönü Square

Reşadiye Caddesi

Tahtakale Caddesi

EMİNÖNÜ

Kennedy Caddesi

Sirkeci Train Station

Hamidiye Caddesi

Pehlevi Caddesi

Firinilar Yok

Asir Efendi Caddesi

Ankara Caddesi

Orhaniye Caddesi

GÜLHANE PARKI

CAĞALOĞLU

Ebussuut Caddesi

Taya Hatun Caddesi

Topkapı Palace

Vezir Hanı Caddesi

Türkocağı Caddesi

Ankara Caddesi

Hükümet Konağı Sokak

Alemdar Caddesi

Grand Bazaar

Nuruosmaniiye Caddesi

Babıali Caddesi

Yerebatan Caddesi

Çatalçeşme Sokak

Alemdar Caddesi

Kennedy Caddesi

Yeniçeriler Caddesi

Divan Yolu Caddesi

Hagia Sophia

Babı Hümayun Caddesi

Ishak Paşa Caddesi

Hippodrome

Piyerloti Caddesi

Imran Oktem Caddesi

Mimar Mehmet Ağa Caddesi

Kabaskal Caddesi

Railway

SULTANAHMET

Blue Mosque ■

Kadirga Limani Caddesi

Sultan Ahmet Square

0   1/2 mi

0   0.5 km

Exploring on your own

Ships drop anchor on the **Bosporus** (the strait between the Black Sea and the Sea of Marmara) on the European side of the city. Taxis are relatively inexpensive and wait at the pier (you can also find plenty throughout the city). The starting rate is about $1, and the drivers apply a surcharge after midnight. You can check out the bus and tram service; cruise lines usually provide shuttle buses to downtown (they typically drop you off outside the expensive rug shops, within walking distance of the **Blue Mosque**). The best way to explore the old section is on foot.

Within Walking Distance: It takes a healthy walk to get from the pier to the Blue Mosque, so with all the crazy drivers in this city and the generally hectic pace, your best bet is to take the cruise line's shuttle or a cab.

After your vehicle service drops you off, visit the **Ahmet Mosque,** built in the 17th century; admission is free. It features dazzling blue and white Iznik tiles and six minarets. Guests must remove their shoes at the entrance. The park in front of the Blue Mosque, the **Hippodrome,** once held great chariot races. Nearby is **Hagia Sophia,** the sixth-century basilica famous for its gigantic domes and magnificent mosaics. Historians regard the church as one of the best examples of Byzantine architecture. Admission to Hagia Sophia is $6.

From the 15th century to the mid-19th century, **Topkapi Palace,** located at Kennedy Cad. Sultanahment, served as the residence of sultans. The complex includes the chamber of the Sacred Mantle, harem quarters, crown jewels, holy relics, and the throne room. Admission is $6; the guided harem tour costs $3.

The **Grand Bazaar** (Kapalı Çarşascdısı), with your best bet for entrance at the Beyazit Gate or the Nuruosmaniye Gate, is the world's largest covered market. More than 4,000 vendors sell carpets, leather goods, jewelry, antique reproductions, and other items. You can buy maps of the Bazaar at newsstands for $5. The setting is a trip in itself, even if you don't buy anything. If you want to buy, make sure you bargain.

Beyond Walking Distance: The **Dolmabache Palace,** Dolmabache Cad., is sometimes called the Ottoman Versailles. The extravagance includes a 4-ton Baccarat chandelier that was a gift from Queen Victoria. Admission is $7 for a long tour (including the Sultan's Quarters and Harem) or $4 for a short tour (of one room or the other). You must pay a fee of $7 to use your video camera.

Kuşadasi

A favorite port for travelers interested in history, the once sleepy little village of Kuşadasi is now a bustling seaside resort. The reason? Its proximity to **Ephesus,** one of the most fascinating and best-preserved ancient historical sites in the world, as well as other major early Christian and historical locales. If the past isn't your bag, you can stay in town and shop (the best place in Turkey to bargain for Turkish rugs) or go to one of the excellent nearby beaches for a swim.

Cruising into port

Celebrity, Costa, Crystal, Holland America, Orient, Princess, Royal Caribbean, Seabourn, SeaDream, Seven Seas, Silversea, Star Clippers, and Windstar all have ships that visit Kuşadasi.

Seeking out the best shore excursions

Ephesus: One of the world's best-preserved ancient cities. Your guide leads you down marble streets to the remains of the Baths, the theater, and the incredible library building. Along the way, you pass columns, mosaics, monuments, and ruins. The tour may include a stop at a rug shop. (3 to 4 hours; $40 to $44)

Ephesus and The House of The Virgin Mary: This tour combines a visit to Ephesus with a trip to the House of the Virgin Mary, a humble chapel located in the valley of **Bulbuldagi** on the spot where historians believe the Virgin Mary spent her last days. The site was officially sanctioned for pilgrimage in 1892. (3½ to 4½ hours; $44 to $52)

Ephesus, St. John's Basilica, and House of the Virgin Mary: This tour combines the two preceding tours with a visit to St. John's Basilica,

Kuşdadasi/Ephesus Region

another holy pilgrimage site. Historians believe that St. John wrote the fourth book of the New Testament at this site (4½ hours; $56). Tour operators may also offer the tour as a full-day excursion, including lunch in a local restaurant and a visit to the museum of Ephesus. (7½ hours; $72 to $98)

Three Ancient Cities: This tour takes in the ruins of the region, including Priene, known for its **Athena Temple** (bankrolled by Alexander the Great); Didyma, known for the **Temple of Apollo;** and Miletus, which includes a stadium the Greeks built and the Romans expanded to hold 15,000 spectators. A light lunch is included. (6 to 8 hours; $68 to $89)

Exploring on your own

Ships dock right downtown. Stores and restaurants are within walking distance of the harbor. Minibuses (available from the town center) and taxis (yellow and metered) can get you to the beach.

Within Walking Distance: You can find plenty of places to shop and haggle.

Vendors generally bump up prices when cruise ships are in port, and they expect you to bargain. Shopkeepers often offer you tea or soft drinks as negotiations get underway as part of Turkish hospitality; accepting their hospitality in no way obligates you to buy.

Beyond Walking Distance: Book a shore excursion to tour Ephesus or the other historic sites to get the most out of your visit. Law requires Turkish guides to be licensed, so you can expect guides who are quite knowledgeable about their subject matter.

Kadinlar Denizi is Kuşadasi's most popular beach, located about five miles from the port. Also known as *Ladies Beach,* the small stretch attracts a large crowd, including women who like to sunbathe topless and macho posers.

Kuşadasi isn't known for culinary artistry. Still, if you want to try the local cuisine, check out the restaurants along the harbor that specialize in the catch of the day.

Chapter 21

Exploring Other Destinations

In This Chapter

▶ Strolling on North American rivers and lakes
▶ Cruising to Canada and New England
▶ Taking cruises to Bermuda
▶ Enjoying South and Central America
▶ Finding your way to Hawaii and Tahiti
▶ Experiencing transatlantic and Northern European cruises
▶ Discovering European river cruises
▶ Going to the extreme: Cruises to Antarctica

*H*ave a yen to sail off the beaten path? Although the Caribbean, Alaska, and the Mediterranean are the most traveled cruise routes, they by no means represent your only choices. In this chapter, we talk about other cruise destinations. We include listings of which cruise lines sail in these regions, and you can cross-reference these with the ship-review chapters (14, 15, and 16) to find out more about the lines. In instances where the lines didn't make the cruise-review chapters — because they don't operate in any big way in the Caribbean, Alaska, or the Mediterranean — we include a phone number that you can call for more information.

The American South and Midwest

Mark Twain discovered America's heartland while traveling down the Mississippi River, which he described as "the great Mississippi, the majestic, the magnificent Mississippi, rolling its mile-wide tide along, shining in the sun." You can explore the America that so enticed the writer by traveling down the very same river and in the very same way as Twain: aboard a real paddlewheel steamboat.

The **Delta Queen Steamboat Company** operates paddlewheelers on the Mississippi and other major rivers, including the Ohio. Offered year-round, the mostly weeklong cruises take passengers past quaint towns and stately mansions to Civil War sites, plantations, and other historic places. Cruises depart from cities including New Orleans, Memphis, St. Louis, Cincinnati, and Nashville (☎ 800-543-1949; www.deltaqueen.com).

RiverBarge Excursion Lines (☎ 888-GO-BARGE; www.riverbarge.com) also operates year-round river cruises on waterways including the Mississippi, Cumberland, Ohio, and Missouri. The company offers 4- to 10-day cruises on a unique vessel that combines two hotel barges propelled by a tugboat.

American Cruise Lines (☎ 800-814-6880; www.americancruiselines.com), based in Haddam, Connecticut, operates two small ships on weeklong itineraries that include Chesapeake Bay, the St. Johns and Tolomato rivers in Florida, and the Intracoastal Waterway (between Charleston, South Carolina, and Jacksonville, Florida). The line also offers New England cruises (see "New England and Canada," later in this chapter).

If you want to feel like you're sailing the ocean without being on the ocean, you can also cruise on the Great Lakes with American Canadian Caribbean and Clipper Cruises. The Traverse City, Michigan-based **Traverse Tall Ship Company** (☎ 800-678-0383; www.tallshipsailing.com) also offers sailings on Lake Michigan and Lake Huron aboard Windjammer sailing ships (refer to Chapter 16 for more info on Clipper and Windjammer).

The Columbia and Snake Rivers

So, reading *Undaunted Courage* by Stephen Ambrose sparked an ambition to copy Lewis and Clark? You're in luck — several cruise lines tread the Columbia and Snake Rivers in the U.S. northwest. As the second-largest river in the United States (only the Mississippi is bigger), the Columbia River winds between the Cascade Mountains and past the Columbia River Gorge's waterfalls and lush forests. Cruises depart from Portland and follow the Columbia River east between Oregon and Washington, sometimes going as far east as Idaho. Visits can include the **Bonneville Dam**, **Hood River** (the windsurfing capital of the world), **Hell's Canyon**, and the historic towns of the **Oregon Trail.**

American West Steamboat Company offers cruises that depart from Portland year-round. Cruise West, Lindblad Expeditions, and American Safari (see Chapter 16 for more on these lines) also offer small-ship Columbia and Snake River cruises in the spring and fall.

New England and Canada

Maybe because Fran lives in New England, she loves cruising this region, but even non-New Englanders can appreciate the quaint, often un-touristy towns and the striking natural beauty of the northeastern Atlantic coast. We highly recommend taking a fall cruise and feasting your eyes on the turning foliage. Attractions on the 7- to 14-day cruises typically include stops in Boston, with its historic Freedom Trail; Newport, Rhode Island, with its gorgeous mansions; Bar Harbor, Maine, with its splendid hiking trails and scenic vistas; the trendy and picturesque island of Martha's Vineyard, Massachusetts, where notables (including the Clintons) have been known to summer; the Canadian coastal provinces of Nova Scotia, New Brunswick, and Newfoundland; and Quebec City or Montreal, two historic Canadian cities in bilingual Quebec. Shorter cruises out of New York City, such as Carnival's, may make just a stop or two in the Canadian provinces.

Cruises generally depart from New York or Boston and travel northward, but you can also board in Montreal or Quebec City and sail south. Some smaller ships sail in Canada's St. Lawrence and Saguenay rivers, or up the coast to Labrador.

American Canadian Caribbean, American Cruise Lines, Carnival, Celebrity, Clipper, Crystal, Cunard, Holland America, Norwegian, Princess, Royal Caribbean, Seabourn, Seven Seas, and Silversea all have ships on New England itineraries.

For a totally different New England experience, you can take a rustic, fun cruise vacation onboard a schooner. A fleet of tall ships based in Rockland or Camden, Maine, sail from May to October in Maine's scenic Penobscot Bay, with itineraries depending on the weather. The fleet of schooners includes the historic *Stephen Tabor* (☎ 800-999-7352) and *Victory Chimes* (☎ 800-745-5651), and other members of the Maine Windjammer Association (☎ 800-807-WIND; www.sailmainecoast. com).

Bermuda

Cruises to Bermuda, a self-governing British colony in the Atlantic Ocean, usually combine several relaxing and fun-filled days at sea with several relaxing and fun-filled days on the island. You can spend your island time exploring by the preferred and fabulously fun means of transport — mopeds or scooters (rental cars are banned here) — and enjoy activities such as golf, tennis, horseback riding, beach-sitting on the island's famous pink-sand shores, snorkeling, scuba diving, glass-bottom boat tours, visiting museums and historic homes, and enjoying very proper High Tea. Opportunities abound for shopping, too, especially for British goods such as wool sweaters and Wedgwood china — and don't forget the lively pub scene.

Bermuda's ports of call are Hamilton, King's Wharf, and St. George's.

Celebrity, Norwegian, Royal Caribbean, and Seven Seas have ships that sail Bermuda routes weekly, from late April to October, with most of the cruises departing from New York (or in Royal Caribbean's case, New Jersey) or Boston on Saturday or Sunday. Norwegian also has Bermuda cruises from Philadelphia and Baltimore, and Celebrity has Bermuda cruises from Philadelphia and Norfolk. Cunard, Princess, Seaborn, and Silversea also visit Bermuda as part of transatlantic crossings or in combination with coastal Atlantic itineraries.

Costa Rica

Most cruises to Costa Rica ("rich coast" in Spanish) explore this Central American country's wildlife areas, offering tours of beaches, rain forests, and mountains. Highlights include the indigenous plant and animal life, including thousands of varieties of butterflies. In addition to the numerous national parks, you can visit historic sites and ruins.

Costa Rican ports of call include Bahia Herradura, Cano Island, Corcovado National Park, Curu, Golfito, Golfo Dulce, Manuel Antonio Park, Marenco Reserve, Playa Flamingo, Puerto Caldera, Puerto Limón, Puntarenas, Quepos, and Tortuga.

Cruise West operates 8-day cruises in Costa Rica year-round (except in the September to October hurricane season). Most are on the country's Pacific coast, with stops including Corcovado and other national parks and remote wildlife habitats. The line also offers longer sailings that combine Costa Rica with a trip through the Panama Canal (see the next section).

Lindblad Expeditions operates 10-day Costa Rican and Panama Canal cruises (including three hotel nights) in the winter, summer, and fall, and also offers special weeklong family cruises in the summer.

American Safari has a yacht in Costa Rica for part of the winter season that sails from Los Suenos. And Clipper does 8-day Costa Rican/Panama Canal cruises (including a hotel night in San Jose) in March and December.

Also cruising from Costa Rican ports (but on an occasional basis) are Crystal, Oceania, Seabourn, Seven Seas, and Silversea. Celebrity, Crystal, Holland America, Norwegian, Orient, Princess, Royal Caribbean, Seabourn, and Seven Seas all have ships that visit Costa Rica as part of Caribbean, Panama Canal, or Central American itineraries, stopping at Puerto Caldera or Puntarenas on the Pacific coast or Puerto Limón on the Caribbean coast.

The Panama Canal

Ships pass through this eighth wonder of the world as part of one-way repositioning cruises in the late fall and early spring as the cruise lines move their vessels from the Alaskan market to the Caribbean market and vice versa. Some lines also include the Panama Canal as part of longer Caribbean, Central American, and South American itineraries in the winter. The reasons are both practical and scenic. Use of the canal trims some 8,000 nautical miles off a trip from, say, New York to San Francisco, because without the continental passageway ships must go south around Cape Horn, the tip of South America.

Traversing the 51-mile canal takes just nine hours and provides a unique and fascinating experience. The water level lifts and lowers your ship 85 feet through a series of locks, gates, and dams.

Panama Canal cruises can include stops at Central American ports such as Cartagena, Colombia; Puerto Caldera, Puerto Limón, and Puntarenas (all in Costa Rica); and Panama's San Blas Islands — home of the Cuna Indians, who are known for their colorful needlework. The cruises may also stop in the Caribbean or Mexican Riviera. Itineraries often last ten days or more.

Cruise lines that make full or partial Panama Canal crossings include American Canadian Caribbean, Carnival, Celebrity, Clipper, Crystal, Cruise West, Cunard, Holland America, Lindblad, Norwegian, Orient, Princess, Royal Caribbean, Seabourn, Seven Seas, and Silversea.

The Mexican Riviera

With its scenic beauty and emphasis on fun in the sun, the west coast of Mexico, known as the Mexican Riviera, offers great cruising. Many of the area's historical features are hidden behind souvenir stands and fast-food restaurants — not that most folks visit for the history anyway. Instead, the glorious beaches are the main attraction, and the accessibility of golf, tennis, deep-sea fishing, and water sports contributes to the something-for-everyone appeal. Three- to seven-day cruises leave year-round from Los Angeles, Long Beach, or San Diego. Cruises of up to 11 days depart in the winter and fall from San Diego. Ships sail the Pacific Ocean, and longer cruises usually include a stop in Acapulco. Some lines also visit the region as part of longer itineraries that include the Panama Canal.

Weeklong cruises usually stop at Cabo San Lucas at the southern tip of Baja California, where you may spot sea lions and gray whales. Mazatlán and Puerto Vallarta are other popular ports of call. Shorter cruises may call at Catalina Island and Ensenada, both in Baja.

Carnival, Celebrity, Crystal, Holland America, Norwegian, Princess, Royal Caribbean, Seven Seas, and Silversea all have ships that sail in the area. Small ships visit the region as part of their Baja itineraries (see the next section, "Baja and the Sea of Cortez").

Baja and the Sea of Cortez

Smaller ships sail to the smaller-scale attractions of the region known as Mexico's Galapagos. History and wildlife are the focus here rather than wild nightlife (although some do make stops in touristy Cabo San Lucas, a party town if ever there was one). The history of many of Baja's coastal communities dates to the 16th and 17th centuries, and many of the stops in this region are in sparsely populated or unpopulated areas such as Isla del Carmen and Isla San Jose. Wildlife-watching (especially whale-watching) is a major attraction, and you can hike, kayak, snorkel, and swim from beautiful and isolated beaches.

Lindblad Expeditions has brought its small expedition ships here for more than 20 years and offers 7-day winter cruises (mostly sailing from La Paz, with a few departing from Guaymas on the Mexican mainland). The line also offers a 7-day package that combines a 4-day cruise from La Paz with 3 days in Baja's Copper Canyon, ending in Chihuahua.

Cruise West bases a ship here for the winter season. The 7-day cruises sail from Cabo San Lucas, and Cruise West offers an optional pre- and post-cruise excursion to the Copper Canyon, home of the Tarahumara Indians. The canyon covers an area four times the size of the Grand Canyon. Think about that one.

American Safari Cruises also brings its *Safari Quest* south for the winter season. It sails from La Paz.

Clipper Cruise Line offers 7-day cruises and 11-day *cruisetours* (combination package of cruise and land tour) in the spring and fall, combining a 7-day cruise from La Paz on the line's *Yorktown Clipper* with a train trip to the Copper Canyon.

The Hawaiian Islands

Rugged coastlines, majestic volcanic peaks, dramatic waterfalls, lush forests, and magnificent beaches await vacationers on the Hawaiian Islands. Cruising to Hawaii provides you with a unique opportunity to experience Hawaiian culture and food at a traditional luau, explore ancient sacred places on land, or visit underwater reefs. Hiking and bird-watching are popular excursion offers; you can shop for that Hawaiian shirt you've always wanted; or you can enjoy a variety of water sports in the blue, blue water.

Cruising around the rules

U.S. law prohibits ships not built in the United States from sailing directly to Hawaii from the contiguous 48 states, or even from sailing within the islands themselves without calling at another country. Yet the spectacular beauty of the islands and their beaches make the 50th state an increasingly popular cruise destination, and cruise lines do everything they can to get around the rules. In 2003, Norwegian Cruise Line (NCL) successfully got Congress to agree to a provision (with big help from Hawaii Senator Daniel Inouye) that allows the Malaysian-owned line to cruise the islands without calling at a foreign port, as long as NCL flags its ships American, pays U.S. taxes, hires an all-American crew, and abides by U.S. laws. Norwegian began all-Hawaii cruises in July 2004 when it introduced the first of its new NCL America brand ships, *Pride of Aloha*, with more to follow.

To get around the restrictions we mention in this chapter's sidebar, some ships start in Mexico or Canada or stop in those countries en route to the islands. These cruises typically last more than a week and visit ports on several Hawaiian islands, such as Hilo, Kailua-Kona, and Kona (all on the Big Island); Honolulu (Oahu); Nawiliwili (Kauai); and Kahului and Lahaina (Maui). Some lines also include Hawaii as a stop on the way to countries in the southern Pacific — New Zealand and Tahiti, for example. Holland America offers a round-trip, 2-week sailing from San Diego (including stops in Mexico), which allows access to Hawaii even for people who don't fly. Norwegian operates the *Norwegian Wind* on 10- and 11-day itineraries from Honolulu that leave the United States by calling at tiny Fanning Island in Micronesia.

Carnival, Celebrity, Norwegian, and Royal Caribbean all have ships that depart from Hawaii. Crystal, Cunard, Holland America, Princess, and Seven Seas have ships that visit Hawaii as part of longer itineraries.

Tahiti

Cruising here is like spending a week in paradise — literally. The ships cruise to some of the most beautiful islands in the world, where volcanic peaks rise above crystal blue lagoons and nearly every beach area is unpopulated, delighting the scuba divers, snorkelers, and beach enthusiasts (the brave can even try shark-feeding). Even if you're not into water activities, you can find plenty to do at visits to ports such as Huahine, Moorea, Raiatea, and Bora Bora, including helicopter tours, visits to black pearl farms, and Jeep safaris. Or you can just rent a bike and explore (the Tahitians are particularly friendly).

Seven Seas, with the *Paul Gauguin*; Princess, with the *Tahitian Princess*; and Windstar, with the *Wind Star*, offer Tahitian cruises year-round. All the cruises are from Papeete on the island of Tahiti.

Also cruising Tahiti year-round is **Bora Bora Cruises,** a Tahitian-owned small ship line that specializes in the islands of French Polynesia. The offerings include 3-, 4-, and 7-day sailings (☎ **866-907-8148;** www.bora borapearlcruises.com).

Cunard, Holland America, Princess, and Seven Seas visit as part of longer itineraries.

Transatlantic

Most cruise lines offer transatlantic cruises because they have to move their ships from the Caribbean to Europe. The actual crossings can take anywhere from six days to two weeks (without stopping!). The itineraries may include several days before or after the crossing, exploring ports in the Caribbean, Europe, New England, or Canada (and sometimes the lower eastern seaboard of the United States, too), or a combination thereof.

Cunard is the only line that offers a regular schedule of 6-day transatlantic crossings from April through November aboard the brand new, $800 million *Queen Mary,* the largest ship in the world. Who can resist a cruise on a vessel with its own planetarium?

Carnival, Celebrity, Costa, Crystal, Holland America, Lindblad, Norwegian, Oceania, Orient, Princess, Royal Caribbean, Seabourn, SeaDream, Seven Seas, Silversea, Star Clippers, and Windstar ships also make occasional crossings.

Northern Europe

Northern Europe cruises visit several different areas, including the Baltics, the British Isles, the Norwegian coast, a number of European capitals, or any combination thereof. Generally, Baltics cruises combine visits to Scandinavian ports, such as Copenhagen (Denmark), Stockholm (Sweden), and Helsinki (Finland) with St. Petersburg (Russia) and Tallinn (Estonia). British Isles cruises include any combination of England, Scotland, Ireland, Wales, and, across the Channel, France. European capitals itineraries include port cities such as Amsterdam and Copenhagen and offer an opportunity, via short excursions, to visit inland capitals such as London, Paris, Brussels, and Berlin. Norway and North Cape cruises take you to the gorgeous land of the Midnight Sun, with its breathtaking fjords. All these cruises offer museums (including some of the best art museums in the world), great shopping, dining opportunities, and scenic delights. The itineraries range from five days to two weeks, with cruises departing from ports such as Dover (England), Copenhagen (Denmark), and Bergen (Norway). Some cruises even depart from Mediterranean ports like Barcelona (Spain).

Cruise lines visiting Northern Europe include Celebrity, Clipper, Costa, Crystal, Cunard, Holland America, Lindblad, Norwegian, Oceania, Orient, Princess, Royal Caribbean, Seabourn, Seven Seas, Silversea, and Windstar.

Although the main cruise season is May to September, **Norwegian Coastal Voyage** (☎ **800-323-7436;** www.coastalvoyage.com) operates a fleet of working (cargo/passenger) ships that bring passengers up and down the coast of Norway (including above the Arctic Circle) year-round.

River Cruises in Europe

Cruising on Europe's rivers and canals gets you inland without having to take bus tours or car treks and gives you a close-up view of the countries you visit. The pace is leisurely and the ambience informal. We liken it to being in a floating country inn or, in the case of the small barges, to floating in a bed and breakfast.

Take a river cruise on the Danube, Moselle, Elbe, or Seine rivers in Germany, Switzerland, Hungary, Holland, France, Austria, and the Czech Republic (as well as on other rivers, including some in Russia). Hop on a barge cruise in France (throughout the country, including Burgundy, Provence, the upper Loire, and Loire Valley), Italy, Ireland, the Netherlands, Belgium, and so on.

Top operators include **Abercrombie & Kent** (☎ **800-323-7308;** www.abercrombiekent.com); **The Barge Lady** (☎ **800-880-0071;** www.bargelady.com); **French Country Waterway** (☎ **800-222-1236;** www.fcwl.com); **Peter Dielmann EuropeAmerica Cruises** (☎ **800-348-8287;** www.deilmann-cruises.com); **Uniworld** (☎ **800-733-7820;** www.uniworld.com); and **Viking River Cruises** (☎ **877-66-VIKING;** www.vikingrivercruises.com).

Antarctica

If wildlife, such as giant albatrosses, penguins, and seals (including the giant elephant variety), fascinates you, and you appreciate icebergs as big as mountains, a tour of the Great White Continent may be for you. But Antarctic cruises aren't for everyone. For one, the water can get quite choppy, especially in the Drake Passage. For another, the port calls are not what you call high-traffic tourist areas (no souvenir stands). Instead, you visit scientific research stations and islands reachable only by Zodiac landing craft. Talk about the final frontier!

Most cruises depart from Ushuaia, Argentina, although some sail from ports in Chile or from Port Stanley in the Falkland Islands. The cruise season is January and February, and the offerings mostly range from 8 to 15 nights.

Adventure cruise pioneer Lars Lindblad was the first to bring passengers to the southern end of the world in 1965, and the company his son founded, **Lindblad Expeditions,** still cruises here. Upscale tour operator **Abercrombie & Kent** (☎ **800-323-7309;** www.abercrombiekent.com) also cruises here with the 102-passenger *Explorer.*

Orient Lines has the biggest ship regularly operating in the market, the 800-passenger *Marco Polo,* which takes only a half-load of passengers on these sailings in deference to the environment (and local regulations). Celebrity Xpeditions' chartered *Kapitan Khlebnikov* (operated in partnership with Quark Expeditions), Clipper Cruises' *Clipper Adventurer,* Oceania's *Insignia,* and Seven Seas' chartered *Explorer II* also sail in the region. Holland America has its *Amsterdam* going as far into Antarctica as regulations allow as part of its 16- and 20-day South American itineraries.

Part VI

The Part of Tens

"Oh Ted, this Alaskan cruise is everything I'd ever imagined! The sweeping vista of the salad bar, the breathtaking dessert tray, the majesty of the carving station..."

In this part . . .

At the risk of sounding like David Letterman, this part is our Top Ten List. Welcome to the place where we clue you in to the onboard activities and romantic experiences that we consider the cream of the crop, the best of the best, the cruise things we do before all others.

Chapter 22

Nine Classic Cruise Experiences

*I*n other chapters, we talk about what you can expect to see and do on a ship, but this chapter contains some of our favorite experiences and activities. You don't have to do them all, of course, but we recommend you try some to make the most of your time on board.

People-Meeting and People-Watching

Who are these people you're vacationing with? Find out. You live within a small onboard community, and you can discover a lot about fellow passengers and crew just by observing. If you're shy, park yourself off to the side on the deck or in a lounge and just watch the action. But striking up a conversation is even better.

Making Believe at the Martini Bar

Think glamour. Think rich and famous. Put on your tux or ball gown and head to the fancy bar before dinner. While you sip that dry martini (shaken, not stirred, if you please) or enjoy fine champagne and caviar, think Hollywood. You're Lauren Bacall, he's Humphrey Bogart, and you're off on your latest adventure. Have fun pretending.

Relaxing with Shipboard Massages

As if cruising isn't relaxing enough, you can turn into jelly at the ship's spa. Drifting off as the massage therapists perform their finger magic is the ultimate shipboard indulgence and well worth the price of admission.

Competing in Silly Contests

What is it about cruises that bring out women who reveal their entire sex lives or men who take off their shirts and put their chest hair on full display in front of an audience just to win a refrigerator magnet? Have these people no shame? (Maybe not, but they sure are fun!)

Filling Up at the Midnight Buffet

At the stroke of midnight, the chefs truly go culinary-crazy. They present mountains of food and inventions such as vegetable flowers, chickens dressed like little men, and fish cut up and put back together to look like fish again, all surrounded by extravagantly decorated cakes and awesome ice sculptures. You need to bring photos home to show your friends!

Entering the Passenger Talent Show

Watch the proud parents when their kids perform, see a man croon romantically to his wife on their anniversary, hear the dirty old man who insists on telling off-color jokes, and enjoy a singer who shows so much promise that you wonder why you haven't seen her on *American Idol*.

Watching Movies in Your Cabin

With all you can do on cruise ships, why would you stay in the cabin and watch movies? Because many of the movies are free, with no commercials, and you can enjoy a comfortable place to catch up on the flicks you missed at home. But mostly, because you *can*.

Ringing for Room Service

Feel like a Caesar salad or a corned beef sandwich at 3 a.m.? Pick up your phone and order it. Don't like to appear in public before you have a few cups of coffee? Go ahead and ring for a waiter to bring some java to your cabin. You can call as many times as you want. And the service is free (although tipping the waiter is a nice gesture).

Gazing at the Deep Blue Sea

You can watch the sea during the day to see the water, the shoreline, and maybe some sights, but one of the best times to stare at the ocean is in the dark of night. Breathe in the fresh air. Howl at the moon if you like. Feel at one with the sea.

Chapter 23

Eight Ways to Enhance Romance

· ·

In This Chapter

▶ Staying in for intimacy
▶ Exploring your ship's romantic options
▶ Playing *Titanic*

· ·

*S*omething about being at sea brings out that feeling of *amore*. Maybe it's the gorgeous views, the relaxed vacation ambience, the rocking action of the ship, or maybe it's all those romantic tunes the lounge singers perform. Whatever your motivation, if you're at sea as a couple, enjoy it. And if you're single, make the most of the atmosphere and start looking for a partner!

Make a Splash

Book a cabin with a tub and squeeze in for a little together time (warning: shipboard tubs can be small) and a game of submarine. Suites may even have hot tubs with jets for that extra buzz.

Watch Romantic (or Steamier) Movies

You can't find steamy movies playing in the ship's movie theater, but if your cabin has a VCR, you can bring along your own or rent one from the ship's video collection. (Hint: Look on the top shelf at the video library.) Some lines, including Celebrity, also offer televisions programmed with pay-per-view adult titles.

Hit the Secret Spots

We hear (without firsthand experience, mind you) that behind the smokestack on the top deck on most ships is a popular hiding spot for couples seeking a little outdoor privacy. More timid lovers can book a cabin with a balcony or veranda (be aware that you may not be completely hidden from your neighbors).

Make Your Cabin Your Own

Bring along some of your favorite items from home — maybe your favorite romantic music (check to see if a CD player is available in your cabin) or perhaps some massage oil. And don't forget the silky lingerie.

Get Rubbed Down

Not up on the latest massage techniques? Book a couple's massage and you have his and hers massage therapists to put you both in a relaxing state of mind.

Have Dinner in Bed

Skip the dining room and order dinner in bed (or breakfast, if you prefer). Or have your meal served on your balcony so that you can take in each other as you take in the sea. Don't forget the whipped cream!

Share Love Songs

Serenade each other at the karaoke bar or in the passenger talent show. If you're too timid (or off-key), go to the dance lounge and slow dance. You can ask the band to play your favorite romantic tune.

Create Your Own Titanic Romance

Okay. We all saw the love scenes with Jack holding Rose. So if you must, stand as close as you can to the edge of the ship and let the wind whip your face, and pretend you're in the movie. Be the king of the world. But be careful, your majesty: Don't climb on the railing. It's dangerous!

Appendix

Quick Concierge

● ●

*T*oll-Free Numbers and Web Sites for Cruise Lines and Charter Companies

All numbers listed are for the United States unless noted otherwise.

Abercrombie & Kent
1520 Kensington Rd., Suite 212
Oak Brook, IL 60523-2156
☎ 800-323-7308
www.abercrombiekent.com

American Cruise Lines
1 Marine Park
Haddam, CT 06438
☎ 800-814-6880
www.americancruiselines.com

American Safari Cruises
19101 36th Ave. W., Suite 201
Lynnwood, WA 98036
☎ 888-862-8881
www.amsafari.com

American West Steamboat Company
2102 Fourth Ave., Suite 1150
Seattle, WA 98121
☎ 800-434-1232
www.columbiarivercruise.com.

Bora Bora Cruises
P.O. Box 9254
98715 Papeete, Tahiti
☎ 866-907-8148
www.boraborapearlcruises.com

The Barge Lady
101 W. Grand Ave., Suite 200
Chicago, IL 60610
☎ 800-880-0071
www.bargelady.com

Carnival Cruise Lines
3655 NW 87th Ave.
Miami, FL 33178-2428
☎ 800-CARNIVAL
www.carnival.com

Celebrity Cruises and Celebrity Xpeditions
1050 Caribbean Way
Miami, FL 33132
☎ 800-437-3111 or 305-539-6000
www.celebritycruises.com

Clipper Cruise Line
11969 Westline Dr. / Intrav Building
St. Louis, MO 63146-3220
☎ 800-325-0010
www.clippercruise.com

Costa Cruise Lines
200 South Park Rd., Suite 200
Hollywood, FL 33021-8541
☎ 800-33-COSTA
www.costacruises.com

Cruise West
2401 Fourth Ave., Suite 700
Seattle, WA 98121
☎ 800-888-9378
www.cruisewest.com

Crystal Cruises
2049 Century Park E., Suite 1400
Los Angeles, CA 90067
☎ 800-820-6663 (for brochures)
www.crystalcruises.com

Cunard
6100 Blue Lagoon Dr., Suite 400
Miami, FL 33126
☎ 800-7-CUNARD
www.cunard.com

Delta Queen Steamboat Company
30 Robin St. Wharf
New Orleans, LA 70130-1890
☎ 800-543-1949
www.deltaqueen.com

Disney Cruise Line
P.O. Box 10210
Lake Buena Vista, FL 32830
☎ 888-325-2500
www.disneycruise.com

Oceania Cruises
8120 NW 53rd St.
Miami, FL 33166
☎ 800-531-5658
www.oceaniacruises.com

French Country Waterways
P.O. Box 2195
Duxbury, MA 02331-2195
☎ 800-222-1236 or 781-934-2454
www.fcwl.com

Glacier Bay Cruiseline
107 W. Denny Way, Suite 303
Seattle, WA 98119
☎ 800-451-5952
www.glacierbaycruiseline.com

Holland America Line
300 Elliot Ave. W.
Seattle, WA 98119
☎ 800-426-0327
www.hollandamerica.com

Lindblad Expeditions
720 Fifth Ave.
New York, NY 10019
☎ 800-762-0003
www.expeditions.com

Maine Windjammer Association
251 Jefferson St. MS-06
Waldoboro, ME 04572-6011
P. O. Box 1144
☎ 800-807-WIND
www.sailmainecoast.com

Norwegian Coastal Voyage
405 Park Ave.
New York, NY 10022
☎ 800-323-7436
www.coastalvoyage.com

Norwegian Cruise Line
7665 Corporate Center Dr.
Miami, FL 33126
☎ 800-327-7030
www.ncl.com

Orient Lines
7665 Corporate Center Dr.
Miami, FL 33126
☎ 800-333-7300
www.orientlines.com

Peter Deilmann EuropeAmerica Cruises
1800 Diagonal Rd., Suite 170
Alexandria, VA 22314
☎ 800-348-8287
www.deilmann-cruises.com

Princess Cruises
24305 Town Center Dr.
Santa Clarita, CA 91355
☎ 800-PRINCESS
www.princess.com

RiverBarge Excursion Lines
201 Opelousas Ave.
New Orleans, LA 70114
☎ 888-456-2206
www.riverbarge.com

Royal Caribbean International
1050 Caribbean Way
Miami, FL 33132
☎ 800-327-6700
www.royalcaribbean.com

Seabourn Cruise Line
6100 Blue Lagoon Dr., Suite 400
Miami, FL 33126
☎ 800-929-9595
www.seabourn.com

SeaDream Yacht Club
2601 South Bayshore Dr.,
Penthouse 1B
Coconut Grove, FL 33133
☎ 800-707-4911
www.seadreamyachtclub.com

Seven Seas Cruises
600 Corporate Dr., Suite 410
Fort Lauderdale, FL 33334
☎ 800-477-7500 or 800-285-1835
www.rssc.com

Silversea Cruises
110 E. Broward Blvd.
Fort Lauderdale, FL 33301
☎ 800-722-9055
www.silversea.com

Star Clippers
4101 Salzedo St.
Coral Gables, FL 33146
☎ 800-442-0553
www.starclippers.com

Traverse Tall Ship Company
13390 S. West-Bay Shore Dr.
Traverse City, MI 49684
☎ 800-678-0383 or 231-941-2000
www.tallshipsailing.com

Uniworld
Uniworld Plaza
17323 Ventura Blvd.
Encino, CA 91316
☎ 800-733-7820
www.uniworld.com

Windjammer Barefoot Cruises
P. O Box 190120
Miami Beach, FL 33119-0120
☎ 800-327-2601 or 305-672-6453
www.windjammer.com

Windstar Cruises
300 Elliott Ave. W.
Seattle, WA 98119
☎ 800-258-7245
www.windstarcruises.com

Viking River Cruises
21820 Burbank Blvd., Suite 100
Woodland Hills, CA 91367
☎ 877-66-VIKING or 818-227-1234
www.vikingrivercruises.com

Web Directory

Here are some great Web sites to discover all kinds of information about cruising.

Information sites
http://travel.state.gov/
This section of the U.S. State Department's site offers information on the travel situation in every country.

www.astanet.com
Operated by the American Society of Travel Agents, this site is a good place to find a reliable agent. You can search by zip code or post a trip you want to take and have an agent contact you. The site also provides advice on how to avoid travel scams.

www.cdc.gov/travel
The Centers for Disease Control's site details their Vessel Sanitation program and offers other health-related travel information.

www.cruisecritic.com
(or AOL keyword *Cruise Critic*)
Cruise Critic features reader and expert reviews, chat, and cruise advice.

www.cruisemates.com

Cruisemates offers an online cruise community, expert reviews, chat, news updates, message boards, first-time cruiser advice, and links to special deals.

www.cruise-news.com

Check here for industry news.

www.cruising.org

The site of the Cruise Lines International Association, the industry's marketing group, offers contact info for accredited travel agents, information on the cruise lines, and articles.

www.icta.com

Search for qualified travel agents at this Institute of Certified Travel Professionals site.

www.nacoaonline.com

Look for members of the National Association of Cruise Oriented Agencies (NACOA).

Online cruise agencies and cruise bargain sites

www.bestpricecruises.com

This is the Web site of Cruise Holidays. You find a "request a quote" feature, cruise specials, and a limited number of featured cruises.

www.cruise.com

Omega World Travel operates this site, offering a large cruise inventory, links to cruise line sites, videos, and deck plans. You call an 800 number to book.

www.cruisebrokers.com

This cruise discounter offers a frequent cruiser program, weekly specials, a "request a quote" feature, and links to cruise line Web sites.

www.cruisecenter.com

This is the site of a large national agency that features hot deals, members-only discounts, and brief cruise line descriptions.

www.cruise411.com

Cruise411 is part of Rosenbluth Travel of Philadelphia. The database allows users to search by cruise line and destination, and the site also offers cruise reviews, message boards, and how-to-cruise info.

www.icruise.com

Icruise is a user-friendly online cruise seller with an extensive database that allows you to search by ship name, itinerary, budget, and date. A live agent feature lets you talk online with a cruise expert, and the site also has a quick quotes feature and offers articles and how-to advice on cruising.

Travel and auction sites that sell cruises

www.allcruiseauction.com

As its name implies, this site focuses on cruise auctions. Features include a weekly newsletter, basic ship facts, and a "cruises wanted" bulletin board (agents can respond to requests).

www.expedia.com

The cruise pages of this major online travel agency are linked to uniglobe.com and allow users to search by destination, month, and price feature. The site also offers ship reviews, a cruise community, and cruise news.

www.lowestfare.com

This discount travel Web site has a section listing cruises offered at discount prices.

www.mytravel.com

This all-purpose travel agency site is part of Travel Services International, which bought a whole bunch of top cruise agencies and merged them into a mega-agency a few years back. Here you find cruise deals, ship reviews, the latest cruise news, chat, and message boards, as well as virtual tours of ships, basic facts, and a "request a quote" feature.

www.travelocity.com

This major online travel agency site offers cruise deals and a good cruise finder (you can search by destination, cruise length, date, departure city, price, or specific cruise line).

www.uniglobe.com

A major travel agency site that features search by destination, last-minute deals, first-time cruiser advice, a cruise club (with e-mail updates on specials), and ship reviews.

www.priceline.com

Hit the cruise button to find cruises at heavily discounted prices.

The Top Brick-and-Mortar Cruise Agencies

The following are some of the top cruise agencies in the country that aren't specifically Web-based (although some have a significant Web presence). We list only the main offices.

Abracadabra Cruises
1735 Roswell Rd., Building 100
Marietta, GA 30062
☎ 800-474-5678
www.cruisemagic.com

Crown's Adventures At Sea
6601 Veteran's Blvd.
Metairie, LA 70003
☎ 800-330-1001
www.crownsadventuresatsea.com

Cruise Directors, Inc.
300 N. Washington St., Suite 104
Alexandria, VA 22314
☎ 800-405-7955 or 703-683-6535
www.cruisedirectorsinc.com

Cruise International (C.I.) Travel
800 World Trade Center
Norfolk, VA 23510
☎ 800-647-0009
www.citravel.com

Cruise Planners
3300 University Dr., #602
Coral Springs, FL 33065
☎ 800-683-0206
www.cruiseplanners.com

The Cruise Shoppe
1525 Lapalco Blvd., Suite 4
Harvey, LA 70058
☎ 800-392-3639

Cruises-N-More
725 Primera Blvd., #215
Lake Mary, FL 32746
☎ 800-733-2048
www.cruises-n-more.com

Cruise Specialists
221 First Ave. W., Suite 210
Seattle, WA 98119
☎ 800-544-2469
www.csiseattle.com

Cruises & Tours Unlimited
8030 Phillips Hwy., Suite 13
Jacksonville, FL 32256
☎ 800-935-2727
www.iwantacruise.com

Liberty Travel
69 Spring St.
Ramsey, NJ 07446
☎ 877-442-7847
www.libertytravel.com

Mann Travel & Cruises
4400 Park Rd.
Charlotte, NC 28209
☎ 800-849-2301
www.travelcruises.com

National Leisure Group
100 Sylvan Rd., #600
Woburn, MA 08101
☎ 800-690-2210
www.vacationoutlet.com

Omega Travel/Cruise.com
3102 Omega Office Park
Fairfax, VA 22031
☎ 888-333-3116
www.cruise.com

World Wide Cruises
8059 W. McNab Rd.
Fort Lauderdale, FL 33321-3254
☎ 800-882-9000
www.wwcruises.com

Worldwide Travel & Cruises
8784 SW Eighth St.
Miami, FL 33174
☎ 800-441-1954 or 305-223-2323
www.worldwidecruises.com

Index

• *E* •

Notes

Notes

Notes

FOR DUMMIES®

The easy way to get more done and have more fun

PERSONAL FINANCE

0-7645-5231-7   **0-7645-2431-3**   **0-7645-5331-3**

Also available:

Estate Planning For Dummies
(0-7645-5501-4)

401(k)s For Dummies
(0-7645-5468-9)

Frugal Living For Dummies
(0-7645-5403-4)

Microsoft Money "X" For Dummies
(0-7645-1689-2)

Mutual Funds For Dummies
(0-7645-5329-1)

Personal Bankruptcy For Dummies
(0-7645-5498-0)

Quicken "X" For Dummies
(0-7645-1666-3)

Stock Investing For Dummies
(0-7645-5411-5)

Taxes For Dummies 2003
(0-7645-5475-1)

BUSINESS & CAREERS

0-7645-5314-3   **0-7645-5307-0**   **0-7645-5471-9**

Also available:

Business Plans Kit For Dummies
(0-7645-5365-8)

Consulting For Dummies
(0-7645-5034-9)

Cool Careers For Dummies
(0-7645-5345-3)

Human Resources Kit For Dummies
(0-7645-5131-0)

Managing For Dummies
(1-5688-4858-7)

QuickBooks All-in-One Desk Reference For Dummies
(0-7645-1963-8)

Selling For Dummies
(0-7645-5363-1)

Small Business Kit For Dummies
(0-7645-5093-4)

Starting an eBay Business For Dummies
(0-7645-1547-0)

HEALTH, SPORTS & FITNESS

0-7645-5167-1   **0-7645-5146-9**   **0-7645-5154-X**

Also available:

Controlling Cholesterol For Dummies
(0-7645-5440-9)

Dieting For Dummies
(0-7645-5126-4)

High Blood Pressure For Dummies
(0-7645-5424-7)

Martial Arts For Dummies
(0-7645-5358-5)

Menopause For Dummies
(0-7645-5458-1)

Nutrition For Dummies
(0-7645-5180-9)

Power Yoga For Dummies
(0-7645-5342-9)

Thyroid For Dummies
(0-7645-5385-2)

Weight Training For Dummies
(0-7645-5168-X)

Yoga For Dummies
(0-7645-5117-5)

Available wherever books are sold.
Go to www.dummies.com or call 1-877-762-2974 to order direct.

FOR DUMMIES®

A world of resources to help you grow

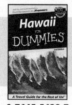